ANCIENT GREEK
LITERATURE
AND SOCIETY

ANCIENT GREEK
LITERATURE
AND SOCIETY

CHARLES ROWAN BEYE

ANCHOR BOOKS

ANCHOR PRESS/DOUBLEDAY

GARDEN CITY, NEW YORK

PA
3052
.B4

Library of Congress Cataloging in Publication Data

Beye, Charles Rowan.
Ancient Greek literature and society.

Bibliography: p. 425.
Includes index.
1. Greek literature—History and criticism.
I. Title.
PA3052.B4   880'.9
ISBN 0-385-06443-8 Trade
0-385-06446-2 Paperbound
Library of Congress Catalog Card Number 74–21235

Anchor Books Edition: 1975
Copyright © 1975 by Charles Rowan Beye
ALL RIGHTS RESERVED
Printed in the United States of America
First Edition

FOR

Howard
Willis
Helen
Gile

CONTENTS

PREFACE

Let me advise you to study Greek, Mr. Under-
shaft. Greek scholars are privileged men. Few of
them know Greek; and none of them knows anything else; but their position is unchallengeable.
Other languages are the qualifications of waiters
and commercial travelers; Greek is to a man of position what the hallmark is to silver.

G. B. Shaw, *Major Barbara*

The ancient Greek language and its literature have never
really recovered from their nineteenth-century role of con-
ferring respectability and status upon emergent bourgeois in
England and on the Continent (especially Germany). Antiquity became equated with gentility, with odious, smug, snobbish propriety, so much so that, for instance, the founders of
Stanford University, who wanted to establish something innovative, felt called upon to advertise in their founding pre-
amble that the new university was not intent upon creating
gentlemen out of their knowledge of Greek or Latin. But
there was a time before all that when anyone with a serious
call to being educated studied the Greek language. Nor was
the literature thought to be an embellishment or garnish to
life's feast, but the very entree, the center, guaranteed to
satisfy the deepest spiritual cravings. Now all of this is
changed.

It is curious that there was a time when people were passionately involved in literature, when they felt that it satisfied
great social needs rather than being a narcotic escape from
life's demands. And it is hard for us to imagine that for
centuries people seriously and earnestly studied the literature
of ancient Greece because it gave them their major spirit-

ual and cultural foundations; for we have relinquished our literary past, not as China's Red Guard did with the torch and the ax, but with the far more devastating yawn.

This book is dedicated to the importance of ancient Greek literature.

I have not written a systematic survey of the literature. I omit the literature composed in the centuries after the Alexandrian Age (third century B.C.). Plato and the orators are excluded from my pages. I have ignored or dismissed most fragments and minor pieces such as drinking songs. What remains is the exposition, analysis and discussion of the major pieces of the preclassical and classical periods from Homer to Thucydides. The chapter on Hellenistic poetry with which the book concludes is meant to isolate by contrast the very singular features of the earlier literature as well as to demonstrate how many of our critical suppositions come from the Hellenistic world.

Certain preoccupations reveal themselves in these pages. One is estimating the implications of the very *public* character of this literature. With few exceptions ancient Greek literature was (at least until the close of the fifth century) a necessary feature of community life, supported by the whole society, pervasive, a useful form of identification for all individuals, a means to establishing social cohesion, a source of socially valuable conformity. The responses anticipated and the responses achieved to this literature were in the truest senses of the word popular. Nothing could be further from the experience of what passes for higher literature in our own time or indeed in the immediately preceding centuries. Therefore the critical conceptions and the aesthetics which we have developed and unconsciously or consciously use do not necessarily apply to ancient Greek literature. The subject of ancient Greek literature is also of real anthropological interest because here is a literature highly refined, sophisticated, contrived, obedient to the profoundest aesthetic principles, probably the greatest literature of the Western world (if that does not sound too much like P. T. Barnum), which is at the same time as socially desirable and efficacious as an imprecatory rain chant or a work song. It was as obvious a staple of the community as the religion. Indeed because of the absence of a priestly caste and established dogma and because of the notable Greek tendency to locate things divine in a terrestrial setting, to measure god by man, the literature is perhaps the greater social institution.

The public quality of the major part of these pieces is linked directly to the fact that they were intended for oral presentation. Nothing so markedly distinguishes ancient Greek literature from the other great literatures of the world than the fact that much of it was not written to be read but rather to be heard, and heard communally. The implications of this, together with the psychological potentials inherent in the vastly expanded role of memory, again demand aesthetic and critical principles quite foreign to those evolved in completely literate cultures.

Another concern has been to gauge the continuing influence or role of the *Iliad* and the *Odyssey* in subsequent literary production. The Homeric poems must have been a heavy and peculiar burden for the Greeks to have borne. Most peoples can look back to the crude beginnings of their literary creation and sense their creative evolution or progress. The Greek on the contrary looked back to his earliest literary beginnings and found standing as monuments to an unexplored, unknowable prehistory these two poems which are sophisticated, complicated, finished, and what is more, complete and full statements of human existence. These poems impressed every art form that followed; we can easily see this. But their imposing presence must also have shaped the Greek creative faculty. To contend with so remarkable and excellent an example in one's tradition is often inhibiting and stultifying. And yet, as we know, the subsequent three centuries in Greece were a period of greatest creativity.

When read together most pieces of this literature reveal themes in common. I have tried to relate them. Most of all ancient Greek literature is preoccupied with mortality. On the one hand, death is a personal problem and a social problem; its frequent portrayal in the literature served to accommodate people individually and collectively to the fact of dying, not unlike the funeral rite. On the other hand, like romantic love in the nineteenth-century novel and sex in the twentieth-century novel, death functioned as the metaphor for the human condition. Corollary to death is the significant act, the response to death, really, whether it is Hesiod's justification of life through work or the Sophoclean Oedipus struggling, fighting against obstacles to learn the all-destructive truth of his being. Even Herodotus' Hippocleides dancing on tables makes the significant act.

Above all the literature celebrates awareness. For mortality demands to be recognized. This is one of the most impressive and consistent themes throughout Greek literature. Awareness seems to be finally the highest kind of heroism, available to all, to Achilles, to Sappho, to Socrates. More than anything else perhaps this compulsive drive for self-consciousness characterized the ancient Greeks, or at least the image which they made of themselves in their literature. If awareness is the premature acting out of death then the response to it is hope, analogous to the concrete significant act. Hope is an idea which appears and reappears in a great range of puzzling variants in the literature. Ambiguously good or bad, hope lies pent up in Pandora's box when every malady has escaped from it into the world. Hope or expectation leads Odysseus home, fuels comedy's fantasies, fatally beguiles Croesus and Clytemnestra. Hope and awareness form the opposing bulwarks in the hostile dialogue between the Melians and the Athenians which Thucydides describes so ironically in his history.

In the fifth century the city of Athens sponsored performances of tragic drama and comedies. The former is a distillation of the Greeks' tragic sense of life which we can discern everywhere from Homer's portrait of Troy to Thucydides' conception of Athens. It is the most persistent life view in Greek literature. But the Athenians wanted comedies, too: and one can contrast the tragic view of things with what we can call the comic view. It, too, seems to be a constant part of the literature from Homer's narration of Odysseus' travels and struggles to Herodotus' anecdotes to certain of Euripides' more experimental plays. So it is that one is tempted to mark out two poles between which ancient Greek literature may be situated, the tragic and the comic.

This thought leads in turn to considering the implications of antithesis in Greek literature, in Greek thought, indeed, in their entire culture. It is obvious from the language that the ancient Greeks had a pronounced tendency to pose things in antitheses. What most Western languages say in conjunction the Greek says in antithesis. This habit of mind culminates in Aristotle's law of the excluded middle. Along the way it achieves some notable polarities. Finally one must ask himself whether the complementary and antithetical nature of the

Iliad and the *Odyssey,* for instance, explains their existence or their survival or both. Or, for another instance, do Herodotus and Thucydides survive because they are antithetical? The question arises, then becomes compelling because it is unsettling to realize how many pieces of ancient Greek literature appear to be so neatly in contrast.

Perhaps nothing is more exciting in the study of ancient Greek literature than to see how an entire vision of human existence is built up throughout the literature. It is a vision as contradictory, ambiguous and vague as we know human life to be. The early Greeks did not depend upon logic and reason. The fifth century advanced upon rationalism but never became an age of enlightenment. Mythopoesis rather than reason was the chariot for the Greek mind. The literature reveals a genius that can encompass impossible contradictions, illogicalities and absurdities, can make them ring true in synthesis, reflecting reality in a way that rational discourse does not know.

My ambition in writing this book has been to account for the extraordinary beauty and power of the literature, to assay its social function and to lay the pieces out in a broader humanistic context. I have often felt it necessary to guide my reader since even well-educated people today are ignorant of ancient Greek literature.

I hope, however, that this book will be useful to all students of literature, from novice to literary critic to classical philologist. To that end I have omitted notes and scholarly argument so as not to impede the flow of exposition. There is, however, an essay on the scholarly research into ancient Greek literature (pp. 421ff.) which should be a sufficient introduction for anyone who cares to pursue the subject.

The transliteration of Greek words is always bothersome. My principle has been to transliterate all obscure words into the closest phonetic approximation of the original Greek. Famous words, however, which are part of the Western tradition have been kept in the Latin spelling in which they entered the tradition and as they are known to most persons.

I am very grateful to the people who have helped me in writing this book. In particular I should like to thank G. Cabisius, D. Frame, J. Mejer, B. Parry, B. Peick and J. Vaio for reading and criticizing parts of the manuscript. I should like to thank Brigit McCarthy for her care and assistance.

Once again I must thank my mother-in-law, Mary Willis Pendleton, for her great aid and encouragement.

Most of all I should like to thank William M. Calder, III, Casey Cameron and Richard Sáez for their close reading of the manuscript and their many criticisms and suggestions.

The debt which I owe to the inspiration and insight offered to me so many years ago by G. F. Else, J. F. Gilliam and T. G. Rosenmeyer can never be adequately estimated. Nor can I forget how I was first taught to read a poem by Mary Powers Beye, in whose memory much of this book is written.

I should like to thank the Harvard University Press for permission to use parts of my "The Rhythm of Hesiod's *Works and Days*" *Harvard Studies in Classical Philology* 76 (1972) copyright 1972 by the President and Fellows of Harvard College; the editors of *Greek, Roman and Byzantine Studies* for permission to use parts of my "Jason as Love-Hero in Apollonios' *Argonautika*" published in Volume 10 (1969); the University of Chicago Press for permission to use portions of John Moore's translation of Sophocles' *Ajax* in *The Complete Greek Tragedies* (eds. D. Grene & R. Lattimore) copyright 1957 by the University of Chicago; the editors of *Ramus* for permission to use parts of my "Male and Female in the Homeric Poems" published in Volume 3 (1974) copyright 1974 by Charles Rowan Beye; and the editors of the *Boston University Journal* for permission to use parts of my "The Criticism of Greek Tragedy" published in Volume 21 (1973) copyright 1973 by Charles Rowan Beye.

THE SECOND MILLENNIUM (The Bronze Age)	● Mycenaean dominance of the Mediterranean c. 1600-1200 ● Troy destroyed c. 1180 ● Dorian invasion c. 1000
THE EIGHTH CENTURY	● Invention of the alphabet ● Beginnings of colonization in Sicily ● Hesiod composing *Works and Days, Theogony* in Ascra (Boeotia) ● Homer (or whoever he or they were) composing *Iliad, Odyssey*

THE SEVENTH CENTURY

c. 680 Gyges seizes the throne in Lydia

c. 675 Sparta crushes revolt of Messenians and acquires a conservative, severe constitution

c. 650-600 the spread of tyrant governments in Greece

c. 640-630 standardized coinage begun in Lydia and soon adopted by Greek city-states

c. 650 Archilochus (born on Paros) writing poetry (mentions the eclipse of April 6, 648, in a poem)

● Tyrtaeus writing poetry in Sparta in the second half of the century

c. 630 Mimnermus writing poetry in Asia Minor

c. 612 Sappho born in Mytilene on Lesbos

594/3 Solon appointed chief magistrate at Athens to reform the constitution

May 8, 585 an eclipse predicted by Thales

561 Peisistratus becomes tyrant at Athens

560 Croesus succeeds to the throne

546 Croesus dies

c. 540 Polycrates becomes tyrant on Samos

c. 556 Simonides born on Ceos

540 Theognis writing poetry in Megara

c. 535 Thespis wins first prize when tragedy first introduced at the Greater Dionysia in Athens

528 Hippias succeeds his father Peisistratus at Athens

c. 523 Polycrates of Samos dies

525 Aeschylus born at Athens

c. 524 Bacchylides born on Ceos

518 Pindar born in Boeotia

510 Hippias expelled from Athens

508 Cleisthenes begins his reforms of the Athenian constitution

c. 500 satyr plays are added to the tragic festival

THE FIFTH CENTURY

499 Ionian cities in Asia Minor revolt from Persia with Athenian aid

494 revolt collapsed, Ionians flee to Athens

490 Persian retaliation; invasion of Greece defeated at Marathon

c. 495 Pericles, Sophocles born at Athens

● Herodotus said to have been born "before the Persian War" at Halicarnassus

c. 490 Phidias born

488/7 comedy introduced at the Greater Dionysia festival

487 first use of ostracism at Athens; public officials now elected by lot rather than popular election

c. 485 Protagoras, Euripides born at Athens

484 Aeschylus' first victory

483 discovery of rich new vein of silver at Laurium; building of a large fleet at the direction of Themistocles

480 August Xerxes enters Greece; battle of Thermopylae; September battle of Salamis a great Greek victory

c. 480 Anaxagoras comes to Athens

479 battle of Plataea, battle of Mycale; Greeks victorious, Persians withdraw

478-476 fortification of Athens

477 formation of the Delian League on the island of Delos

476 Pindar writes Olympian I, Bacchylides writes Ode V

472 Aeschylus' *Persians*

472 discontent appears in the League: Carystus (472), Naxos (470), Thasos (465) try to withdraw, are crushed and subjugated by Athens

469 Socrates born

468 Sophocles defeats Aeschylus at tragic festival

467 Aeschylus' *Seven Against Thebes*

463? Aeschylus' *Suppliants*

between **460-455** Thucydides born at Athens

458 Aeschylus' *Oresteia*

458 building of the long walls from Athens to the harbor

456 Aeschylus dies at Gela in Sicily

455 Euripides first competes at the Dionysia

454 treasury of the Delian League moved to Athens from Delos

c. **455** Aristophanes born at Athens

447 the Parthenon is begun; Euboea revolts, is subdued and made subject to Athens

444 Herodotus goes to assist in the founding of Thurii in southern Italy

441? Sophocles' *Antigone*

441 Euripides wins first victory

438 Euripides' *Alcestis*

438 Pindar dies

436 Isocrates born at Athens

411 oligarchic revolution in Athens

410 democracy restored in Athens

        409 Sophocles' *Philoctetes*

        408 Euripides' *Orestes*

        406 Euripides dies in Macedonia, Sophocles dies at Athens

405 battle of Aegospotamoi; Athens' fleet destroyed

        405 Euripides' *Bacchae, Iphigenia in Aulis*

404 surrender of Athens   **404** Thucydides, returns to Athens

        401 Sophocles' *Oedipus at Colonus*

                            c. 400 Thucydides dies at Athens

THE FOURTH CENTURY

394 battle of Coronea ends Sparta's pretensions to leadership of Greece

399 Socrates dies at Athens

387 Plato starts the Academy at Athens

384 Aristotle is born in Chalcidice

362 battle of Mantinea ends Thebes' pretensions to leadership of Greece

356 Alexander born in Macedonia

347 Plato dies at Athens

342/1 Menander born at Athens

341 Epicurus born at Samos

338 battle of Chaeronea won by Philip of Macedon against the combined forces of the Greeks

338 Isocrates dies

336 Alexander succeeds to the Macedonian throne

335 Zeno born in Cyprus; Aristotle comes to Athens, founds school

331 foundation of the city of Alexandria in Egypt

323 Alexander dies

322 Aristotle dies

307 Epicurus starts his school

c. 305 Callimachus born in Cyrene

304 Ptolemy declares himself King in Egypt

c. 300 Theocritus born in Alexandria

THE THIRD CENTURY

297 foundation of the Mouseion at Alexandria

c. 295 Apollonius is born

293/89 Menander dies

282 Ptolemy I dies

270 Epicurus dies at Athens

263 Zeno dies

c. 260 Theocritus dies

247 Apollonius steps down as librarian

240 Callimachus dies

ANCIENT GREEK
LITERATURE
AND SOCIETY

CHAPTER ONE
THE LANGUAGE

Speech man taught himself and swift
thought, the temper that makes a state . . .

Sophocles *Antigone* 354–5

Speech is one of those things lodged in man by
nature; when the technique of persuading others
and of indicating to ourselves what we wanted developed then not only did this signify a departure
from animal life, but also by gathering together we
built cities, made laws and founded the arts.

Isocrates

In the beginning was the Word . . .

Gospel According to John

Most people know Greek literature through translations.
These are often pathetic, pale shades of the vigorous and
sensuous original tongue. Translators confront the problematic fact that literary English or American is far removed
from the way people ordinarily speak, whereas standard English or American has surrendered to the banalities of television speech and government double-talk. Our literary tradition is much influenced by the Roman experience when the
spoken language and the literary language sharply diverged.
The Greek literary language, by comparison, although ex-

traordinarily rich, with a large and subtle verb system and an enormous vocabulary, always retained a strong flavor of the spoken tongue. Less artificial than literary Latin, or literary English, for that matter, it flows more naturally, more sensually than rationally. Since it is easier to learn and more easily remembered than Latin it is a pity that it was not retained in the secondary school curriculum.

In the late nineteenth century, however, America's secondary schools had to choose between keeping Greek or Latin in the curriculum, and the decision was for Latin to stay, whereas compulsory courses in Greek were abandoned. Jettisoning Greek was probably a major error. For it left youngsters with Latin and Roman literature, a language and literature elegant, compressed and contrived, subtle by arcane convention, snobbish and hierarchical, mirroring a people insecurely cloaked in a derivative culture. It is not an experience to which many teen-agers are sympathetic. The result has been the erosion of Latin from the curriculum and eventually the absolute decline and general disappearance of all antiquity from the curricula of both the school and the college.

Anyone who reads much Greek in translation or who contemplates the criticism of Greek literature should have some idea of the nature of the language and its history and development. Poetic translations particularly, whether in English or American, sound alike because there is no longer a poetic diction in either dialect of the language. The great stylized dictions of our time—rock and roll, blues, country western—just will not do. In the translation of ancient Greek one gets either English upper class rhetoric trying for noble simplicity or something like a Chicago newspaperman reaching for grandeur. But that is not what Greek is all about.

Therefore, I shall introduce the literature of ancient Greece with some brief remarks on the language of the Greeks and even more skeletal statements about the period when the language was first formed. The Greek people have always had a passionately tenacious grip on their language. At the start when dialects of the language developed in each valley settlement, the local inhabitants clung steadfastly to their peculiar speech. The literature displays dialect differences and these matter. When the Romans ruled the world they obliterated whole cultures in what is now Western Europe, but they did not at all challenge the Greek language in the East, imperturbable in its dominance. Throughout Turkish rule the Greek language remained alive, banked like coals under ash in the Greek Orthodox Church. There are enclaves today in southern Italy below Brindisi which show an even greater tenacity, where the people speak a Greek which is descended pure from the Greek of the mainland in the classical period. The Greek spoken today in downtown Athens is closer to the ancient Greek of twenty-five centuries ago than modern English is to the English of Chaucer.

The period between the Greeks' arrival in their historical land and the beginnings of their recorded history in the eighth and seventh centuries is continually ambiguous. Next to no written documents survive within Greece or in foreign cultures which can offer positive facts upon which to stand a chronology or historical narrative. The best of the consequent guesswork maintains that peoples moved down into what is now Greece toward the end of the third millennium B.C.

The people coming down out of the Balkan peninsula at the end of the third millennium settled themselves part among the indigenous population in northwest Greece from present-day Albania south to the Gulf of Corinth and part in the Peloponnesus. The two groups evidently lost contact with each other finally because each area evolved a separate dialect of the language. Their cultural achievements were also diverse. The group in northwest Greece has left us little indication of what we commonly consider an advancing civilization, whereas the group in the Peloponnesus was the author of that glorious Mycenaean civilization which through much of the second millennium rivaled the Minoan civilization on the island of Crete and eventually overcame it. The Mycenaeans whom Homer calls Achaians derived their culture not only from the resources which they brought with them, but from contacts with the native people of that part of the Mediterranean as well as association with the Minoans and the older civilizations of Asia Minor. There was an international culture throughout the eastern Mediterranean in the second millennium, which may account for elements in the Homeric epics and in Hesiod's poems which also appear in more eastern literatures.

The Mycenaeans possessed a script (Linear B) which, to judge from what has been deciphered of it, was used for archive reports. The society probably was not literate and therefore dependent upon the oral poetic transmission of their culture. This suits our understanding of the *Iliad* and the *Odyssey*. Although they appear centuries later, at times they recall elements of the Mycenaean world, so the oral poetic tradition which created the two epics may have had its beginning and development at Mycenaean courts. It explains as well the relative easy lapse into total illiteracy when the Mycenaean Empire came apart. When there were no longer archives there was no further need of clerks and accountants and the script vanished; at least we have no later trace of Linear B script.

The Mycenaean world was stable, a political and economic entity extending throughout southern Greece and many of the islands, exhibiting a uniform culture, complex and essentially original. All this came to an end in the twelfth century B.C. when the northwest Greek-speaking peoples began to move down into the Peloponnesus, taking over by force or otherwise (it is unclear) the established Mycenaean centers. The archaeological evidence shows that considerable disruptive events at this time fragmented the culture and destroyed the sources of its stability and quality. A memory of this episode was retained in Greek tradition in the story of the "Dorian invasion." The name Dorian refers to the incoming people (their language and culture as well) who settled throughout the southern Peloponnesus at this time. In the north of the Peloponnesus another group of the invaders settled who spoke a dialect slightly different from Doric and considerably different from Mycenaean. The dialect is called Northwest Greek; it is also the language of the people who lived in Aetolia north across the Corinthian Gulf and as far east as Delphi. Together the two linguistic groups constitute what is known as West Greek. This category meant more to the Greeks than a linguistic distinction. Through much of their history the Greek in the east and west saw basic differences in their cultures. In the west it was the Dorians who created a way of life which was in clear contrast to that of eastern Greeks. Among the Dorians the Spartans are always singled out as representative of the western way of life because of their power and because of the eccentricity of their way of life.

The movement of people into the rich centers of the Mycenaean civilization forced most of the Mycenaeans out. We can tentatively trace their movements through the loca-

was the language of oral poetry which centuries of trial and error had created from all the dialects for the sole purpose of narrating in dactylic hexametric lines the events of saga. As such the dialect was artificial, not meant to approximate spontaneous human speech. Just as the *Iliad* and the *Odyssey* exerted major influence on all later poetry, the majesty of the epic dialect was such that every style of poetry thereafter incorporated epic forms freely, words, phrases, the formulae. Dialects simply amplified the potentials of poetic expression. Instead of one poetic diction, for instance, there were available several dialects and styles each with its own associations. The Aeolic love lyrics of Sappho, the Ionic elegies of Mimnermus, the Doric choruses of Alcman, the Attic iambics of tragedy—in each of these the variation in dialect offers something which does not exist in contemporary literature. The effect is *not* like dialect stories or poems in American letters; these dialects are the speech patterns of minorities in contrast to the one common language. In ancient Greece all dialects were equal; only the Attic dialect, the speech of Athens, where most of the literary production took place, was, so to speak, more equal.

We know of the many, many dialects to be found in Greece because they are preserved in writing. The Greeks invented their writing when they became acquainted with the Semitic alphabet through their trading association with the Phoenicians. Sometime in the eighth century they adapted this script to their own language, but with change. The Semitic alphabet makes no provision for the representation of individual vowels. The Greeks had the genius to take certain Semitic consonant symbols which they did not need for consonants and use them for their vowels. They created a truly phonetic alphabet, a singularly efficient device which promoted the spread of literacy and was certainly the *sine qua non* for the formation of the enlightened democracy in Athens in the fifth century. The Greek invention was taken up by the Romans and has subsequently spread around the world as the most efficient method of writing language.

At the same time as the emergence of dialects the Greeks were beginning to recover from the shock and dislocation of the Dorian invasion. Life formed itself fragmented, hidden away in small groups in mountain-ringed valleys. Their political instincts were strong; they organized each valley into a microscopic state, the city-state. So *local* was the spirit of these centuries that every town spoke a little different dialect; man was alien beyond the borders of his birthplace. The ancient Greeks are sometimes accused of being provincial and parochial, of being too anthropocentric, limited to the terrestrial view of things. These criticisms stick, I believe, but they are also the sources of the strength of ancient Greece. The limits which such habits of mind imposed caused a kind of communal introspection from which sprang concerns that in turn motivated and shaped much of Greek literature. The long preservation of dialects and regional distinctions in an area so small (yet so mountainous and difficult to traverse) is testimony to that innate parochialism. The facts of history as well turn upon the absence of a common view in Greek lands. Many argue that the failure to unite in common cause destroyed any chance of a Greek nation; this is true and parochialism is again at fault. The literature, however, largely created in the small city-state of Attica, in the city of Athens, within one century eventually produced a common cultural view that transcended ideas of nationality, in fact transcended finally the temporal, geographical and spiritual limits of Graeco-Roman antiquity to shape a considerable part of the art and institutions of the Western world. Such was the intellectual and spiritual power of a small city-state.

Athens became the superior political power among the Greeks in the fifth century. From tribute paid by subject cities sprang a building program that in its beauty and grandeur paralleled the superlative nature of the outpouring of literature. Coincidentally or not the end of Athens' imperial dominance in the debacle of the Peloponnesian War came at roughly the same time as her literary fecundity began to vanish. The fourth century saw the power struggle go to Sparta and Thebes; in Athens prose replaced poetry and philosophy replaced mythology. Athens was becoming a university town. As Alexander ended the city-state forever in his establishment of an eastern Mediterranean empire, the creativity moved to his new city, Alexandria.

Classical Greece was succeeded by Hellenism, an international Greek culture, spreading uniformly over the eastern Mediterranean, lasting until the creation of the Byzantine Empire eight centuries later. The cultural uniformity of the emergent Hellenistic world was reflected in the linguistic unity. Dialects disappeared. The literary productions and the long political and longer moral dominion of Athens made the Attic Greek dialect become increasingly standard, although modified to suit its enlarged and catholic status. From mid-fourth century on Greeks increasingly spoke what was called the common tongue (*koine*), which eventually became a written language as well; it is for instance the language of the New Testament. Dialects remained a staple of learned, pedantic poetry, cultivated for their associations, their recherché vitality. The new world center at Alexandria found a large part of its creative energies in a nostalgic looking back, to making a Greek literary history, codifying, purifying and commenting upon the facts. Hellenistic literature as most literatures of the Western world is a back glance and a criticism of classical Greek literature. The latter is fundamentally different from other literatures in the Western tradition. As it came into being there were no genres, no genre rules established, no models, nothing. In the briefest span of time a small group of people created precise forms of literary expression, each of which had the means to express certain things best. Somehow their experimentation went immediately to the heart of the literary problems and found the potentials. Despite analysis the literary history of those centuries, especially the fifth, remains a mystery bordering on the miraculous.

Alexandria was Alexander's creation and the spirit of the new age which this youthful ruler invoked found its sponsors here. The third century is called the Alexandrian period, signifying the new artistic energy pouring out of the Egyptian city. Alexandria remained one of the great cities of the ancient world, but her absolute cultural dominance was shortlived. By the middle of the second century B.C. Rome became the major power in the Mediterranean; the world began to be measured in Roman terms rather than Greek.

In the following pages I should like to give an account of some of the pleasing peculiarities of the Greek language. It must be somewhat technical, but I hope valuable for those who know no Greek. It is naïve of me perhaps but I am in love with the language and like all lovers I imagine that I can easily convince the world of my beloved's charms.

Ancient Greek is a musical language; it has a number of features lacking in contemporary Western languages (except Welsh and Irish) that create musicality. First, the underlying rhythmic element of Greek is the varying lengths of time established by convention for the voicing of each syllable. So-called "long" syllables are held twice as long as "short" syllables. Therefore metrical units such as the dactyl ($-\smile\smile$), the iambic ($\smile-$) or the trochee ($-\smile$) do not have the nervous, tympanic effect which is often found in stress rhythms. The rhythmic effect is an understated play in time sequences. Because the Greek language has a large number of short syllables the poetic line is often lighter, more rapidly changing, faster. One can compare the greater number of dactyls in the *Iliad* and *Odyssey* with the greater number of spondees in the *Aeneid*. Then, there is the high percentage of vowels to consonants in Greek; they are usually sounded separately from the adjacent consonant. The clarity of this articulation means a greater variety of distinct sounds contributing to the general musicality of the language. The Ionic dialect particularly has a large number of vowels often occurring next to each other, sounded separately, a very musical effect. The number of different vowel sounds in ancient Greek is large, unlike modern Greek, in which many of the inherited vowel sounds have been reduced and combined, not quite as bad, however, as contemporary vernacular American, where many of the vowel sounds are ambiguous, indistinct, little more than articulated grunts. The instinctive prominence given to vowels in ancient Greek is such that words generally end in vowels. The only consonants with which words end are *n*, *r* and *s* (the first two of which in fact function as quasi-vowels in various languages). Then too, a natural melody was derived from the system of pitch accent. Most modern languages, including modern Greek, have a stress accent on one syllable of each word. In ancient Greek, on the contrary, one syllable of most words was pitched higher than the others; this in turn adds to the range of vowel sounds because a change of pitch invariably changes the quality of the vowel shape. Stress accent eventually replaced the pitch accent by late antiquity, as the effort required, however slight, to raise one's voice gradually created a stress accent upon the syllable formerly pitched up. Some believe that even in early antiquity there was a modest amount of stress accent in poetry not necessarily coming on the pitched syllables—which would of course create a contrapuntal effect with the pitch accent.

Greek is an inflected language, that is, elements added to the semantic root indicate such things as case, gender, number, and person. These elements frequently indicate as well the relationships of the words; as a consequence the Greek sentence is not at all as dependent upon word order to achieve meaning as, for instance, English (where order determines meaning there is a great difference between "the dog bites the man" and "the man bites the dog"). Poetic expression is much enhanced by the freedom of the individual words in Greek sentences; since any arrangement is possible there exists beside the natural meaning derived from inflection another kind of meaning through the juxtaposition of words, a meaning often irrational and ambiguous but nevertheless strong. Another peculiarity of Greek that is hard to render in translation (mainly because of their peculiar economy) is the particles. These are words, generally monosyllables, that give a sense to the expressed meaning that our pitch, gestures and facial expressions do in contemporary speech. Often they add a nuance or shade to the meaning in ways that are impossible to express other than in acting out the statement. The particles, for instance, give much of the dramatic quality to Plato's dialogues and charge them with emotion. In a language in which neither pitch nor stress is available for emphasis the particles are immensely valuable.

Although inflection released Greek from the demands of word order the prose sentences generally fell in the order of subject, verb and object, each element with its attendant modifiers. The style of the sentences varied considerably over the centuries. The earliest style reflected natural conversational narrative patterns, that is, short ideas brought together by the simplest connectives. This style the Greeks called *paratactic,* which means one thing set side by side another. Juxtaposition is the clue to meaning, as in "it was raining hard and we didn't go on the picnic," where causality is not expressed but implied. This style appears in prose and poetry often with epic associations, in which an initial idea, theme, image or name causes the writer to spin out his narrative by constantly amplifying the original element in a series of short ideas set one after the other.

Eventually there came about a style better suited to the demands of logic and abstraction, a style which coordinated ideas in such a way as to subordinate some to the creation of a central point. The style is known as *syntactic.* Clauses particularly but all the refinements of grammar make this style. In its most complex form the result is the periodic sentence in which the meaning is not clear until the final word of the sentence is introduced. A simple example is the sentence above transformed: "since it was raining hard we didn't go on the picnic." Because the Greeks used all the elements of the verb far more than modern languages, especially participles and infinitives, and because the inflection made word relationships clearer, periodic sentences could attain great length without being unduly tiresome, artificial or, more important, confusing. Intellectually a periodic sentence could indicate in one intellectual consortium all the ramifications of an idea and in the exposition of its parts show the logical hierarchy of the whole.

Very few authors, however, completely surrendered their taste for spontaneity and the vernacular to the rigidity and formalism which periodicity demands. The conventions of formal grammatical usage were there, but writers often chose to ignore them, seeking the immediacy and *verité* of simpler, bolder, more vernacular expressions. Here again translations fail because they cannot convey the exquisite combination of an objective, logical use of grammar and an intellectualized vocabulary with the emotional, majestic use of vernacular and popular idiom. This confident, precise yet relaxed use of language marks Plato particularly, yet from translations he appears to be a philosophy professor. This is a great deal due to the separation in the English language between the spoken and the written word. Our convention does not allow the styles to mix freely, at least not in academic or so-called learned writing. Therefore Plato's Greek comes across in translation as something much stiffer than the original, and perhaps also more dogmatic, assertive and authoritative. Actually, Plato is in the profoundest sense playing games much of the time.

The separation in English is in the tradition of the Latin language, which, when first the Romans confronted literary matters, was continually molded, self-consciously made a vehicle for grand literature and ideas. The language, therefore, went two quite separate paths—the literary language and the language of the people—ending in the cultural alienation of the upper class and a general sterility in the literary language. Greek by contrast continually refreshed itself in the pool of vulgar idiom. Everyday speech helped create the immense vocabulary of literary Greek; the language was alive to growth through new combinations of suffixes and prefixes much as American English is.

The precise combination of casualness (with its freedom to originate) and seriousness (the concern to say something, to be exact rather than to be a vocal extension of the instinct to animal togetherness—the goal of much random talk) is one of the marked qualities of ancient Greek. This feature has helped the language survive these thousands of years, always adapting, assimilating and never losing its freedom. The language of Homer can be seen in the language of tragedy and of philosophy which in turn with vast simplifications became the language of the New Testament. Greek was the language of the Byzantine Empire and when that succumbed to the invasions of the Turks the Orthodox Church provided the underground in which Greek culture survived Turkish domination.

The modern Greek poet Cavafy achieves in many of his poems a sense of the marvelous continuity in the Greek language. He uses words and phrases that are at once altogether contemporaneous and at the same time evocative of Homer and the fifth century. In a Proustian way the passage of twenty-five centuries is made to fade and we are simply in the presence of the Greek language and things Greek.

CHAPTER TWO
WINGED WORDS

They began to serve the meat and mix the wine
and the herald came near leading the excellent singer
Demodokos, honored by the people. He seated him
among the feasters, the chair next to a broad column.
Then clever Odysseus said to the herald . . .
"Here, herald, give Demodokos this meat so that he
may eat and I may offer my respects, miserable though I
am.
For among all the men who inhabit this earth singers
deserve honor and respect since the Muse
has taught them their songs and she loves the race of
singers."

Odyssey 8.470–81

We cannot imagine the silence of ancient Greece. A countryside empty of people, settlements devoid of mechanical clatter, every call of a bird, the blowing of the wind must have been significant. Into ears so rarely assaulted the sound of the rhythmically chanted word must have rung like a symphony. The history of the earlier centuries of Greek literature is the story of oral poetry, made to be spoken and to be heard. Not until the latter half of the fourth century do we gain the impression that words were meant to be written and read. And not for centuries thereafter did persons read to themselves silently as we do. They sounded the words as they read. The winged words of which Homer often speaks, flying from lips to ears, were a long time dying.

The technical problems for an oral poet are materially different from those which confront a literate poet. Furthermore the expectations and talents of the preliterate audience are special. These are essential factors in contriving an aesthetic for oral poetry. Moreover, since the influence of the Homeric poems was so pervasive and long-lived, the special qualities with which oral poetry is endowed remained influential in later literary production when considerably less emphasis had to be put on communicating to preliterate people. Reading and writing were commonplace in Athens of the fifth century, but, as the works of Herodotus make clear, the oral mentality resisted the intrusion of literacy.

There are periods of history from which so much data survive that they become as familiar to us as our recent past. Some figures loom out of history's shade distinct and recognizable down to the merest wart. Greek literary history begins with the *Iliad* and the *Odyssey*. The period when they were composed, the men who made them are utterly obscure. Freed from the moorings of objective fact the two poems have become legend, creating their own milieu, their own poets. Describing a moment in time and ways of looking at things which are separated and gone from us like the stars in the sky, the poems themselves remain among us, remote and mythical. One thing is clear: these are no primitive, inchoate attempts at poetry. They are sophisticated, fully developed narrative poems of unusual subtlety and control.

The Homeric poems are the only complete surviving examples of Greek oral epic poetry. Other epic poems existed, we know, even other kinds of smaller, occasional poems, but so far as we can understand from the evidence the *Iliad* and the *Odyssey* came at the end of the oral poetic tradition and survived because they were the best of their kind. Thereafter new forms of literary production came into being. The *Iliad* and the *Odyssey* are therefore not only an end but a beginning, the end of a tradition of oral poetry, but because they are the earliest specimens of Greek poetry in existence, they are the beginnings of Greek literature and Western literature in general.

The ancient Greeks believed that these two poems had been composed by a blind poet from the island of Chios, by name Homer. The actual circumstances of their creation, whether they were by one man or several, how they got to be written down, where or why, whether indeed they are simply specimens of oral poetry transcribed—all is problematic, controversial and ultimately requires an act of faith on the part of the critic. For, as the ancient Greek wit, Lucian, pointed out, the only person who has the answer is Homer, and he is dead.

During the twentieth century a scholarly consensus has emerged, an orthodoxy perhaps, based on numerous statistical surveys of the language and style of the two poems and comparison with similar poems in other cultures. Scholars maintain that the *Iliad* and the *Odyssey* are specimens of oral poetry that somehow came to be transcribed, dictated perhaps, and therefore survived. Truly oral poetry cannot survive without some form of transcription. In our time it is recording, a technological aid which is able to preserve in various backwaters of the contemporary world the remnants of oral poetry in disappearing preliterate or semiliterate societies. The internal evidence for the *oral* quality of the poems while convincing to some is disputed by others. The comparison with the oral poetry of other cultures also has its proponents and objectors. One may object that the poetry of the two poems is hard to quantify and therefore a body of evidence is difficult to acquire, or that the *Iliad* and the *Odyssey* are far and away so superior to any other oral poems reported from any culture that the technique of comparison falters.

Nonetheless the manner of the poems is different in subtle and penetrating ways from, say, Apollonius Rhodius' *Argonautica* (third century B.C.) or Virgil's *Aeneid* (first century B.C.), which are epic poems, in various ways self-consciously in the style of Homer and yet composed in writing. They are demonstrably *literate* poems. The *Iliad* and the *Odyssey* are something else, and the theory that they are specimens of oral poetry best accounts for this difference. And superficially it accounts for the fact that these two sophisticated poems can sometimes refer vaguely and sometimes concretely to details of the Mycenaean period, which was several centuries before the Greeks were known to be literate, and also that these two poems can exist in their obvious length and complexity. In some way they must be the product of a centuries-long tradition.

The oral theory had its important beginnings in the observation that unlike normal human speech, which uses individual words as its building blocks, oral poetry is made up of phrases which have a metrical value. Greek epic poetry has a rhythm called dactylic hexameter, that is, six units of timed sound. The basis of the timing is the individual syllables of the words. All but the last of these six units of timed sound are made up of either one so-called long syllable followed by two short ones, or two long syllables. The difference between a *long* and *short* syllable is that a short syllable is timed to be sounded half the length of time accorded to a long syllable (see the preface on language). The symbol commonly employed for a dactyl is $-\smile\smile$ (*dactylos* in Greek means the finger, which is indeed sectioned into two short and one long segments). The alternative, $--$, is called a spondee.

The metrical scheme even with all the possible variations inherent in changing from dactyls to spondees is highly constraining. No word for instance that contains the metrical value of $-\smile-$ in three successive syllables can appear in a dactylic hexametric line. Over a period of centuries poets who chanted the deeds of the Mycenaean kings gradually developed a metrically controlled vocabulary of phrases which functioned for them as a language does for mankind in general.

The most obvious example of this phenomenon is the commonplace name-adjective, sometimes noun-adjective combination, a hallmark of Homeric poetry. We all know the wine-dark sea, the hollow ships, Menelaus of the loud war cry, swift-footed Achilles. It is difficult to demonstrate to the Greekless what is significant here. Essentially it means that the poet by always using an adjectival epithet with these names and certain common nouns immediately has control over a larger part of the line; he knows in advance how he will fill more of the metrical requirements than if he were using each word individually. Greek is an inflected language, that is, the nouns and verbs vary in their endings in differing grammatical situations. This alters the metrical value of the word. This is true of the very limited vestigial inflections in English, for instance the nominative case of the pronoun "he" takes less time to sound than the genitive form "his." We can see how the poets worked with this fact in creating their metrical vocabulary. For instance in the *Iliad* the name Odysseus is generally qualified with "shining" in the nominative case, "god-like" in the genitive case, "great-hearted" in the dative case, and "like unto Zeus in counsel" in the accusative case. The ending of the name Odysseus, as it changes for each grammatical inflection, becomes metrically different and requires a metrically different element to make up a common and easily remembered piece of the line.

This must have been the product of centuries. That is most obvious in the fact that almost *never* do there exist two phrases which are semantically and metrically identical. That would be as intellectually useless and as unnatural as a language having two words that meant precisely and exactly the same thing. At the same time there are formulaic phrases to cover a very wide range of human expression. Obviously centuries of experimentation were required to create the range while at the same time culling out inferior duplicate phrases.

There are other examples of centuries of experimentation and refinement. One which again cannot be easily demonstrated is the fact that many words have been discovered to appear invariably at certain places in the line although metrically they can hold still other places. That is to say, every word clearly has a metrical value. Some of its syllables are long and some are short. By confining key words to certain conventional metrical niches the poets again were contriving a device to control larger blocks of meter. In beginning to formulate an idea the appropriate key word would come to mind, usually a verb. If the poet instinctively felt where that key word would fall he had the means instantly to feel the metrical shape of the vacant areas to either side. Such key words often come in the first third of the line; the name-adjective combination often finishes the line. If the poet were instinctively sure of these two elements, his metrical grasp of the phrases of his poetry would allow him to select the other semantically and metrically suitable components. All this is guesswork on our part. But what we have learned from other cultures is that oral poetry is *not* remembered verbatim, but created afresh on every occasion out of a very stylized vocabulary and with recognizable stock story elements. But created new; so the poet had to be ready to put together line after line of verse moving forward his plot with whatever variations came to him on any occasion. For this formidable task he needed language that would come to him already metrically identifiable. He had to feel his phrases. It is like the way words come automatically to us and we instinctively use them in the correct order (the semantics of "man bites dog" and "dog bites man" are unmistakable, instinctive products of word order), except that the poet had the added factor which, of course, materially altered everything and made his work distinctive, that is, the words or phrases had to come to him as workable metrical components of a line and metrically bondable in juxtaposition. The *Iliad* and the *Odyssey* give ample evidence of this process at work. There are even examples of words which became localized in a phrase and in that context over the centuries acquired another connotation and then appear with the new meaning in another phrase; so that there is in the same poem the identical word in two different phrases meaning different things. That is to linguistics what fossilization is to paleontology.

The language of the *Iliad* and the *Odyssey* is also remarkable in that it was never used for any other purpose. That is, it is nowhere identifiable with the spoken language of either the aristocracy or the people. It is, in fact, an amalgam of dialects. After the breakdown of the Mycenaean Empire in the period of dislocation and wanderings, as dialectal variations of Mycenaean Greek arose, the poets in their movements would encounter these different dialects. Different poets in fact speaking different dialects and encountering phraseology or words from one or another dialect superior or originally good would incorporate this material into the stock of their epic vocabulary. Certain words will only fit into the dactylic hexametric line in certain dialectal variations because otherwise the alternating long and short syllables will not produce part of a $-\smile\smile$ or a $--$ rhythm. Gradually, we assume, there came into being a language markedly dactylic in quality, an artificial language divorced from the vernacular made for the oral spontaneous narration by professionals. The language is so contrived that one cannot imagine amateurs using it well, although in a lifetime of hearing the recitation of this poetry presumably the people acquired a good deal of the phraseology in their memory. This would be something akin to the nineteenth-century American custom of quoting from the King James Version of the Bible, a language apart from daily speech to be used for special purposes, with a very special context.

The oral poet did not create his language primarily in the effort to produce an effect; rather he was interested in some means to facilitate his memory and incidentally make comprehension easier. Nonetheless hearing oral poetry must have been a unique verbal, intellectual, imagistic experience. Special demands are made, vaguely analogous to the special demands which in our time music makes upon auditors in distinction to language. It was a poetic diction with great numbers of its own rules, rules far different than those of vernacular speech. The auditor must have had to prepare himself, to submit, to enter into the verbal experience in distinct ways. While we cannot gauge successfully the nature of the controls and submission we can note that the oral performance in this respect, a very basic one at that, altered the circumstances of the auditor, brought him into a strange (though familiar) land, away and apart from his nominal ordinary day-to-day existence. We might liken it to a trance or a dream.

Other features of oral poetic narration which came about because they were a mechanical aid to the poet became the special strength and vision of the oral poetic utterance. Most important after the idiosyncratic language is the continual emphasis upon the typical. A hallmark of ancient culture is the pervasive tendency toward the static, the normal, the general, in sum the typical. Was it always in the Greek soul, we may ask, or did oral poetry put it there? The chicken or the egg . . . At this distance we cannot easily assess the immense informative power of oral epic poetry, yet we must remember that in the silence of the early ancient world these poems spoke out and made impressions without competition, that thereafter the *Iliad* and the *Odyssey* were recited annually, that every schoolboy memorized them. And then we must remember that the language and story narrative is formulaic and typical. There are no surprises, no changes; this is the poetry of rehearsal. Whether or not it created the classical Greek genius, it obviously suited it.

Typical scenes and typical characters dominate both poems. The *Iliad* is made up of battle narrative, known as *androktasiai* (man-killings). They vary little; hero encounters hero, sometimes descriptive or biographical detail of one or the other follows, then comes a detailed description of the fatal wounding of the victim and his death. Thousands of lines of the poem are repetitions or variations on this. The *androktasiai* are sometimes modified to describe the wholesale killing by one major hero. This event is known as the *aristeia* (the moment of supremacy). Both *androktasiai* and *aristeia* are very like lists, and they share in the characteristics of the catalogue, a technical term used by Hellenistic critics of Homer to describe such dactylic hexametric lists as the Catalogue of Ships in the second book of the *Iliad* or the

Catalogue of Noble Heroines, the phantom legendary great ladies whom Odysseus meets in the Underworld. The eating of meals especially in the *Odyssey* is described in language very similar or exactly parallel. Arrival and departure, again especially in the *Odyssey*, is structured the same and described the same.

The heroes of the *Iliad* are all of them much alike, again typical. Ajax, Diomedes and Achilles are all variations on a theme; the most obviously typical of these is Diomedes and he is most thoroughly presented in this fashion and for this reason in books 5 and 6 of the *Iliad*. Everything he says and does in the *Iliad* is an extension or dramatic realization of what all the other heroic warriors do or hint at. Nestor is an old man; Phoenix, who goes to see Achilles in the ninth book of the *Iliad*, is his double in every way. Priam is the other side of the coin, the old man as destroyed. In no case do we find idiosyncrasy, even the barest manifestations of personality. Achilles' seeming difference derives from his excessiveness; he is the logical extension of the others, extended too far, beyond the point where the heroic world makes sense. There he finds himself alone and naked and his anguish begins. The women of the *Odyssey* in turn derive from types, Circe and Calypso, Helen and Arete; all four share in certain qualities, and Penelope is their summation. Again there are no personalities. Perhaps nowhere is one so struck by this as in Andromache's lamentation for the dead Hector (*Iliad* 22.477ff.) or Calypso's speech of resentment at having to give up Odysseus (*Odyssey* 5.118ff.). There is no hint in either one of a unique, special personal point of view, but each speech builds from the natural, inevitable demands of the situation. They are thus typical speeches.

One can in fact often recognize that speeches are built upon a stock structure. Consider, for instance, the speech in which Paris encourages Helen to come to bed to make love to him. "Never have I loved you so," he says (3.442ff.), "not when first I took you from Lacedaimonia . . ." Substantially the same structure occurs when Zeus submits to Hera's seduction (14.315ff.): "Never before has any goddess or woman so melted my heart . . . no, not the wife of Ixion, . . ." The first version is meant to have a list of place names as the second has a list of Zeus' loves. When we are tempted to consider Zeus' list crude and offensive to Hera in the circumstances and perhaps therefore conceive it to have been humorous, we must reflect that perhaps the original audience was so conditioned to a list speech of this sort that they did not notice what we would see as its incongruity.

Or perhaps similar situations or the repetition of a phrase produces unconscious parallelism. A speech by Agamemnon to Menelaus (4.155–83) and one by Hector to Andromache (6.441–65), containing exact repetitions, are also formally very similar. Both contain the following: "For this I know full well in my mind and in my heart; there will come a day sometime when holy Ilium shall perish, and Priam and the people of Priam of the strong spear" (4.163–65 and 6.447–49). The two speeches have many similarities. Both are speeches of compassion delivered by the stronger of the two persons most immediately concerned. Roughly the same length, they begin by acknowledging one point of view (155–57; 441) but preferring another (158–62; 441–46) for the same reason (the lines have been quoted). After a few more lines the concern of both speeches turns to the person being addressed (169ff.; 454ff.); a situation in which each is humbled (Menelaus dead; Andromache a slave) is envisioned; imaginary remarks delivered at each in their humbled state are evoked (178–81; 460–61). In both cases the imaginary remarks reflect back upon the speaker (Agamemnon; Hector). Both speeches end with a prayer for death if the alternative is to witness the misfortune being conceived.

What are we to make of this? The speeches are separated by roughly one thousand lines so that it is unlikely that the poet is consciously playing the one against the other. Very likely the poet worked out the first speech and when creating the second, as the exactly parallel lines came into his head unconsciously the *structure* of ideas in the subsequent lines of the first speech came to him as well, for it is only after the parallel lines that the two speeches grow to be similar. The important matter here is to accommodate ourselves to parallelism and repetition.

It is instructive to compare the fictitious identities which the disguised Odysseus contrives when he returns to Ithaca (*Odyssey* 13.256–86; 14.192–359; 17.415–44; 19.165–202). Here we find repeated ideas, e.g. he is a native of Crete, a man of rank, victimized in some way. We find exactly repeated language, e.g. 14.258–72 equals 17.427–41, and we find some of the language of descriptions of storm at sea similar to other storm passages in the poem, e.g. 14.314–15 equals 7.253–54; cf. 14.301ff. and 12.403ff. Here repetition plays perhaps a role in the story, that is, these fictions with their parallelism in detail are Odysseus' "routines," so to speak. The exactly parallel lives are effective indicators of the stock and routine nature of the fictions. The approximate similarities in storm scenes are, on the other hand, what one expects from formulaic poetry and no more.

As literate persons we consider parallelism and repetition to be highly emphatic. Because we are never at any moment confined to our text, but can reread or read forward, obvious structural devices seem all the more obvious to us. Unlike the written word, however, a line of oral poetry does not have any existence beyond the moment of the poet's verbalizing it. Once spoken, the line is heard and gone. Parallelism and repetition, like typicality, are at once only a poet's means to organize his material so as to ease the constant burden placed upon his memory. This is particularly obvious in Archilles' description to his mother (1.365ff.) of the events of the quarrel, where a verbatim repetition of the initial narration (11ff. equals 370ff.) appears, omitting the direct discourse, or in Odysseus' repeating to Achilles verbatim (9.122ff. equals 264ff.) the gifts which Agamemnon wishes to offer him. The poet knows a good thing when he has made it and uses the lines again while they are still with him. His auditor, who has no way of reviewing the material, accepts, I should imagine, each moment of utterance as more or less fresh or unique. Furthermore estimates are that we hear no more than 50 per cent of what is said to us. The percentage would naturally rise for serious occasions of recitation. Nonetheless to some extent the auditor who cannot study or go over this material as a literate person can, must indeed, fill in the lacunae from his understanding of the story, the manner of narrative, the language. Subliminal repetition or parallelism is therefore a great aid to him. On the other hand, he is not looking for meaning.

But there is far more to this than the mastery of a technical problem. For here is a world free of accident. Ships that rot on the shore are consistently called "swift"; Diomedes enters the battle described very much the same as Achilles will be later; heroes eat, drink, arrive and depart in a precisely similar way. One hero after another is described as dying on or being buried in "the life-bearing earth," whereby the poet announces the immutability of things. What we have called a poet's technical aid is also a vision of life as sacred, beyond time, laid up, completed before it was begun. Here lie the wellsprings of the ancient Greek overabundant and ever-flowing sense of irony, this inexorable narration of events. In Gaelic cultures the oral poet is a seer; Homer is the high priest of the *déjà vu,* his audience is led again and again to an awareness of what "has been, is and will be," as it is so often expressed in the early poetry. Few things could have been more formidable in the Greek experience than this thoroughly worked-out conception of life and action which has such devastating finality to it. Everywhere the poetic narrative reinforces itself, emphasizes its own validity through repetition, parallelism, typicality and the like. This gives to the *Iliad* and the *Odyssey* their monumental quality, the stability and security of a narrative that acknowledges nothing tentative and no alternative. The choral poets and the tragic poets borrow this technique, at least to the extent that by using epithets and objective and formal phraseology they manage to remind us of the Homeric view of things and thereby to confer upon their own scenes the timelessness and inevitability which can either invoke notions of heroism or prepare us for the irony of the tragic awakening. Plato's search for the immutable reality which lies transcendent beyond the accidental ephemeral congeries of this world we see is a restatement of the fundamental of his childhood education, namely the memorization of the *Iliad* and the *Odyssey.* For he was conditioned to the notion of a transcendent absolute by Homer. His Republic was already caught in the fix of ideal time, the time of never-never land, at Ithaca, at Troy.

The inevitable limitation in focus in oral poetry, the concentration upon the moment, allows for what a reader would call contradictions. There are very real ones, the reappearance for instance of a minor character who has earlier been described as dying. These are insignificant, of course. But there are more considerable contradictions, for instance the apparent contradictions in Achilles' seeming ignorance in the eleventh and sixteenth books of the *Iliad* of Agamemnon's attempt at reconciliation and restitution in the ninth. Achilles angrily resists returning to the fight because he has been dishonored (16.49ff.), and yet we know that Agamemnon has promised gifts and the return of Briseis. It is as though the poet had forgotten what he had narrated before. Indeed it is an omission of this sort which moves many critics of the poems who are steeped in the technique of literary narrative to insist that no one man could have woven a narrative texture so full of holes. Still on the theory that some later editor pieced together a variety of narrative pieces into what we call the *Iliad,* it is more unlikely that such an editor did not catch, as editors invariably do, so enormous a gaffe. It is an omission that no oral poet or audience of an oral poet would probably notice.

In the beginning of the sixteenth book Patroclus makes a strong emotional plea for a return to the fighting. Achilles is made to answer him equally emotionally. If the subject of restitution had come up, Achilles' reply would have had to become legalistic, complicated and indeed quite petulant. The moment does not call for that mood. The argument that so short a time has elapsed between the ninth and the sixteenth book is only suitable, if even then, to realistic novels. It is to assume that Achilles is a real person, that a real span of time exists in the story of the *Iliad.* But Achilles is a creation of the poet and he will be manipulated like a marionette. He has no other existence. Likewise, time is the poet's creation. The distance between even the ninth and the eleventh book—where also Achilles speaks as though ignorant of the offer of gifts—is a great distance, however small mathematically and logically, great by virtue of the interruption which the tenth book provides; for that episode changes the focus and mood significantly. What we have is the poet's concentration on the properties of the moment of narration, a concentration that can exclude any number of story details.

Because every moment of narration has equal value, equal narrative strength, the poet often moves discursively. What we call digressions are common. They cannot be truly called digressions until someone can definitely show what is the *essential* story line of either poem. This is a crucial issue. Repeated hearing of these stories as well as of the numerous other commonplace saga adventures—for instance the many exploits of Hercules or Jason and his pursuit of the golden fleece—must have bestowed upon the memory of every lifetime habitué of this poetry an immense reservoir of saga and mythological information. Again the familiarity must have made the plot movement of the story so anticipated, so inevitable that the tension inherent in getting from one point to another in the story must have been nil. Therefore perhaps the shortest distance between two narrative points was not at all the straight line because the very idea of narrative points in this boundless field of overlapping well-known lines was nil. There are therefore no digressions.

The Catalogue of Ships (*Iliad* 2.484ff.) and the description of Odysseus' scar (*Odyssey* 19.392ff.) are often called digressions. In the first case since the social disorder so vividly described throughout much of the second book and Nestor's strategy to quell it all lead to the Catalogue, one could not in the strictest sense call the Catalogue digressive. Yet because it does initiate action and because it draws attention far away from what we might label the immediate narrative concerns, that is, Achilles' withdrawal and Zeus' promise to Thetis that the Trojans will achieve instant success in battle to demonstrate the Achaians' real need for her son, in this sense the Catalogue can be called a digression. Yet seen in the over-all structure of the poem it provides as a practicality a rehearsal of many of the names of the poem's major figures and structurally and aesthetically it gives the sense of introduction and panorama that a poem of this length and scope needs. Since the poet has an audience secure in its anticipation of the plot, he need not pursue it; he may reveal instead what we find irksome but what his original audience would accept as fulfilling other of their needs than plot information. Furthermore, reports from the field indicate that the audiences of oral poets are keen for catalogues, consider them *tours de force*, and well they might, since the fabrication of hexametric lines from almost nothing other than proper nouns, many of them conforming less to the metrical norms of the language, must be a considerable feat. The poet of the *Iliad* certainly implies that he is up to something grand, contriving six similes as his bridge from the narrative to the Catalogue (2.455–83), and then invoking the Muse again for aid and inspiration, and even, which is very rare, introducing himself into the narrative ("I could not name them all, not if I had ten tongues and mouths . . ." 2.488ff.). At this relatively early point in the long poem the poet by offering a catalogue is perhaps among other things demonstrating his *bona fides*, his poetic credentials and vitality.

The description of the scar of Odysseus leads as well into his birth and the story of his grandfather naming him. Since the departure for this so-called digression was Eurykleia's recognition of the scar we may seem to be rather far afield. Yet there as well the audience is not hot in pursuit of the story, which is obvious, but perhaps more engrossed in the phenomenon of recognition and revelation, which is the constant theme of the entire poem. The recognition of the scar leads to the revelation of his name. Autolycus says (19.404ff.), "Since I have come to this place as an object of odium to many, hated by many, let him be called object of hate, child of woe [in Greek Odysseus]." The scar is the flaw, the mutilation of the heroic skin or texture, and therein stands revealed that strange quality of character in Odysseus, his apartness, aloneness, his nature that commands respect from men, but toleration and no affection. In this sense nothing about the passage can be considered digressive.

Because the poet does not observe a tight narrative line he breaks down the artifice of an arranged view of action. Reality is presented as vast, complex, multi-faceted and spread out in time as we know it to be. This feeling comes through the paratactic grammatical style in which the Homeric language is cast (see pp. 27f.). Parataxis is a feature of archaic Greek language; more than that it is a habit of mind and an aesthetic principle as well, just as we should expect from the all-powerful fact of language.

How the paratactic style produces a kind of reality in the Homeric epic may be seen in the following simile. Menelaus has just been wounded in the thigh by an arrow.

> Straightaway the dark blood flowed from the wound. Just as when some woman stains a piece of ivory with purple, a Maionian woman or Karian, in order to make a cheekpiece for horses, and it lies in a chamber, and many are the horsemen who long to carry it, but it lies there to be an adornment for some king, both an ornament for the horse and a thing of glory to its rider. Just so, Menelaus, your thighs were stained with blood (*Iliad* 4.141ff.)

The immediate comparison is excellent, but the act of staining the ivory has a reality, a history, a vitality of its own, and we are made to move farther, from the shouting moment at Troy to the quiet of a woman's chamber, anywhere in the Eastern world—two places are suggested—then to the living desire which the beautiful object engenders, and finally we are reminded of its universal and ideal function, its inner virtue—an ornament for the horse and a thing of glory to its rider.

The example makes clear the Homeric disinclination to subordinate human experience. Every experience is of equal value, one placed against the next, a progression of equivalence. We may say that this is in essence the highest realism, for it is true that in the daily living of our lives no editor cuts out or shapes anything; we must experience each thing and live each moment, and it remains true when all is said and done that the consummation of a great love affair can often occupy far less time and command far less concentration than the picking of one's teeth.

One of the more important problems in criticizing oral poetry is assessing the effect of its being so much repeated. When the poet describes an audience in the *Odyssey* calling out for certain episodes we can imagine that the aesthetic pleasure came in hearing what was already well known, of hearing it revealed in that special language always just inaccessible to the amateur, and at the same time experiencing the slight or even larger alterations that a unique poetic personality will inevitably give.

The familiarity of his audience with the saga poetic material seems to have given the poet a certain freedom in developing his plot. This may also have been influenced by the naturally episodic nature of oral poetry with its restrained or narrowed focus upon the moment of oral delivery. One finds episodes which seem to be misplaced, but like digressions, misplacement may be altogether illusory. Some are minor and may be nothing more than a matter of taste. Hector and Andromache's farewell in book 6 of the *Iliad,* for instance, is a rather definitive one although realistically there is no reason to suppose that they did not encounter each other again before the fatal moment in book 22 when he meets Achilles before the walls. Still it is the great good-bye, loaded with melancholy foreboding; its very natural sequence is Hector's death, the sentiments seem to be building to that. Yet more than two thirds of the action intervenes. In terms of narrative line, however, the original audiences were so familiar with this melancholic, tender and brave farewell between a woman and her man who is immediately to be killed that they did not need the juxtaposition. The events could exist independently. And here the farewell creates an effect in the over-all description of Troy which we see in book 6, Troy the city, a society, a family, life-supporting, all seen through the women of Troy; Hecuba nourishing and cherishing her exhausted son; Helen, charmingly, warmly talking with her brother-in-law; and finally Andromache worrying over her husband. Hector's farewell shows the fatal vulnerability of this, of the tragic doom of Troy, which is another theme running through the poem. Here in that tearful farewell occurs the one truly deeply affectionate exchange in the poem: the laughter between the couple over the infant fears of their son. (How much it differs in seriousness and humanity from the gods' laughter at Hephaestus in another scene of society, this time divine, with which the first book closes!) Andromache and Hector's relationship rounds out the vision of Troy which Homer has contrived partly in the third book—that is, the fatal and destructive love of Helen and Paris—and mostly in the sixth. The death of Hector, on the other hand, comes as the natural culmination of Achilles' mad rampage, his surrealistic *aristeia* of books 20 and 21. In the twenty-second book the poet takes the elements of battle narrative, that is, the tactics of meeting and killing the victim, brought together with some biographical detail of the victim—often remarks about his parents or his homeland or his wife whom he will never see again. The poet has taken this and enlarged it into Priam and Hecuba beseeching their son from the walls, the chase of Achilles and Hector around the city, Priam and Hecuba looking down on the killing, and finally, Andromache's lamentation from the walls. The poet has separated these two elements—the farewell and the death—in order to use them as components of other narrative formulations.

Still other episodes seem to a greater degree out of place. When, for instance, in book 18 Thetis comes to grieve over her son's sorrow at the dead Patroclus, it seems excessive and out of focus, that is, Patroclus' death is set aside by the poet. As she cradles Achilles' head it is the primal *Pietà*. She is grieving for the dead Achilles, it seems. Some scholars indeed argue that the scene was lifted, so to speak, from another epic narrative describing the death of Achilles. First, however, we may acknowledge what Homer himself so well states (19.301ff.): "The women about her made every appearance of grieving for the dead Patroclus, but in fact each was crying over her own lot." Thetis' grief like any mother's will be for her own son. But more than that. Patroclus' death is the end for Achilles, since, as we all know, it will goad him into returning to battle. Thereby, he will have made the choice to die young and gloriously on the field of battle rather than living out a serene and uneventful inglorious life to old age. Thetis' excessive grief here is an episode taken out of natural narrative sequence. But in a field of action where all is known, and in that sense everything has already happened, the grieving mother at the side of her as-though-he-were-dead son makes perfect sense. Time has been telescoped.

The description of the funeral of Achilles in the final book of the *Odyssey* is another example of misplaced action which serves still other ends. Certainly it has no organic connection with the story of the *Odyssey*. Critics from Hellenistic times on have, in fact, argued that the entire ending of the *Odyssey* is not genuine, largely because of the anomalous funeral description. Here again, however, we have an episode so fully familiar to the original audience that it can exist independent of its logical narrative nexus. And in this way we may in fact see that the poet has succeeded with this description in gaining two ends. On the one hand, he has contrasted Achilles' decent, full, ritually correct burial with the way that the suitors ignominiously and helter-skelter arrive in Hades. This is part of a contrast elsewhere developed; the suitors in their debauch, gauche in their improprieties, are contrasted with Nestor at his ritual sacrifice, knowing the correct thing to do, and with Menelaus, host at a grand banquet, reminding his doorkeeper what is *comme il faut* on that occasion. Secondly the poet has used the funeral to bring the poem to a formal close, a funeral being inherently a conclusion. The poem rather dwindles away otherwise. The poet of the *Odyssey* who everywhere reveals himself to be concerned for structure and organization has taken this episode and used it as a structural piece completely apart from any narrative logic.

The poet of the *Iliad* in keeping with the great and unusual (we presume) size of his poem has created a very large sense of introduction or commencement. He has done this again by taking known narrative elements and using them not so much for their narrative value as for their sense of introduction. The Catalogue of course is truly introductory. The scene on Troy's walls, however, in book 3, as Helen points

out certain Achaian chiefs to Priam, is a truncated catalogue; the same situation with a full catalogue appears in
other poems; and the scene in book 4 when Agamemnon
goes about to encourage his chiefs, naming them and defining them, bears all the traces of a formal catalogue. It
too is brief. But they both (often referred to respectively as
the *teichoskopeia* and the *epipolesis*) induce the sensations of
overture and entree which is a mood the poet contrives to
have dominate books 2 through 7.

Then too, the poet like many another after him manipulates
situations for aesthetic strategy rather than for narrative
ends. The best example is the decision by the Greeks to
build a wall and a trench around their ships to protect them
from the very successful Trojan onslaught. There is not much
real value to this military idea and Homer is quick to say
later on (12.10ff.) that the wall was destroyed and disappeared following the Trojan War, as though to make it clear
that he and his audience know that it was not really part of
the Trojan War saga tradition. It serves him, however, at
the moment. This is an extraordinarily long poem; many
heroes are accommodated in many battle scenes. The language of battle narrative is unusually repetitive, and here
the wall and trench serve Homer by allowing him to describe
another kind of fighting, hence, use a vast repertoire of
formulae that does not suit open fighting on the plain. But
as an integral part of the narrative the wall and trench
tactic amounts to little.

Sometimes a particular narrative development seems to
be rehearsed so as to guide the auditors' responses the
second time around. In the ninth book when Phoenix cautions Achilles against being so obdurate he recounts the story
of Meleager (9.529-99), who refused to go out to fight
despite the pleas of first the community elders who offered
him gifts, then his father, then his mother and sister and
finally his friends. At last at the pleading of his wife he returned to the fight, although, as Phoenix remarks, it was in a
sense too late because they would no longer give him the
gifts. In the ninth book we have Odysseus, offering Agamemnon's gifts, Phoenix speaking *in loco parentis* or for the
family at large, and Ajax pleading for Achilles' comrades.
In the sixteenth book when Patroclus in tears beseeches
Achilles we know that he will yield, Patroclus being for him
his tent mate and soul mate, very much like a wife, like

Meleager's wife in her pleading, and true to the rehearsal we know that it is too late, all in vain. The doomed fact of Patroclus' entry into battle is established in many ways and the Meleager story is an important one.

Repetition of the stories and the common reappearance of various story devices very likely conditioned audiences into certain responses which a modern novelist would be at great pains to generate. Today's narratives need psychological motivation and the justification of realism; ancient epic did not and this sometimes confuses critics. A very striking example of this is Penelope's decision in the nineteenth book of the *Odyssey* to arrange among her suitors a contest of stringing the immense and difficult bow with the purpose of offering herself as prize to the winner. Throughout the poem Penelope has remained steadfast in her loyalty to Odysseus despite her suitors' protestations and importunities. Now she is given several rather strong hints that her vigil will soon end. Theoklymenos, who appears in the story for almost no other purpose than this, prophesies (17.165ff.) that Odysseus is already in his homeland; Odysseus in disguise offers (19.165ff.) powerful proof of this certainty that Odysseus will soon return. Penelope dreams (19.525ff.) a prophetic dream which the disguised Odysseus interprets optimistically. At this Penelope quite abruptly decides to hold the archery contest on the following day and give herself away. In a similar vein a little previously (18.158ff.) Athena puts it into Penelope's head to descend and appear before the suitors whom she has consistently insisted that she loathes, not only to influence them but to ask them for gifts, something rather overtly bridal. The atmosphere throughout is hot, humid and tense.

But why does Penelope suddenly decide to hold the contest? Critics generally consider it to be madness to accept defeat when victory is obviously so close at hand, but they are dealing in logic and psychological realism whereas the poet on the immediate level is not. The poet is playing with a number of well-known storytelling devices to achieve a maximum climax here. One is the winning of the princess in a contest where all but one of her suitors die; the winning of Hippodameia by Pelops is such a story. Another is the arrival of a stranger underdog who turns out to be Prince Charming. We have had a kind of rehearsal of this at Scheria when the unknown and old-seeming Odysseus enters the contest of the Phaiacians and wins. Nausicaa should have been, might have been the prize except that our poet was moving things another way in that episode. Finally there is the common device of the Husband or Protector Arriving in the Nick of Time. Here in our narrative at this moment the poet brings together all these techniques. When Penelope announces the contest his audience would consider it not only immensely exciting but altogether natural.

Much has been said of the mechanical and formulaic in the making of oral epic poetry. The narrative is generally straightforward and obvious in its presentation of action and events. Yet there remains one aspect of this poetic tradition that is consistently beguiling, subtle and allusive; that is, the similes.

The extended simile, that is, a comparison of some length, is a hallmark of literary epic, found again and again in Virgil or Tasso or Milton. It is a direct inheritance from the Homeric epics. While extended similes are common to literary epic, they are unusual in oral epics at least of other cultures. Nowhere but in the *Iliad* and *Odyssey* are they found in such number or so skillfully contrived. Oral epic is an art form in which many of the techniques, motifs and attitudes are common from one culture to another regardless of the language or the nation in which the epic appears. For this reason the Homeric simile is remarkable as a peculiar feature of the Greek oral epic tradition.

The simile may in fact be more remarkable as a demonstrably late feature in the Greek epic tradition. In fact some scholars choose to believe that the "last Homer," so to speak, he who composed the *Iliad* and *Odyssey* as we know them, created the similes. The human world which the similes sometimes describe displays customs and artifacts that anthropologists and archaeologists contend belong to a period toward the end of the epic tradition, rather than to Mycenaean times. Many words used in similes occur in forms that linguists can date as late developments in the Greek language. Furthermore, there are only eight similes repeated in the whole of the two poems. Repetition is, of course, often a criterion of an early date, since the more common a phrase or motif is the more obviously it seems to be worked into the very fabric of oral epic poetry. On the other hand, the phraseology of the similes observes all the other mechanics of oral formular poetry, for example, the traditional metrical positioning of words, commonplaces of meter, the repetition of theme, formulaic phrase, etc. For this reason, and because they work so well in the poetry, and perhaps, most important, because a number of them seem to have developed out of one theme, they are probably the work of some time and many minds. If any synthesis can be made of this information we may say that the evidence suggests that similes were a little-used device which toward the end of the period of oral epic poetry in Greece became a far more important feature of the poetry.

There are other odd aspects. The *Iliad* is filled with similes, varying from nearly two hundred long ones to about thirty short ones. The *Odyssey* has only about forty long and fifteen short similes. The great majority of similes in the *Iliad* (about three fourths of all) occur in battle narratives. Since the *Odyssey* has few battles and considerable dialogue in which similes are almost never found, the lesser number of similes there is reasonable. It is odd, however, that similes, which are supposed to be a late development, occur far more often in the *Iliad,* which is generally considered to be earlier, and in battle narrative, which seems, at least to me, essentially more traditional, hence perhaps older.

Similes do not appear in dialogue. So the first, sixth and ninth books of the *Iliad* do not have many. The focus is always on the action in epic, and in these books the action is redefined by the emotional, verbal reaction of the speakers. Where there is little speaking, as in battle narrative, similes supply the means to reconsider the action.

The extended simile often makes its point of comparison with the narrative action, then evolves organically, true to the dynamics of its own image. At the same time it leaves behind and does not return to any further parallel with the narrative. The comparison of Menelaus' wound with the staining of ivory is of this sort. On the other hand, the simile comparing Paris to a horse seems to adhere at every turn to points of similarity. The majority of similes, however, work like the former example.

Very likely the extended simile grew from simple little comparisons, like "he went along like the night," said of Apollo, or "she rose like a mist," said of Thetis. The development of the simile probably reflects the manner of the poet in creating the entire poem, that is, his beginning with an idea that is a whole, and creating by simply redefining what he has said. The style is one of evolution. In the following simile I have tried to translate as literally as possible to keep the word order. The poet states his thesis immediately (the joy of welcoming the moribund father back to life), then proceeds to reveal the dramatic potential behind the original statement:

> As when to his children appears their father's life as something joyfully to be welcomed back, when he is lying in sickness, suffering strong pains, wasting away for a long time, and a malevolent spirit was hanging onto him, but then the gods freed him from this evil, to the children's joy, so did the land and the trees strike Odysseus as something sweet to see again. (*Odyssey* 5.394ff.)

Although style encourages the poet to leave the original point of comparison, often the secondary elements of the simile reflect the elements of the plot as a whole. For instance, in the one just quoted the malevolent spirit can be equated with Poseidon who holds Odysseus back, and the gods who finally free the man of his sickness can be the consensus of the Olympian council that Odysseus should get home. The children's joy at having their father restored reflects the yearning of almost everyone at Ithaca.

Often closely spaced similes seem to reflect one another. In the first real battle scene of the *Iliad* in a short space (4.422–56) there are three similes. Each relates to a specific moment, yet all three are unified. In the first, as the armies are coming together, the Greeks are compared to resounding waves breaking on a beach. Homer is true to the fact that they are the invading army, beached on the shore and attacking the city. The Trojans are shortly thereafter compared to sheep waiting to be milked, bleating when they hear the sound of their lambs. The Trojans are throughout the *Iliad* portrayed as the defenders of their city and their families, to which the sheep crying for their lambs corresponds. Further, the sheep as victim is a common enough idea in the *Iliad*, fitting to the Trojans. Also the bleating seems to me to imply weakness set against the sound of crashing waves. The effect is much like the opening of the third book, where the sound of the Trojan approach is compared to the clamor of birds followed by Homer's chilling remark that the Achaians came on in silence. The poet of the *Iliad* always finds something ominously frivolous and unpredictable in the Trojan psyche for which Paris is the grand symbol.

The third simile moves the reader away from the immediate scene to a kind of poetic high, describing the battle as a clashing of storm-filled rivers, heard from afar by a shepherd. By bringing together the shepherd and the furious water, the poet has united the other similes, helping to give the simile world a real coherence and consistency. The known and partially visualized simile world becomes another dimension of the entire narrative scene.

In the fifth book of the *Iliad* when Diomedes takes the field he is compared at some length to a winter torrent that sweeps everything away in its path (5.87ff.). As the battle progresses Diomedes triumphs, but he is finally stopped at the sight of Ares, the god of war, fighting at the side of Hector. In his hesitation he is compared to a man who halts in dismay at the prospect of crossing a storm-swollen river (5.597ff.). With this simile the poet implies that the thrust of battle, which is the energy of rushing water in both similes, has been taken from Diomedes. The comparison remains when, toward the end of the book, Ares leaves the battle likened to the black air of storm clouds, source, as we all know, of those sudden violent rains that produce rapid torrents (5.864ff.).

Correspondences between the similes are often to be found. Nonetheless, there is certainly not the one-for-one ratio that appears in the literate poets. Nor is it likely that all the analogies were worked out consciously by Homer. Everything is suggestion, sprung from the subconscious or intuition in which enough ambiguity lies.

The world described in the similes is more homely than the heroic situation of the main story. Farm people and their occupations, the little people caught up in the necessary details of their existence form a world more like that which Hesiod describes in his *Works and Days*. Since Hesiod was not fictionalizing we take his description to be the world of the eighth and seventh centuries. Homeric similes therefore perhaps are the ground line that keeps our perspective. Although there are not enough similes to make this really so, one can almost see a saga world, a divine world and a simile world, all three of them restatements of the human condition. Certainly Homer had no sense of such a schematization; nevertheless, it is there in part, contributing to the extraordinarily ecumenical vision of Homer. The other continuing theme of the simile is the world of nature. It, too, is not of the heroic world. Such similes treat mainly of animals, trees, rivers, or the ocean. There appears, especially in the battle sequences, one theme handled countless ways. It is the wild lion seeking his prey—usually domestic animals in the care of a shepherd. In all its variations this simile rehearses the archetypal confrontation of an invading army and a beleaguered city. Because the simile describes a situation from nature, it reiterates in the comparison the natural rhythm of death and survival that underlies the elaborate heroic war ritual. The development through similes of two worlds is akin to what Gerard Manley Hopkins saw in the imagery of Greek tragic choruses, which he called underthought and overthought. Overthought refers to the immediate surface meaning and underthought to the conception built up simply through imagery.

The significant aspect of Homeric similes is that they work through suggestion. Ordinary epic usage is direct. Scenes and attitude are fully described. But the similes have an economy of language after the fashion of lyric poetry. More is demanded of the reader.

Consider the scene when King Alkinoos feasts Odysseus for the last time at Scheria, and the Ithacan waits for nightfall to be taken home. After several lines describing a lavish banquet scene Homer notices that Odysseus turns his head toward the setting sun, "As a man yearns for his supper for whom the whole day long the oxen have been drawing the plow . . ." (*Odyssey* 13.31f.).

Obviously the supper is Ithaca and the day's labor is ten years of wandering. Ironically, however, the Phaiacian surfeit of plenty produces hunger in a man who, by nature, moves on, lives off wits and a lean belly. The rest and recreation at Scheria, too, has only produced fatigue—the fatigue of impatience at delay, as well as the fatigue of manipulating a strange environment. The simile illuminates the complexity of Odysseus' personality.

The similes show a poet who is exercising close control over his material. Such control, subtly extending into minutiae, somehow seems contrary to the manner of the practitioner of the formulae, the traditional theme and the mechanical response. The relationship between the similes and the remainder of the narrative will always be enigmatic; but more than anywhere else in the two epics one senses in the similes the personal quality of poetic creation.

CHAPTER THREE
THE HEROIC AGE

... and when the earth had covered over that generation, then Zeus, son of Kronos, made still another, a fourth, upon the much nourishing earth, a juster, braver god-like race of heroes who are called demi-gods, the race previous to ours upon this broad earth. Evil war and dread battle killed some of them at seven-gated Thebes, in the land of Cadmus, fighting for Oedipus' flocks, and some, when they had been brought in ships across the great gulf of the sea to Troy for the sake of fair-haired Helen; and there death's end came over and covered them. But to the others Zeus, son of Kronos, gave a place to live apart from men at the ends of the earth and there they dwell, calm in heart, in the islands of the Blessed by the Ocean's deep, happy heroes . . .

Hesiod, *Works and Days* 156–72

Two thousand years before the birth of Christ the Greeks had arrived in the land where they have lived ever since. They moved south into the relatively fertile valleys of the Peloponnesus and established palaces and fortifications which constituted social and political centers. The most impressive remains are at Mycenae, which is why the culture and its people are known as Mycenaean. Homer calls them Achaians and the evidence shows that this was the name by which they were known in the eastern Mediterranean. The Mycenaeans left remains from the Levant to Britain testifying to a far-reaching trading system. Their rich palaces and their eventual domination of the Minoans on Crete suggest empire. They have left us much brilliantly wrought gold, vases, other artifacts, some mammoth palace construction, a rather barren archival record and a tantalizing hint at what the Mycenaean world was like in the *Iliad* and the *Odyssey*. Toward the close of the second millennium shortly after the city of Troy in Asia Minor was heavily damaged in what must have been a large enemy invasion effort, the Mycenaean society perished or underwent profound changes. At roughly the same time the extensive use of bronze gave way to iron.

Serious archaeologists when they try to reconstruct the ambience of the Bronze Age avoid using the Homeric poems as evidence. For contemporary research into the making of these poems has established as an agreeable hypothesis that several centuries of creative effort went into their creation. What we have are probably poems of the eighth or seventh century, four or five hundred years after Mycenae's greatness was played out. Therefore the poems are unreliable, for they reflect different lives at different times. Agamemnon's overlordship may indeed reflect Mycenaean hegemony, there may indeed have been a devastatingly protracted war between the Achaians and the Trojans, but one does not imagine that Mycenaean kings supervised the hitching of horses as Alkinoos does, nor that princesses did the laundry as Nausicaa does. More seriously, could the sense of personal loss and social instability that pervades the background of the *Odyssey* mirror a time when a great empire securely controlled the land?

Yet the *Iliad* and the *Odyssey* are traditional poems. Over centuries stories were passed on from one generation of singers to another and perhaps some kind of continuity with the Mycenaean world persisted. What at the least is true is that the poems describe a world (and people in it) that is different from that of the eighth and seventh centuries when the poems came to be written down. Achilles, Odysseus, Diomedes, all of them are, as Hesiod says, known as heroes. We call this world the heroic age, and make it a reality sometimes equivalent with the Mycenaeans, sometimes more vaguely placed in the never-never land of our imaginations, that once upon a time, part of the Mycenaean age, part of the period thereafter, mostly that time when no written record existed to offer an alternative to the powerful authority that the *Iliad* and the *Odyssey* exert. For we know that there was a time when the Achaians fought at Troy, Hector died, Penelope waited and Odysseus sailed the ocean. No material remains turned up by archaeologists can ever challenge the formidable authority of these poems. Before the seventh century there is only the Homeric Age, that is, the Heroic Age.

For the Greeks themselves with their considerably less efficient techniques at getting at the remote past, the *Iliad* and the *Odyssey* were incontrovertible records of prior times. Most of all the poems preserved—caught in the amber of tradition and sanctified by being taken out of time—a way of life, a system of belief, a vision of life's meaning that became the *a priori* truths of Greek society. Much of this has passed into the general stream of Western culture. The heroic world and the heroes of that world are in some mysterious way apart from the problematical humanity which we must claim, just as Hesiod describes them in the *Works and Days,* but what they did and said in the *Iliad* and *Odyssey* speaks to us directly now as it has for over two thousand five hundred years.

Sometimes, however, the message has been obscured. Today there is a reaction against the *Iliad;* it does not receive the esteem that has been lavished upon it at other times. In the last fifty years, for instance, the major pieces of Homeric criticism in every country have dealt with the *Iliad* and ignored the *Odyssey.* Now when man's killing of man has made outrage shopworn, the ancient Greek heroic tradition begun in the glorious hexameters of Homer's *Iliad* stands suspect. There survives from antiquity a curious essay, its author unknown, entitled *The Contest Between Homer and Hesiod.* It recounts an occasion when the two poets contested in Chalcis for a prize at the funeral games of the last king. Although the contest turns on the skill with which each poet fashions lines of hexametric verse in response to the other, the author tells us (322):

The king gave the crown to Hesiod saying that it
was right for the man who called out for peace and
farming to win, not the man who recited wars and killings.

A lonely voice in antiquity, that, for Homer's supremacy was otherwise not often challenged. He was "the divine poet" or simply "*the* poet"; no name was needed.

The present-day disenchantment with the *Iliad* is an over-reaction to the common German reading of the poem. Nine-teenth-century German romanticism was obsessed with the idea of the hero. The romantic movement coincided with the first serious scholarly work done on the Homeric poems and that ideology entered the scholarship. Seduced by the figure of Achilles, German scholars and critics tended to ignore every other facet of the poem, and there are many. The anguish and ordeal of Achilles were suffused with a projected self-pity and sentimentality that persisted well into the period of the Third Reich when the Nazis positively adulated Achilles, the true Aryan man of strength, the hero par ex-cellence. By contrast Odysseus was often portrayed by Nazi schoolmasters as the prototype Jew. This ideology, at least in the form of excessive enthusiasm for Achilles at the expense of the rest of the poem as well as a tacit dislike for Odysseus and the *Odyssey*, spread to England and America with the arrival of massive numbers of German émigré scholars in the 1930s. It remains a barrier to appreciating the poems. For the *Iliad* is far greater than Achilles' role, although his is the most conspicuous personal drama, and Odysseus, despite certain uneasy-making aspects of his personality, is a testament to the more enduring qualities of human beings.

The French Jewish philosopher Simone Weil reacted to this German philosophy in her celebrated essay of the late '30s, entitled in English translation *The Iliad or the Poem of Force*. She is one of the few critics of the *Iliad* who look long and hard at the battles and the deaths of that poem. In his invocation to the Muse the poet asks that she sing of Achilles' wrath, but he goes on to define the wrath in all of its consequences, the woes to the Achaians, the early deaths, bodies left on the land for the birds and dogs. Mostly critics overlook this. They overlook the long narratives, one upon another chronicling the deaths of warriors, often because they find them boring, while they fasten instead upon the peculiar sorrowful, even tragic, drama of Achilles that is played out in the poem.

Weil's essay will not let us escape so easily to the redeem-ing story of Achilles. Her analysis reduces the poem to a grimness and despair that cannot be redeemed by the per-sonal drama of Achilles. Perhaps she is more impressed where Homer's original audience would have been more matter-of-fact, for in a military society, supported, as the scanty evidence implies, by plunder, violent and untimely death is the one constant. In any case she is too literal. The killings, the deaths, like Agamemnon's heavy-handed suzerainty, are Homer's projection of the inexorability of things. After centuries of recitation and fashioning, the battle narratives had become a distillation rather than specific history. Weil's essay is important, however, because it does emphasize the context against which as well as in which Achilles' story unfolds. When Achilles tells those who have come to him in the ninth book that there is a choice for him of early, glorious death on the battlefield or easy life and quiet death at home in Phthia this is no abstraction. All the battles, gruesome in their detail sometimes, make the choice vivid. This same narrative reminds us that Achilles' ultimate affirmation of life comes from his confronting death, that the dynamics of heroism are bound up in killing and violence. In this early period the Greek word that later came to mean the psychological state of pride (*hybris*) meant quite literally assault and battery. From a late-twentieth-century perspective this is the awful continuing fact of notions of heroism. This may be the reason why the *Odyssey* has been rediscovered these days. Perhaps now the *Odyssey* will receive the critical attention it deserves. But the *Iliad* should not be rejected; it is the best expression of that moment when mankind opens wide his eyes to behold his mortality.

In the nineteenth book of the *Iliad* when Achilles' anguish over his beloved friend Patroclus' death has evolved into a relentless fury, and he seeks to lead out the Achaians supperless against the Trojans, Odysseus coolly encourages a respite for food, advice that seems to sum up the basic difference in the tempers of these two heroes. In turn the difference perhaps reflects the contrasting philosophies that underlie the *Iliad* and the *Odyssey*. Odysseus says:

> Men quickly get their fill of battle
> and the harvest is slight, the bronze
> sword cuts mostly straw on the land;
> Zeus, the battle steward, weights the scales so.
> The Achaians can't mourn the dead with their belly
> for too many fall each day, one after another
> —when does anyone rest from this labor?—

but we must bury the man who dies,
keeping a stout heart, after crying for him all day;
whoever survives this hateful battle let him
turn his mind to food and drink, so that
we will fight the enemy strongly hereafter. (19.221–32)

Everything in Odysseus' remarks reflects the concerns of the hero of the *Odyssey*. The harvest image brings up the notions of the neat, tidy, profit-minded farmer lord who throughout his wanderings yearns to be united to home and possessions again. The observation that an empty belly is a meaningless act of mourning shows a mind bent on practicalities, cuts through Achilles' grief coolly, opposing the common heroic tendency to largeness, formality and theatricality. It is the typical observation of one who could remain a hero while disguised as a beggar. Odysseus' remedy for grief is also typical of him. To bury the dead is to accommodate the unknowable and unworkable to a human scale of things, to act in the face of death which is the ultimate denial of all action; to return to food is to affirm living, to affirm humanity and at the same time to accept its inevitable frailty.

Throughout the *Iliad* Achilles seeks meaning for his life in the face of death. Death is the background against which all action is played and every speech is made. The poem does more than chronicle the psychological disposition of Achilles' wrath; it shows the ceaseless agony of war. War confers heroism upon some, and the poem tells this. Patroclus' entry into the battlefield (book 16) is his triumph before he is at last cut down by Hector. This is Patroclus' *aristeia*, the moment when he alone triumphs and outshines on the field of battle. The Homeric hero is reared to be a "speaker of words and a doer of deeds" (9.443). Thus he is urged to strive for the superlative physically and mentally, in excelling to reach the outermost limitations imposed upon mankind.

The gauge or measurement for any hero lies within; it is what Homer calls his *arete*. Like all concepts, *arete* is difficult to define adequately. It is the realization of the person, his excellence, the achievement of his potential, when he becomes what he has within him to be. For a hero before the walls of Troy this means the most intelligent manipulation of a body at top physical strength and coordination on the field of battle. Wits and physique are pushed to their utmost

limits in battle striving. Although unsaid, it follows that the
moment of fullest realization, of greatest striving, comes in
the contest with death. In this sense Patroclus' *aristeia* in
book 16 is the ideal one.

Death becomes, then, the measure for *arete*. So it is that
the *Iliad* concentrates so much on battle, for only on the
field will the participants to this drama find sufficient dimension. The fighting narrative, the *androktasiai,* must have been
a very popular part of oral poetic saga, for they occur in the
Iliad far more often than one would believe necessary to establish a point or convey a mood. These passages frequently
bore the twentieth-century reader, they are so repetitive, although paradoxically enough contemporary films and television cannot seem to satisfy the craving for violence and
physical mayhem.

The formulaic language that is a major part of the artistry
of the epic bard is never more prominent than in battle
narrative. It must have been the staple of epic tradition, the
first- and best-learned element upon which each apprentice
oral poet built his own creations. Even in formula the details
of death and killing are explicit. From the fifth book, for
instance, there are these:

Famous Menelaus, son of Atreus, struck him [Skamandrios]
with his spear as he tried to get away in front
struck in the middle of the back and drove the spear right
    through.
He fell on his face and his armor crashed down upon him.

(55ff.)

Meriones when he caught up with [Pherekles]
stabbed him in the right buttock. The sharp point
went straight through under the bone into the bladder.
He fell to his knees shrieking and death engulfed him.

(65ff.)

The famous warrior son of Phyleus came near [Pedaios]
and struck him with his sharp spear in the neck tendon.
The bronze spear cut through the teeth and under the
    tongue.
He fell in the dust, and he held the cold bronze in his teeth.

(72ff.)

There are so many descriptions, so close together, of no
tactical value to the audience, surely, and too formulaic to

be personal stories. What remains is the fact of death and dying, rehearsed again and again in a short span of lines. The twitching of hands, the failing of limbs, the stumbling, the shrieking all go to show the frailty of the human vessel, the utter insignificance of man before death.

Not so often there appears in battle narratives an element standing contrapuntally to the descriptions of death. This is the biographical detail given to the victims, sometimes to the victors as well. This detail offers a view of humanity different from the description of dying. Victims are identified similar to the following:

. . . son of Strophios, Skamandrios, skilled in the hunt.
. . . For Artemis herself taught him
how to shoot all kinds of beasts that live in the woods of the
    mountains.
But Artemis who delights in arrows helped him not at all
then, nor the arrows, in which he took such joy before.

(5.49ff.)

Pedaios . . . Antenor's son,
who was bastard born, but shining Theano reared him
with equal care alongside her own children, to do her husband
    kindness. (5.69ff.)

. . . Shining Hypsenor
son of highhearted Dolopion, who was priest
of the Skamander river, and he was honored like a god in the
    neighborhood. (5.76ff.)

If there is one theme common to a majority of these biographical anecdotes it is genealogy, an obvious means of identification. Traditional saga poetry identifies its figures by genealogies; intensified genealogies can be called primitive histories. But the theme has been expanded, or refocused. It is love, marriage and birth that are emphasized in these genealogical references. The story of the love encounter that resulted in the young warrior's birth (6.23ff.), the story of the new groom who left his bride to die at Troy (11.225ff.), or the story of the district's most resplendent bride who married the finest groom who now lies dying at Troy (13.427ff.), all turn on what is traditionally held to be the remedy against thoughts of one's mortality. Marriage and childbirth, whatever they imply—love, sex or both—are the great affirmation of life. These anecdotes animate the narrative and personalize the victims. More generally they provide the true length of horror in death's dominion. Additional pathos is achieved by such fairy-tale motifs as the sons who go out to their doom ignoring their prophet father (11.328ff.) or the youths who are caught, ransomed and caught again (11.104ff.). Through thousands of lines in the *Iliad* man is cut down again and again.

The mood of the *Iliad* is painful, bitter, desperate. At the very end Achilles offers to Priam a description of the divine workings of the world which sheds no more comfort upon man's estate. The gods plan for mortal men to live in misery, he says (24.525ff.), while they live without care (if not uncaring). There are two jars, one of good, one of evil. Zeus sometimes mixes them to give a man an alternately good and bad life; at other times he gives evil alone. The universe is indifferent, the world a place where man appears alone and weak. As Glaukos says (6.146ff.), man is like the leaves of the trees, which the wind scatters to the ground and the spring renews upon the trees.

The suffering and despair are reinforced in the story of the death of Hector; it is also the personification of Troy's fall. The modest reminders of man's reversal on the field of battle, the slight stories of his prosperous yesterdays juxtaposed to the flesh-gouging and bone-breaking of his death are pieces of a theme. The Trojan story with its elaborate dramatic pathos pulls these elements into a common focus of woe. Hector appears as the man of family and city, sharp contrast to the Achaian warriors. In the sixth book he is shown with his mother, his sister-in-law, his wife and his son. Throughout the poem he appears in conversation with his brothers. His mission is to defend his city, his family, his friends. His death signals catastrophe for all. The outcry at his death (book 22) and the lamentation at his funeral (book 24) describe the collapse of the social and familial fabric. Andromache describes the fate of the now orphaned Astyanax (22.477), who will be turned away from banquets without a father to protect him. Helen calls Hector the only kind person at Troy (24.767ff.). In Hector's death civility and community perish too.

The third, sixth, twenty-second and twenty-fourth books give glimpses of the Trojan world. The poet skillfully establishes the essence of Troy in brief sketches; we find the city through Helen, the rather mindless, bewildered adulteress; her paramour, the prince Paris, gentle, sensual and frivolous. They are balanced by Priam's womenfolk, his wife, Hecuba, sharp, bitter, and his daughter-in-law, Andromache, nervous and dependent. These characters project the values and attitudes of Troy, of a settlement of civilization. They are each linked with Hector; when he dies the core of Troy is taken. The fate of Troy, never explicitly described in the *Iliad*, remains as a muted but ever present threnody within the narrative, as present as the never quite stated death of Achilles. Troy's doom is a large tragedy, an expansion of the pitiful theme of the many biographical anecdotes of the battle narratives. The *Iliad*, considered apart from Achilles, is almost unendurably doleful. Like fifth-century tragedy, its spiritual heir, the *Iliad* seeks the meaning of life confronted with death and asks for man's justification. Achilles' anguished demands of Agamemnon in the first book are simply the overture to the greater question, for in taking Achilles' prize Agamemnon has rehearsed the greater and final deprivation.

Epics are generally more highhearted than the *Iliad*, especially epics drawn from martial saga. Fighting, city-sacking and the like are the subjects of these epics, personalities are little apparent and there is little of the speeches that mark the *Iliad*. While action matters in the *Iliad*, what it means to the participants matters even more so. Hector's death, for instance, is described brilliantly by Homer; we see it as though it were a tableau painted on a geometric vase, the men running, the family imploring from the walls. Yet Hector's death becomes vivid in the speeches of his family, who verbalize the agony of bereavement. Thus the anxieties and sorrows that war engenders engulf the simple line of action. Perhaps the tradition that lies behind the *Iliad* in its earlier stages was made up of epics that stuck to the simple story of invasion, siege and destruction. Passages such as the Catalogue of Ships, the more mechanical *androktasiai*, the funeral games and so on probably predominated; they resemble the elements of early epic in other cultures.

The catalyst for change perhaps came in the arrival into the Mycenaean or post-Mycenaean world of the story we can piece together from the surviving passages of various epic poems about the Near Eastern hero Gilgamesh. The epic story of Gilgamesh was common to many areas of the Levant in the second millennium; it bears remarkable similarities to both the *Iliad* and the *Odyssey*. Of particular interest here is the spiritual agony Gilgamesh suffers following the death of his beloved friend Enkidu; he is driven to wander, questioning the meaning of life. Throughout his travels he never finds what he seeks; the story has a profound pessimism to it that is only partially dispelled at the end by the heroic, grand funeral for the dead Gilgamesh.

Certainly the Gilgamesh-Enkidu relationship immediately reminds one of the Achilles-Patroclus story in the *Iliad*. While some will say that the two are physically lovers, Patroclus *is* Achilles' alter ego, and his death engenders in Achilles the feelings of a man who looks in his mirror and sees that he is doomed. Apart from that, the bitterness and despair of the Gilgamesh epic may well have infected the original Mycenaean saga of siege and destruction; like Gilgamesh, Achilles is driven to ask why. The answer is certainly not to be found in the stars. The gods of the *Iliad* seem indifferent to human suffering. Thetis can weep for Achilles, or Zeus for Sarpedon, but these are parents crying for their children. As keepers of the universe the divine family on Olympus is indifferent. The extreme anthropomorphism of these deities not only in bodily attributes but in mental attitudes as well produces creatures endowed with all the drives and wants of mortal man without the restraints which he knows. The divine mind in Homer's epics seems self-indulgent, and often petty. Homer, we must remember, served no priestly caste nor was he slave to dogma; he (or his tradition) was free to portray the gods as he chose.

The poet of the *Iliad* is ambivalent in his conception of the deities. The Zeus who scatters good and evil whom Achilles describes, the Zeus who holds the scales of destiny over the mortal combat of Hector and Achilles, the Zeus who never descends from Olympus to mix in the field of battle as his divine colleagues do, this Zeus is austere, impartial, truly the majestic father of men and gods, less human, more remote. Hephaestus, on the other hand, can appear the true working man wiping sweat from his brow (18.414ff.), Artemis can whimper as shrewish Hera beats her (21.489ff.), while Aphrodite and Ares can be so negligent as to be wounded in human battle (5.334ff.; 855ff.), not to mention being caught in bed together by her husband (*Odyssey* 8.266ff.). Zeus seems truly different from these. Yet Homer has contrived humorous scenes for Zeus as well. The close of the first book finds Zeus, after having assented in deep secret to Thetis' request that he honor Achilles by letting the tide of battle go to the Trojans, returning to Olympus. He appears very much the king of Olympus.

Zeus went home. Straightaway all the gods
rose from their seats at the coming of their father. No one dared
await his arrival, but all stood up to face him.
And so it was that he then sat upon his throne . . . (533ff.)

The majesty hereafter seems to be lost in a domestic squabble.

But Hera when she saw him
knew right away that he had been making plans
with Thetis the silver-footed daughter of the old man of the sea.
Straightaway she addressed Zeus son of Kronos with a sneer . . . (536ff.)

The ensuing quarrel is all too human except for a brief unveiling of power and hardness that seems Olympian when Zeus threatens to stretch out his "untouchable" hands against her (567). The resolution of this scene is both peculiarly human and not, as well. The god Hephaestus reminds his mother Hera of Zeus' power, mentioning the cruelty once inflicted upon himself from which he is now crippled.

Thus he spoke, and shining white-armed Hera smiled;
Smiling she took in her hand a goblet from her son . . .
[Hephaestus then pours wine for the other gods.]
Then laughter without end arose among all the blessed gods
as they watched Hephaestus bustling about through the room.
(595ff.)

Gods, like humans, can laugh and smile; but humans would not laugh so readily in these circumstances. Humans, in fact, throughout the *Iliad*'s first book have been particularly grim and angry in circumstances much the same as this Olympian scene. An angry Achilles challenges the authority of his overlord, Agamemnon. The latter angrily retaliates. Old Nestor attempts to mediate, but the rift is irreparable. Agamemnon takes Achilles' gift of honor away from him and

Achilles withdraws, angry and bitter. The similarity between the two scenes is so obvious that Homer must consciously have planned it so. Hera plays Achilles to Zeus' Agamemnon while Hephaestus replaces Nestor. The humorous incongruity of the Olympian scene approaches the ludicrous set beside the serious and sullen business at Troy below. Why this humorous moment?

Some scholars call the Olympian scene in the first book a parody of divine behavior, but the scene has another kind of seriousness. Olympus is a place where no crisis exists—the inconsequential nature of Aphrodite's wounding (book 5) and Artemis' beating (book 21) substantiate this—and there is no crisis because there is no testing. The gods have the attributes of humankind except that they are also immortal. It is the story of Tithonus in reverse, the man who got immortality but not eternal youth and thus hideously grows eternally older. For the gods have human qualities, but unlike man, they have no capacity for change. Change is the symbol of death. Every day man dies a little, but the gods cannot; man is born to die, but the gods are not. For the gods there is no testing, no identification, no measure to their passions, fears and wants. The Olympian scene shows gods who are inconsequential, all the more so set against the intensity of an Achilles or an Agamemnon. The view is sustained in setting Aphrodite and Ares in the field of battle with Diomedes. The seriousness, the commitment of the mortal hero, his energy and passion come from his facing death. The gods face nothing.

Homer does not mean, however, that suffering is ennobling. It is an ugly thing, indeed, and Zeus sorrows for Achilles' divine horses because of their proximity to it:

You poor things, why did I give you to Lord Peleus,
a mortal man, you who are ageless and deathless:
just to have misery down among wretched mortals?
for nowhere at all is there anything more sorrowful than
    man
of all that breathes and creeps upon this earth. (17.433ff.)

Toward the end of the poem god and man are juxtaposed after the fashion of the first book. The twentieth and twenty-first books contain together one continuous episode (which begins at 19.349), which is Achilles' mad onslaught as he returns to battle. It begins in seriousness; all the gods participate. They gather together at Olympus, every nymph, every river and meadow sprite, the great gods as well (20.79), and Zeus bids them descend to earth to do battle. The *androktasia* that follows is also the *aristeia* of Achilles. As Trojan faces Greek, god faces god; furthermore gods intervene in human action, notably when Poseidon takes Aeneas from battle and Apollo takes Hector. Divine action and statement reveal only superhumanly powerful creatures with the noblest human concerns, i.e. the protection of favorites. The gods' behavior is a match for the earnest striving of the mortal participants until shortly before the end of this episode when the mood changes (21.385–513). It pleases Zeus, the poet says, to see conflict stirred up among the gods. Ares is felled by a stone thrown from Athena's hands. The description of his fall to the ground (406ff.) uses many of the same words that occur in formulaic expressions describing the fall in death of the victims in battle narrative. A grandeur is added in the size of his fall—"he covered seven acres as he fell," a god-like equivalent of such expressions as "he fell like a tower comes down," commonly applied to the mortals. At this Athena laughs. Aphrodite's attempt to help Ares provokes Athena to strike her in the breast, knock the wind out of her to send her sprawling. This is followed by Hera's attack upon Artemis, beating her with her own bow.

As the language describing Ares' fall is formulae reworked, so the passage itself is a perversely created battle narrative. The scene on Olympus in the first book bears strong affinities with the human events, but here there is more than affinity. The typical battle has been peopled with creatures who don't fight fair, so to speak, whose emotions, cynical (Athena's laugh) or child-like (Artemis' whimper), contradict the heroic ethos. The poet seems to be making a statement again about the essential superfluity and vacuity of the divine anthropomorphized being. The typical *androktasia* projects victors enclothed in the glory of their triumphant conquests and victims wretchedly destroyed, cast away forever from the goodness of their past. The *androktasia* is a battle of life and *death*, exactly what the gods cannot share. So they retreat into nonsense.

It is difficult to speak of "ancient Greek religion," there being so many diverse strains always apparent, and difficult even to speak of "Homeric religion" because contrasting ideas of god appear everywhere. Both the *Iliad* and the *Odyssey*, for instance, are filled with many acts of simple piety in which humans demonstrate their acknowledgment and reverence for forces stronger and more creative than themselves. Libations are made, prayers offered, sacrifices performed and so on. The recipients of this religious expression are often stated to be the very Olympian figures whom we are discussing, but often they are not, or Zeus alone is the recipient, addressed more in the spirit of abstract deity than the personalized anthropomorphized god. In some way the poets of the epic tradition have taken the elements of the human personality and created divine figures apart from, greater than cult expression. These are the Olympians; they appear as a group, a family, and as such they form a coherent counterpart way of life and scale to the scene at Troy. They are the workings of the universe, the reality behind the half-understood human moments; for instance, Athena's preventing Achilles from an overt expression of his anger (1.193ff.) is part of the Olympian scene, a facet of the universal order. When the poet shows the gods to be light or silly, set against the seriousness of the terrestrial scene, he reveals a universe dancing to a tune the earth will never know. This is the terrible truth of Homer's gods, a truth with which every successive poet had to deal.

But this terrible truth is also the source of an ennobling strength which shines out in most of the pre-Platonic literature. It is the great redeeming power of the *Iliad*. Man is superior to god, something the Greeks intimate, assume, but never say outright. Man must die, the universe is bleak, there is no reward. Man settles his mind to this truth, chooses and acts, commits himself. Through the looking glass his divine counterpart lives on, playing at life in an Olympian Petit Trianon, never committed, never choosing, without definition, through horrible eternity. So Odysseus spurns Calypso's offer of immortality, so Ajax magisterially kills himself while Athena can only mock, so Oedipus fights and rages to know the terrible truth. The ancient Greeks were not at all pessimistic people, as they are so often portrayed, for they found a glorious affirmation in their steadfast gaze at death. Like Wallace Stevens, they would have said: "Death is the mother of beauty." Much later on in the debacle of the politics of the city, the Olympian religion and the much dimmed heroic tradition, it was Plato, under the relentless, destructive teachings of Socrates, who finally surrendered and turned his eyes to the gods.

Some writers fasten on what they see as an inexorable fate which holds the characters of the *Iliad;* Troy is doomed, Hector is doomed, so many figures seem beyond the agency of god, free will or whatever. The poet, however, is ambiguous about the relative strengths of fate and the gods (who are some kind of projection of free will). The colloquy between Zeus and Hera (16.431ff.) over the impending death of Sarpedon illustrates this. Zeus ponders whether to snatch Sarpedon to safety out of battle. Hera rebukes him for trying to alter the fate of a doomed man, but indicates that the restraint upon him is only ethical. The same ambiguity resides in the scene of Zeus' holding up the doom scales on which are balanced the fates of Hector and Achilles (22.208ff.). True, free will and fate are irreconcilable if set too close together; any poet intent upon a vivacious narrative will be vague. Homer's use of fate or destiny is less rigidly philosophical, and more commonsensical. For instance, in the twentieth book (293ff.) Poseidon rescues Aeneas from what looks like a fatal encounter with Achilles. Poseidon explains to Aeneas his concern that the Trojan prince be killed when otherwise he is fated to survive the Trojan holocaust to lead the remaining Trojans another day. What this means is that all things being equal Aeneas will survive to lead, but if he foolishly or imprudently tries too many heroics, especially in the vicinity of Achilles, this natural expectation will be thwarted.

The gods, fate and the battle narrative make for the bleakness of things. The hero, however, at the center of the narrative, provides a human affirmation and redeems the action. We can call Achilles an existential hero who by his action creates meaning in a meaningless world. The beginnings of the concept of a heroic person (in contrast to the literary term, hero) or heroic ethos derives from oral epic poetry. The heroic person does not differ radically from culture to culture where oral epic poems have been recorded. While Achilles is considered the representative hero in Greek culture, this is only partly true. He is the prototype of hero in tragedy, but not the true exemplar of heroic man in a heroic society. This, in fact, is his personal dilemma. Diomedes in the

Iliad is the figure truest to the standards and values of heroic society. This, too, is Achilles' dilemma.

Diomedes, lord over the cities adjacent to Mycenae, has come to Troy accompanied by his follower and charioteer Sthenelos, with whom he is so close as to insist that they could fight the battle of Troy alone. Tydeus is Diomedes' father, an illustrious man, whose exploits are introduced twice into the narrative as reminiscences (4.370ff.; 5.800ff.). The glory of his father gives Diomedes the support to speak out in council ("Don't be annoyed because I am so much younger than all of you, I also boast that I spring from a noble father . . ." [14.111ff.]), and in his exploits Diomedes identifies with his father's renowned prowess (10.285ff.). Yet because Tydeus is dead Diomedes is not in danger of being eclipsed in the family.

Sure of his valor and his position, Diomedes is yet modest; he understands the hierarchical world in which all the heroes exist. He waits before speaking in assembly to be sure that no other has something to say (9.29ff.); when Agamemnon harshly and injustly rebukes him for unseemly delay before the fight, the poet chooses to underscore Diomedes' sweetness by contrasting his quiet reply with the angry rejoinder of Sthenelos, in turn an echo of Odysseus' angry remarks (4.411ff.; 403ff.; 349ff.). On the battlefield Diomedes can talk tough to his enemies (for instance, 11.384ff.), but then again show characteristic courtliness. The celebrated conversation between Diomedes and the Trojan ally Glaukos (6.119ff.) shows the pride of lineage, self and a common heroic code that prevails among the major figures of this heroic world. Conversely Diomedes is rough in talking with Paris, whose archery and womanizing mark him as perverse.

Diomedes' *aristeia* in the fifth and sixth books is the longest devoted to any one hero. It is the practice of the poet to develop a typical theme or scene completely once and subsequently suggest the form with a minimum of content. Diomedes' *aristeia* is typical and fully developed, Diomedes as he appears in it is the typical hero. He is the measure for Achilles deliberately set up by the poet.

Diomedes enters battle lit by fire, the crown of his superior energy and formidable position. Here as elsewhere he is called "the best of the Achaians" (103). To some he seems to be a god (183ff.), and quite rightly. So superlative is his performance that he is admitted to the divine world as no other hero in the *Iliad* is. Athena removes the obscuring mist from his eyes so that he can see the gods in the field (127f.). He wounds Aphrodite and Ares both. Athena acts as his charioteer (835ff.). Moreover Diomedes talks to Athena in the language of equals (814ff.). Yet he observes the gods' superiority, too (818), and when after three times (surely the enchanted three) he tries a fourth time to rush the stricken Aeneas (436ff.) and Apollo stops him ("Don't try to rival the gods in your designs") Diomedes prudently yields, avoiding the inevitable disaster that comes after the fairy-tale motif of the enchanted three repetitions.

As Homer shows, Diomedes' every action is in tension between the extravagant potentials of his superior body and mind and the limits imposed upon him by the group of warriors about him and by the gods. This is the dramatic activation of the ideas involved in the concept of *arete* which was discussed earlier. Diomedes' thought and action are normal, the Greek hero is normal, and as he moves to extremes, these are the extremes of normal behavior. The association of heroism with abnormality, a Faust or a Captain Ahab, a commonplace of Western tradition, derives from the otherworldliness of the Christ and is foreign to Greek thinking, which continually celebrates the typical.

But Achilles, too, is a typical hero. Throughout the *Iliad* Achilles is uniformly portrayed as the Achaians' greatest defense, the Trojans' greatest fear, pivotal to the entire action of the poem. Temperament, birth and circumstance, however, combine to force him to hold the fabric of his society up to the light of reason. The despair that ensues is an agony with which he struggles throughout the poem. Agamemnon, who does not like Achilles, says of him that he always wants to be superior to all the others (1.207). Patroclus, who loves him, says that Achilles is the kind of man who makes people afraid and who could accuse the innocent (11.653f.). Frightening, quick to anger, Achilles rides the demon ambition of heroism hard. Then too, Achilles has the exaltation that comes with a divine parent. Diomedes can converse with a god from time to time; it is Achilles' birthright. There was a story that Thetis was perhaps to marry Zeus. If it happened, their male child born of that union would be superior to his father (in structural terms overthrow Zeus as Zeus had overthrown Kronos, and Kronos had overthrown Ouranos). But Zeus managed to learn of this doom from Prometheus and gave Thetis to the mortal Peleus as a wife. There is another story that Thetis, wishing to make Achilles immortal, dipped him in the waters of the river Styx, only forgetting that the heel by which she held him remained dry and thus vulnerable. Both stories project the inherent tragic plight of Achilles although whether the stories were known to Homer is immaterial. For the ambition and egocentricity of Achilles come from some mysterious sense of what the best is in fact all about, that best at which the princes are forever aiming, while knowing that it cannot be had.

The quarrel between Achilles and Agamemnon at the poem's start is a crisis for Achilles. The girl, Briseis, whom Agamemnon takes from him is not an object of his affections (although he makes a rhetorical claim to this later [9.342f.]), but a prize given by the troops in recognition of his superior valor and success in battle. Heroic society is hierarchical and public where the esteem and disregard of the group determine a man's status. However valorous and noble Achilles may in fact be, the gift of Briseis establishes and confirms its social truth, just as Odysseus' striking the lowly Thersites proves the latter's impotence and insignificance, although Thersites had just spoken truthfully and to the point (2.265ff.). As the assembly of fighting men accept the social meaning of the blows directed against Thersites, so they may be presumed to react to any public addition or diminution of a man's position.

When Agamemnon seeks arrogantly to take Achilles' girl he is in effect stripping Achilles of epaulets and braid. The anger with which Achilles reacts swiftly places him at the very edge of the conventional world he knows. Anger, which is the extreme of individualism, sets Achilles outside the group and produces some cynical questions about the nature of the heroic world (1.149ff.). Achilles questions the hierarchy but, more important, he questions the motives of war. Suddenly the heroic logic of *arete* and *aristeia*, glory through battle and status through valor, is no longer enough for Achilles. Abstractly Agamemnon's taking Briseis causes Achilles to lose group esteem, so to lose his place in the group. Instead of that abstraction being dramatically realized the poem moves to a more profound level. Achilles' cynical questions take him out of his place; he is isolated from the group and the philosophies which sustain it. This is dramatically realized by his retiring from the field of battle. Some time passes before we see Achilles again; in the interval the principle of hierarchy is pressed more than once. It is originally abstractly presented in Nestor's speech to the angry leaders (1.247ff.), then dramatized in Odysseus' striking Thersites and in the marshaling of the forces by their leaders (Catalogue of Ships, Catalogue of Trojans, 2.484ff.), then finally portrayed in the visit by Agamemnon, the overlord, to his allied chiefs (the *epipolesis*, 4.223ff.). Diomedes is presented sympathetically as the hero in his milieu whom the hierarchy shapes, from which he derives his sustenance.

Hierarchy and the heroic logic of fighting are all that Achilles knows. They are the only comforts available against the cold emptiness of human existence. When Achilles rejects Nestor's pleas and withdraws from battle, he sets himself adrift: It is then that the poet contrives perhaps the most memorable episode of the *Iliad*. The Greeks grow desperate, they seek to enlist Achilles once more in the common cause. Odysseus, Phoenix and Ajax are dispatched to see him in the ninth book. There the poet has created something extraordinary in the poem, he has managed a control and subtlety which to an extent defy the dicta of the theories of oral poetry. For one, the scene is almost allegorical. Odysseus arrives with gifts of recompense for Achilles. He analyzes the gifts as symbols of restitution and Achilles' role as fighting man in an army depends upon public acclaim. But Achilles says no to the lure of public honor. Then Phoenix, the old man, loving guardian of Achilles' youth, speaks tearfully and emotionally of the love he bears the young man, then speaks to the obdurate, proud personality, counseling him to yield. It is in part a refrain of what old Nestor had said of hierarchy in the first book, and again Achilles says no, this time to the sympathetic wisdom of a surrogate father. Finally Ajax speaks briefly of the desperate fate of Achilles' comrades in arms, there dying on the battlefield. For the third time, in folk tale the fatal time, Achilles again says no, here to the loyalties and love that a man feels for his peers. Alone, in physical isolation, Achilles has now cut himself off from all society, rejecting any claim which it might make upon him.

When Achilles rejects Agamemnon and withdraws from the army to brood alone in his tent he has rejected life, for the heroic milieu is the only one he knows. His environment forsaken, Achilles is naked before death. The choice his mother gave him comes foremost to his mind since death is the only reality still with him for sure. The hero Gilgamesh forsakes his normal life and wanders in search of life's meaning only after death has come to him in his companion Enkidu's death. The *Iliad* is more complicated. Achilles' rejection of the heroic life brings on his alter ego's death. In this way death finally comes to Achilles too as it had come to Gilgamesh. But as the ninth book testifies Achilles is already alone with death. Patroclus' death is only the acting out of those feelings.

But, of course, one must not lose sight of the story. The hotheaded young man, clear-eyed and angry before Agamemnon's arrogant and hypocritical ways, the distaste, the hurt and the withdrawal; then later, the contempt for Odysseus, the obduracy bordering on childlike petulancy with Phoenix all set beside the thoroughly noble, restrained, solid but not at all too sensitive Diomedes. The *Iliad* is first of all a story, one that gains forever in the retelling. One reason why the *Iliad* may be so satisfying is that the story incarnates the human response to death. We are the animals who must confront our own mortality. From the first day we become aware that we too must die until that moment when the death rattle grows in our throat we must accommodate ourselves to death. Recent studies of the psychology of terminally ill patients show striking similarities of feeling with that which Homer gives to Achilles. Denial and isolation, anger, bargaining, depression and acceptance in that order are what passes through the dying person's mind at successive stages of his last career on earth. They are Achilles' feelings as well, for as the story unfolds Achilles comes to meet his death.

The rejection of the ninth book comes dramatically alive in the death of Patroclus, his close friend, his alter ego, whose departure signals Achilles' own death. His enduring wrath against Agamemnon like his mad anger at the death of Patroclus are furious forms of sustenance against this emptiness. The poet has contrived an awful battle, almost surreal, that stands symmetrically against the earlier *aristeia* of Diomedes; it is the wild cry of his agony as he tries all extremes to shake off the burden of nothingness.

Finally it is the sight of Priam come to ransom Hector's body that frees Achilles. The old man makes meaning in an indifferent universe when he approaches the young, brooding hero in his tent, kneels before him, takes his knees in supplication and kisses "his hands, the terrible hands, man-slaying, which had killed so many of his sons" (24.478f.). The courage breaks Achilles, he cries and the wrath and the fear are over; he has not come back to the hero's world, but simply to life. He has come to accept the frailty of life, the fact of mortality. So finally it is he who can urge the old man to lay aside his grief and turn to food (24.601ff.); he has come to affirm life as Odysseus does.

In the *Odyssey* Odysseus is offered immortality and he rejects it and he visits Hades and returns. The first act is a philosophical affair, the second bears intimations of cult ideas, however obscured, of death and rebirth. Both give to Odysseus a logical extension of the personality with which he is endowed in the *Iliad*. Nowhere else in fact is there such consistency between the two epics as in the character of Odysseus.

When Calypso offers Odysseus immortality and warns of the impending dangers if he should continue to head for home, he replies that he must go home, that he has suffered too much already to worry about the misery ahead. He has rejected immortality for home; the greater value lies in humanness even with or perhaps because of its temporal limitations. In that direction lie both homecoming and suffering. The return is in a way a reinstatement, a rediscovery of self. Strange environments and the disorientation that they cause do, it is true, make for self-examination. Expatriates are forever finding their true self. Odysseus himself, according to later tradition, could not endure to remain in Ithaca, but set out himself on additional voyages. Still, wandering precludes complete integration into an environment, that absolute spatial realization of self which the Greeks especially insisted upon. Suffering, in turn, is the process whereby a man learns his uniqueness, which is the other side of environmental integration. Suffering integrates one internally, because one can only suffer alone (using "suffer" in the sense both of experiencing pain and enduring it). God, immortal, omnipresent and invincible, can never know suffering or exile. Eternity, ubiquity and insensibility are not only hard to grasp, they are stultifying in their implications. Odysseus' essential heroism is the rejection of Calypso's offer, despite the grayness of afterlife in the Underworld (as it is described in the eleventh book).

Odysseus' refusal of immortality is a paradox. Homer has

shown us what life means to Odysseus in the contrast he draws between the adventuresome hero and his craven crew. The chasm is vast that separates the noble from the ignoble lust for life. Odysseus is concerned with living, whereas the crew is concerned with survival. At each dangerous turn of the journey Odysseus seeks to learn the new while the crew looks for escape. Everywhere they seek food, he seeks information. Ironically, the crew's efficient concern for survival brings about their own death. Confronted with hunger and surrounded by the Sun God's taboo cattle, they cannot look beyond the physical act of immediate survival to spare the sacred beasts. Thus they perish, whereas Odysseus, the much-enduring, the much-exploring, the gambling man, survives through a sophisticated prudence. The paradox seems important to the poet because he mentions the episode in the opening lines of the epic.

The mentality behind Odysseus' actions is found in the reply that Paris gives Hector in the third book of the *Iliad* when he is reproached for his constant sexuality. "The gifts of the gods are not to be thrown away," he says (3.65). In one sense Paris is saying that once the human condition is set, it should be exploited to the full. For Odysseus this exploitation becomes the search for the new and the strange wherever he is on this earth.

Here is the background for Odysseus' refusal of the gift of immortality. Immortality betrays the fairy-tale mentality, and the hero wandering in the land of marvels rejects it as alien. Immortality—eternal stagnation—must finally be beyond the ken of one who lives completely in this world. Immortality is for the survival-minded, not the venturesome. Eurylochos persuades the crew to eat the cattle of the Sun God with this argument.

All deaths are hateful to us wretched mortals, but most
pitiable is to die of starvation and meet your doom that
    way. . . .
If the Sun God is angry because of his straight-horned cattle
and wants to kill us, and the other gods follow along with him,
I should rather die drinking down at one fell swoop the ocean
    wave,
than to die slowly on this desert island. (12.341ff.)

The survival-minded fear death; the crew is afraid of the experience of dying as Odysseus is not. Not a little of his

objection to immortality is that the experience of living makes
sense only in the dying. No curious man would give this up.
Beyond this Odysseus understands man's essential weakness
and insignificance. The weakness and insignificance make living, being alive, the central good. Therefore to live fully, to
experience all life's ramifications, is to participate in the good.
It is to experience joyousness. Immortality by removing
frailty and transitoriness also denies to life its supreme value.
Odysseus' advice to the suitors says just this:

> Of all the things that breathe and crawl on this earth,
> nothing does earth produce of less consequence than man.
> For as long as the gods give him manliness, moral integrity,
> virtue [the word *arete* means many things] and his knees
> work, he thinks that he won't suffer evil in the future. But
> when, as will happen, the blessed gods make things
> wretched, these too he must bear with an enduring spirit
> though he be suffering. For man's mind and disposition is
> no more or less than what the father of men and gods
> causes it to be each day. . . . Wherefore let no man ever
> ignore the unwritten laws of this universe, but keep in
> dignity and silence whatever gifts the gods may happen to
> give. (18.131ff.)

Telemachus, alternately despondent and helpless before the
outrages of his mother's suitors and wide-eyed in amazement
at the life-styles of the princes of Pylos and Sparta, moves
through the opening episodes of the *Odyssey* in a quest for
news of his father that serves as his voyage of discovery into
the ways of the world. A goad to his inaction is the story of
Orestes, an example (*paradeigma*) of filial loyalty and courage that is served up to the hesitant Telemachus more than
once. Throughout the first half of the *Odyssey* the poet often
returns to the story, of which Orestes' vengeful slaying of
his mother's paramour, Aigisthos, is only the final act. In
adding other details, Clytemnestra's seduction for instance or
Agamemnon's murder upon his return from Troy, the poet
has created a leitmotif which illuminates certain potentials in
the drama being played out at Ithaca. At its simplest there
are marked similarities: a queen alone, suitors on the prowl,
waiting; a husband making his return from Troy; a son who
detests the suitors. The similarity animates the story with
suspense; could Penelope behave as Clytemnestra did? Agamemnon's angry denunciation of Clytemnestra and praise of

Penelope (*Odyssey* 11.444ff.) is only one occasion in which the suspicion is naturally raised.

Questions more profound than suspense, however, are engendered by the juxtaposition of the story of Orestes, Clytemnestra and Agamemnon to the drama at Ithaca. There are many things to be learned from it by Telemachus besides examples of courage and piety. In his own way Telemachus is as deprived and desperate as Achilles in the *Iliad* but he learns different lessons. This is apparent from the very beginning of the *Odyssey*. The author of the *Odyssey*, in fact, seems to have in mind Achilles' bitter observation about Zeus' jars of good and evil when he contrives in his very first scene to have his Zeus criticize human irresponsibility.

Great Heavens! How mortals do go on blaming the gods,
insisting their miseries come from us, whereas they themselves
contrive woes beyond measure out of their own stupidity.

(32ff.)

Zeus presents as his example Aigisthos, who seduced Clytemnestra despite the gods' grave warnings and in the end paid with his life for it. Humans *are* responsible, Zeus is saying. Furthermore the notion of warnings from god bespeaks a rational scheme to the universe, for which the gods are keepers. Instead of the bleak picture Achilles draws for Priam of an arbitrary and random dispensation of evil (24.527ff.), the Zeus of the *Odyssey* makes good and evil the natural and inevitable fruits of man's behavior.

As the suitors stalk Penelope, then, larger questions are raised. Will the beleaguered queen avoid the stupidities of Clytemnestra and Aigisthos and so spare her family the dissolution that was the fate of the House of Atreus? Penelope is indeed different. Her constancy and chastity only reflect the sense of responsibility and self-control, the coolness that marks all successful people in the *Odyssey*. Agamemnon, Aigisthos and Clytemnestra are destroyed because they are witless, self-indulgent or unsuspecting. Prudence on the contrary marks all of Odysseus' family.

And awareness too, for as Odysseus often demonstrates, he recognizes the forces and rhythms to his universe. For instance after being buffeted about in the storm sent by Poseidon while daring a landing upon a rocky shore, he senses a river flowing into the sea, and in his heart prays:

O Lord, whoever you are; hear me I beseech you, the answer
to all my many prayers at sea. . . .
Even the immortal gods reverence a wandering man
. . .
pity me, o Lord; I throw myself upon your protection.

(5.445ff.)

Piety of this sort is one of the first lessons Telemachus is
made to learn when he visits the kingdom of Nestor at Pylos
(book 3). He arrives as Nestor is offering sacrifices to
Poseidon and when he departs Nestor offers a sacrifice to
Athena. Sobriety and humility accompany the feasts that
follow the religious offering. The poet makes much of the
correctness of the ritual; he presents an abundance of detail
and includes a charming exchange between Nestor's son,
Peisistratos, and the disguised goddess, Athena, that turns on
the correct mode of libations (3.36ff.). The immediate contrast is with the chaotic and anarchic banqueting among
the suitors at Ithaca, but Nestor's family's common sense
and knowledge in turn touch at other points of the poem. For
instance, the initial description of Eumaios (14.5ff.), the
swineherd, has immediate similarities. Odysseus comes upon
Eumaios busily engaged just as Telemachus came upon
Nestor. The description of the swineherd's farmstead and his
making sandals is again a picture of knowledge, rules, the
imposition of order on nature, here in the secular rather than
religious part of life. Organization and the knowledge and
discipline that lie behind it are important to the poem; it
appears in the description of Calypso's home (5.55ff.), the
elaborate description of Alkinoos' palace (7.81ff.) and elsewhere. It is an affirmation of man's control, his responsibility
in the universe.

Conversely the episode in Cyclops' cave has all the horrors
of the unknown and unmanageable which come from passions
and attitudes not tempered by the conventions man has drawn
to order his relationships. Odysseus' stories of his fabulous
travels involve men and beasts from the realm of magic and
fairy tale. Their estrangement from the human scene is nowhere greater than among the Cyclopes, who will not observe
man's laws of hospitality, for a stranger arrived was sacred to
the ancient Greeks, as the *Odyssey* everywhere affirms. Part
of the horror of Agamemnon's death is that he is struck
down newly arrived, unawares, thus most vulnerable; the

reason for the exquisite delay in learning Odysseus' identity at the court of King Alkinoos is that a stranger must have the opportunity to recover himself from the exhaustion of the road before he must indicate himself to be friend or foe. The action of the poem moves from one arrival to another, permitting the characters to be caught up again and again in the machinations of greeting that require tact, an adroit manipulation of autobiographical details, patience, all the qualities developed by persons anxious to hold the social fabric together.

The *Odyssey* in this respect is a moral poem; man's conduct toward man has paramount importance. To be sure the failure to protect a newly arrived stranger violates Zeus' laws of hospitality and is therefore an act against god. That fact of religion, however, which motivates the good will of every reception, is not stressed; the emphasis shifts to the matter of human good will. Nowhere is this clearer than in the lovingly developed encounter between Odysseus and Nausicaa (the sixth book), where the most subtle considerations affect every move the two make.

In his relationship with Nausicaa Odysseus shows equal portions of sensibility, grace and intelligence, so that the episode is as subtle and complicated as his reunion with Penelope. The Nausicaa episode has a frame beginning with Homer's comparing the young Phaiacian princess to Artemis, virginal, chaste and robust. Odysseus repeats the idea in his initial speech to the girl ("If you are a goddess . . . I myself would compare you to Artemis" [6.150ff.]). The frame closes with the story of Aphrodite and Hephaestus where exactly the opposite qualities are presented, that is, indulgent sensuality, foolish adultery and public scandal. The Aphrodite story, furthermore, re-creates in microcosm the theme of the entire poem: the wife and suitor, the revenge of the husband. Odysseus' role is redefined at this moment. Clearly enough his destiny is not to stay at Scheria. Not long after the song Nausicaa says farewell to Odysseus. In the entire episode Nausicaa is almost a protagonist. She tries to seduce Odysseus, politely enough, to be sure, and she rejects him at the end. Her sensibility to the possibility of marriage and later to its impossibility makes her one of the cleverest, most sensitive girls in literature. She is testimony to the poet's conscious elevation of intelligence, sensitivity and verbal skill over all other human attributes.

Athena picks up the theme of marriage when she appears to Nausicaa in a dream. The dream itself, as we moderns know, is Nausicaa's subconscious wish in any case. Athena talks of the need of clean clothes, for the time of Nausicaa's wedding must be near at hand ("You won't remain a maiden very long" [6.33]). Nausicaa upon awakening alludes to her bachelor brothers' need for fresh clothes, because, as the poet says, she is too shy to speak of her own possible marriage. Only here does the poet introduce that sort of stage direction. Once having established the conflicts between desire, propriety and maidenly shyness, he unfolds a superb scene of human beings reacting to one another. When Odysseus steps forth from his hiding place he supplicates Nausicaa in alternating allusions to her physical comeliness and to her marriageable state. The speech is intensified by Odysseus' naked predicament, which the poet amplifies by noticing his concern to cover his manliness, his decision not to embrace Nausicaa's knees, as any ordinary suppliant would, and his determination to wash himself, although young girls customarily wash men in the *Odyssey*. These contradictions to normal behavior show his sensuality and that he is conscious of it. He is in the midst of lovely young girls, virginal and naïve, as he knows. His defenses are down and he wants to avoid trouble.

Nausicaa's response is flavored with the idea of marriage. She even mentions it openly to her maidens ("Would that such a man were called my husband" [6.244]). When she apologizes to Odysseus for not wanting to walk with him through the city, she demonstrates her cool prudence, her middle-class good sense, as well as a conception of public good behavior that contrasts with Aphrodite's spectacle later on. Nonetheless, the whole speech is a none-too-subtle hint that Nausicaa would like to marry Odysseus. She has presented her case indirectly and at an early stage—as befits a girl in a position of power who desires a defenseless male.

Everywhere the episode is marked by taste and intelligent subtleties. The Phaiacians are obviously the most civilized people in either epic. As Alkinoos says:

> We are not great boxers or wrestlers, but we can run swiftly on foot, and are the best when it comes to ships. For us the banquet, the lyre, dancing, changes of clothes, warm baths, and couches are always the nicest things.
> (8.246ff.)

The Phaiacians possess all the ingredients for enjoying human existence. Their *politeness* shows how they cherish human beings.

Notice how Alkinoos asks by indirection if Odysseus is perhaps a god, in a subtle attempt to get Odysseus to reveal who he is before the ritual moment for asking identities has arrived after the dinner. In turn Arete quickly notices that Odysseus is wearing palace clothes and uses it as an opening to his identity. ("Who are you? I thought you came from overseas. How did you get those clothes?" [7.238f.]) Odysseus, stalling, answers her several questions in reverse. As soon as he has finished describing where he got the clothes, Alkinoos cuts in, thereby freeing him from further identifying himself, which by now it is clear Odysseus does not care to do. Notice how nicely Odysseus lies for Nausicaa when her parents object to her not having had the manners to lead Odysseus up to the palace. ("I didn't want to [go with her] out of fear and shame" [7.305]) Alkinoos puts his case for Odysseus marrying Nausicaa very cleverly, if suddenly. After rather abstractedly offering the marriage, he speaks longer about the means of transporting Odysseus home. As persons of sensibility know, if one has a shocking or daring proposition to make, he had best offer at greater length an alternative, far less drastic course of action, so his prey will not feel desperately cornered and react desperately. Odysseus effectively says no to the idea of marrying Nausicaa by saying nothing. Alkinoos understands this, and quietly assumes that Odysseus has a wife and children elsewhere, to whom he alludes in a later speech ("When you are dining in your halls with your wife and children, you will remember our manliness" [8.242ff.]). The farewell between Nausicaa and Odysseus vibrates with all the things left unsaid. She gives him a chance to mention why he is leaving when she says, "You owe to me first your life," but the brevity of her speech eliminates any real need to answer anything. Odysseus, the perfect gentleman, says no more than Nausicaa. He does not mention his family as he had to Calypso with whom he had been sleeping. He subtly alludes instead to the moment of their meeting when he says that he will pray to her as to a god, echoing his comparison of her to Artemis in his initial speech of supplication. He thus returns them to their nicest moment, when everything was fresh and possible for them.

The divine entourage of the *Odyssey* in turn has been accommodated to the intensely human scale of the poem. Olympian gods are scarce—Zeus at council, Poseidon among the Ethiopians; minor and strange deities crop up in fairy stories. Only Athena remains, demonstrably an Olympian, prominent in the action, even appearing in her natural guise to Odysseus (13.288f.) rather than in disguise. Yet Athena appears so frequently in the action that her presence becomes less a deity and more a human companion, at most a guardian angel. Greek gods are so anthropomorphized that they need mention of Olympus or reminders of their immortality to keep the perspective. Athena in the *Odyssey* has little of that. In turn she is therefore not available to give a theological context to human actions, which as a result seem all the more relevant only in terms of fellow humans. Hence the distinctly moral quality of the poem.

Conduct, organization, behavior, know-how, all key ideas in this poem, imply a world of rules, or conventions, both on the unseen divine level and on the human social level. The battle between Odysseus and the suitors has these implications beneath the surface. The suitors, as their defense of their position in the second book of the *Odyssey* shows, have a certain right on their side. King Odysseus is long overdue, missing and presumed dead. The implication is that the succession passes to the husband of his widow since there seems to be no idea of regency (although beneath the so-called realistic level on which this is played one can discern an earlier matriarchal point of view where the queen is the key to the throne if not the holder herself; this is also Jocasta's position in the Oedipus story). The suitors therefore are right to seek Penelope's hand, she is somewhat in the wrong to deny them. But whatever justice the suitors may find for their cause is dissipated in the course of the poem, first in their outrageous behavior in the missing king's palace, but more importantly in their confrontation with Odysseus disguised as a beggar.

The marvelous suspense that is engendered in the extraordinary delay between Odysseus' first appearance before the king and queen of the Phaiacians and his revelation that he is Odysseus (7.145–9.19) is repeated and considerably amplified in the suspenseful passage of time between the disguised Odysseus' arrival at the palace (17.328) and his successful handling of the great bow followed by his acknowledgment that he is Odysseus (22.35ff.). Again and again the suitors and the sluttish female house slaves, their whores (a male's point of view, of course—what choice had they?), irrevocably place themselves in the wrong. The wrong is their maltreatment of the disguised Odysseus the man, Odysseus the stranger and Odysseus the favorite of Athena and several other gods. They are acting out the wickedness of Clytemnestra as it is so often described in the poem. Their error is both human, personal and a crime against the divine system. After Antinous has struck the beggar, one suitor calls out to him:

Antinous, that wasn't a good thing to strike that miserable beggar; you're ruined if he turns out to be a god in disguise.
(17.483f.)

Odysseus, of course, is no god in disguise, yet Antinous has in this way outraged the gods; the poet does not say this directly but the tenor of the confrontation between Odysseus and the suitors throughout these passages has the feeling of divine testing. Again the suitors are committing a moral offense, and the gods' anger is manifested in that terrible and sad scene as the suitors sit to laugh at Telemachus' earnestness. They are drunk and their laughter suddenly dies:

But then they were laughing with jaws over which they had no more control;
the food they had was splattered with blood; their eyes filled with tears, their minds with sorrowful thoughts.
(20.347ff.)

Here is the suitors' doom; they have broken the laws of the universe; they are almost sinners in Christian terms.

By contrast Odysseus is a man who seems to have done good and whom good attends, and who seems to get the reward because the suffering, the wandering, the daring and enduring have meaning finally in heaven's terms. Particularly Christian poets found the epic form congenial, the epic form as it crystallizes in the *Odyssey*. It is the *Odyssey* indeed that is paradigm for most later epics for this very reason.

Yet the *Odyssey* itself is no philosophical tract or even a philosophical poem. Because it was created at a time when poetry's function was profound and social it breathes with meanings and questions and further questions. Despite the poet's announcement that there is a rhythm apparent in the universe, which fosters goodness and puts down wrongdoing, Odysseus is a hero too complicated to be analyzed as the allegorical good man. He is a man aware, thus prudent and humble. In the latter half of the poem Odysseus manipulates the suitors so that they act in the wrong and the ensuing contest can appear in part as one between good and evil. But he is not actively good, rarely well-meaning.

Odysseus can show no sympathy for the legitimate beggar Iris who haunts the suitors' sides, he can countenance the cruel torture of his slave Melanthios for his insolence, he can play a teasing game with his lonely, sad old father, and time and again he quite arrogantly can force his crew into situations that destroy them or nearly so. And then he lies. He lies every chance he has, practices cunning and deceit absolutely instinctively. To be sure, the times the *Odyssey* supposedly mirrors were desperate, it seems. The aftermath of the collapse of the Mycenaean Empire was political, social and very often personal chaos and the poem reflects this. Then too, the goddess Athena particularly admires and favors Odysseus for his consummate skill at deception (13.291ff.). Odysseus has many attributes of the trickster god, Hermes. Perhaps this is owed to the atmosphere of fairy tale which pervades the *Odyssey*, an atmosphere that confers its own ethos. Nonetheless he succeeds where others fail in this poem; he does not succumb to stupidity. His wisdom, his sense of the universe sustain him, yet he is not a "good" man. Masking inward joy with outward cool, humble in his understanding of the powers that hold man, arrogant in his assumption of his own worth, sociable and personable toward every kind of person, though never sympathetic, always private, sensual and fastidious, cruel and cunning, serious and dignified, Odysseus is the most exciting and profound character that Graeco-Roman paganism ever conceived.

Odysseus' success faintly evokes the turnabout of events familiar to fairy tales. Apart from his heroic stature ensured him by the frequent references to his role in the saga story of the Trojan War Odysseus is a little like Cinderella, a man with all the odds against him—Poseidon, the suitors, the inexorable passage of time, among others—who with the help of his fairy godmother, Athena, arrives in the nick of time to triumph quite incredibly over his adversity. This is a thrust within the story as strong as the idea of the victory of good over evil, paralleled by Telemachus' change from a sniveling ineffectual boy to a commanding young man. Odysseus actually sees himself as a kind of Cinderella figure. The false identities he invents, for instance, cohere in certain essentials; they create a portrait of the underdog. Odysseus is always a family man in these stories, true to the peculiarly strong homing instinct in this hero. He is a victim often; in one story someone of greater importance tries to force him to serve under him, and elsewhere his half brothers try to do him out of an inheritance. He is an outcast as the bastard but best-loved child of a ruler surrounded by jealous legitimate brothers. He is a misfit when he cannot serve another because he is too talented, or when he, penniless, acquires a rich wife on his own merits. He is the runt as the younger brother of Idomeneus, and aware that he is not so competent or heroic. He is unheroic when he kills one man by night in a sneak attack, or when he sees that a battle is being lost, throws away his shield and turns suppliant before the conquering general. The psychological facts of these supposedly false stories which he tells coincide so well with the character traits which both the *Iliad* and *Odyssey* give Odysseus that it seems clear the hero is finally paradoxically creating truth out of fiction. What emerges is the inner Odysseus, not too different from the Norse figure Loki, who is mischievous, sly, cunning and underhanded time after time. This is the Odysseus who looks on pleased and amused as Penelope is given another round of presents by the suitors whom he will shortly destroy, or the Odysseus who teases his own father. This is not the personality of a hero nor is it Odysseus' public personality. But it is there to be caught like that of Proteus (*Odyssey* 4.385ff.), who magically transforms himself in a kaleidoscope of changing identities until when held tight, he must take on his true one. So it is that back in Ithaca as Eurykleia prepares to bathe the disguised Odysseus she comes upon his scar, the token of his true identity, which prompts the poet to tell the story of his getting it. Within the story of the scar we learn that Odysseus is so named because his grandfather Antilycus, "the greatest thief and liar of his time" (*Odyssey* 19.395-96), said, "Since I come hated [in Greek a word similar to "Odysseus"] by many . . . let his name be Odysseus [the hated one]." Here is the deep core of Odysseus, his suspicion, his cunning, his covert self, suddenly revealed, the scar upon his being.

In a story that turns so much upon the repeated motif of

the identification of voyagers, as one after another arrives in
new situations, Odysseus' magnificent progress across the social and familial landscape of Ithaca is a mighty tale. First
he is integrated as lord of the manor when he makes himself
known to the faithful swineherd Eumaios, then he reveals
himself to his son, after that his old dog Argo recognizes him;
disguised as a beggar he enters the palace where once he was
king and the subsequent revelations are more momentous.
His personality comes with the scar. His manhood stands
revealed when he triumphs over the suitors in a feat of
strength that might be considered sexually competitive as
well. Stringing a bow and shooting an arrow through successive holes so as to win a woman for marriage in competition
with other males—even without Freud—is an exceedingly
virile deed. Thereafter he identifies himself to Penelope when
he describes the intimate features of their marriage bed which
he himself built, as it were offering as his *bona fides* the
subtlest details of his sexual/conjugal personality which only
a wife would be likely to observe.

Penelope tricks him into revealing himself when she implies
that the marriage bed can be moved whereas he knows that
it is made from a living tree and rooted to the ground.
This is the moment of Penelope's triumph before a man who
has throughout the poem controlled every situation and
manipulated those around him by his lying. The very adventures which he recites to the Phaiacians at Scheria are
themselves suspect. But his falsehoods are his virtue. Athena
loves him for this, as she says fondly to him:

You stubborn man, full of so many plans, deceits,
not even in your own land have you any intention
of stopping your cheating, your lying words,
which you know you love from the bottom of your heart.
                                        (*Odyssey* 13.293–95)

And yet the poem is a progress in revelation as Odysseus
moves out of the strange and unknown to the familiar.
Odysseus is going home where he can become once more
what he is meant to be, husband, father, lord of Ithaca. Yet
the qualifying adjectives with which Homer endows him,
crafty, much-enduring, man of many devices, many personalities, describe the traveling man. It is as though the real
Odysseus can only exist upon the journey. And so the modern

Greek poet Cavafy sees it as he describes Odysseus in his poem *Ithaca*. It is the journey, says he, which matters.

> Better that it last for years,
> so that when you reach the island you are old,
> rich with all you have gained on the way,
> not expecting Ithaca to give you wealth.
> Ithaca gave you the splendid journey,
> Without her you would not have set out . . .

And yet Cavafy has overlooked what makes this poem unique among extant heroic epic poems, what it is indeed that shapes Odysseus when first the poet describes him to us sitting at the edge of Calypso's island gazing out to sea. It is the treasure at Ithaca for which he must return, his wife Penelope. Indeed the great presence of women in the *Odyssey* gives the poem its extraordinary flavor.

The ancient literary critic Longinus made the celebrated observation that Homer must have written the *Iliad* in his youth and the *Odyssey* in his old age because the attitude was so different in the one than the other. He was not the first or the last to observe fundamental differences between the two poems.

There are certainly profound differences in the representation of women, differences that suggest diverse authorship, because they frame very different points of view toward life. Of course, the *Iliad* is a war poem, indeed a battlefield poem in general, and one would not insist that many women appear; the *Odyssey*, on the other hand, is the chronicle of a man bereft of all male companionship, continually confronting and relating to women. This is very obviously the poet's doing; there are no special demands of the traditional story that call for it. There is a certain desolation in the *Iliad*. Could the author of the *Odyssey*, we ask ourselves, have seen life so bleak? Do not the women in fact emphasize a certain affirmation of life?

Let us, however, think again of Longinus' statement. Psychologists often remark on the morbid, death-oriented life view of adolescence as opposed to the attitude of a male's later years when he is first of all a part of home and family, secure, usually loving life, yet, of course, also en route through life, and in a certain sense consciously voyaging toward his end. Perhaps Longinus was exactly right: it was the genius of Homer to have created in these two poems two of the most important reactions to life which dominate a man, one in his youth, one in his old age.

The *Odyssey* is a poem of many women and one man. We first meet the goddess Athena, who comes to prod Odysseus' son, Telemachus, out of his melancholia and impotence. She guards him and guides him through the poem as she does his father, Odysseus. Then there is warm, motherly Calypso, who wants to keep Odysseus with her forever on her lonely sea-girt island, promising him immortality and all the joys of her bed, and, one feels, great *Gemütlichkeit*. There is Circe, the sorceress, who challenges Odysseus with magic once he has entered her bedchamber, a kind of symbolic sexual duel which she loses, but evidently charmingly so, for Odysseus proceeds to spend a year enjoying her pleasures and would have stayed on, it seems, if his crew had not complained of the delay. At Scheria there is the young virgin princess Nausicaa, fantasizing, just like Snow White, that someday her prince will come, only to find Odysseus, a shipwreck on the beach, naked and very desirable, right before her eyes, but alas unobtainable. Then there is Helen, powerful, self-possessed, beautiful, and Arete, Nausicaa's mother, obviously queen in her palace, real lord over her bumbling, kindly, ineffectual husband, Alkinoos. There is Eurykleia, Odysseus' old nursemaid, now still doing for Telemachus. There is Melantho, a serving girl in Odysseus' palace, who is carrying on with the suitors. Even in the Underworld Odysseus meets up with a great bevy of the world's famous heroines and beauties, and when the court minstrel sings at Scheria, he sings of the adultery of Aphrodite. And finally, most of all, there is Penelope, object of the suitors' desires and Odysseus' dreams. Nary a man in the whole lot save Odysseus himself.

Women are furthermore a part of every facet of the narrative: scenes of arrival, often the meeting with something strange, where character is revealed; scenes describing food, music, drink, often bed, the sensual enjoyment of the ambience. We may indulge our penchant for Jungian perspectives by relating these to man's greatest arrival, the arrival through sexual intercourse at the very locus where he had his origin; or to a man's relationship with a woman which is the most truly significant discovery of the other, the meeting of the fantastic; or to a man deriving from a woman many of the sensual experiences of his life, principally food and sex, but also as a baby simply voice sounds and touch; and of course it is the food of his mother's milk that first starts him on the voyage of living. Even without any or all of these observations to reinforce it, the notion that this is a woman's poem in some way or another, is hard to resist. A hundred years ago Samuel Butler wrote *The Authoress of the Odyssey*, a peculiar and uneven book emphasizing the predominantly feminine quality of the observations made by the poet in the *Odyssey*. The book seems silly today when Butler sets out to judge what a woman could or could not know and understand. He does, however, point up how often the poet is concerned for the female point of view. Robert Graves turned Butler's idea into a fiction in *Homer's Daughter*. The idea persists.

In several epic traditions there are poems especially for women, poems about women and perhaps some poems composed by women. Sometimes they are folk stories with a moral, often they tell the story of the wives of heroes. Marriage is often the central feature. And marriage for a woman who was as housebound and family-bound as they were in those days represents a very fearful and courageous adventure analogous, one would imagine, to Odysseus' pursuit of the unknown, although, of course, marriage was not undertaken voluntarily. The *Odyssey* seems much like some of these. Because of Odysseus, his adventures, his prowess, we say that the *Odyssey* is heroic. But there is also magic, a fairy-tale ambience, contrivance, cunning, plot complexity, a moral story or a story with a moral (certainly we are meant to learn something from the *Odyssey;* learning is one of the main themes of the poem, too), and all the women. Then too, there is a special amused self-consciousness to the *Odyssey* which one might consider feminine. The poet of the *Odyssey* several times seems to be parodying the *Iliad*, or saga narration like the *Iliad*, for instance the military adventures described at 14.462ff. which have been called mock-heroic, or the peculiar *androktasia* when the suitors are killed (22.8–389), or Odysseus disclaiming lies in the celebrated words of Achilles (*Odyssey* 14.156=*Iliad* 9.312), or Helen and Menelaus recounting heroic anecdotes, the very stuff of epic recital, but in their mouths used for very personal, argumentative communication. This is feminine in the sense that parody—or more particularly mockery—is the natural weapon of those who cannot participate in something to which they are attracted. Such would describe the attitude of women before war-oriented, male-oriented heroic poetry.

There are distinctly female roles in the poem. There are definite parallels in characters and situations in the *Odyssey*. For instance, Calypso, Circe and the Sirens can be linked as the three temptations for Odysseus; Nausicaa at the Phaiacian games, Penelope at the bow-stringing contest, we may say, are modeled on the example of Hippodameia and Atalanta; then too, the parallels of the arrivals on an island with a woman waiting there may be noted: Ogygia and Calypso, Scheria and Nausicaa, Aia and Circe, to which we should add Ithaca and Penelope, so that we do not forget the degree to which Penelope is part of the typical as well. The parallels accrue; what grows more certainly possible is that all the women of the *Odyssey* are in some quite definite way manifestations of a female who is archetypal to the poet or the tradition.

Penelope, of course, is a more obvious figure. Is she different from the others in degree or kind?

The immediate and constant fact of Penelope is her great dependency upon Odysseus. So she appears forever in tears and shows herself to be passive. But the poet of the *Odyssey* is a very great poet indeed, and he chooses to reveal still another Penelope, the Penelope of Odysseus' anticipation. He does not develop the life they lead after their reunion; Penelope disappears from the narrative after that first night together in bed. Some would say that this is also true to the male apprehension of the female, particularly true to more specifically erotic situations, that it is the prelude to the relationship that exercises the male more than the realization of it. So it is that the poet has created a relatively passive figure, but he offers a number of powerful suggestions or hints as to what this ambiguous figure may offer. Just as *Odyssey* books 1–4 help to set up an idea of Odysseus before he appears, so all the women encountered in the poem, because they derive from a type, go to developing our notion of Penelope, introducing and reinforcing numerous expectations of her. That these expectations are not necessarily realized in the poem is beside the point. This is true to the idea of homecoming; it is arrival and not residence, as Cavafy so brilliantly shows in his poem *Ithaca*.

All the women of the *Odyssey* are similar, although not

self-consciously created so by the poet. They are typical in the epic sense of the word, so the poet can develop certain values and associations through the introduction of one after another of these women, each with minor but suggestive variations. Penelope is a kind of summation of them as Ithaca is also the sum of all arrivals in the poem.

The ever recurring feature of the women of this poem is their dominance in the male-female relationship. With dominance goes the manipulation and frustration of males, which is the other side of female dependence as psychoanalytic study sees it today. Beside even minor details such as the providential help of the nymph Ino, we have Calypso keeping Odysseus, Athena protecting and guiding Odysseus and Telemachus, Helen dominating the hearth at Sparta as Arete does on Scheria, Nausicaa offering shelter and clothing to the naked, vulnerable shipwreck, Penelope tricking Odysseus in the matter of the marriage bed. Even Zeus yields consistently to his daughter Athena.

These women are all beneficent. Some of them save Odysseus' life. Their dominance is clearly benign. But the subtlety of the poem saves the story from being simply a fairy-tale success. For there are certain disquieting details that make Penelope in our anticipation sometimes suspect. First, there is the important leitmotif of Clytemnestra's story. It is the exact parallel of Penelope's except that there is but one suitor and he has been successful in his suit. The Clytemnestra story charges Odysseus' homecoming, however, with the suspense of betrayal. Suddenly Penelope's yearning, her tears, the declaration of constancy and loyalty go beyond the cliché and routine to the chance, occasion and potential for infidelity and betrayal. In fact, seen in terms of Clytemnestra, Penelope is not passive, but actively faithful.

Relevant to this is Penelope's defense of Helen (23.218ff.) on the ground that chastity is a very chancy thing. Penelope's continued protestations of fidelity and loyalty are, to be sure, natural to epic technique, which depends upon reiteration; nonetheless the consistent protest is a defense against a wish ("the lady doth protest too much, methinks"). For this ambivalence we see a kind of pairing, that is, Penelope and Clytemnestra, two ways for women to resolve the repressed rage of a woman deserted. One cannot say that the condemnation of Clytemnestra in the poem argues for male authorship. The pair is there to give expression to both sets of feelings, but the one, murderous rage, is so antisocial that its expression must be coupled with condemnation.

Circe particularly increases the scope of Penelope's potential behavior. Circe appears without personality or motive. She is a fairy-tale figure who embodies stark action or inevitable action without qualifiers. Nothing explains her. She is perhaps the abstracted projection of two well-attested male fears: submission to the female through orgasm, and submission through the fundamental male dependence upon the female for food. Circe and Penelope are very similar. Circe is dominant and malign in a way that can be related to Penelope. Like Penelope she is surrounded by males. They have become her victims and in the same way one can recognize the suitors at Ithaca as Penelope's victims. Penelope descends the stairs, seduces the suitors with her beauty, writes them notes, strings them along while weaving the shroud. They in their impatience, their desire and boisterousness have become animal-like in their behavior. Eventually they are destroyed in a setting that derives from the common motif of suitors contesting for the princess. Which is to say, they are gathered together for a woman as a prize and in this setting they are destroyed. What could be more poignant commentary upon their victimization than their own premonition so sympathetically described (20.345ff.)? Even Penelope's weaving the famous shroud takes on a faintly sinister aspect; she is like a spider upstairs in the women's chambers weaving a magical doom.

For Odysseus, the man of action and daring, there never is any doubt that home and Penelope are all he ultimately wants from his life. Not Calypso, not immortality. Penelope is the constant focus except for that dangerous year at Circe's. Penelope represents the eternal seduction, temptation, the eternal *need*. Like the marriage bed rooted to the earth, she is the all-encompassing stability at the end of man's adventuresome travels outside the home. And in the man's viewpoint Odysseus' return to Penelope represents man's utter dependence upon women.

Yet nothing is ever simple and the *Odyssey*, like all masterpieces, is true to life's complexity. Man's acceptance of the woman is of course accommodation to another person, and that can be sometimes seen or imagined as submission. We think of the hero and his autonomy, his happy male freedom. The loss of it can only produce resentment, the thought of losing it hostility and fear. The *Odyssey* superbly captures these two conflicting forces in a man's being, the need for women and the fear of submitting to this need. Certainly, if this is so, then the *Odyssey* was composed by a man because this is a man's dilemma. Yet composed by a man who understood that a man's identity could only be found with his woman. It is a wise child who knows his own father, but a wiser man who finds his own wife.

CHAPTER FOUR
HOMER AND THE POETS

One man gets his knowledge from another, both
yesterday and today;
It's not easy, you see, to open up the gates of words
as yet unsaid.

Bacchylides

The Homeric epics are relics of a kind of poetry that
transcended personal authorship or resisted the obvious impress of an individual poet. The surviving poetry thereafter
betrays the author's presence. Poetry becomes the vehicle
for some one person's private expression. Poets no longer
asked the Muse for the poem as Homer had done; they
sought assistance and no more. Acute self-consciousness marks
the poetry after Homer as the poets freed themselves from
the epic tradition enough to take an objective stance toward
its language, style and conceits. It was an age of tremendous
experimentation when a verbal construct that had provided
a vision of life was tested, fragmented and eventually reshaped. The temporal span from Hesiod to Pindar and
Aeschylus is two or three centuries. What results is a distillation of the hexameters of saga and wisdom poetry,
their transformation finally into myth in the public institution of
Attic tragedy. The personal lyric poetry did not survive as
an art form; even Pindar's great choral odes seem weak set
beside tragic odes. This poetry had no social role. The epic
saga tradition, on the other hand, with its social and even
political claims, reinforced by the needs of the city-state,
returned in tragedy; it overrode the private voices of the
private Muse.

Despite the fact that only the *Iliad* and the *Odyssey* and the name Homer stand out in the obscurity of early Greek poetry, the oral poetic tradition was pervasive. The merest fragments of other poems are enough to allow us to assume that all the events of early Greek saga tradition—Jason and the Argonauts, Oedipus, the fighting at Thebes and so on —were as much sung and celebrated as the stories associated with the Achaian war against Troy. Some of this body of saga was put together at a later date into a continuous story, called the Epic Cycle. Individual poems were gathered together into a collection in chronological order. The collection began with the birth of the gods and ended with a quaint story of the death of Odysseus at the hands of his son, Telegonus, born to Circe. Telegonus promptly marries Penelope and Telemachus marries Circe. And where could the saga tradition go after that extraordinary minuet of loose ends tied up? When the Epic Cycle was gathered, how complete at any given time the collection was we do not know. The events of these other poems were popular in the fifth and fourth centuries, in tragedy, for instance, and in vase paintings. The fragments are not enough to judge how oral these poems seem to be, although they are certainly in the manner of the *Iliad* and *Odyssey*. Although the entire saga tradition came into existence and was preserved through the medium of oral poetry, no doubt when the conditions for oral poetry passed there were still poets who created long narrative poems in the style and diction of oral poets.

The great influence of this oral epic style is apparent in a collection of poems known as the Homeric Hymns. These are not strictly speaking hymns nor are they necessarily by Homer. The Homeric Hymns are mainly narrative poems, stylized, very organized, self-consciously like Homeric narrative. Their difference from Homeric epic lies in their small size and their narrative simplicity. The hymns to Apollo, to Demeter, to Hermes and to Aphrodite are by far the best; of these the Hymn to Aphrodite is probably the most successful. It is a charming story: the love goddess who never falls in love but only brings love madness to others is made to fall in love by Zeus; so she goes disguised as a mortal maiden to the tent of Priam's brother, Anchises, shepherding the flocks. Though he is wary of her, because he is afraid that she is a goddess, he succumbs at last to her blandishments. After their love-making she prods him awake standing there revealed as the goddess she is and she tells him the future of the son which she has just conceived. Unlike the Homeric poems it is a sensual story; there are emphatic details of Aphrodite's preparation for love, her ointments and jewels, described again as she removes them in Anchises' tent; there are also descriptions of the flowers and trees, and of Aphrodite's and Anchises' beauty. The sense of physical love is everywhere in the poem. Structurally the story is a variant of the theme of the Great Mother Goddess and her consort male god. Aphrodite takes Anchises, uses him and discards him. "Tell no one that you slept with Aphrodite," she cautions him (281ff.). "After going to bed with you," exclaims the enthusiastic Anchises (153–54), "I would gladly die." And when he discovers who his bedmate really was he says in fear (188f.), "Don't leave me to lead a feeble life among men, but pity me." Aphrodite describes the fate of Tithonus, who was granted immortality but not eternal youth, doomed to eternal senility ("His voice flows on without end but there's no strength to him" [237]), and adds "If only you could live on as you are now in shape and looks and could be called my husband then no sorrow would enfold my heart, but soon enough old age will enfold you, ruthless old age which stands near mankind, deadly, destructive, which even the gods hate." So the story is melancholy as well. Its moods and its elements, however, are brought together in a coherent statement of action and emotion. The language is Homer's but the control is far greater.

Poems such as the Homeric Hymns were said to have been recited at public gatherings as a prelude to a recital of a portion of either the *Iliad* or the *Odyssey*. These two poems evidently swiftly became so popular as to be almost sacred. Their recitation was no small matter; there came about a guild of men whose occupation it was to recite correctly the poems, maintain the texts, if only in memory, since in the period of transition from a completely preliterate to a literate society, variant versions of the Trojan story and the homecoming story must have been sung in every village and hamlet where Greek was known; furthermore the value of a written text of a particular version, or of a received version, however it was maintained, could scarcely have been apparent to everyone. The guild of men, called Homeridae, were truly pioneers therefore, reciting another man's poem verbatim. These rhapsodes, as they were also called, yielded, however, to their normal creative impulses, to the traditional role of performer, by reciting something of their own composition first. Such was the genesis of the Homeric Hymns. The four best and longest bear interesting affinities with the *Iliad* and the *Odyssey* apart from similar diction, that is, each has taken an element of the Homeric narrative and enlarged upon it, or rather cast a much smaller poem integrated upon one idea or theme: the Hymn to Aphrodite with its sensual descriptions of the material world; the Hymn to Apollo with its catalogue-like listing; the Hymn to Demeter, which is an attempt to encapsule epic sequential narrative in a smaller frame; and the Hymn to Hermes with its comic, cunning action. The experimental nature of the Hymns is remarkable.

The Homeridae maintained the traditions of Homer, even preserving the correct pronunciation of words, and they were considered by the general rhapsode as superior and authoritative. Plato's dialogue *Ion* presents a portrait of a rhapsode and while there is the usual confusion which Socrates' compulsive irony introduces in the dialogues, one is able to get a certain idea of what a rhapsode (at so late a date as the latter part of the fifth century) thought of himself and imagined his role to be among others. Ion considered himself valuable. We may assume that a seventh- and sixth-century rhapsode or Homerides in a society without the range of cultural alternatives that came later must have had a considerably higher opinion of his own worth. Particularly those who were keepers of the Homeric tradition in a society without priests or scribes were guardians of the society's past and its most articulated ethical, moral and theological statement.

The early Greeks called Homer one of the seven wise men and creators of their tradition. Another was Hesiod, whose place in time is obscure enough (roughly 700) but who has put so much more of himself into his poetry that we can get a rather good idea of the man. He is thought to be the author of two poems: the *Works and Days,* which is often called the first didactic poem, for he preaches rather much in it at his brother Perses; and also the *Theogony,* a poem of the creation myth found among the Greeks and similar to the creation stories of the Near East. His poetry is extremely influential; reflections of his kind of thoughtful verse appear throughout Greek history particularly in the choral odes and in Hellenistic poetry. Then too, the peculiar way in which he manages an idea through imagery and through word association is an excellent manifestation of the mythic way of seeing things which persisted throughout the next two centuries. Born in Boeotia, in a small village ("bad in winter, wretched in summer, never any good," he says [*Works* 639]), in an agricultural world, Hesiod was a shepherd who got the gift of poetry. Although there are indications that Hesiod is roughly contemporaneous with the authors of the *Iliad* and *Odyssey* and that he too is part of the oral tradition, the circumstances of his life seem far removed from the kind of life we can imagine for a Phemius or Demodokos. Furthermore his is not narrative poetry but reflective poetry, especially his poem called the *Works and Days*.

Some dismiss Hesiod as a poet, but he created verbal images of great beauty. There are several first-rate passages in both his poems. The description of Zeus' fight with Typhoeus is one (*Theogony* 820–68), the battle between the Titans and Zeus' generation is another (*Theogony* 617–753), and there are glorious descriptions of natural life in the *Works and Days*. Here, for example, is a description of a hot summer's day and a recipe for a mild wine cooler:

When the artichoke flowers, and the chirping grasshopper
from his tree pours down his shrill song constantly
with his wings, in the season of heat that wears you out,
then goats are plumpest, wines the very best;
women are hotter then, but men are weakest.
The Dog Star dries out the head and knees;
the heat dries out the skin; but then what is needed is
the shadow of a rock and some Biblian wine . . .
I'll drink some glistening wine, sitting in the shade
turning my face to the west wind coming fresh
and from the everflowing spring coming clean
I'll pour out three parts and from the wine a fourth. (582–96)

Best of all is Hesiod's description of winter (504–63). His description of the cold winter gale is masterful and reaches perfection in the sensation of chill evoked in the contrast between the old man bent in the fierce wind and the naked girl in her bedroom.

[The wind] goes through an oxhide; it cannot stop it.
And through the fine hair of the goat. Through sheeps' wool
  so thick
Boreas' cutting wind cannot penetrate
but it makes an old man curve like a wheel.
Nor does it blow through the soft-skinned maiden
who stays within the house with her mother
a girl who does not yet know the works of golden Aphrodite
who washes her tender skin and anoints herself with oil
lying in the inner room of the house on a winter's day.

                  (515–24)

Often, however, Hesiod's poetry is misjudged because one is
not certain what he is about. Some critics, for instance,
feel that in the *Works and Days* the poet clumsily attempts
an idea but the attempt falters because Hesiod introduces
elements completely foreign to his main point. And this is
so because Hesiod was an early intellectual who had to use
poetry when no prose medium was at hand; had there been
a developed prose, goes the argument, he would certainly have
had more control. But Hesiod, as he himself proclaims, is a
singer. The medium of poetry shaped him as surely as he
shaped it; his ideas therefore in part derive from the exigencies of his medium. In fact, we had best rid ourselves
of the notion of Hesiod's *ideas;* it becomes too easy to
imagine the intellectual making notes or an outline which
he then casts into the poetic mold. There is no "idea" apart
from the poem; indeed the poem is so innocent of the self-
consciousness of its creator that it is more the *evolution* of
an idea, in the sense that Hesiod was not exactly sure where
he would end when he began. The creative tension lies in
Hesiod's juxtaposing traditional elements in his poem and
allowing these juxtapositions themselves to constitute the sense
of the poem.

Hesiod has been called a representative of a Boeotian
school of poets who left heroic poetry to the bards of Asia
Minor while busying themselves with lists and catalogues.
But Hesiod could probably handle heroic poetry in addition
to the catalogue style. His account of his participation in
the singing at the funeral of King Amphidamas (*Works and
Days* 654ff.) has been thought to be a reference to his
career as a heroic epic poet. Then too, the invocation to the
Pierian Muses with which the *Works and Days* begins cer-

tainly has to do with epic poetry. Homer's poetry has enough well-integrated Hesiod-like passages and Hesiod's enough Homer-like passages that we can easily imagine heroic narrative and cataloguing both existing on either side of the Aegean.

The distinguishing mark of Hesiod is phraseology that does not belong to the Homeric poetry. Despite the lack of any real substantiating evidence we may imagine that this area on the mainland shared in the common language of epic but that there were local stylistic variations in phraseology. Perhaps also there was a different attitude on the mainland; at least Hesiod, whose extant works show a penchant for cataloguing and listing, takes a different attitude toward oral narrative from what we imagine to have been Homer's. The former attitude is expressed in the famous account of the Muses' visitation to Hesiod: "Yokels," say they to him and his fellow shepherds, "you wretches, we know how to tell lies that seem true, although, when we choose, we can also speak truth" (26–28). The anecdote, however obscure, contains critical attitudes, one toward chronology—that is, Hesiod will sing of things in time past and future—and one toward veracity—Hesiod will be able to sing of true things. In short, his mission as he sees it is more than to sing the famous deeds of heroes lodged in some vaguely timeless past. As he says to Perses at the beginning of the *Works and Days,* "I shall tell you the truth." This is what has been called the antiquarian mind, the mind that receives and collates what tradition has created.

While he may share a tradition with Homer, Hesiod seems, in the *Works and Days* at least, to differ from Homeric poetry in style as well as substance. He was not working under the influence of the Homeric poems specifically and trying to adapt their phraseology to a set of ideas that he himself had worked up. The evidence now suggests that Hesiod himself was an oral poet or very close to the mechanism of the oral poetic tradition. His language and themes cannot be said to derive from any one source after the manner of imitation or adaptation among literate poets.

Hesiod's sources are also becoming better identified as the poetry of the Near East becomes known to classicists. Hesiod shares many themes and stories with second-millennium poetry. These so-called "foreign" elements are there in verse that comes from the oral poetic tradition. This implies generations of creative amalgamation of theme and phrase, which, of course, seems to point at a very early acquisition of these stories. Perhaps we may thus take Hesiod's tradition back to the Mycenaean period, the next most recent moment when communication between the Greek-speaking world and the eastern Aegean was common.

Hesiod is different from Homer in an important way. Homer creates narratives out of metrically defined phrases and metrically assigned key words. The metrically defined phrase for the oral poet is the linguistic building block just as the word is for literate verbal production. The *Works and Days,* however, sometimes reveals another, longer, semantically more complete building block. This is the aphorism. Line after line is a self-contained idea. Often one sees what may well be aphoristic elements combined to make a greater whole. For instance, lines 21–24—

Anyone will want to work when he sees his neighbor
wealthy, who is anxious to plow and to sow,
to keep the house in order; neighbor competes with neighbor
going after wealth. This strife is good for mankind.

—are three loosely connected statements that can with very little grammatical adjustment be easily made into a set of six observations free of any connection:

1. Anyone will want to work when he sees his neighbor.
2. He who is anxious to plow and to sow is wealthy.
3. Keep your house in order.
4. Neighbor competes with neighbor.
5. Go after wealth.
6. Strife is good for mankind.

The aphorisms of Hesiod bear a strong resemblance to the earliest quoted responses of the Delphic oracle. The oracle dealt out sacred wisdom as, we might say, Hesiod seems to be offering secular wisdom. Herodotus in fact quotes a line (*Works and Days* 285; quoted at 6.86) common to Hesiod and to a Delphic oracular utterance. Perhaps we can see in these two places, in the one institutionalized, and in the other at least regularized, the phenomenon of verbal elements in dactylic hexametric verse that are self-contained, complete ideas in a way that the characteristic Homeric phrase is not.

This is a striking difference between Homeric and Hesiodic poetry; that in the latter we find a poet using complete thoughts—however brief (however trite)—as remembered units, or units at the ready in the creative subconscious. We need a different criticism for this poetry. It is what these elements mean *in combination* that becomes important or more important than what each one means intrinsically, separately. Hesiod's act of creation, after all, his attempt at making meaning, comes in the combination, not in making each individual metrically discrete thought. It is there where we must seek his intent.

Hesiod's style is, however, remarkably various; the *Works and Days* contains other kinds of passages such as the celebrated description of winter (504ff.) or the discussion of justice (249ff.). These are distinctly less aphoristic; so are the agricultural calendar, the Ages of Man scheme, the Prometheus/Pandora story and so on. But in one way the aphorisms are like the stories (passages like the Prometheus/Pandora narrative, for instance): they are elements Hesiod got from the tradition of which he was a part. In the case of the aphorisms the elements are whole—even the very words and their order—whereas the stories, just as those in Homer, were very likely in his memory in outline which he could flesh out in words.

As we have noted, Hesiod's *Works and Days* bears marked affinities to many texts of the Near East. The odd fact, however, is that Hesiod's poem incorporates elements that are, so to speak, of different genres in the earlier Eastern literature. On the one hand we have something like proto-historical cosmological or cosmogonic stories, that is, the Prometheus/Pandora story and the Ages of Man—man's fall—and on the other hand we have the wisdom literature. In turn it is of two sorts, one, practical/ethical proverbs, and two, an agricultural calendar. The combination of these three different poetic species seems unusual and remarkable. It does not happen that way in the Near East. There is also the added element of the poet's reaction to this traditional material (which is how I would characterize Hesiod's discussion of justice). This last recalls the sardonic voice of Qoheleth, the Preacher of the Old Testament (still known to some as Ecclesiastes), as he views some elements of the traditional wisdom of his culture.

This unusual combination suggests that Hesiod's purpose was something other than reconstructing history or offering an encapsulated, codified education. He is not using any one of these themes or traditions straight, to come to the obvious. Rather the fact of their combination inhibits the exposition of the obvious. Thus we may look to see how these elements relate to each other as the projection of some meaning for the poem, a meaning that will transcend its parts.

A rough analysis of the poem reveals habits of mind very characteristic of the archaic period in Greece. The poem falls roughly into three parts, the first being the invocation, the initial discussion of wrath, the Prometheus story, the Ages of Man and the fable. In the second part Hesiod strives to make the ideas of work and justice synonymous. This portion ends with the triumphant and almost operatic:

> So if in your heart you want wealth, then
> get to it, work and pile work upon work! (381-82)

Properly speaking, only the third part is the works and days. A panorama of agricultural life is set out in an orderly schema based on the seasons. It commences with plowing (383-492), the activity of autumn; then there is a description of winter (493-563), then spring and early summer (that is, February to June, 564-96). The passage ends with a description of the harvest (July to October, 597-617), by which point Hesiod has gone through a year. After two passages, one dealing briefly with the maritime calendar and one offering a variety of maxims mostly relating to the taboos in man's life, the poet moves into the lucky and unlucky days, which close the poem.

In this last part it is easy to see how Hesiod has joined the elements, for it is more obvious here; it helps in analyzing the first part of the *Works and Days*. To repeat, there are an agricultural calendar, general and particular remarks about the life of a sailor, a series of maxims relating to behavior, and a list of lucky and unlucky days. Altogether these elements combine to provide a strong reaffirmation of the first and second parts of the poem. Nonetheless moving from one to another of these very distinguishable passages, trying to "maintain the thought," as the expression goes, is difficult, to say the least. This is because the transitions are of another sort than logical.

To begin, the remarks on the sea proceed easily out of the close of Hesiod's description of the agricultural year. The latter ends as it began, in autumn, now late autumn. Hesiod mentions the setting of the Pleiades to locate it in time, just as he has been using the stars as a frame throughout this discussion. The reference to the Pleiades either allows for, we may say, or, as I think, more probably, *provokes* in Hesiod the transition to the ships, for he again (619) notices the setting Pleiades now as the sign to draw up the ships and leave off seafaring for the winter. Hesiod's remarks on winter gales and the dangers they engender at sea set the tone for a relatively pejorative account of the sailor's life, which is more general and abstract than the preceding agricultural calendar.

In turn the end of the passage on sailing provokes perhaps the series of maxims that follows. Hesiod concludes his description of sailing by saying: "Keep the measure; to everything there is a season" (694). Then he turns to say: "When you are ripe take a wife" . . . etc. The sense of "ripe" is a natural concomitant to the preceding; furthermore, "ripe" and line 694 both underscore the idea of aphoristic wisdom poetry which has to do with propriety or rightness of one sort or another.

Then, finally, the list of lucky and unlucky days, because they have to do with magic, relates directly and proceeds naturally from the discussion of taboo acts which the maxims are. Furthermore, the days are the calendary particulars for which the previous description of the agricultural year was the overview.

In this fashion Hesiod moves from one distinguishable passage to another. In one case two references to the setting Pleiades provide the link, in another the common idea contained in "measure," "season" and "ripe." What we are here observing is that there is no ideological or logical transition between the passages. The same is true of the first part of the poem where Hesiod lays the ground for the presentation of works and days. This is important to remember because the first section appears especially obscure to many readers, for there seems to be the kind of structuring that ought to derive from logic.

Hesiod's medium is poetry, either truly oral or suggestive

of an oral culture or oral mentality. Therefore, we can expect: transitions that are other than intellectual; presentations of what we may choose to call ideas, which when they are conceived in images are not at all made up self-consciously from agreed-upon symbols; and a focus upon the immediate presentation of each segment rather than a development of the whole. Architecture in oral poetry is evolutionary and nowhere more than in a cataloguing style where the fact of juxtaposition is central; the additions in listing continually alter the main theme or idea. Let us consider the poetic development of the first 212 lines. At the very first of the poem, the poet begins after his invocation by advancing on a piece of traditional wisdom which he chooses to redefine. His definition of the two forms of strife links, on the one hand, competition, work and the idea of underground or more generally the idea of "within": 19–26, ". . . in the roots of the earth . . . prods . . . to work . . . strive . . . compete"; and on the other, hostility, idleness and talk: 13, 28–29, "Fosters war and hate; Strife keeps you from work . . . makes you a hanger-on at the market place."

The sense of "within" leads him to his story of Prometheus, 30–31: "no time for quarreling when you haven't got enough provisions for the year within," 40–41: "silly kings, who don't know the benefit to be found in mallow and asphodel." "For," says Hesiod next, "the gods hid the provisions from man." The transition lies in the in-ness of hiding, back through the benefit in mallow, "provisions within," to the gods having hidden the good strife in the roots of the earth. The transition certainly is not logical but the images are congenial: the hiding of healthy struggle or competition in the roots of the earth; there being something of benefit tucked away in mallow and asphodel; and the gods' having hidden the means to man's sustenance. Indeed the notion of containment and hiding gets us well into the Prometheus/Pandora story.

The idea of concealment or containment in fact holds the Prometheus/Pandora passage together. The gods *hide* the means of life for man; a few lines later Zeus is said to have *hidden* something unspecified in anger; then Prometheus steals the fire from Zeus and *hides* it *in* the hollow stalk of a plant; whereupon at Zeus' bidding the gods adorn Pandora and by this means *conceal* her malevolent nature; Pandora a little later clamps down the lid on the jar, thereby keeping hope or delusion *within*. Most of these images relate back in an ambiguous way to the fundamental fact that something much needed is hidden within and must be ferreted out, that things are not as they seem and must be understood. Commentators are often puzzled at this section. For instance, the gods' hiding the means of life and Zeus' hiding fire are two very different things which Hesiod manages to equate. A common critical refuge from this confusion is to say that Hesiod passes lightly and allusively over tales wellknown depending upon his audience's knowledge of the relevant passage in the *Theogony*. However true it may be that both Hesiod and his audience knew much fuller versions of what he here merely touches upon, it is an important critical principle that we must concentrate on whatever details he *does* offer as being significant for his present narrative. The idea of "within" has permitted him to assemble certain facts. Let us consider what the aggregate suggests.

Man has fire, Pandora (or womankind *per se*), work and misery—that is what the story tells us. And these are all inextricably linked; that is Hesiod's use of the story.

He brings work and life's sustenance together in the idea of hiding, first good strife or struggle in the roots of the earth, and then sustenance hidden by the gods. If this had not been so, says Hesiod (43ff.), one could leave off tilling, again equating work with life's nourishment. Then he equates life's nourishment with fire by means of the confusing remarks on Zeus' hiding at first something unidentified, then specifically fire. Since fire seems to have been understood as man's first contrived means to sustain himself it relates naturally to the idea of provision. The natural relationship of contrivance and fire implies work. The two are in turn tied in with the description of Pandora's arrival in man's world. Pandora is woman, Pandora is punishment for stealing fire; Pandora and fire arrive almost simultaneously. Fire and Pandora are evocative of house and family, craft and society—in sum, the organized life of which routine, planned work is part. And work in a primitive agricultural society is a kind of evil, very often fatal, generally debilitating and crippling. Members of advanced, technological, urbanized societies do not realize or forget the agrarian realities that form the poem's context. There is the fear that the crop will not come to maturity, fear that the stored harvest will not last the barren season and fear that a decent planting season will not recur.

There is the disfigurement of agricultural labor, the permanently bowed limbs, cracked skin and squinting eyes; there is the danger of agricultural accidents that bring blood poisoning, tetanus and gangrene. Perhaps most of all there are the imperious, daily demands of the agrarian routine.

The fact that Pandora is a woman allows Hesiod to emphasize that work is something intrinsic and natural, however evil. Thus it is *more* than an imposed punishment from god. Hesiod relates work to the arrival of woman, and just as woman is a natural and inevitable feature of this world, so is work. The shift here from an emphasis on work as punishment, work as evil, to the barest suggestion of work as natural plays with the idea of good *strife,* desirable competition or struggle. This may indeed be Hesiod's original addition to the traditional concept of work. In any case, Hesiod is faced with the not uncommon problem of justifying or at least legitimizing an evil. His equation of work-fire-woman-evil accepts the pessimistic assessment of work but also makes it natural and social.

In sum, Hesiod tells us man must inevitably work; his life will be harsh. Pandora has closed the lid on hope. As he concludes the Prometheus/Pandora story he says, "And so there is no way to escape the will of Zeus" (105). After this grim observation he moves to a restatement: "If you like, I shall tell you another story." This is his transition from the grim observation to the description of the Ages of Man. As "another story" the Ages of Man represents an alternative paradigm; we shall look for a correspondence. This kind of restatement is in a larger scale like the appositional style of the Homeric poems. In detail the Ages of Man is a moral chronology which reveals man's growing antisocial behavior. Men of the Silver Age, long in childhood, incapable thereafter either of social communion or of the responsibility toward their gods, are followed by the men of the Bronze Age, whose outstanding trait is bellicosity, to which their deaths, so lengthily described, are a natural corollary. Bad strife is certainly ascendant, even though Hesiod pauses in his pitiless narrative for a moment to acknowledge the literary fact of a mythopoetic heroic world. Then on to the Iron Age, too awful to live in, Hesiod's present day, characterized by the disintegration of the family, by the perversity of the machine of justice. The emphasis on the evil of words and of the market place harks back to the initial description of bad strife, which Hesiod related to the market place. The horrors of Iron Age families, on the other hand, are an abstraction of Hesiod's very own quarrel with Perses. These are the details of the Ages of Man. Overall, it reinforces and isolates the central fact of the Prometheus/Pandora story—the inexorability of evil. The emphasis on the ever increasing degree of this evil heightens the desperation.

And now, says Hesiod, thereafter, I shall tell you a fable. The "now" like "another" presents an alternative again in apposition, again a refinement. The fable of the hawk and the nightingale being brief and non-human is an abstraction, the sum and cap to the whole sequence. The fable is a commonplace; it articulates most succinctly and most clearly the sense of desperation that the previous two stories have engendered. The fable says that the rhythm of this world in which mankind is the victim is inexorable (the hawk has the nightingale fast in his talons), arbitrary ("I shall make you my dinner if I will or maybe let you go") and amoral ("You're mine to take where I will even though you are a singer"). This is the natural world with which on its most intimate level a farmer has to contend.

The relationship between the description of the Ages of Man and the fable of the hawk and the nightingale is repeated —it is hard to say whether consciously—toward the close of the poem in the relationship between the agricultural calendar and the lucky and unlucky days. In the earlier part of the poem, Hesiod's history of the inexorable march of degeneration is rephrased in the fable's projection of invincible force. At the poem's very end the agricultural calendar displays a panorama of annual activities dictated by the stars. Like the Ages of Man this is a chronology, although of another sort, but just as inexorable. The list of lucky and unlucky days refines and emphasizes, projects the mechanical and inevitable nature of that calendar.

The extreme pessimism Hesiod reflects is a typical feature of wisdom literature. It relates very definitely to the cyclical view of time which an agrarian culture, especially its religion, presents. The agrarian world, inexorable in its seasonal, even daily, demands presents a recurrent and fixed chronology from which there is no escape. Hesiod has said, "There is no way to escape the will of Zeus." His stories have demonstrated this idea, partly as a refrain, but also showing the truth of this assertion in details of another order. The stories in the first part have to do with history whereas the end of the poem, the wisdom poetry, deals with personal behavior and daily tasks. The maxims, the calendar, the lucky and unlucky days are, we may assume, just as traditional as the stories, and in that sense, they are again the "truths" which Hesiod has assembled—the verities of the tradition. They are not there as a farmer's calendar or as a complete guide to rural behavior. As is often noted, they seem sketchy and incomplete. This is so, because they are parts standing for the whole, to illustrate the fact of inexorability in the day-to-day existence of man. The aphorisms and calendar are as arbitrary and inevitable as the grip with which the hawk holds the nightingale, as the harshness of life which Zeus through Prometheus and Pandora brought to mankind. One is reminded of the pessimism of Qoheleth, for instance, when he says (1.4ff.), "One generation passeth away, and another generation cometh: but the earth abideth for ever. The sun also riseth, the sun goeth down . . ."; or when he says (1.9), "that which hath been is named already, and it is known"; or the celebrated passage which is most directly analogous to Hesiod's *Works and Days* which begins: "To every thing there is a season, and a time to every purpose under heaven . . ." (3.1ff.).

This idea of the right moment, the concept of ripeness, is a continual refrain in Hesiod's poem. Hesiod, however, manages to escape the melancholia of the cyclical rhythm which, for instance, Qoheleth manifests at every turn. This is because Hesiod has managed in the central portion of his poem to find a positive stance to take toward the inexorable rhythm of his life, to have converted necessity into choice. While this is perhaps no more than verbal legerdemain, nevertheless man has very few other ways to escape the fact of his elemental nothingness. Speech is the futile revenge of the disinherited, as one man said.

In the central portion of his poem duality becomes significant. This theme is in the poem from its beginning; the invocation is based upon it (man will be spoken of *or* not, Zeus can make a man strong or he can bring the strong man down). Indeed the very idea of strife or competition depends upon duality. Furthermore, there is a duality in good and bad strife, Hesiod versus Perses, Zeus versus Prometheus, Epimetheus versus Pandora, the Silver and Gold ages versus the Bronze, the hawk versus the nightingale. The sense of duality, however, while present is not emphasized at first.

The quarrel between the brothers is, as we have said, expressive of the general duality throughout the poem. And the duality becomes the mode by which Hesiod saves himself from the extreme pessimism which one may note in Eastern wisdom literature. From the first there lurks the hint that if Perses is the bad, then of course, Hesiod must be the good; so there is an alternative.

The dispute that Hesiod describes between himself and his brother and his constant admonition to Perses seem the perfect metaphor, or the living paradigm of the speculations he contrives within the poem. The natural competition between siblings turned to hostility by Perses' actions shows good and bad strife as well as the human tendency to degeneration, particularly in the family arena, and the local judges' ruling in favor of Perses is both an arbitrary exercise of power like that which man must face in the hierarchy of nature and an illustration of the distinction between the basic malignity of the forensic scene and the spoken word and the goodness of work and the farm. Admonitory literature of the Near East is similar. There is even a specimen of poetry involving a dialogue between Good and Bad brother.

The poem perhaps arises from the inevitable synthesis between the particulars of Hesiod's experience and the universal *données* of his tradition. Sibling rivalry is typical, private ownership makes dispute inevitable, law courts and litigation serve to make clear the distinction between the doer and the speaker, admonitory literature demands an expressed object of the admonition. Fact and form combine perfectly in the *Works and Days*. Perses is an expression of the arbitrary evil in this world which men must accept positively or to which they must resign themselves in pessimism.

The first part of Hesiod's poem is a bleak account of man's fate. It corresponds to the earlier experience of Hesiod's life, the heartless judgment that went against Hesiod in favor of Perses. The second portion of the poem is an attempt to make something of this fate, and at the same time Hesiod projects the expectation of a changed situation in his landholding. What we have is a psychological correspondence.

The second part of the poem is curious because Hesiod awkwardly goes about defining justice in two ways which are not necessarily complementary. Hesiod somewhat briefly tries out the possibility of an ethical basis of justice, and then returns to the matter of inexorability and there locates his idea of justice.

The most prominent features of this second part or central portion of the poem are: the image of the race track, where arrogance and justice compete for victory; an ideal portrait of the good city to which a brief pendant portrait of the evil city offers contrast; the image of the two roads, one leading to virtue, the other to evil; and a composite of the virtues of work, interspersed with aphoristic comments on the slothful man.

The least structural, most improvised passage is at the center (248–85). It is Hesiod's extreme venture into some kind of theology of a deity who presides over ethics and morals. This is a change from the earlier portion of the poem; there Zeus was not benevolent but rather harsh. The act of hiding men's sustenance shows Zeus to be devoid of compassion. Some critics would like to believe that Hesiod means to imply that Zeus did it for mankind's own good. But Hesiod does not say this, no matter how much we may imagine that he had tendencies in that direction. The shift to a conception of an ethical deity is motivated by the material of Hesiod's poem; he is in this sense led to it. Zeus at the outset of the *Works and Days* is simply power, pure power; he is the hawk, mankind is the nightingale. Hesiod did not have intimations of divine benevolence lurking, waiting to be expressed.

The new, ethical dimension to Hesiod's Zeus comes out of the material he is at this point developing. The immediate transition following the fable of the cruel hawk and the helpless nightingale is Hesiod's own exhortation to Perses to leave off acts of arrogance. Although the fable had begun as a pendant commentary on the naked power of the order of things it is also a portrait at the same time of unalloyed arrogance; hence the appeal to Perses follows naturally.

The descriptions of the good city and the bad city, together with the portrait of the Age of Iron, also relate to the Perses/Hesiod quarrel. As Hesiod develops his case, always set against the larger issues of the human condition, he leans heavily on the picture of a family torn with dissent. The healing in this familial situation comes from compassion. This ingredient is central to his present conception of Zeus, who is guardian of man's conduct to his fellows, the god who will punish those who maltreat others and bring down the unrighteous. With his conception of the good and bad cities, but more on the basis of his fable, Hesiod makes a special case for mankind's behavior. When he remarks (275ff.) that Zeus contrived for the animals to eat one another but to men he gave justice, Hesiod is perhaps saying that man cannot do violence as the senseless, instinct-driven or mechanical natural powers—whether animal or meteorological—can. Because man is frail, he is vulnerable next to god and nature; the Prometheus story is an example. Man is of another order from those creatures who naturally do violence to each other; witness the hawk and the nightingale.

At this point Hesiod continues to say: "to him who knows how to speak justly Zeus gives prosperity . . . for him who lies and injures justice . . . his descendants shall be dim and obscure." Justice here means just dealings among men. In that sense the relevance of justice to Hesiod's present plight with Perses is strongest, yet the passage is ambiguous in terms of the whole poem, for Hesiod by introducing the cosmogonic stories and the wisdom poetry has established a much larger if quite unwieldy field for his speculative adventures. Maltreating another may set in motion special punishment, stemming from Zeus' thirty thousand spirits who ever watch mankind from the entreaties of Justice, enthroned next to Zeus in the heavens. But rectitude in one's dealings with his fellow man will not necessarily spare a man from the anguish, aches and pains which the Prometheus/Pandora story and the portrait of the Iron Age reveal as man's natural lot. Nor does this conception of justice show one the way in confronting the inevitability of man's grim estate. True enough, Hesiod has left all that behind in the manner of an oral poet and turned uncomplicatedly to this new conception. But he just as easily turns back again, so that it is dubious to give too much emphasis to the ethical position. That is not Hesiod's main concern.

It is the idea of work, instead, that offers the most complete expression of justice. Hesiod reaches it through several images that convey the sense of duality. Competition between personified moral conditions and acts points the way out of hopelessness and pessimism. Suddenly instead of the static picture of the hawk and the nightingale we have the open-ended, ongoing chancy race track and the competition of arrogance and justice. Following this the descriptions of the good and bad cities manage to bring together important ideas so as to begin to achieve the synthesis between justice and work. The good city where justice is kept is described in vegetable or at least organic terms. The city blooms, its people are in blossom, the earth bears, oaks and bees flourish, the grain-giving earth brings forth its harvest and so on. The portrait of the bad city, brief as it is, speaks of war, plague and commerce; women sterile, armies destroyed, ships at sea swept away. The bad city is of a piece with the Bronze Age, the Iron Age and the ideas of wicked strife, whereas the good city is an agrarian phenomenon; the language of prosperity is from the field and the blessings of justice are flourishing crops. Justice in the good city is the concomitant if not the agency of agricultural success. Hesiod, following his description of the good road and the bad road, changes the emphasis and links agrarian prosperity to work. But the very description of the road turns the emphasis that way naturally: "The gods have placed sweat on the road to goodness; the road to goodness is long and steep, rough-going at first." In other words it is hard work to get to goodness; the association is natural. Goodness becomes hard work, justice lies in working hard, and working hard is going along the assigned route.

The image of the two roads is in part a restatement of the race-track image of thirty lines earlier. But the freedom of the race track is gone. Hesiod returns to the fundamental idea of inexorability that dominates the thinking of the poem. There is a road to good and a road to evil. The road is a system, a way, in that sense closed, inexorable. The image of the road is a natural corollary to the control and rigidity implicit in the fable of the hawk and the nightingale.

Now Hesiod is able to portray the man whom the gods love as the hard-working man. "Gods and men hate him who is idle . . . thus let your work be done in measure, so that your barn will be full in season . . . men who work are loved by the immortal gods . . . if you work you will grow rich . . . goodness and honor come to him who is rich." With this Hesiod leaves the ethical idea of justice, with which he had toyed only briefly. He further cements the relations between work and justice by talking of knowledge. But it is not enough to work hard, one must comprehend the way things are. Hesiod says, "The really best man is he who himself thinks through everything and comes to knowledge, next best is the man who will trust in the advice of one who knows. He who won't listen is useless." Comprehension or understanding emerges as a natural component of admonition or something didactic, and Hesiod utilizes it fully.

There is another sense of justice which becomes the more substantial one for Hesiod, justice in the sense of the way it is supposed to be. This is the justice of the race track, the right road and the wrong road, but more important it is the binding link between the stories and the aphorisms and the agricultural calendar. The earlier portion of the poem sets forth the inevitability of man's life but Hesiod by establishing the ideas of Good and Evil, Right and Wrong, imposed a notion of freedom and choice upon the basic sense of the stories. Man like the nightingale is caught in the talons of the hawk, but if he knows it, can learn the nature of this power, he has in some sense mastered it to his own advantage. To the ideas of Good and Evil, Right and Wrong, Hesiod conspicuously adds and often reiterates the temporal dimension of "timely" and "untimely." The hawk's talons are the rhythm of agricultural life, from which there is no escape. If one can live by it, accepting it and the equally inevitable necessity of work, one becomes rich, god-blessed. The third section of the poem at first seems only to restate the basic premise of the first section, the necessity of work. But the wisdom is more than that; it is traditional proof of the nature of the just life. It is not at all a guide to agriculture or clean living. The calendar is much too incomplete and the maxims are random and incoherent; rather it is proof of the nature of justice, of the very existence of justice, because it shows the pattern of inexorability man can know and become triumphant in his acceptance of it. These are the "spiritual exercises," so to speak. Work is the actualization of them. In the *Works and Days* Hesiod like Homer seems to show a characteristic of the Greek mind when juxtaposed and compared to the mentalities of the East. The poet of the *Iliad* is preoccupied with the problem of death, which nullifies the importance or dignity of human existence. The poets of the Gilgamesh tradition approached this problem, too, but as far as we know they never overcame the sense of desolation. Homer's Achilles, however, by his actions, his heroism, if you will, creates an existence that is equal to death. Achilles forces meaning on life. Hesiod, too, faces the desolation of life. Incessant agricultural labor, hard work, nature's forces—these are the living death, life's nullification. Death itself is not even a problem. The pessimistic wisdom literature of the East often prefers death in fact to the incessant routine of life. Hesiod has, however, taken the tradition, reshaped it and imposed upon work meaning and dignity.

Whether Hesiod is truly the author of both *Works and Days* and *Theogony* and in that case which of the two is the earlier work we do not know. The *Theogony* is thought to be earlier because it is simpler in structure ("more primitive"). Certainly the *Works and Days* seems more ambitious. If anything could go as proof, it is that the *Works and Days* implies a concept of god that the *Theogony* has worked out. Their diction is similar, but the *Theogony* is much more simply a collection of catalogues, of the same style as the Homeric Catalogue of Ships.

The *Theogony*'s genealogical catalogues unfold a world, a universe and its history, marvelous in its complexity and diversity. Its enormity in space and time is in sharp contrast with the steamy closet of domestic relations that the Homeric Olympic gods represent. Yet Hesiod starts with the anthropomorphized gods as his premise; their description in the Homer epics was probably the common one at the time. The hymn to the Muses that provides a prelude and program to his poem invokes a divine order as human as Homer's as for instance when Hesiod describes the Muses and the unending sweet song that flows from their mouths. "And the house of their father loud-thundering Zeus laughs with joy as the flower-delicate voices float about" (40ff.).

The genealogical catalogues that make up the *Theogony* provide the natural point for Hesiod's inquiry into the nature of god, for god's birth provides the basic link between the divine and human conditions. The gods are immortal; this constitutes the never-to-be-crossed chasm separating the gods from humankind. But these gods are born, unlike the God of Genesis, who remains outside of time ("In the beginning God created Heaven and Earth"). As Arthur Darby Nock used to say, "The Greek gods are this side of creation." In their birth and growth the Greek gods exhibit change and development, the source for their link to humanity, partial inspiration for their anthropomorphization. Greek religion is filled with stories of divine birth. Hesiod seeks the permanent meaning of this transitory, change-laden and altogether human event.

One way in which Hesiod invests genealogy with significance is in his categorization. Family after family appears in his listing; the sheer volume of names seems often confusing, yet unmistakable patterns emerge. In details, too, Hesiod is sorting and ordering experience. As has been pointed out, for instance, his list of the offspring of the sea (233ff.) assembles names that symbolize various mythological and meteorological facts of sea life. In turn the first several hundred lines of the poem detail the family lines of figures who are not cult figures nor much anthropomorphized nor central to mythology. These are the natural facts of the universe—heaven, earth, mountains and so on. The children of Night also (211ff.) are more representative of the human condition than individually realized, personalized figures of myth. The natural and physical quality of these phenomena is still clearer in the list of children of Ocean, Sea and Heaven. It is astronomy, meteorology, geography and geology.

Hesiod's material—the genealogies, the very idea of change, growth, progression or evolution in some supra-terrestrial sphere—is not unique with him. Traces of this interest lie in the *Iliad,* for instance 15.187ff., where the poet mentions the dispensation of divine powers and touches on divine genealogy after the manner of Hesiod. Much more important is Hesiod's connection with the East. Babylonian and Hittite documents show very similar ways of organizing human experience in environmental metaphors and the same intimations of supernatural forces. The parallels are not sufficient to show direct borrowing. Much more, the poetic style seems to serve or better, to create, the same end, and the poetic style is similar, arising no doubt from similar instincts in these cultures.

The *Theogony* is sometimes considered to be a *Handbuch* of mythology for the poets of Greece. Nothing could be further from the truth. True, Hesiod's interest is strongly antiquarian, he is devoted to codification, but consistently he goes further, he moves toward an analysis of Zeus. Here is the greater importance of the poem, the revelation of Zeus as an all-powerful and eternal god, apart from all other deities. It is this conception that gives validity to the traditional assertion that Hesiod along with Homer, Orpheus and Musaios is one of the great teachers of the Greeks.

Moreover his cataloguing and genealogies are also the first experiment in analysis.

Within the poem's structure lie the identification and analysis of Zeus' power. After the natural phenomena with which the poet begins, the story of the generations of gods prepares for the central fact of the poem, the life of Zeus. Not only does this primitive mythology concentrate on divine births, reflecting a cult interest in the divine child, but the stories reflect a rhythm of the warring between divine father and son. Ouranos is castrated and cast into impotence, Kronos, in turn, loses his power. What seems to be a natural Oedipal construct of the archetypal family is converted by Hesiod to a fact of evolution. The earlier generations of gods are essentially characterized as monsters, fabulous creatures of one sort or another, far removed from the standard of Greek mythological thinking, which is to say that they are inhuman and unhuman. The *Theogony* betrays an obsession with monsters, but there is nothing quaint or primitive in this, as it might appear. Rather the poet is intent upon isolating the superior strands in the divine fabric and true to the Greek point of view these are distinctly human.

So it is that the *Theogony*'s generations of gods cleanse the tradition, so to speak, of supernatural elements that are alien to the human dimension. The monsters are banished; Zeus reigns. Hesiod's poetic instinct led him to underscore this fact with the celebrated Titanomachia (battle with the Titans) and the battle against the monster Typhoeus. The *Theogony* has in fact been called one great *aristeia* whose hero is Zeus. The two battles serve different ends. The Titanomachia is a collision of two world systems; the descriptions of the fighting emphasize vastness and as Zeus and his cohorts win out over the older order of gods, the monsters, ogres and implacable demons, the vision is that of a change in world orders, the movement of eras, not unlike the feeling Karl Barth found in the birth of Christ; that is, Zeus' victory signals the beginning of history. The battle with Typhoeus seems to some redundant, thus an interpolation, to others, an example of the lack of discipline, the garrulity of epic poetry, yet the picture of the single figure of Typhoeus pitted against Zeus is first of all a formal piece of epic, the duel between heroes, and then it is the realization of the individual power of Zeus, now the new king of the gods. The poem is historical because it is genealogical; the Titanomachia is part of the history of the gods. The poem is also analytical, an attempt to define the mythological and religious phenomenon of Zeus. The fight with Typhoeus serves that analysis.

The poet, having brought Zeus, single victor, into a new moral dimension, is not afraid to introduce a story of primitive religiosity that immediately seems to contradict the essence of the new dispensation, that is, Zeus' swallowing of Metis. The stories, however, that exhibit primitive or early religious ideas are in fact the strength of Hesiod's account, for as he says, he speaks the truth. The old stories have truth to them because they are traditional, because the actions they describe are elemental, such as the castration of Ouranos (*Theogony* 178ff.). The *Theogony* is built upon the theme of overthrow; in essence Oedipal, it is expanded by Hesiod to cover the whole nature of things. The overthrow of Zeus is therefore inherent in the story. The description of his swallowing the goddess Metis who is pregnant by him with an offspring destined to overthrow him is grotesque yet strikes at the heart of the problem; for in this act Zeus has now assured himself of eternal power, hence the fostering of moral absolutes and eternal justice.

The ensuing generations' criticisms of Homer's only too human portrait of the gods never touch upon such stories as these for they transcend human action. Their stark power leaves no direction for criticism, unlike the final portions of the *Theogony* where Hesiod chronicles the goddesses and mortal women with whom Zeus has lain. Here again the intent is clear. He has established Zeus as focus of the universe and obscures or denies the implications of the earlier genealogies, that is, the multiplicity of the supernatural world. Zeus is focus, and from him must emanate the gods and heroic mortals who people legend and mythology. The conclusion foreshadows monotheism, although the encounters mentioned are themselves amorous and erotic in theme. They are a parallel to the more obvious passage in the fourteenth book of the Iliad when Zeus crudely attempts to compliment Hera on her physical charms by listing a number of his conquests who were her sensual inferiors. Homer's use of this material is meant to be humorous; there is no theology there.

The progressive evolution within the genealogical stories and the just victories won by Zeus later in the poem contrive a vision of the universe of moral order, rather than the brute, neutral environment that surrounds man. The *Works and Days* is complementary to this work for it develops a farmer's conception of human existence and purpose that derives from a belief in not only a moral universe, but most particularly a moral scheme of things in nature.

But at times one can only wonder that the *Theogony* and the *Works and Days* are thought to be by the same man; for they betray such different senses of time. The former with its story of successive generations of gods, the battles and triumphs of newer and more refined deities, shows a linear sense of time; a notion of progression and change that is altogether absent from the *Works and Days*. And yet the cyclical time sense of the *Works and Days* is the rhythm of agricultural life woven into the fabric of its aphorisms and calendars. One could not exactly expect otherwise. Where they are alike is in their positive affirmation, and in this they differ markedly from their Near Eastern sources.

To the ancient Greeks Hesiod and Homer were legendary, they were the primeval poets who created the gods and the heroes, who laid down the vision of life which was memorized by generation after generation. Between them and subsequent poets there lay a great abyss.

The seventh and sixth centuries were a period of great change in the Greek world. The beginnings of the spread of literacy, the invention of coinage, widespread migrations, the decline in power of the aristocracy coupled with the emergence of tyrants who spoke for a proto-bourgeoisie, together these factors brought social dislocation, upheaval and crisis. The sense of change and experimentation is reflected in the poetic fragments that come from this period. Unfortunately the fragments are little more than that so we can make only minimal estimations of the poetic production as a whole as well as of the quality of each individual poet. Sappho, for instance, enjoyed a high poetic reputation throughout antiquity, as indeed she does to this day. But we have little evidence for that judgment.

The new movements in poetry are directly related to the language and style we find in the *Iliad* and *Odyssey*. There were other kinds of rhythmic language at the time of Homer and his contemporaries. Both poems describe other kinds of formal verbal play, often with singing or chanting, like the little boy singing the Linos song, a song of grief, while his friends dance, described on the shield of Achilles (*Iliad*

18.570), or the wedding song of the shield (*Iliad* 18.493ff.), or random singing such as Calypso's while she works (*Odyssey* 5.61–62). And there are other examples. But we can only trace the relationship in language between the epics and later poetry and the reaction in the later poets to the epics. Other influences and relationships are completely obscured.

One poetic development is the elegiac meter, a dactylic hexameter line alternating with a line made up of two hexameter half lines made into one line, i.e. $-\cup\cup-\cup\cup-//-\cup\cup-\cup\cup-$. Possibly it was originally accompanied by the flute. The poetry in this meter because of its dactylic quality has much of the language of the epic and much of the epic's public, social quality. Elegiac was, for instance, the medium of epitaphs, the most famous probably being that which Simonides composed for the dead Spartans at Thermopylae.

> Tell the Lacedaimonians, stranger, that here,
>   obedient to their commands, we lie.

Elegiacs were also used for exhortation. The Spartan Tyrtaeus, for instance, has a long poem of Homeric character on the virtue of dying in battle, defending one's city. It begins:

> To die is beautiful falling in the foremost rank
>   when it's a good man fighting for his fatherland.

And the Athenian political figure Solon uses elegiacs to display his personal philosophy, which is best and most simply caught in these few lines of a seventy-five-line poem.

> We humans good or bad think alike
> each has wonderful expectations
> before suffering. Then comes the grief. Till then,
> however, we're happy, agape with airy hopes.

> (33–36)

Elegiac was also used to make more personal statements but nonetheless obviously pronouncements, such as those of Mimnermus on love:

> What is life what is joy without golden Aphrodite?
> May I die when these things no longer move me—
> hidden love affairs, sweet nothings and bed,

you know, the blossoms of youth there to be snatched
by man and woman both. For along comes painful
old age, makes a man repulsive, feeble, to boot.
Ugly cares eternally wear at his mind,
he gets no pleasure looking at the rays of the sun,
there he goes repulsive to the boys, without women's esteem;
that's how god makes harsh old age.

or Theognis on social change:

Kyrnos, my boy, it's the same city, but different people;
who formerly knew neither justice nor laws
who wore to shreds goatskins around their ribs
who went about outside the city like deer.
Now they are the gentry, son of Polypaides. Those once noble
are the lowly now. Who can bear seeing it?

The earliest known poet is Archilochus, born on Paros,
who lived somewhere from 680 to 640 more or less. He
made elegiacs, and also poems in iambic meter ($\smile$–) and its
reverse, the trochaic (–$\smile$). Later poets and critics developed
the convention that the iambic meter, because it was so close
to common speech rhythms, was the meter of satire and
abuse (on the aristocratic theory, I suppose, that the com-
mons opened their mouths only to rail at one another). But
Archilochus, who had the reputation in antiquity of being
especially vicious, does not show this or a predilection for
being abusive in iambs. He uses the meters well, which
implies that there was a technical tradition behind him.
And he mocks certain epic pretensions in his poetry in various meters. For instance, in contrast to the epic hero's
excessive anxiety over the keeping and taking of weaponry,
Archilochus has this to say:

Some Saian is enjoying the shield, pretty little thing
that it was, I ditched by a bush, quite against my will.
But I myself escaped death. And that shield, to hell with it!
Tomorrow I'll get me another no worse.

Or in contrast to the heroic general, the Homeric "lord of
hosts," Archilochus says:

I don't like a great general, one walking legs astride,
nice hair, shaved, proud of it.
No, give me a little fellow, legs you can see between—
that bow legged—standing firm on his feet, full of heart.

Most of all, Archilochus' poetry reveals himself. This is
private poetry although it is abroad and public, different
from Hesiod, Solon or Mimnermus, because Archilochus is
intent upon revealing his feelings as well as his intimate situation. Nothing, for instance, could better describe how it
feels to be a soldier of fortune, the aloneness, the self-
sufficiency, than these lines:

In my spear is my bread kneaded, in my spear wine,
Ismarikan wine, I drink leaning on my spear.

He sounds like Odysseus on his storm-tossed raft when he
cries out:

Heart, heart, stirred round in sorrows beyond repair,
up, escape, press your chest against the evils,
in the enemy ambush, take your stand nearby.
Steady. Neither in victory rejoice too high
nor beaten fall down at home and grieve.
Take pleasure in delights and at evils grieve
not too much—get to know the rhythm which holds mankind.

Among the few extant pieces perhaps Sappho most of all
can describe intimate feelings. Her sensuality is matched by
the wide variety of meters she uses, far more sensual themselves than the accustomed conventional meters. She sings of
her feelings at seeing a man and a girl talking and laughing
together and of her jealousy at not being able to be in the
man's place.

Seems just like the gods
that fellow sitting across from you
and near, hearing you
    sweetly talking
and your sexy laugh. Makes my
heart fly up in my breast
looking at you even a second, my voice

won't come any more,
but my tongue breaks, all at once
a little fire runs up and over my skin
my eyes can't see, my ears,
        they roar.
Sweat starts pouring down, trembling
comes on all over. I am greener
than grass, and I seem like
    I could die.

Elsewhere she evokes in her reader a great series of sensual impressions. The following fragment of poetry was found written on a potsherd in the third century, although parts of it are quoted by two ancient critics. The poem is addressed to Aphrodite.

. . . .
Come to me here from Crete to the holy temple,
to your sweet grove of
apples, altars smoking
incense.

Here the water is cold, it rushes
through the apple tree leaves, roses
make shadow patterns everywhere, quivering
leaves stop in sleep
. . . .

Sappho uses language self-consciously, deliberately breaking the epic linguistic patterns, which must have fallen upon her auditors' ears as twelve-tone scales once did on ours. For instance, the common epic phrase, *gaiă mĕlāină*, "black earth," is used by her in a certain case (accusative) and thus a new metrical situation impossible in epic, that is, *gās mĕlāinăs*. The sequence −◡− cannot, may not occur in dactylic hexameters. To hear the accustomed words in the impossible rhythm is to make the language new again, to rediscover the *words* in the phrase. Likewise the common phrase *ptera pukna* (hard to translate clearly: "thick wings" or "wings rapidly") is separated by her "thick rapidly flapping wings," *pukna dinnenter ptera*. These are subtleties, but they fracture and recast obvious language.

The poem from which these two examples are taken is

Sappho's most famous and possibly only complete poem. She has taken two moods and brought them together in an unusual way in the twenty-eight lines. She begins with the typical elements of prayer to a goddess, using epithets, getting a sense of great size and great space.

> Clever-minded immortal Aphrodite,
> child of Zeus, cunning, I beseech thee
> don't break with worries and cares my
>   heart, lady,
>
> but come here, if ever another time
> you heard my cry and came from
> afar, leaving your father's golden
>   house, you came
>
> hitching up a chariot. Beautiful sparrows
> brought you swift over the black earth
> rapidly flapping wings out of heaven through
>   the middle air.
>
> Swiftly they came, and you, blessed one,
> a smile on your immortal face,
> asked what I was suffering, why
>   I had called
>
> and what most I wanted for myself and my
> crazy heart. "Whom should Persuasion
> bring to you in love, who, Sappho,
>   hurts you?
>
> For if she now flees, soon she'll pursue.
> If she refuses gifts, nevertheless, she'll give them,
> If she won't love, soon she will love
>   even against her will."
>
> Come to me even now, free me from
> harsh cares, get me what my heart
> tells me get, you yourself
>   be ally.

In the third and fourth stanzas she has a bit of narrative. Then the pace changes, staccato questions, first in indirect statement, repeated in direct quotation, then the more breathless sixth stanza. One feels the power of the goddess and yet as the seventh stanza returns to the prayer we realize that the intensity of the sixth was the increasing passion of Sappho's fantasy. In this way Sappho has endowed the formality of the prayer with the intensity that initially motivated it.

More remains from Pindar than any other poet before the Hellenistic period except for the tragedians and Homer. Of eleven books of his poems we have the last two preserved, the so-called victory hymns. Pindar wrote for hire, and he is reputed to have made a lot of money composing hymns in celebration of victories in contests, notably those held at Olympia in honor of Zeus every four years. The victor was not necessarily considered the man who contested but in fact his backer. As in many other periods of history it was a chance for someone of wealth to gain additional status. Pindar's clients were often Sicilian tyrants who wished in every way to legitimatize their rule. The particular glory of mounting a winning horse at a contest so noble and hallowed as that at Olympia conferred immense status upon tyrants. The victory celebration was further ennobled by having a choral song of victory composed by someone like Pindar. Crude as it may be as an analogy, it was not unlike having Lester Lanin or Meyer Davis personally lead the orchestra at a Mafia daughter's debut.

Pindar's worth is a subject of controversy. Few claim to understand his poetry. Many will say that it in fact means little. Apologists will argue that the music and the dynamics of the banquet of celebration gave to the words a context and significance that made a meaning we with only the verbal text cannot possibly recapture. Voltaire put the matter very well indeed:

> Sors du tombeau, divin Pindare,
> Toi qui célèbras autrefois
> Les chevaux de quelques bourgeois
> ou de Corinthe ou de Mégàre
> Toi qui possédas le talent
> De parler beaucoup sans rien dire
> Toi qui modulas savamment
> Des vers que personne n'entend
> Et qu'il faut toujours qu'on admire.

The Pindaric ode nonetheless is a familiar if formidable phenomenon. The form is a series of strophes answered by metrically identical antistrophes or it is triadic, strophe, antistrophe followed by epode. The language and manner of expression show that this poet like all the rest in the archaic age (he lived quite beyond this time, 518–438, but his sentiments and manner resisted the fifth century) was in the spell of Homer and Hesiod, yet invoking their language, thought and manner to contrive an absolutely new structure of reality. The Pindaric manner can be immediately detected in the earlier tragic choral odes, which become clearer in meaning when it can be seen that they owe much to this other style.

Yet we would be wrong to attribute too much to Pindar alone. His contemporary Bacchylides was a similar poet for hire, his odes also celebrating victories. Both in fact were hired to celebrate the victory of Hieron, tyrant of Syracuse, on the occasion in 472 when his horse, Pherenikos ("Victory Bringer"), came in first. We are unusually lucky to have both choral odes preserved since they show us how two poets approached the same assignment.

Bacchylides recounts the story of a meeting in the Underworld between Hercules and Meleager. The latter has died because his mother in revenge for his killing her brother (by accident) has taken an enchanted stick from a chest and set it afire, an act doomed to end Meleager's life. This is typical saga narrative but Bacchylides sets it forth in brief phrases and images, here literally translated.

> Thestios' fierce daughter
> for me a mother of evil fate
> plotted my destruction, fearless woman that she was;
> from the carved chest
> she took the stick of quick death,
> burnt it, the stick fate once had ordained
> would be the end of my life.
> At the time I was in the act of slaying
> the blameless body of Klymenos, Daipylos'
> bold son, before the walls;
> for they were fleeing toward
> the well-built city

of Pleuron. My sweet life grew short,
I felt my strength decline.
Oh me, breathing my last, I cried,
wretched at leaving my glorious youth.

Like epic narrative the epithets are there, the action is
there, but the details are not, the extension of the essential
action is not. There are affinities with those moments in epic
when the poet wishes to allude to something beyond his
narrative; for instance the description of the betrayal of
Agamemnon's house by Aigisthos (*Odyssey* 3.254ff.), especially that chilly, terse line following the description of
Aigisthos' having killed the chaperon whom Agamemnon left
in the house: "then he willing her willing led to his home"
(3.272). The best example deals incidentally with the story
of Meleager (*Iliad* 9.527ff.). It is typical of a tendency
throughout Greek literature to offer examples while instruct-
ing. Much ancient Greek literature is self-consciously instructive if not formally didactic. Instruction by example is
a commonplace technique throughout. In the *Odyssey* Telemachus is constantly offered the example of Orestes as a way
to understanding and solving his dilemma of the suitors who
surround his mother. In the *Iliad* Phoenix instructs Achilles
in the necessity of yielding, its virtues and its psychology. He
offers the example of Meleager as a man who yields too late.
What is significant and relevant to the narrative art of
Bacchylides is that Phoenix does not tell an extensive story
of Meleager, does not bring in those numerous details and
asides that mark epic narrative. It is in the examples particularly where the epic poet tries the technique of letting
the less stand for the more, a technique that is essential to
the choral lyrics.

Likewise in this poem Bacchylides *suggests* the meaning of
his narrative in a way quite unlike the explicit epic. Meleager
describes his undoing at the hand of a woman, his mother,
as close a relationship as a man can have. Hercules shudders,
then says (164), "It is best to speak of what man has the potential to do," that is, let the past alone and look to the hope
and success of the future. He then asks, "Have you any
sisters at home?" Meleager replies, "Dejaneira," and here the
narrative part of the ode ends. This is extraordinarily condensed, for there is much implied but unsaid. Dejaneira, as
Bacchylides' audience knew, marries Hercules and ultimately

is the cause of his death, however unwittingly, out of jealousy. It is Meleager and his mother all over again. Therefore Bacchylides seems to be saying, look to the future with caution, expect little. Success is failure. For a victory ode these are the proper commonplace Greek sentiments.

While comparisons are misleading and singling out so little from so large a preserved *oeuvre* as Pindar's is doubly so, nonetheless I have done so. One can see certain distinct tendencies in poetry manifest in Pindar's work which are not in Bacchylides.

Pindar's poem Olympian I, as it is called, is one of Pindar's extremes, the very opposite, say, of Pythian IV. The latter is much more narrative, an account of Jason. Olympian I on the other hand is allusive, obscure, moving by imagery from one point to another. To demonstrate this through an English translation is very hard and perhaps nonsensical. Those who champion the virtue or indeed even the possibility of translation are quickly refuted by a poem like Olympian I. Let us, however, try, because Pindar is especially important as a revelation of that transition in narrative from Homer to tragic choruses. He is virtuoso, mostly technique, and we see more clearly here what content will sometimes obscure in Aeschylus. The poem begins:

Strophe I
Water is best, but gold like shining fire
that stands out in the night is man exalting wealth's high mar

If one tries to *study* Pindar, he is in danger; it is the same danger of intellectual anarchy which overcomes us when we stare too hard at or listen too long to a word and suddenly it loses its meaning, dissolved into unintelligible units. The same is often true of a Pindaric ode. The two lines quoted seem to be ideas or propositions; as such they are nonsense, or at least trite. But if we get away from an "idea," we may say that Pindar instead has begun a mood. The poem celebrates victory. These lines introduce the spirit of contest and do so monumentally. "Water is best" evokes Hesiodic maxims. Furthermore, it is a statement like those of the Ionian philosophers of the sixth century who were seeking to reduce reality to its absolute core. So there is the sense of final, irrevocable truth, the very beginning of it all in these few words. The poem begins solid and monolithic. The fire simile that follows is a Homeric commonplace, associated intimately and consistently in Homer with all manifestations of heroism, thus construing the high heroic mood. The idea of contest has to do with superiority, and the two lines reinforce that idea in several ways.

> If, my heart, you will
> sing of contests,
> 5   look no further than the sun,
> no other star hotter in the day
> shining through the desert of the air,
> or sing no contest greater than Olympia

Pindar reinforces eminence, glitter and contest (through comparison) and then continues

> (Olympia)
> whence comes the oft-sung hymn
> 10   thrown around the wisdom of the wise,

These are confusing lines which I take to mean Olympia the source and inspiration of hymn after hymn which cloak, or are made to settle around and hence mold, the minds of the poets.

> (hymn)
> to sing of the son of Kronos,
> as they [the wise] arrive at the blessed hearth of Hieron

Hymns aim at the best, that is, praise of Zeus; poets in hymning arrive at the blessed hearth of Hieron; the poet has placed his patron next to Zeus and in a passage devoted completely to superlatives, Hieron becomes a superlative himself. Clearly the poet places himself in the superlative regions as well.

> Antistrophe I
> (Hieron) who wields the scepter of natural law in
>   Sicily
> abounding in apples, plucking the tops of every *arete;*

A Homeric description first, thus somewhat heroic if commonplace, then an image that reinforces the notion of contest and also relates "plucking" to "apples."

(*arete*)
he is made bright in
the choicest music*
15   which we men play often
around his table.
        Come take down the Dorian lyre from its peg
if the pleasure that comes from Pisa and Pherenikos
puts any sweet thought in your mind,
20   when by the Alpheus river he raced,
no need of spurs to his body on the course;
he mixed with his strength his master
the horse-loving lord of Syracuse.

The root of the word "play" above is the same as the root of
the word for "child," so there is some sense here of "we men
make music, are thus children to the tyrant Hieron's role of
our father." The poet continues to glorify Hieron and to set
the scene of the occasion of the hymn. "The choicest music"
in the sense of selection recalls plucking the tops; "he is
made bright in the choicest music" means, of course, Hieron
has luster because it is Pindar who sings his praises. Pisa is
the town nearby the sacred precinct and racecourse of
Olympia; Alpheus is the local river. Pherenikos in his
victory brought Hieron into it by virtue of his ownership.
But the language is from cooking, or mixing water with wine,
which leads us to the caldron with Pelops cooking.

        Epode I
        the horse-loving lord of Syracuse; his fame lights up
        here in the colony of good men, colony of Lydian
            Pelops
25   whom the Earthshaker, great in his strength
        Poseidon once loved and wanted when Klotho seized
            him out of the caldron
        outstanding with his shining ivory shoulder.
        Yes, there are many wonders, and somehow
        some way stories tricked with glittering cunning
        lies deceive the talking of men beyond the true account.

There existed a mythical account of Tantalus who cut up his
son, Pelops, to serve as dinner for the gods. They refrained

* Literally the very finest-quality wool of music, or as we might say,
the flower of music.

from eating except Demeter, who absent-mindedly brooding
over her lost daughter, Persephone, ate the shoulder. Pelops
was miraculously reassembled in a boiling caldron and fitted
out with a new ivory shoulder. Pindar denies the truth of this
myth. Skill at storytelling, clever stories, these are not necessarily truth.

> Strophe II
> 30 Pleasure which makes all sweet things for mortals
> brings honor, makes the incredible credible often.
> But the days thereafter
> are the wisest witnesses.

Which must mean that however seductive and delusive pleasure is, time will reveal all. Song is a source of pleasure and
seductive; but reality will surface.

> It is fitting for a man to say
> 35   good things of the gods; for the blame will be less.
> Son of Tantalus, I shall say things of you
> opposite to what they said before,
> how when your father invited the gods,
> a most respectable banquet on his Sipylos,
> returning in this way an invitation from them,
> 40   then the Bright Trident seized you,

> Antistrophe II
> overcome in his mind with love, on golden horses,
> went off on high to the mansion of wide-honored Zeus.
> There another time, a second time,
> came Ganymede as well
> 45 for Zeus, for the same reason.

Ganymede, the cupbearer to Zeus, was a beautiful Trojan
youth like Pelops, whom Zeus could not resist.

> When you were missing
>   all men searching and no one brought you back to
>   your mother
> then a jealous neighbor began to say behind your
>   family's back
> how in the water's high boiling point on the fire

> they cut you up with a knife limb for limb,
> 50 then finally at table served you out
> as meat and ate you.

Line 48 with "water," "fire" and "high point" is some kind of restatement of the first line, but what? The occasion of the banquet is also that implied at the end of strophe I and into the antistrophe, "hearth of Hieron" (11), "around his table" (17), if not again the idea of Pherenikos mixing his master into his strength (22). But what is the sense of it? This portion of the poem is perplexing. Envy breeds slander? Hieron in his high position analogous to Pelops being god-loved is thus equally vulnerable. False stories are pretty stories dependent on pleasure rather than truth, so Pindar says at 28–31. Slander deriving from envy, false, pretty stories, they must be somehow the same. Pindar will set himself apart as the poet who speaks otherwise.

> Epode II
> I cannot call one of the Blessed a glutton; I revolt.
> Many losses are the fate of those who speak maliciously.

Somehow in this murky poem Pindar is talking about truth and falsehood in stories; at the same time he insists that he will not say anything unseemly, for instance "it is fitting" (35), now here more fully. The word "losses" means principally the absence of profit. He has already implied some equation between Hieron and the gods; the end of the first stanza, for instance, contains the word "blessed," which by itself as used here (52) means a god or the gods. Is he somehow talking of his poetic responsibilities toward Hieron and the liabilities in the relationship? "Losses" and "seemliness" would both be apt. After all Pindar was in this for money, and clients are touchy. But is that what he is saying and does he expect Hieron and the other celebrants on this occasion to take this meaning? True enough, he elsewhere refers to poetry, his poetic rivals, the competition in the business, so allusions of this sort would not be impossibly obscure.

> If the guardians on Olympus loved any mortal
> 55 man, it was this Tantalus. But digest
> his great good fortune he could not, and stuffed
> as he was, he got himself in high trouble;

> the Father hung above him a heavy stone;
> as he forever tries to get it way from his head he strays
>   from happiness.

The idea of gluttony is taken up here, Tantalus, well-fed or overfed, hungers for more and brings on his own grief. Banqueting, or at least eating, remains with us. This section otherwise is a poetic commonplace, natural to victory songs, that is, nothing too much; overwhelming success can only remind us of devastating failure, a result in Greek culture of the emphasis upon the contest system. The logic here is from Pelops, the son, to Tantalus, who is a stock (notice "this Tantalus") example of excessive pride. The Father is Zeus. Pindar's audience, because the poem deals so extensively with excellence and competition, would expect something like this. The gastric metaphor, however, is the significant link with other parts of the poem, eating having been first implied in "hearth" (11), "table" (17) and then in the reference to the ivory shoulder (27) and elsewhere thereafter.

> Strophe III
> He has helpless life misery that won't go away,
> 60   along with the three a fourth labor, because he stole
>   from the immortals for his drinking friends
>   nectar and ambrosia,
>   gave it to them, which made them
>   immortal. But if any man
>   hopes to deceive a god at whatever he does, he errs.

Pindar's audience knows that the other three legendary great punishments are those of Tityus, Sisyphus and Ixion.

> 65   For this reason too the immortals again cast the son
>   back among the short-lived race of men.
>   When he blossomed in stature,
>   the hairs covered his chin and it darkened,
>   he thought of marriage as ready

Pelops goes in disgrace, but also the beautiful boy has become a man. Pindar's audience would certainly have thought of the latter. Pelops left because of his father's disgrace, but it is time for him to depart Olympus. Beauty has its place only fleetingly. He goes back to short-lived men even as his

adolescent beauty was short-lived, even as his father's favor
with the gods was short-lived. Try or not, good things pass.

      Antistrophe III
      (marriage as ready)
70   to take from her father Pisatas famous
      Hippodameia. Going near to the gray sea alone
      in darkness, he called to the Deep Thunderer
      the Good Trident god. When he appeared
      right at his feet, close by,
75   to him he said: "Now then, Poseidon, if the dear gifts
         of Kypria bring about any pleasure,
      restrain the bronze spear of Oinomaos,
      get me to Elis in your fastest chariot,
      give me strength.
      Since he has killed thirteen men
80   suitors, and throws off the marriage

Oinomaos, father to Hippodameia, established a contest for
those who sought her hand. They tried to ride away with her
in the chariot while Oinomaos pursued trying to spear the
suitor. Pindar makes Pelops' success the simple matter of a
god's love. Pindar wants to introduce the enduring nature of
pleasure here in contrast to its fleeting, ambiguous nature in
line 30. Though Pelops is no longer Poseidon's beloved,
the pleasure that he gave endures.

      Epode III
      (marriage)
      of the daughter. Great risk comes not to a weak man.
      Since we must die, who would sit
      in the shadow stewing an old age, nameless, pointless,
      without a share in all that's beautiful? No,
85   this is the contest set for me; give me success out of
         love."
      Thus he spoke; he got to him; his words
      worked. The shining god gave him golden
      chariot and horses untiring, winged.

      Strophe IV
      He overcame Oinomaos' strength, got the maiden to
         bed.

She bore six sons, leaders, striving in their excellence.
90   Now in blood offerings
glorious he is mixed.
Lying by the path of the Alpheus
he has a celebrated tomb by the
much visited altar.

Pelops is mixed as Hieron was mixed in his horses' strength.
There is no real correspondence, yet it suggests something
immanent. The subject of fame which follows brings us back
to one of the initial themes of the poem.

The fame of the Olympic contests looks out afar from
the racecourse
95   of Pelops, where swiftness of feet is in contest
and the high points of boldness and the struggle of
strength.
The winner all the rest of his life
has honey-sweet good weather

Antistrophe IV
because of the contests. Nobility that goes on day after
day
100   is highest for all mortals. And I must crown
this man with a horseman's song
in the Aeolic mood.
I know no man knowing
more of beauty, holding greater power
105   of those whom I adorn with noble folds of hymns.

"Nobility, etc." is a Hesiodic commonplace, true as an as-
piration, a wish, a belief, which nevertheless, as Pindar often
states in the poem, is contradicted by the evidence. If we
keep away from meaning or idea the preceding lines all
work together, that is, "the fame" looking out "afar," "the
high point," "winner," "rest of his life," "good weather,"
"nobility," "day after day"—all of it true to the exhilaration
of winning. The poem overall is ambiguous, waffling between
what is fleeting and what is imperishable, but that is immensely and successfully true to what seems the basic archaic-
age manic-depressive swing in feeling.

"This man" may refer to either Pelops or Hieron and is
ambiguous, provides the link and transition between Pelops

and Hieron. "The fame" here at line 94 reminds one of
Hieron's fame in line 23.

> God turns to you, cares for you
> has this regard, Hieron, for your concerns.
> And if he does not depart
> still sweeter, I hope, a concern
>
> Epode IV
> 110 with swift chariot shall I celebrate finding
> a helping road of words coming to far-seeing Kronion.

A god watches over Hieron as Poseidon watched over Pelops,
he cares but he may go, Pindar will advance Hieron's glory
in the chariot of song as his jockey has done on the back of
Pherenikos (Pindar also imagines himself in a chariot as
Pelops has one in winning Hippodameia), "coming to far-
seeing Kronion" the road of Hieron's glory leads to the sacrifices to be performed here, a hill sacred to Zeus at Olympia.

> For me the Muse nurses in courage her strongest
> weapon;
> great men are great in different ways. The extreme is
> reached by kings. Look not still further.
> 115 May you walk this time on high.
> May I for this length of time mingle with victors
> outstanding in wisdom among all Hellenes everywhere.

Greatness, acme, we are back at the beginning, with a
typical personal advertisement by Pindar.

The year in which Hieron's victory occasioned these two
poems also saw the performance of Aeschylus' *Persians*. Unlike other extant tragedies, the *Persians* dramatizes a reality,
the Persian defeat at Salamis, although since the action consists of the reaction of the Persian court at Susa to this doleful event, about which Aeschylus would have known nothing,
we would be better off calling the *Persians* a fiction. But the
way in which Aeschylus uses geographical distance and
stresses the exotic nature of Persian culture together with
his refusal to refer to the contemporary Greek world mythologizes the real event. "Seawashed Ajax' isle, soil bloodied,
holds all there is of Persia," sing the Persian chorus (595–
97), making epic out of the topical reference to the corpse-

strewn beaches of Salamis following the naval battle in
September 480.

The chorus enter in anapaests, the marching meter (⌣ ⌣ –
⌣ ⌣ –), singing a lyrical catalogue of the Persian forces. Unlike
Homer's catalogue, however, reminiscences of which give
this choral ode that typically Aeschylean "epic" flavor, the
Persians' song has the names combined in a mosaic that
gives the texture of mighty vastness rather than supplying a
register of place names:

> And they, Susa and Agbatana
> and the ancient bulwark of Kissa,
> leaving, went on horse,
> on ship, by foot they went,
> bringing war's close array of men,
> Amistra and Artaphrenes,
> Megabates and Astarpes,
> lords of Persia,
> kings, to the great king subservient,
> they rush, overseers of a great army,
> bowman and cavalry,
> fearful to behold, terrible to fight
> in the show of their courageous heart.
> Artembares, horseman lustful of battle,
> Masistes, archer conqueror,
> the noble Imaios, Pharandakes,
> Sosthanes, driver of horses.
> Others the Nile sent, the great
> and greatly nurturing Nile; Sousiskanes,
> Pegastagon, Egyptian-born
> ruler of holy Memphis,
> great Arsames . . . (1–37)

So they continue proudly, boastfully until once in place in
the dancing area of the theater. Then the meter changes to the
usual strophe-antistrophe lyrical structure which we saw in
Pindar. The chorus grow more reflective, commencing with
the description of Xerxes' frantic and exultant advance upon
Greece until they break out* in fear. The initial choral utterance which recalled Homer changes to the axiomatic
Hesiodic structuring of things, here posed in questions:

* The corruption of the text has caused lines here to be transposed.
These quoted are 93–96 which follow upon line 114.

> god's deceit and deception—
> what mortal man avoids this?
> Who masters his flying leap
> with swift enough foot?

Throughout this opening chorus, Aeschylus translates the historic fact of the Persian expedition into a sacral truth in the way in which Pindar removed himself from the immediate victory of Hieron's horse.

Fourteen years later in 458, two years before his death, Aeschylus won first prize with his Orestes trilogy. The first play, the *Agamemnon*, has lyrical choral passages of unusual force and grandeur which show what Aeschylus chose to do with the techniques we have observed in Pindar. There are significant differences, for Pindar was creating relatively brief occasional poetry whereas each choral ode in the *Oresteia* is an integral part of a very long, elevated, enduring view of human action enough abstracted by its mythical and logical properties as well as the universal, to which our attention is constantly directed, that the lyrics pass together with such pieces as the Old Testament Psalms into the body of sacred poetry.

The first two choral passages in the *Agamemnon* are unusually long; they are also relatively obscure, which conveys the quality of prophecy suitable to the highly metaphysical conception of human action which Aeschylus presents in this trilogy. Their length and formality also serve to introduce the mighty train of events that takes us from the sullied sheets of Atreus' bed to the citizens' court on the Areopagus at Athens.

The *Agamemnon* begins with a lively piece of characterization. A watchman, loyal family retainer in the house, describes his years-long wait for a beacon signal from over the Aegean which will tell that the war at Troy has ended. Then, suddenly there is the light. Euphoria breaks out, followed by gloom as the foreboding he feels settles back on him. The advent of light is the first great image of the trilogy, for the play's action moves out of darkness until finally it is bathed in the full light of Athens as the dark and sinister Erinyes are changed into gladsome, kindly spirits, the Eumenides. But out of this first light, however, comes the next movement in the *Agamemnon*, the entrance of the chorus, who begin with these lines:

40   This the tenth year since Priam's
            great plaintiff
      Lord Menelaus and Agamemnon,
      two-throned, Zeus-born, two-sceptered
      stout yoke of honor in Atreus' line,
45   launched from this land
            myriad ships in expedition
            a defense of soldiers
      crying great Ares from their heart
            like eagles
50   in grief at the nest departing of their young
      high over their beds wheel about
      plying the oars of their wings
            child care gone now
      which kept them at their beds.
55   Someone on high whether Apollo
      or Pan or Zeus heard
      the high-pitched cry, bird lament
      of these visitors to god's domain
      afterward sent punishment upon the transgressors.
60   So Zeus, the Lord, protector of the stranger, host
            and guest,
            sent Atreus' sons to Alexander [Paris]
            because of a woman of many men
            great wrestlings, weighing down of limbs,
            when the knees are planted in the dust, and
65   the spear snaps at the outset,
            laying it all on Trojans and Danaans
            alike. Now things are
      where they are. It will fall out to what was fated.
      No sacrifice, no libation
70   of wine or of tears
            will soften stiff wrath.

The choral ode is complex at the beginning and continues
that way, so much so that from time to time editors of the
text must assume that there are errors of copying in the lines.
Much of the complexity is Aeschylus, however, as he paints
and delineates the manifold faceting of human experience.
The initial ambiguities in the metaphors and other images
here build a powerful impression of the cruel contradiction
and complexity of the universe which is an impression sustained throughout the trilogy as Clytemnestra is transformed

from a mother revenger to an adulteress, as Orestes hesitates to kill his mother, as the Erinyes go to defeat in the *Eumenides*.

Aeschylus dresses Menelaus and Agamemnon in epic costume. Lines 42–44 have the quality of the language of Homer, 43 particularly, which is like the repeated drum stroke as the three main words in that four-word line (all beginning with a *d* sound in the Greek) are heard. In lines such as these the chorus seem to be singing an epic, and thereafter Aeschylus contrives to have action and character ring often with epic reminiscences. Throughout this choral ode and the next Aeschylus alludes to the war at Troy as the high adventure which Homer describes. Then characteristically at the close of the second he reiterates the epic motif with a totally altered significance. The grand epic sense returns in such phrases as "Ares (money-changer) of bodies and the weigher of spears in battle (437)." Aeschylus creates a stunning combination of images: for behind Ares with his scales of death stands the commonplace idea of Zeus, weighing upon his scales the fates of men fighting together in battle as he does in the twenty-second book of the *Iliad* with the fates of Achilles and Hector. Like the image of Ares, the words which follow are bitter: dust exchanged for bodies, beautiful young men buried at Troy, the parents angry. The motif of concerned parent/endangered child is repeated from lines 49ff. also from another, ironic perspective.

Agamemnon and Menelaus are "plaintiff" (41), a word from the law court as is "defense" (47), although not so specifically. The war is fought for justice; the gods have heard them and aid them (55ff.): justice will inevitably be done. The images forecast the triumphal end to the trilogy in a court of law. As is typical with Aeschylus, the ending of the trilogy begins with this choral ode, which poses the sons of Atreus as instruments of justice before a city-state's legal machinery has been established. The word translated as "punishment" (59) is Erinyes, the name given to those grim spirits who avenge family murder who will hound and pursue Orestes after he has murdered his mother until he is set free in Athena's court, when the spirit of punishment which the Erinyes represent has been transmuted. Yet the jury decision at the close of the play, while it frees Orestes, does not change the nature of things. The force of revenge, the need for vengeance are still among men although the resolution of them will perhaps take different forms. The Erinyes are, therefore, natural and unnatural, good and bad at the same time.

Where the ode is most exciting is in the image of the soaring eagles. In all of its complexity the eagle-parent image is one of the most important to the trilogy. (Parallel to this is the introduction of the idea of the net at the beginning of the next ode [355–66], which is also fundamental to the trilogy.) The eagles are, as the poet says (58), entrants into the gods' world, dread enemy shrieking for their young. Eagles are traditionally agents of Zeus. They will avenge Paris' seduction of Helen, who has left the nest. But there is also the true child gone from the nest, that is, the slaughtered Iphigenia, a notion reinforced when the chorus describe (114ff.) the portentous omen of the eagles who rip open a pregnant hare. The avenging eagle, the proud father, the war lord are cast in another light. In the prayer to Artemis which follows shortly (139ff.) the poet poses things in terms of male and female: Artemis, the pregnant hare, Clytemnestra and Iphigenia against the sons of Atreus and Zeus. What man has done to women will be done again.

> Holy Artemis in anger and in pity
>   at her father's winged hounds
>   eating the unborn children of the hare
> hates the banquet of the eagles. (125ff.)

We remember the banquet of Thyestes, how Atreus killed the adulterous Thyestes' children and served them to him unbeknownst and we ponder the inexorable return or more still the eternal sameness in different guise. Specifically, Artemis will demand through Calchus the sacrifice of Iphigenia, a rehearsal of this dread slaughter of the eagles. A similar demand whatever it means will be repeated when Clytemnestra forces Agamemnon to walk upon the carpet as a kind of reiteration of the killing of Iphigenia.

The choice which Artemis forces upon Agamemnon and his subsequent sacrifice of Iphigenia are treated by Aeschylus in the allusive manner so common to Pindar and to Bacchylides. A different effect is achieved here because it is lodged within the drama. As the chorus describe so briefly and abstractly the ships becalmed, Calchus' answer, Agamemnon's response and Iphigenia's death, no names are used. It is the prophet, the father, the chieftain, the child, the daughter. Flashback window openings onto action that has become already greater than its participants. Action that has become mythology. The true drama of this scene becomes apparent when we remember that as the chorus so vividly illuminates one moment, then another of that proud but sad and horrible story, Clytemnestra, the mother, the wife, moves back and forth before the altars. Like the action which the chorus describes, she becomes herself symbol in a paradigm. The abstract nature of the choral odes is apparent from the overtly gnomic, Hesiodic passages such as 160ff., 367ff. The brilliance of Aeschylean tragedy lies in the theological, philosophical line which he establishes to play in counterpoint to the ambiguous and conflicting story line. The first two odes are lyrical evocations of that view. They establish a way to view the action, a manner of accommodation that lasts throughout the trilogy.

Choral lyric is not usually so ambitious; sometimes it seems to be mainly ornamental. But often at its best the lyrical chorus describes another truer world, more complicated, profound, of which the tragic action is only the merest surface iceberg-like projection.

Aristophanic comic choruses do not have the complex metrical schemes of tragic choruses but they often have an unsurpassing musicality to them which those who do not read Greek cannot clearly get. Yale's football cry, for instance, breka kekex-koax koax, comes from a chorus in the *Frogs*, an attempt to render the sound of frogs. Aristophanes' bird sounds in the *Birds*' chorus is a remarkable feat because the poet has surrounded the senseless bird sounds with lines of verse whose words echo the sounds of the bird calls. The passage has become famous: part of it (685–723) was translated by Swinburne unusually well.

The chorus of birds set out to demonstrate the central role of birds in the history of creation. The long passage (676–800) is essentially a parody of Hesiod's *Theogony*. Just as Hesiod begins with an invocation to the Muses the birds call upon the nightingale (676ff.) in lyric meters:

> o beloved, golden,
> dearest of birds,
> partner in all my songs,

> childhood friend, nightingale,
> come, come, present yourself . . .

Thereafter, the chorus turn to anapaestic tetrameters in which they describe the origin of the world from Void and Night, passing on to a marvelous, full description of the multitudes of different birds which take the place of the many Hesiodic elements in the *Theogony*.

At 737 begins a seventeen-line ode which is later repeated metrically in the antistrophe of lines 769–784. The ode's lyrical meters and bird calls distinguish it sharply from the preceding anapaests and subsequent trochaic tetrameters (◡–◡– etc.). Even in this crude translation its inherent beauty, its musicality, just barely revealed in the bird calls, help to remind us that Greek tragic and comic choruses were first of all splendid sensual experiences, indeed the best surviving lyric poetry:

> Thicket Muse
> tyo, tyo, tyo, tyo, tyo, tyo, tyotingx
> many colored, with you
> in the valleys, on the mountaintops
> tyo, tyo, tyo, tyotingx
> sitting upon the leaf-crowned ash
> tyo, tyo, tyo, tyotingx
> singing from my golden throat
> holy songs to Pan I render
> sacred dances for the mountain mother
> totototototototototingx
> Here is the source just like honey
> where Phrynikos gathers the fruit
> for his ambrosial tunes
> ever stealing our sweet song
> tyo tyo tyo tyo tingx.

CHAPTER FIVE
ATHENS IN THE
FIFTH CENTURY

O, glistening, violet-crowned and awful,
bulwark of Hellas, famous Athens, holy city . . .

Pindar

. . . if any ambassadors come to town to trick you
the first thing they call out is "violet-crowned." If
anyone says that, then you sit right up on the crowns
of your ass. Then if anyone adds "glistening Athens,"
they've made it on account of that "glistening," although it describes little fish better.

Aristophanes, *Acharnians* 636ff.

Athens is the teacher of Greece.

Pericles (quoted by Thucydides 2.41)

The history of ancient Greek literature of the classical
period is the history of the city of Athens. The city is the one
consistent theme that goes from author to author. Most of
them lived and worked in Athens. Whether it is simple
description, or praise or blame, whether a discussion of city
government, the obligations of the citizen, Athens is never
far from the center of attention in every piece of literature,
poetry or prose. It was the one all-encompassing fabric; it was
family, religion, education, government, security all in one.

The life of the city is so intimately reflected in the literature from description to metaphor and allusions that the literary remains are major historical documents. All of it is political literature calling for a knowledge of the ways of life in the city. Whatever way the facets of this life are explored all roads lead back to Athens.

Moreover this small city, or *polis* as it is called in Greek, produced or welcomed in a span of one hundred years more than a dozen of the small number of acknowledged masters of Western thought, art or letters. As residents of a small city they probably knew each other. Such a cluster of genius is amazing.

A historical period is hard to get down; the details are so many, the perspectives various. Narrative historians let wars or political events form the skeletal backbone of their story. But one could fix the perimeters of the period of Athens' literary glory from the birth of Aeschylus (525 B.C.) to the death of Socrates (395 B.C.) or Plato (347 B.C.) or Isocrates (338 B.C.), or one might say that when Euripides and Sophocles died in 406 B.C. the poetic Muse went with them just as the tutelar goddess Athena deserted her city in its defeat at Aegospotami at the end of summer in 405 B.C. The latter notion has the kind of stagey quality to it that historians sometimes use to reinforce artificial temporal categories such as these.

The concept of fifth-century Athens can, however, best be fixed by wars and politics. The cultural energy of the fifth century came out of the reforms in government that commenced about 510 B.C. and brought on a new kind of democratic vigor. That vigor was matched by the enthusiasm with which the Athenians received their victories in the Persian War and their subsequent military might. In turn the decline in artistic activity that becomes perceptible at the close of the century is related to the economic and human loss and the spiritual fatigue brought on by the excesses of the long-fought Peloponnesian War and the defeat in 405 B.C. at Aegospotami. See Euripides' *Andromache,* which is a reflection of this mood.

Perimeters matter only because all historians, literary or otherwise, from antiquity on are obsessed with an organic view of this period, treating it as a patient which sickened and died after a gloriously healthy life. Actually, the more common metaphor is the seasons. So it is that with the fateful battle of Aegospotami in 405 and so perfectly *at the end of summer,* Athens entered upon her autumnal years, which culminate for literature in the so-called New Comedy of the late fourth century. This autumn is then followed by a long, long winter as Athens becomes the ancient world's university town, sleepy and uneventful. From this vantage, Athens of the fifth century may indeed seem an exceptionally lively, healthy organism or a particularly beautiful springtime. The trouble with this approach is that critics are forever looking for the first telltale wrinkle or white hair. The criticism of Euripides is particularly susceptible to this. Many critics conveniently ignore that he was Sophocles' exact contemporary (although sixteen years younger) to make him a symbol of decline and decay. The Alexandrian period as well is described in terms that doctors reserve for their terminal patients or more often in terms that the clergy heap upon the unrepentant in their flock.

If, however, we take the long view and consider that humankind has a remarkable repertoire of responses to the environment, we may see change as something neutral at least, if not positive. A second-century A.D. epic poem by one Quintus from the city of Smyrna (modern-day Ismir) is instructive. Called the *Post-Homerica,* the poem is a plodding, if not sedate, narrative in unoriginal hexameters of the events of the Trojan War not covered by Homer. If read as the latest in a succession of increasingly blurred and inferior copies from Homer's engraving plate, the *Post-Homerica* fulfills all the expectations of decadent literature. Yet, if we stop to examine what the poet is doing, to notice the enormous number of similes in the poem, then we might say that he is trying to change rather dramatically the quality of the traditional epic narrative, through imagery and a kind of lyricism inherent in similes, contriving another kind of vision. And yet . . . and yet, when everything has been conceded, there are few who would not turn back to the earliest centuries, particularly to the fifth century, as the truest, clearest, freshest spring from which to drink.

Athens was a quiet and unassuming town in the seventh and early sixth centuries, a center in an aristocratic, land-owning, farming community, called Attica, which was roughly the size of Rhode Island. The excitement was all in Asia Minor, where the Greek-speaking people along the coast, the Ionians, were already noted for their cities, their arts and philosophy. The older, richer civilizations of Persia and Lydia lay to the east, providing stimulus and inspiration. Later, the other Greeks found fault with the Ionians, with their tendencies to elegance, style and languor as though they had been corrupted by their eastern neighbors. Yet when the Ionian cities were subjugated by the Lydians and the Persians, a wave of Ionian immigrants came to Athens who were an immense influence there, providing a sophistication and a subtlety new to the Athenians. In fact these migrants were a major stimulus to the burst of cultural energy in Athens in the fifth century.

Athens began to change when Peisistratos seized control of the government in 561. Born an aristocrat, he ruled in the manner common to the tyrants in Greek city-states of the sixth century, that is, he ignored the aristocracy, looked to the soldier class for his support, improved the lot of the people generally, brought the cultural amenities of the aristocratic life to the city, making the whole city his court. He embarked on land reform and building programs; he started festivals, imported artists and artisans. When he had died and his sons lost their control of the city in 510, the aristocratic cliques wanted to take back the power, but Athens was no longer a city that could tolerate their domination.

Political chaos was avoided by the stratagems of Kleisthenes, who was voted by the people to an office of political reform. Himself an aristocrat, son of the great Megacles and Agariste, daughter of the tyrant of Sicyon, once sufficiently favored by Peisistratos' son that he held office under him, Kleisthenes had political ambitions, led one of the aristocratic factions. But aristocratic feuding was only prelude to anarchy. Kleisthenes chose to work reforms as the outlet for his need to manipulate. His reforms were brilliant, far-reaching and radically reshaped the society of Athens. They placed power in the hands of the people (from the Athenian point of view, which excluded women, children, slaves and resident aliens), providing for a participatory democracy scarcely equaled, never surpassed.

It is true, of course, that an assembly meeting of, say, 5,000 adult males could pass a law with a majority of 2,501 that was binding upon the perhaps 200,000 to 300,000 people of Attica. Not exactly our idea of power in the hands of the people, but the ancient Athenians valued absolutely adulthood, ethnic integrity, liberty and most of all the male sex. Those who did not qualify in these respects could not, were not able, in the sense that they lacked the talent, to vote. It was as simple as that. The handbooks of ancient politics always state that the ancients never really understood representative government whereas in fact each older male adult was representative of some family unit, representative of wife, children and slaves. Whether the Athenian males themselves understood this is debatable.

As far back as the times to which Homer refers, we can see a distinctive tripartite division of the people, the monarch (Agamemnon), his patrician advisers (Nestor, Achilles, Odysseus et al.) and the people (the army assembly represented particularly by Thersites). During the centuries this evolved in Athens into certain managerial offices held by aristocrats, a court made up of retired officials (and therefore also aristocratic), and the popular assembly. The strong, rich and well-born from the coast, the plain and the uplands were in constant rivalry to dominate the city's political life. Kleisthenes undertook to destroy the access to power of any person or group, continually to return the power to the people.

The population had traditionally been divided into four tribes. Without altering that historic and sentimental association, Kleisthenes instituted ten new tribes made up of voting units known as *trittyes*. Each *trittyis* was made up in equal parts of persons from the coast, the plains and uphill. This effectively canceled the pretensions to power of any one part of the country, although when voting time came in the assembly those who had easy access to the meetings, the city-dwellers especially, dominated the vote. When the annual invasions of the Peloponnesians during the latter part of the fifth century brought so many conservative farmers into town, the assembly became a place of increasing tension, as city folk and country folk polarized.

The conception of the *trittyes* is an example of Kleisthenes' thoroughly rationalistic approach to political problems. He and his successors contrived many other ingenious schemes. What follows is a synthetic account of the Athenian governing system once it had evolved over a period of thirty or forty years.

The popular assembly was open to all adult free-born males over eighteen. This was perhaps forty thousand persons; five thousand was an average attendance figure, an unwieldy number for legislative planning. The answer was the *boule* or council, a kind of steering committee, a smaller group of five hundred, fifty chosen from each tribe. This was further refined by the institution of the *prytany,* an executive subcommittee of fifty, in effect the group of fifty from each tribe sitting in the *boule.* The *prytany* rotated each tenth of the year to a new group of fifty from another tribe. This small body of fifty men was intimate enough to discuss among themselves the demands of operating a city-state and to act upon necessity. Of course, the assembly was the sovereign body of the state; it met at least once in each successive *prytany,* that is, ten times a year, to deliberate and to vote legislation. Each day the actual head of state, holding the keys to the treasury, the seal, and having absolute power in emergency, rotated among the fifty in the *prytany.* In a year, then, three hundred and sixty-five men out of the five hundred who at different intervals sat in the *prytany* held office as head of state, or more specifically president of the assembly, if it met that day, for a day. Membership in the *boule* was for a year and could be repeated once, although not in the consecutive year. So it was that most Athenian men in the course of a lifetime sat in the *boule,* in the *prytany* and many held the executive office. This meant that the real exercise of considerable power could and did fall to many men randomly and distributively. Socrates, for instance, describes how as president of the assembly, he voted against an illegal proposal for a vote amid the clamor and fury of the citizenry (*Apology* 32b; cf. Xenophon, *Memorabilia* 4.4.2).

The method of choosing those who served as archons, those who were in the *boule* and those who sat on juries evolved in a curious way toward the purest democratic practice. By 487, candidates to these positions were all elected by lot, that is to say the choice was random and arbitrary, a name plucked from many, like the method of choosing American civil juries. By eliminating popular elections the Athenians were able to destroy the influence of great aristocratic families, to destroy as well the influence that can be exercised by those who have outstanding personalities, charm, intelligence, talent or expertise. Furthermore, the annual rotation of all offices meant that no one could build up a fund of knowledge so as to make himself indispensable, as is the case with entrenched bureaucracies.

Corollary to this was the amazing custom of ostracism, a vote for exile. A man voted into exile had to leave the city and stay a specified distance away for a decade although his family and possessions were not in any way affected by the decree. The arrangements for the vote of ostracism again show strong controls against the formation of blocs or units of opinion. More or less in January, the question was put to the assembly whether they wanted to hold a vote for ostracism that year. No debate was allowed. In essence then, each man consulted himself as to whether he considered there was someone in the community whom he should like to see sent out. If the assembly voted assent, then during one of the next few meetings of the assembly the vote for ostracism was taken. There were no public debates, no accusations of anyone, no defense made. At the time of voting for ostracism, each man decided for himself. Here again the system discouraged alliances, public demonstrations of solidarity, symbolic modes of commitment without which modern political life could not survive.

Each man scratched on a piece of a broken pot (in Greek *ostrakon*, hence ostracism) the name of his candidate for exile. Upon the taking of the vote, the officials first counted the potsherds without reading or tallying the names. If less than six thousand votes had been cast, the vote was declared invalid and the sherds destroyed (many went to fill up abandoned wells where they remained undisturbed for twentieth-century archaeologists). This precaution was designed to ensure that a vote of exile was something desired by a significant portion of the community and that failing this, no opportunity presented itself for gauging or fantasizing trends of hostile tendencies toward various individuals among the populace (reminding us again how essentially undemocratic political polls are).

A great part of the population sat on juries which met almost daily. Juries consisted of up to 6,001 men depending upon the importance of the trial. The members were elected by lot; a simple majority ruled. Eventually, jurors were paid a small sum, making it a kind of valuable daytime occupation for the older members of the community. We have a good impression of the law courts. Aristophanes' *Wasps* has a portrait of an old man whose passion is jury duty. Plato's *Apology*, which is supposed to be Socrates' defense to the jury, is so ironical a manipulation of the jury that its character and personality are continually showing through. Most of all we have the speeches of Lysias and

Demosthenes and other men who composed speeches for the courts. Litigation was a constant feature of Athenian life, so juries were a busy and important activity.

Yet the Athenian native political genius made provision for something like leadership. They popularly elected for a year's term ten generals who could be re-elected. This curious body of ten, called the *strategia,* is a source of much confusion. What power had they? Specifically, what kind of power did Pericles have? We know he was re-elected general often and finally without interruption from 443 to his death in 429. Nineteenth-century historians likened him to the British Prime Minister, the nine other generals being his Cabinet. This in-interpretation subtly colors accounts of the period to this day; yet it is not a good analogy.

The generals were elected popularly, but not as a group. They were therefore independent of each other, owed no political debts. Furthermore, they did not initiate or realize policy. This was the assembly's function. Each time the assembly met it could embark upon new policy, start a war, call for peace and so forth. The generals were there originally to lead men into battle; obviously therefore popular election persisted for generals, since who wants to find the odd neighbor at the helm when catastrophe impends? They remained military men, doers, whether it was Themistocles improving the Piraeus harbor as a general or the civilian Kleon losing his life at Amphipolis when he led troops against an infinitely superior soldier and strategist, the Spartan general Brasidas. What seems, however, to have been their main political function was to stand as a projection of the popular will. The ancient evidence suggests that the generals spoke a good deal in the assembly, urging and persuading to one course of action or another. Insofar as they clearly articulated what the people wanted to hear they were successful. Plato describes (*Protagoras* 319d) how the assembly hooted down those who did not know what they were talking about. Aristophanes' most political comedy, the *Knights,* portrays the people (Demos) as master in the household and the contemporary outstanding figures, Kleon, Demosthenes and Nikias, as the servants below the stairs who will try any wile or stratagem to stay in Demos' good graces. Pericles was probably elected general again and again because he was an expression of what Athenians wanted to be and he encouraged them into what they wanted to do. The debates in the assembly do indeed seem to have aired the essential positions on any subject so well that the assembly could vote from conviction. The power, therefore, of the generals was something that had to be renewed constantly by the people. Sovereignty was never delegated in any real sense.

The political life of Athens is reflected in the literature of the period. We must imagine a community where the men actively participated in the management of the city, on many levels, where the fate and purpose of the community were matters of constant discussion, where the taking of ethical and moral decisions was a continual adult communal activity. Nothing, of course, could be more remote from the twentieth-century experience; therefore it is hard to imagine. New England town meeting government is the best analogue. Likewise to imagine how communal the reaction to the literature would be is also hard. The Greeks had no real concept of a private person. The term *idiotes,* which for obvious reasons becomes our "idiot," meant simply someone withdrawn from his true self, which was a political man. Whether at a party singing poems, in a body listening to Herodotus read from his *Histories* or Gorgias lecturing, or in the theater at a tragedy or a comedy, every man of the audience was a social person, a political person, intensely involved in the city, closely relating to the fellow members of the audience. This social cohesion is the remarkable feature of an anecdote about Socrates. When Aristophanes presented the *Clouds,* which parodies sophistic teaching, the character of the Sophist was represented by an actor wearing a mask made to resemble Socrates, who was notorious for his singularly ugly countenance. At the moment when the character first appeared, Socrates is said to have stood up so that the audience could note how well the mask maker had done his job. This intimacy and camaraderie among so vast an assemblage is frequently apparent in Aristophanic comedies. For instance, the characters and the chorus speak not only to each other, but turn often to speak to the audience, which they almost assume into the play. Indeed, they speak to individuals in the audience. We must remember that there was no proscenium arch and that the chorus becomes by metonymy the entire group in the theater. This is often vividly effective in tragedy, for example in the opening of the *Oedipus Tyrannus* when Oedipus addresses the suppliant populace of Thebes as represented by the chorus to which the entire audience is empathetically assumed, or when Clytemnestra defends her actions before the townspeople in the *Agamemnon*. The audience participation in Aristophanes' comedies is notable because often some rather dangerous ideas are being discussed. For instance, Dicaiopolis in the *Acharnians* (produced in 425, five years into the Peloponnesian War) launches into a long defense of Sparta in an exchange between himself and the chorus and statements are made that we would consider definitely seditious. But perhaps that is because we see theater as inherently alienated, therefore able to propagandize, whereas Athenian comic theater, by virtue of the symbiotic relationship of all its celebrants, was able to maintain dialogues that got at submerged concerns and deviant attitudes.

It was like a giant family, you might say. The family and the *polis* are, in fact, remarkably intertwined, forming one of the major metaphors from which all Athenian life flowed. In earlier centuries when the city organization was considerably less evolved and powerful, the extended family was the single cohesive force in the society. Analogous social groupings reinforced the idea of the family. The migrating Indo-Europeans came divided into tribes (*phyllae*). This remained the basic, hoary community division. Then each tribe was made up of brotherhoods (*phratres*), like a giant family since everyone—man, woman, child—was officially enrolled in membership. The brotherhoods contained subdivisions, which were the great dynastic aristocratic families (*gene*), beside which very shortly the non-aristocratic members of the brotherhoods organized themselves into associations to provide a countervailing social identity to that of the aristocratic families. Finally there were neighborhood organizations (*demes*). Each unit had special cults, rites, religious leaders, celebrations, as well as offering some kind of assistance and protection. Where there were no public community agencies promoting the welfare, these societal groupings were extremely valuable. They formed sources of psychological and social strength as well, making the kind of isolation and alienation that marks urban twentieth-century life very rare. No wonder it was abnormal to be considered a private person.

The basis of the family was the husband and wife, for whom very different roles had evolved. What Hector said to Andromache in the *Iliad* (6.488ff.) remained true: "No one can escape his fate . . . Go back to the house, take up the loom . . . and leave war to me." The household of Greek antiquity was arranged to serve the interests of a group who had rights in common to inherited land. Children were desired to maintain the family's ownership of the land, also to succor their parents in their enfeebled old age. Women were needed to produce these children and manage the house. The life of a woman was circumscribed by these needs. To begin with, her life was led within the home and in the women's quarters. Once pubescent, she had to be confined and quickly married. In the early years of marriage, the young wife was again confined so that her contact with males would never be suspect. She was even kept from eating with her husband and his male friends. These practices were to ensure her virginity first and effectively to legitimize her offspring thereafter. Land tenure came from blood ties. Illegitimacy was therefore to be scrupulously avoided and feared. Likewise, premarital rape and seduction posed threats and problems. Nowhere, however, do we find the least concern for the feelings of the female in these strenuous domestic arrangements. Things got better for everyone, however, once the family progeny were born. Women could divorce, dowries were retained, adulterous affairs were not impossible (especially since unwanted children could be killed at birth). Pericles, the great statesman, son of Agariste, daughter of Kleisthenes, the lawgiver, married and divorced, then lived out his life with Aspasia, a remarkably interesting woman from Miletos, gifted, intellectual, very much his peer.

A man of the prosperous or aristocratic elements of the community normally entered marriage after active military service, around age thirty. His wife might be as much as half that age. His experience and education would put impossible barriers between himself and his naïve, house-sheltered, early-teen-age bride. Besides, he would already employ the custom of passing time in the company of foreign-born courtesans of Athens. These were women of style, personality, social and cultural attainments who for a variety of reasons had to find some margin of security outside the family confines and beyond respectability. While they did not have the abiding security that only living with a family could confer and their occupation of sexual and psychic service had its obvious degrading aspects, they were nevertheless free to exercise their minds and to discover a great deal of life their respectable sisters would never know.

A more formidable competition for her husband's affections and interest came from his homosexual connections. Upper-class males generally practiced considerable homosexuality. Respectable men sought the company of handsome teen-age boys. Emotional, intellectual and physical ties grew strong, and, if we can believe our sources, this relationship was the most serious. Conjugal relationships ensured a lifetime of marital well-being, courtesans provided fun and merriment; boys were the source of self-esteem and personal improve-ment. The commonplace attitude to this practice is contained in the speech of Phaedrus in Plato's *Symposium*. However, male relationships command almost no attention in myth or tragedy or comedy. Tombstone epitaphs also show strong affection between man and wife, although it is true that one is disposed to cut a good figure at the graveside. Aeschylus wrote a tragedy upon the homosexual love of Achilles and Patroclus, and Sophocles wrote a satyr play on Achilles' loves, but they have not survived. Indeed, one reason for the lack of extant evidence may well be the censorship exercised by suc-cessive centuries which found homosexuality either odd or immoral and therefore did not preserve the materials rel-evant to this theme. Aristophanes' comedy *Lysistrata* is to my mind, however, evidence that Athenian men preferred heterosexual intercourse and were generally sexually inter-ested in their wives. The play is about a fantasy stratagem whereby the women of Greece deny their husbands sexual relations until a peace treaty is signed. Much of the humor turns on the physical distress of men who have been kept from their wives too long. Of course, comedy always simpli-fies things and the situation demands that there be no alter-natives such as boys or courtesans. Still and all one gets the sense from the play that in ancient Athens as in other societies most men wanted heterosexual relations and out of love, constancy, penury or indolence sought it with their wives. Homosexuality, however, was not reprehensible or ridiculous, unless it was coupled with effeminacy. Nor was it avant-garde. Probably it was an emotional relationship en-dowed with all kinds of intellectual and spiritual potential by its ideological adherents which males of greater curiosity and greater emotional appetites sought out. One must not overlook the fact too that Mediterranean teen-age males can often be, as the expression goes, breathtakingly beautiful. Youth is always sexually attractive and in a society where no teen-age females were ever seen, it is not surprising that teen-age boys would become objects of sexual interest. We have accounts of men lounging about the exercise area watching the nude boys practice. It is the ancient Athenian version of the drugstore cowboy watching the girls go by.

Homosexuality had political and ideological undertones. Among the conservative aristocracy who preferred landowning to seafaring, the claims to superiority by birthright rather than amassed wealth, quiet power in the hands of their class to the vociferous democratic assembly, certainty and stability to passion and the unexpected vote, the social system of Sparta seemed superior. Spartan life was characterized by the practice of homosexuality. Then too, aristocracies achieve their strength through exclusiveness. Kinship is the major mode of exclusiveness, yet homosexuality can also further this. The young teen-age passive partner in anal intercourse is tamed and bonded in a certain sense. The English old boy system had or has at its roots a distinctive physical intimacy in the teen years that is a latter-day manifestation of the same thing.

Ancient tragedy has always been a mine for psychological speculation, quite rightly so, since the family theme incites in us all the most powerful memories and associations. The male-female relationship in extant tragedy is one of conflict or sometimes unwitting disaster: Creusa's betrayal and exploitation by Apollo in the *Ion,* Dejaneira's unsuspecting gift of death to her husband, Hercules, in the *Trachinian Women,* Medea's killing of her children to attack her husband in the *Medea,* Clytemnestra's seduction and killing of her husband, Agamemnon, in the *Agamemnon;* one could go on and on always to find, if not outright hostility or trouble, then at least great coldness between the sexes. Yet one would not expect realistic love scenes; that would be foreign to the theatrical convention and difficult since males took all the roles.

One notices dominant females and inferior males, the latter generally victims of the former. The explanations for this are numerous. Myths of an age when there prevailed a cult of a strong female goddess assisted by an inferior male who died following his association with her are transmuted in a society of dominant males and repressed females to express the latent rage of the latter and the fear or projection of that rage by the former. Children growing up in a home where the father was generally absent as was the case in ancient Greece, if only absent in the sense that he was not in the women's quarters, tend to have the notion of a strong, dominant mother and a weak father. When there is added the child's sense of the mother's rage at this rejection, one sees played out the common tragic male-female theme. Women grow more prominent, more unhappy, more violent in later tragedy. One can only imagine that the increasingly evident individualism and the narrowing of the extended family gave women more a sense of self, more of a chance to act out the emotion that repression gave her. Euripides' *Bacchae* is, among other things, a frightening (from a male's point of view) portrait of female hysteria. Typical of the Hellenistic Age with its greater sympathy and understanding of the female is Theocritus' twenty-sixth Idyll, which sympathetically depicts Agave and her sisters discovering Pentheus and ripping the unfortunate man apart. The point of view in every case is crucial. One wonders how women reacted to tragedies of this sort, to what extent their limited education and limited life experience were obstacles to understanding. Did the ancient Athenian woman always play a passive, weak, introverted Electra to her husband's decisive, wise and seasoned Orestes? Was she always the alien Medea in the self-satisfied Jason's house? Did tragedies teach her something or confirm what she already knew?

In the course of the fifth century the city became the all-pervasive, all-encompassing family. As the city usurped the functions of the family it assumed its attributes as well. The executive body, the Prytaneion, ate a common meal like a family; there was a community hearth. The civic worship of Athena was a cult like that in the household. Athena was the goddess who was translated from keeper of the household to keeper of the city. Her virgin chamber (Parthenon) was situated upon the Acropolis. Her people were Athena's people, Athenians, not like the Spartans or Corinthians, named after a place. The Olympian state gods were arranged into a family unit of some complexity and interaction. Government was participatory but also paternal. In the *Crito* Socrates invokes a sympathetic picture of the Athenians' laws as his true parents; they have nurtured him and raised him up, as a parent would, and he refuses to betray them. As we said, many extant tragedies portray action carried out among members of a family. While the family is the archetypal arena of human action, tragic action also often suggests that the politics of the family are to be equaled with the politics of the city. For example, Sophocles' *Antigone* portrays an urgent and fatal conflict between family and state, niece and uncle, father and son, man and woman, citizen and leader, law and religion.

The Olympian deities, the Pantheon, so-called, those gods of whom it was claimed that their home was on Mount Olympus up northeast in the direction of modern-day Thessalonica, were depicted by Homer as a large family. The idea persisted and was refined; the common relationships of family life, sibling rivalry, parental affection or rejection, conjugal strife, were all there. Herodotus claimed that Homer and Hesiod created the gods, which means no more than that theirs were the first literary representations of the gods. Homer depicted anthropomorphized deities, which are so anthropomorphized as to begin to create theological problems shortly after his time. Homer does seem to be portraying gods who are at times ridiculous, particularly as they are compared to men. The examples from the *Iliad* which we have elsewhere discussed are instructive (pp. 64ff.). Only Zeus, father of gods and men, whose title signifies his sovereignty, stays apart; throughout the succeeding centuries he remains somehow more serious, heavier, more somber. His wife is Hera, eternally malignant toward his many illicit progeny, true to a wife's anxieties in a culture where a woman's worth was so directly tied to childbearing. Hera, associated in cult with marriage and childbearing, bore only one child to Zeus, the dread war god Ares, whom Homer portrays as doltish, brute stupid, somehow the true product of this dread celestial marriage. Each bore a child without intercourse. Athena sprang full-grown from Zeus' head, a goddess of talents, technique and stratagem signifying the intellectualist control over the elements of living; and in perfect symmetry Hera bore Hephaestus, the artisan god, the worker god, an extension of a woman's household, housewifely skills. Unique among the gods, Hephaestus is lame, which is true to the worker's life, where accidents abound and crippling work is normal. Zeus lay with Leto whereupon she bore Artemis and Apollo. The latter is a mysterious deity, an import in fact from the East into the Greek world. Mysticism, morality, healing and oracular utterance are attached to his divinity, which is far less thoroughly anthropomorphized than most of the Pantheon. Delphi was the site of his temple, his worship, his priestess whose inspired garbled response to questions was the oracle the temple priests interpreted. Apollo was in this respect more institutionalized than other deities. Zeus also lay with a minor deity, Maia, to produce Hermes, the messenger, the trickster, the Greek version of the Norse Loki, whose charming cunning is memorialized in the Homeric Hymn to Hermes. Aphrodite sprang forth from the foamy sperm of the severed penis of Ouranos, a powerful image far removed from Botticelli's *Birth of Venus*, which is how we conceive her to be. Poseidon and Hades, brothers to Zeus, are kings in their own right. Hades is an unknown personality; Hades means the unseen one. Poseidon, elder brother, lord of earthquakes, rider of horses, often has a Colonel Blimp personality similar to that of Oceanus in Aeschylus' *Prometheus Bound*. When one reviews the several deities of the Pantheon, it appears that they express most facets in the complex of male and female persons. For instance, Hera, as a jealous wife and mother, Athena, as sexless, clever manager, Artemis, as virgin, young girl in her animal phase, Aphrodite as sexual person present many aspects of a woman's being, just as Zeus, Apollo, Hephaestus and Ares present a man's persona.

The two most important elements of the Greek religious experience come from the earliest times and are the result of the amalgam of two different cultures, the immigrating Indo-Europeans and the indigenous peoples of the mainland of Greece. The Indo-Europeans were nomadic peoples who needed the sky as their map and compass. Their religion centered on a sky god, in Greek called Zeus, a word that is related to the Indo-European root for "sky." Zeus is a weather god, the meteorological phenomena are his attributes, as the Homeric epithets indicate: "Zeus who delights in thunder," "cloud-gathering Zeus," etc. In Greek as well as the other Indo-European instances of his name it is linked with father, father as protector, lord and master more than father as procreator. Thus Zeus is the protector of guests and travelers as the male authority figure in his own home. He is also associated with fertility. There are stories of Heaven (*ouranos*) copulating with Earth (*ge*); sometimes Zeus is the male figure in this union, and the rain is the sperm. Sometimes Hera, the Olympian goddess wife, appears as his mate. Their union is the *holy marriage,* an enactment of nature's fecundity and fertility. Homer has taken the theme of the holy marriage, endowed it with personalities and irony and presented it with the tone of Noël Coward as sharp-witted malicious Hera seduces bumble-headed Zeus to further her own designs (*Iliad* 14.153ff.).

Zeus is a male authority indicative of a religious belief fostered in a culture in which males hold a superior position, a patriarchal society. The stories connected with him have to do with power. He blasts his enemies with thunderbolts. He and his brothers, Poseidon and Hades, have divided up the dominion of the universe: Poseidon the sea, Hades the Underworld, Zeus the heavens. The story of his birth is Oedipal. Ouranos and Ge conceive so many children that Ge finally becomes exhausted. She persuades her son Kronos to castrate Ouranos when he proceeds to his constant mission. Kronos agrees and duly succeeds his castrated father in power and symbolically in bed, every son's dream come true. As Rhea, his wife, who is an alternative of Ge, produces offspring to Kronos he swallows them up one by one, in a sense father competing with mother or taking on her role of carrying a child in the belly, but also father destroying the competition that children entail. When Ge gives birth to Zeus, a stone wrapped in swaddling clothes is handed to Kronos, who finds it a powerful emetic. So he vomits up Zeus' siblings and relinquishes the power to Zeus. Zeus reigns as king, judge, keeper of justice while at the same time his role in fertility is kept alive by the very popular story of his being born and nursed as a small child in a cave in Crete. The baby, the birth, the cave in the earth are all emblems of a vegetarian cult mixed with the sky god figure for which the mediation is always the rain.

The indigenous people whom the Greek-speaking invaders met upon their arrival were agricultural folk and perhaps—and this is a big perhaps—a society in which women had considerable power, dominant, a matriarchal society. The myths and legends suggest this; for instance, when King Laius dies at Thebes the throne is held vacant until a male comes along who weds the queen and gets the throne, and at Ithaca with Odysseus probably dead at Troy and Telemachus a youth the suitors vie for the hand of Penelope, with whom comes possession of the throne and kingship. The preoccupation of these people was making crops grow. Fertility was therefore paramount and women are walking advertisements of reproduction. Indeed, man's reproductive role and value were unclear, the biological necessity for sperm was not established. So it is that women would be accorded respect and power since they seemed to have the peculiar magic for the growing of things.

The technology of the last century makes it very unlikely for the population of the industrial nations to experience the anxieties of agriculture and human survival. Time was when food supplies locally grown could not be supplemented by importation. Refrigeration was non-existent, so the food grown and stored had to suffice until the subsequent harvest time. There was no alternative except to starve. Drought, untimely cold, chance hailstorms could suddenly mean extinction for some members of the community, usually children, in whom the community had made the least investment and whose reproduction was easiest. Religion starts from awe at the unknown, and is an attempt to accommodate the unknown to a human frame of reference and to control the unknown that way. Nothing could be more chancy yet more basic than the annual harvest. The religion of an agricultural society seeks to make the crop grow, to propitiate those forces that can stop or start the earth's fertility, to ward off the dread force of non-life that hovers in nature's catastrophes. The myth of Demeter and Persephone is a projection of seasonal phenomena in Greece of planting in September, harvesting in May, of barren, dry, burnt-over fields through the summer months. Persephone, virgin daughter of Demeter, is snatched away by Hades to be his wife in the Underworld. Demeter, bereft, grieving, wanders the earth, and lost in her grief ignores the crops, which wither and brown. In anguish the humans call upon Zeus, who restores the girl to her mother two thirds of the year, leaving her with Hades the rest of the time. The myth depicts non-life snatching the promise of fecundity away from the principle of reproduction; it also shows fecundity going at intervals to non-life beneath the earth and coming back to reunite with the principle of reproduction. The generative force is always present (Demeter), but is activated or not by the contest of wills between non-life (Hades) and the promise/potential/energy for reproduction (Persephone).

Seen from another perspective, it is the feminine power of reproduction which needs no man (no male father figure worries over Persephone's departure) in conflict with non-life or perhaps in conflict with the male as non-life (Hades). From another perspective, the sorrowing Demeter is the archetypal *mater dolorosa*, the grieving mother, an experience of motherhood that must have been ubiquitous then. For not only would the high infant mortality rate and the normal fatal accidents later decimate the ranks of children, but war, almost a natural pestilence, must have carried off many sons. A mother bore children that they might die and she might sorrow. One thinks of Thetis' crying for Achilles, Hecuba crying for Hector, Andromache crying for Astyanax, Niobe eternally weeping for her lost fourteen. What woman could dare to have children until the tears were ready?

Demeter means "earth mother" (*de* is a dialect variation of *ge*, plus *meter*, "mother"), the eternal source of life. The earth receives the human corpses; the grain was stored in underground granary chambers. Women contain a cavity where the human is stored and from whence it springs forth. The confusion of these observations produced the rituals of propitiation. Dread gods of the earth, spirits of the dead, somehow also source of life ("If a piece of wheat does not fall to the ground and die, it remains alone. If it does fall and die, it brings forth much fruit"—*Gospel Acc. John* 12.24), were controlled, so to speak, by a mimicry of their action. A pig, presumably earlier a virgin girl, was thrown into a crevasse in the earth, there to die and putrefy. At sowing time the remains were brought up and mixed with grain on the altar, then planted. The pig, which is so often pregnant and has such prominent dugs, is the perfect animal symbol of fertility. Prominent breasts on the Artemis of Ephesus or the Minoan snake goddess statuette manifest woman's fertility. The snake is a constant element in the artistic representations of this figure. The snake sheds skin, dying and reborn like the seed; it comes from the earth, from the very underground; it guards the home, the granary by killing rodents; it forms the perfect complement to the breasts, being the symbolic penis sliding in and out of earth's orifice.

Persephone, the virgin, is representative of a range of female figures in mythology, which bear the generic term *kore* (Greek for "young girl"). Corollary to the disappearance of Persephone into the Underworld is the story that appears in different forms of a hero journeying to the Underworld to snatch away the *kore*, a story that plays on notions of death and resurrection or salvation rather. The *kore* figure is the fertile promise of soil untilled, seed unsown, fruit unplucked, crop unharvested, the essence of virginity. One of the finest poetic expressions of the idea is Hippolytus' ode to chastity in Euripides' play (73ff.). The goddess Artemis is the best-known expression of this idea. Sometimes the figure is called the "Mistress of the Beasts," represented in art by a feminine figure with animals, particularly lions, rampant. The Lion's Gate at Mycenae shows lions rampant on either side of a pillar, a variant on the *kore* theme. The pillar stands for a tree, the both are alternatives to an erect penis, which is in some way an alternative to the *kore*.

The erect penis is itself an important part of Greek religion. Many ceremonies and processions were marked by carrying the phallus through the throng. At Delos there was a walkway with gigantic sculptured marble penises complete with testicles on six-foot-tall bases. What exactly was their function beyond a general expression of fertile vigor is not clear. On the surface of things they remind one of the phallic symbolism in the crossed swords held aloft by the groom's men at military weddings. The Greeks were accustomed to the public display of representations of an erect penis. This fact must temper any interpretation of ancient comedy, which was enacted by characters to whom were appended phalli. The plays often derive considerable merriment from these, which could be only a source of embarrassment to persons raised in even these, the last vestiges of Victorian prudery. Comic phalli are humorous from the same perspective that animates most comedy in antiquity, that is, men trying to move naturally while coping with an erection are in a ridiculous state. Contemporary men have long been able to chuckle over this in the locker room. The omnipresent phallus in Greek antiquity, however, made the humor of that situation available to everyone.

Demeter-Persephone, Bride-Mother, earth, eternal life, giver of life, woman appear in the myth of a dominant female goddess in sexual or symbolic association with an inferior male deity who suffers in this association. Aphrodite and Anchises (crippled), Aphrodite and Adonis (killed), Artemis and Actaeon (killed), Athena and Tiresias (blinded) are variants on this theme. The common explanation of this story arises from the eternal earth which annually bears fruit. Annually she is fertilized by a young (rainy season) male figure who then dies (end of the growing season), only to be supplanted the following spring by another. The young man is generally known as the year god; the death of the year god was thought once to be the source for tragedy's concentration upon the death of the hero. While this no doubt influenced tragedy, nothing so simple seems likely. The story is true to the biological fact that a male's orgasm ends his usefulness to the species whereas a woman's role is prolonged, true also to a man's short-lived orgasm and a woman's sustained rushes of sensation. *Animalibus post coitum tristitia* as the ancient Roman saying goes, a truth for the male akin to a woman's *post partum* depressions.

Any number of these ideas play at the edges or in the center of scenes in the tragedies, providing another range of associations in the play. In the *Agamemnon,* for instance, Clytemnestra, *mater dolorosa,* like Demeter laments her daughter, Iphigenia, who is snatched from her by Agamemnon, the weaker male figure. She then seduces him into the house through the door where she kills him in the bath, naked and vulnerable. The door and the bath seem starkly obvious sexual ideas. At 1387ff., when she tells of the killing, the ideas of sperm, sex and vegetation cults all come together as she describes the blood spurting on her, like spring rain which makes things grow.

Throughout classical times the worship of Demeter took place at Eleusis, a suburb to the northwest of Athens. Today by some hideous travesty of fate the site is surrounded by the smog and filth of an unrestrained industrial locale. Then the temple was the site of the mysteries. Initiates were sworn to silence, but we do know that the ceremony turned on ritual mourning followed by ritual joy, darkness turning to light, the fulcrum moment being when the priestess held up a sheaf of wheat.

Demeter was not among the Olympian family, nor was Dionysus, one of the most popular gods of Greece. He, too, seems to be a people's god, probably imported into the Greek world from Thrace; yet his name has now been deciphered upon Linear B tablets so the name and probably the deity are of Mycenaean times. The worship and cults of Dionysus betrayed different origins. There was the vegetation deity, particularly the growth of fruits, of which the grape and wine are particularly associated with the god. Dionysus, the babe, victim of Hera's jealousy, was one characterization of the vegetation deity. He is sometimes known as Bacchus, attended by nurses, in flight, who hide him from Hera's vengeance. The stepmother's wrath he shares with Hercules, doomed to labor in the service of his inferiors to satisfy Hera's jealousies. Like Hercules Dionysus appears as a civilization builder spreading the culture of the vine, which is to say, agriculture as a social enterprise. He is often otherwise attended by satyrs, animal men with phalli, emblems of fertility.

The other, more important side to Dionysus was the emotional, ecstatic, orgiastic religious experience. Some elements of this worship were achieving ecstasy through drugs and wine, through whirling dancing and swinging lights, *omophagia*, the ritual of tearing apart a live animal and eating its still quivering flesh. The ecstasy was to get the celebrant out of his body, the *omophagia* to eat the god. Again as the celebrants put on skins and masks of animals, they were putting on the god. The festival of theater was part of the worship of Dionysus and perhaps the masks and mimetic enactment of action evolved from the skins and masks of god. The mysterious, frightening scene in the *Bacchae* when Pentheus appears, dazed, that is, outside of himself, dressed as a woman, in intimate conversation with the god, submitting to the god, has its roots very likely in this aspect of the cult. The emotional extremity thereafter in that play as Pentheus dies, followed by the depression of his slayers, seems to be mirrored in cult. Exaltation, repulsion, sacrament and pollution are found in a ceremony on the island of Tenedos: a pregnant cow was chosen from the herd and when she had calved, a man was chosen from the community to smash the calf with an ax, reducing it to mush, which the community ate. Thereupon the calf's slayer was stoned, driven down to the sea, where he could wash off the pollution.

The Orphic religion bears affinities with this experience. The god figure, Dionysus or Zagreus, son of Zeus and Semele, is killed and eaten by the Titans, all save the heart, which is saved by Athena, from which the god returns. The Titans blasted by Zeus are reduced to ash from which springs man, who thereafter contains a kind of original sin. The Orphic faith is largely concerned with purification and the afterlife. It represents a distinctly separate vein of religious experience in the spectrum of ritual and belief in the sixth and fifth centuries. The Dionysiac ritual and Orphism were both personal and communal. The oracle of Apollo at Delphi was, on the other hand, political. We are limited in our knowledge of Delphi to the responses that have been preserved and since so many of these come from the ancient historians they tend to be political. There was evidently much priestly concern with morality; purity of the spirit was more important than the purification that ritual brings. Ion in Euripides' play is the young temple boy at Delphi; his innocence, purity, love of the simple life and the country are personifications of the Delphic ideal. The inscriptions at Delphi were "Know thyself," "Nothing too much" and the mysterious letter "E" carved in the pediment of the great temple. By treaty the oracle site was always accessible to all Greek city-states at all times despite varying states of hostilities. As a pan-Greek institution the oracle was political, keeping close watch on the political life in each city, interfering through oracular pronouncements, generally conservative, backing aristocracies or the aristocratic point of view, being used to locate sites for new colonies, encouraging the maintenance of traditional cults, the continuity of religion.

Religion and drama probably indoctrinated more than the school. Formal education in the fifth century was simple, but its staples, while not calculated to instill an appreciation of poetry, were nevertheless a guarantee that this would happen. The aristocratic ideal was a combination of athletic exercise to create a beautiful body and music and poetry to create a beautiful personality. With this came, of course, reading, writing and arithmetic, but the emphasis was upon the development of a noble young man. Aristophanes' *Clouds* contains a debate on the merits of the older as opposed to the newer system of education. There is a charming portrait of the old system (961ff.), which taught a boy how to be modest, sitting so as not to expose his crotch, smoothing out the sand when he arose so that the impress of his buttocks would not be visible, and how to be strong:

> "If you do what I say
> put your mind to it
> you'll always have a glowing chest,
> bright skin, great shoulders.

> small tongue, big ass
> little prick."

(1009–14)

The emphasis was upon beauty. Again the confusion between physical beauty and moral worth is apparent. A beautiful boy is a good boy. Education is bound up with male love, an idea that is part of the pro-Spartan ideology of Athens. Phaedrus refers to the pedagogical value of homosexuality in the *Symposium*. A youth who is inspired by his love of an older male will attempt to emulate him, the heart of the educational experience. The older male in his desire for the beauty of the youth will do whatever he can to improve it. Obviously, Athenian education had little to offer women and in fact tried to do little or nothing for them. Iphigenia, for instance, in *Iphigenia in Tauris* is illiterate. Aristocratic education was also based upon the premise that the quality of goodness was something with which a man was born. The aristocracy were known as *the good*. The education, therefore, was to promote and encourage that innate goodness. The memorization of poetry and the practice of music were exercises to formulate the actions, thoughts, the behavior of the young in accordance with the native impulse to goodness with which they were born. What in effect happened was that the aristocratic young learned certain behavior patterns, certain values and attitudes in the home on an informal basis. Their schooling, the poetry, the music, the athletics simply reinforced on a formal basis this early learning at home. The poetry of Homer and his successors is aristocratic poetry which could only enhance those values. And being conformist literature it is pedagogically ideal. Aristocratic education was an activity of leisure that revealed the person; it was a static work of art. This was opposite to the innovation in education that sprang up in the latter half of the fifth century in Athens.

Literacy was common in Athens in the fifth century, but those who were not aristocrats were cut off from the system of education within the family which gave wisdom and manners and enabled the aristocratic youth to benefit most from the formalized education. As increasingly all the freeborn males were called upon to take part in government, as more and more litigation appeared in the courts, more persons wanted to learn how their society functioned. An aristocracy controls best when it has a monopoly on the culture. In the early period at Athens when only the aristocracy held public office, they alone understood the laws and the operation of government. The wisdom accumulated over a century by this class became an invaluable exclusive oral tradition passed down in these families, not available to outsiders. Eventually, however, the outsiders needed to know how things worked and the educational system was not prepared to show them. This was the impetus for the widespread patronage and popularity of professional educators known as Sophists. The sophistic education was pragmatic and not ideological; the Sophists offered technique, not indoctrination. The ideology of the aristocracy remained unchallenged. The monied class that sprang up alongside the aristocracy never achieved or perhaps never tried for a class identity independent of the aristocrat. There was never a bourgeoisie. By and large the values and attitudes of Athens remained those of the aristocracy. Aeschylus was born an aristocrat; Sophocles was the son of a wealthy industrialist, yet his plays show values perhaps more actively aristocratic than the former's. The *Ajax* and *Philoctetes,* for example, are tragedies of history, with aristocratic heroes who are tragically anachronistic. Both men were more than playwrights. Aeschylus fought at Marathon and chose to record that fact rather than his playwriting on his tombstone. Sophocles, twice over elected general, once holding office as the imperial treasurer (443/2), was also the priest in a healing cult, and while a suitable temple for the god Asclepius was being built, he made his house available for the rites of that cult. Euripides' origins are more obscure and his plays are far more various in their tone. Aristophanes once calls his mother a greengrocer, but that may have veiled meanings. He perhaps came from money. He was said to have passed time with the intellectuals. Certainly, he had no governmental service. Because he is a constant and obvious butt for Aristophanes, he probably represents a really different point of view, intellectualist, progressive, middle class—if one can honestly talk of such a phenomenon at this time—part of the sophistic movement. Despite Aristophanes' criticism he was immensely talented. When Euripides died Sophocles is said to have appeared at the next festival with his choruses in mourning.

Our word "sophist" comes from the Greek *sophistes;* an intellectual, we might say. The word was often used pejoratively as is our word "intellectual." A man who dealt in wisdom could make good money. In a society where one drachma was an average day's wage, Protagoras was said to have offered a three- to four-year course charging ten thousand drachmas; prices had fallen half a century later, Isocrates complains, to a thousand drachmas for something similar. The major Sophists were great celebrities, their lectures were thronged. When Gorgias, for example, came to Athens in 427 B.C. he was a sensation. Their popularity had an unsettling effect upon Plato. He professes great contempt for the whole movement, because he feels it fraudulent to claim that goodness (his conception of social and political behavior) can be taught. Socrates, in Plato's dialogues, is at pains to disabuse everyone he meets of the notion that they know anything technical about goodness, that they therefore cannot teach it as one teaches woodworking or any other craft with a set of standards and rules. The Sophists who have the misfortune to meet Socrates in Plato's pages never have the chance to retort that the science of man was in its infancy, much needed doing and learning, much could be done if Socrates and Plato would stop trying to locate the focus of investigation in the heavens, stop proceeding from *a priori* truths which were not necessarily found in fact, give over the principle of education by indoctrination.

Perhaps Plato's indignation sprang from the same source as the wrath of the judges of the Areopagus when they saw their power eroded in the 460s. The Areopagus court made up of former magistrates in its early days had been the visible expression of the aristocracy's exclusive hold on law and custom. Similarly before the Sophists the education system such as it was was the province of the aristocracy. Xenophon, at the beginning of the fourth century, has a revealing aside in his essay *On Hunting* (chapter 13): "The people have brought an end to athletic exercise and to the practice of music, holding to the belief that it is not a good thing, but in fact they know that they are incapable of doing these things. In the offices of arranging choruses, of managing exercises . . . it is the rich who lead the dance and the people who follow, the rich who arrange the exercise and the people who are exercised . . ." Bound up with the aristocratic tradition, education was a thing offered as a given. The Sophists challenged this by opening it to everyone, especially by declaring that this tradition could be looked at objectively, which is to say, by those who did not have a stake in its maintenance. Protagoras' dictum that man is the measure of all things is a direct challenge to the aristocracy's metaphysical control of things. We know that one of the burning issues of the fifth century was the debate over the relative value of *nomos* (custom) and *physis* (nature). It appears again and again as a motif of central concern in the literature. There are many factors in the immense appeal of this controversy, but an important one is that the aristocracy's notion of education was based upon a belief in the virtue inherent in their class and their progeny. Those who believed in *nomos* as the more powerful force in society were a direct challenge to their primacy. The Sophists, who objectively lectured upon human behavior, trying to establish rules, prototype psychologists, anthropologists, social scientists and political scientists, were saying in effect that nothing is fixed, alternatives exist to human behavior and the existing order. The immediate practical effect of this was in the political life of the *ekklesia*. The right to speak was available to every man, but obviously people who command language and can marshal their thoughts, who can speak from sophistication and inherited information are in a dominant position, certainly in a society that still prized excellence and quality. The Sophists among other things taught rhetoric. They therefore could in theory take men off the street and make them able to compete with the aristocrats for the attention of the assembly. Some of the venom of Thucydides toward Kleon, whom he describes in his *History* as a kind of villain, is resentment at this parvenu who alone of all the major figures mentioned in the *History* on any side—Athenian, Peloponnesian, even Sicilian or Persian—is not an aristocrat. Kleon is Thucydides' Thersites, one might say.

Sophistic education made changes in the fifth century. Analytic thinking and generalities on psychology and social behavior are particularly noticeable in later tragedy. One thinks of Creon's speech in the *Oedipus Tyrannus* on the role of a prince regent, or Ion's speech on country living in the *Ion* (585ff.), or the nurse's speech in the *Hippolytus* (435ff.) on sexual health. Euripides develops marvelous irony in the *Bacchae* (272ff.) when he has Tiresias, once a seer, now turned thinker, deliver a lecture, neutered and pallid, on the meaning of the Dionysus cult while the god himself in all his terrible power in fact stalks the city of Thebes. Euripides'

Medea is almost entirely a debate in intellectual terms, a panel really more than a drama until Medea breaks through the enslaving words with action and kills Creusa and her own children. Thucydides' generalizations upon the nature of revolution (3.82ff.) are a particularly good example of the influence of sophistic thinking in his work, but it is everywhere in the speeches, which are analyses, either psychological or sociological, of human action. Sophistic teaching did not, however, help or foster the art of tragedy. A marked feature of later tragedy is the increasing emphasis upon debate. Sometimes it is almost ornamental, as that between Helen and Hecuba with Menelaus as judge in the *Trojan Women*. It constitutes almost the whole play in the *Medea*. The very large role the juries played in Athenian life seems to have spilled over into the theater. The demands that court activity and litigation made in the society motivated the Sophists and their clients to turn considerable attention to verbal assault, manipulation, defense and control. Disputation and dialectic were at the heart of this education. It responded of course to the Greek instinct for antithesis, but formalized it and intellectualized it. In the last decades of the fifth century it must have grown to be the common intellectual property of everyone, the new way of seeing things however much distorted or simplified. For all that, Plato's Socrates mocks the Sophists; he not only practices dialectic, but aggressively, eristically in the manner of a courtroom assault, scarcely, if at all, masked by his irony and gentle mocking. Analysis is alien to the kind of symbolic language and action that is acutely necessary to ancient tragedy. Then too, tragedy depends upon a belief in the inevitable for its effect. While it remained true in sophistic thinking that we all must die, nonetheless the general tenor of this movement is optimistic, given to problem-solving, and these are not constituents of tragedy. Euripides is therefore interesting as a playwright who begins in the one mode and whose last play is one of the most powerful expressions of it, and yet who could often slip out and over to the other perspective, sufficiently warping the tragic frame to pave the way for New Comedy. In the ancient biography of Euripides, it was written: "Peripeteia, the rape of virgins, substitutions of children, recognition scenes with rings and necklaces, these are the very stuff of New Comedy and it was Euripides who developed them." On the other hand, this could be conceived as the surfacing of the non-aristocratic sensibility in Athens. Engels remarks on the optimism of the bourgeoisie. New Comedy is among other things an optimistic variant on tragedy come at a time when the aristocracy was gone. Again the features mentioned by the ancient biographer are more in keeping with fairy tales than with heroic poetry, which are the poles of difference between aristocratic and folk narrative. So again we may attribute this to the emergence finally of a new point of view if not an ideology in Athens as it grew increasingly and thoroughly democratic.

The paradox of Athens' history in the fifth century is that the city moved toward complete democracy and yet not only were women and slaves exploited at home, but the men who gathered to exercise their freedom in the *ekklesia* believed almost to a man in Athens' rule over all the peoples who were once associates in the Delian Confederacy but finally subjects of the Athenian Empire.

The course of events that mark this development form the tragedy of Athens, a set of historical facts which by the design of those who recorded them for posterity or by nature conform to the most common kind of tragic action. Athens, of course, commanded the attention of its citizens. In its glory it excited their patriotism and their pride. As it commenced to suffer, it exercised their fear and awe. It brought them sorrow. As the center of all major literary activity throughout the fifth century Athens is the one constant in it all from Pindar's famous "Athens, violet-crowned," Aeschylus' praise of the Athenian jury system (*Eumenides* 927ff.), Thucydides' remarks on her material greatness (1.10) to Sophocles' heartbreaking ode in the *Oedipus at Colonus* (694ff.) on the glories of the olive groves of Attica at a time when the Spartans had destroyed them all. The story of Athens remains a staple of the dwindling mythology of the West, its failures, like the fall of Rome, one of the mysterious tragedies of Western history.

Athens' imperial history may be divided into three periods, the first ending with the decisive retreat of Xerxes out of Greek lands in 480 B.C., the second with the commencement of hostilities between Athens and Sparta in 431 B.C.—which marks the beginning of the long-drawn-out Peloponnesian War—and the third ending with Athens' defeat at Aegospotami in 404 B.C.

Athens played a major role in the astounding defeat of the

Persian invasion force at Marathon in 490. The Greeks had some difficulty and took some time absorbing the fact that a modest people limited in material possessions had defeated the army of untold thousands of soldiers led by a monarch with inexhaustible wealth. Herodotus' account of Xerxes' army on the march at the time of the second invasion gives one a sense of the fairy-tale quality of the story as it must have passed from mouth to mouth. The vast numbers of soldiers, so many that at any stop for water they drank the rivers dry; the phantasmagoric quality of the Persian army in contrast to the sinewy reality of the Greek defenders—this is the amazing stuff of folk tale. Upon the second invasion in 480, Xerxes came still more prepared, fortified in men, ships and gold. The first major engagement fell out as expectations would have had it. Three hundred brave and noble Spartans fell at Thermopylae pass before the Persian hordes, their defeat finally coming through treachery and Persian gold. They fought gloriously but nonetheless they were defeated.

In the bay opposite Salamis, however, the Athenian navy utterly routed the Persian fleet, inflicting massive casualties, causing the fleet to withdraw. A subsequent naval engagement at Mycale, in which again the Athenians were superior, and a land battle at Plataea favorable to the Greeks collapsed Persian pretension to power in mainland Greece. Athens faced peace as a military power equal to Sparta, the traditional power in the Greek world. More important, Athens was a naval power. The strategic necessity now was to keep the Persians at bay across the Aegean and to make lightning expeditions into Persian territory so as to wrest enough plunder to pay the expenses of the war. This needed ships. So, the balance of power shifted toward the Athenians. The politics of Athens was also altered by the victory in the Persian War. Traditionally, Athens rested her security upon the protection given by the hoplites, the infantry men. They constituted an economic, social and political class, those men who were able to bear arms at their own expense, for war was no longer fought by the aristocracy from expensive horses and chariots. Now after the battle of Salamis and Mycale and with a continual naval presence in the Aegean in prospect the future defense of Athens rested upon the rowers, a class of men of the most limited financial means. The movement during the subsequent two decades to open all offices to every man, to establish payment for serving in public office is directly related to the new need for the rowers and their demands made upon the community.

Athens and most of the island communities formed a league of mutual assistance and protection against the Persian menace. In 477 they established a league and made its headquarters and treasury on the island of Delos. The member cities were in the main Ionic-speaking Greeks, and Delos had strong associations for Ionians. Therefore the Delian League, whatever its purposes, constituted an Ionic bloc, a tangible antithesis to the traditional league of the Dorians in the Peloponnesus; the polarity the Greek lands had kept latent now became more visible and more active. In Athens, for example, the attitude of the outstanding figures toward Sparta became a political issue. Cimon was ostracized in 464 because of his pro-Spartan stance at a time when Sparta offended Athens. In the Delian League, Athens insisted upon democratic governments in the member cities; conservative, oligarchic governments were suspect. Athens not only had Persia as the official menace. There was Sparta, which increasingly became the focus of hostilities in Athenian political life.

The city of Sparta, which lay in a fertile mountain-ringed valley, remote, isolated, significantly with no outlet to the sea, formed the perfect contrast to Athens. The word "perfect," however, should remind us how we are at the mercy of our meager ancient sources, how the ancients with their deep aesthetic sensibilities strove to give form and structure, to impose meaning upon intractable detail, how therefore they may have so carefully, if fundamentally unconsciously, selected the materials for posterity as an artistic creation or a mythology more than historical fact, whatever indeed that may be.

The Spartans were conservative people, very strong in war, self-sufficient; their government was extremely stable, their society and daily lives offered no surprises. Throughout the fifth century Sparta offered to Athenians who could not stomach the democracy, the empire or the rapid cultural changes a viable alternative. Their virtues correspond enough to the Puritan ideal—minimal talk, minimal baths, minimal self-indulgence of any sort, muscles and endurance—to have charged the concept behind the phrase "Spartan way of life" with a good deal of value. In reality, they were probably more like the caricatures of Spartans created by Aristophanes, that is, crude, thoughtless, macho types. Their celebrated way of life sometimes seems to us most like that of a Hitler youth camp, although it was often praised by the Victorians. But we may say that the Athenian democracy's emphasis upon things Ionian probably represents a strong ideological stance, something more than a conflict between democracy and aristocracy. One must not, however, be led astray by modern interpretations of such words as "liberal" or "conservative." The ancient Greeks had little belief in or interest in change; they were all relative to the modern outlook very conservative. At Locris, for instance, something extreme but indicative was the law that whoever proposed a new law in the assembly had a noose around his neck. If the law failed to pass, he was hanged forthwith. Other states had monetary punishments for the urging of what by subsequent vote would appear to be an extremely minority view. This was on the one hand more against extremism, but on the other, it prevented the airing of ideas whose time perhaps had not come, but which were commencing to be in the air. The oligarchic faction which writes of the wanton and radical Athenian assembly in democracy's heyday misleads us, for we cannot easily calculate how extremely conservative the Athenians must have been.

The Spartans controlled a land where over three fourths of the people were enslaved tillers of the soil for their Spartan masters. Fear of slave revolt molded the society. To maintain the necessary repression, Spartan life was dedicated to soldiery. Men from childhood on were trained to fight. They lived in barracks until thirty years of age and thereafter continued eating at a common soldiers' mess, sharing in providing the food. Men were bonded into a tight emotional unit by the barracks homosexuality, which was an essential feature of Spartan growing up. There were a number of *rites de passage* from boyhood into adulthood, most of them harsh tests of endurance, such as flogging, stealing food, carrying heavy weights; no doubt submitting to anal intercourse over a period of years was more of the same. In contrast to Athens, women were very free in Sparta. They lived much of their life separate from their men, managed the farms, had considerable responsibilities. The promiscuity of Spartan women was a subject of much speculation and gossip in the rest of Greece, prompted in part by the Spartan custom of attempting to ensure that superior physical specimens would

unite to produce offspring despite other marriage arrangements. Old, infirm men, for instance, who had vigorous
young wives were meant to find them vigorous males by
whom they could conceive superior children. There is a
curious play by Euripides, the *Andromache,* in which the
antagonism between Spartan ways and the more conventional
view is brought out. Euripides has fashioned an anti-Spartan
propaganda play (dated somewhere in the early years of the
Peloponnesian War). For this he puts aside his customary
sympathies with the repressed and exploited lives of Athenian
women to launch an attack upon Spartan women, by extension women in general, whose freedom makes them liars and
sluts and for whom Hermione, the main character, decides
total confinement would be the solution (943–53). To avoid
the temptations that new ideas and commerce might bring,
the Spartans chose a system of coinage that made extensive
trading in or out of the country impossible. So it was that
they escaped the waves of social and political change that
moved at varying speeds across the Greek mainland. Foreign
advocates of Sparta looked to the stability, the single-minded
purpose, the devotion to the state and praised Sparta. The
fact of the matter probably was that the single motive that
produced this seemingly poised and excellent society was
fear. Over the centuries, Sparta's cultural sterility became
physical and by the second century there were few Spartans
left in that little backwash valley of the Peloponnesus.

This was Athens' main opponent in the Peloponnesian
War although almost all the Doric-speaking city-states of
mainland Greece were in league with Sparta. Thucydides
claims that Sparta's fear of Athenian growth prompted her
to move against Athens; in truth, by 431 Athens and the
Delian League had changed character considerably.

The League was established as a common defense against
Persia. Since, however, Athens was the greatest power and
from the start the ten treasurers of the League were to be
Athenian citizens, it was not exactly a mutual arrangement.
Every city was to contribute ships to a common armada or
if this was difficult or a city's proportionate share was less
than a full ship, the city could contribute money. Most
favored the latter, either being small or not having the means
to build ships. Either innocently or by design, Athens' ship-
yards and navy were busy turning out ships and maintaining them. The vagueness of law and contractual arrange-

ments made them *de facto* and probably *de jure* Athenian property.

Immediately the League appeared more as empire. In 472 B.C., Carystos, a city on Euboea, the island off the mainland, was forced by the League fleet to join because the city was too strategically located to be neutral. More ominously in 467, when Naxos chose to opt out of the League, the fleet laid siege and broke the will of the city on the argument that no city could withdraw until the League was dissolved by common consent. What was new, however, was that Carystos and Naxos were nakedly made subject states of Athens, forced to pay tribute, having lost their autonomy. All the Greek city-states viewed this development uneasily. And it got worse. More revolted, more were subdued, more were made subject to Athens. In 454—a pivotal date—the treasury was transferred from Delos to Athens to the safe-keeping of the goddess Athena, and the city unashamedly began a building program with this money that made it the glory of the ancient world. The League was twenty-three years old; a generation had passed.

When the League was new in 477, Athens was still amazed at the victories of its fleet, which had been built by Themistocles with silver discovered at Laurium in the south of Attica in 483, six years earlier. They were rebuilding their city hastily after the Persian invasion, especially putting up fortification walls from 478 until 476. Aeschylus celebrated their triumph over the army and fleet of Xerxes with his *Persians* in 472 (young Pericles was the producer), which tells the story as though from the Persian point of view in which the pride of Persia is humbled unexpectedly by these far-off strange men of might. Five years later as Naxos was being reduced to subject status Aeschylus won again with his *Seven Against Thebes*. In 464 the conservative Cimon was ostracized, Ephialtes and his protégé, Pericles, were in the public favor with schemes that gave new power and wealth to the people. The court of the Areopagus, already much reduced by the law of election by lot, now lost jurisdiction over many cases, and so the last visible power of the aristocracy was diminished. Alternative courts became numerous, justice came into the hands of the people, justice became rational rather than part of an unknown arcane aristocratic code. A law to pay the judges so anyone could afford to serve came somewhere between 462 and 460. Aeschylus won with the *Oresteia* in 458, a trilogy about crime, punishment, law and order which speaks to the political events of the time. That same year Athens after taking over Megara in 459 and allying herself with Argos began building the long fortification walls from the city to the harbor. This was a major project of those who favored power for the rowers, money for the traders, empire for everyone; now no matter what happened to their land Athens' umbilical cord to the sea was safe. The Athenians were acting out in another way their resolve of 480 when as the Persians invaded Attica they voted to move all their wives and children out of the city onto the island of Salamis while the men took to the ships. For the farmers, however, and the great aristocratic land-owners the building of the great wall from Athens to the Piraeus was madness, a thrust of energy away from what was sacred, ancient and natural, the land. The tension between these two very distinct visions of Athens is frequent in the literature, especially in Aristophanes' plays, where the conservative voice is often well expressed. Dikaiopolis, for example, the small farmer in the *Acharnians*, is just such a one, the kind of person who suffers most from empire and benefits least, seeing his beloved land ravaged by the Spartans (the play was produced in 425), forced to live in the city.

Athens plunged forward with empire and power. The year after the *Oresteia* Athens went victoriously against the island of Aegina and the land of Boeotia. In 454, the year the treasury was transferred from Delos, they sent an expedition to Egypt. In 451, a law was proposed by Pericles in the city excluding from citizenship any man whose parents were not both Athenians. The pie was becoming so delicious that the people began to cut off the takers. There is a certain irony that Pericles, friend to Sophocles, Phidias, Anaxagoras and many another citizen or alien in Athens, consort if not husband of a woman from Asia Minor, was the one to propose the measure. Of course, he was simply articulating again what was in the air, what people wanted. Yet, at the time of the plague twenty years later his two legitimate sons died and the assembly had to pass a special law making a citizen of his son by Aspasia who of course had only one Athenian parent. Relations with the Dorians were shaky enough so that stabilizing them with a truce seemed good. But the truce that year and peace with Persia two or three years later were illusory events because Megara and Boeotia were lost in 447; a thirty years' peace concluded with Sparta in 446 was gone in war fifteen years later. Still Pericles summoned Iktinos to begin the Parthenon in 451 and Phidias to oversee the sculpture. Somewhere in the 440s Sophocles triumphed with his *Ajax* and on another occasion with the *Antigone,* and Athens founded Thurii in southern Italy, her first move toward the west. Thurii was a colony to replace Sybaris, which had been destroyed. Men from all cities were invited to go together to colonize; supposedly Herodotus, the historian, and Lysias, the orator, went along. Pericles appointed Protagoras, the Sophist, to draw up laws for the new community.

Relations between Athens and the Peloponnesian states ruptured in 431, the year Euripides won third prize with the *Medea,* a play that shows the strong intellectual bent of the playwright. The outbreak and subsequent events of the Peloponnesian War are available in Thucydides and do not need retelling here. It was a long war fought in a desultory fashion by land forces (Sparta) who could not effect any real damage to a city-state (Athens) which could safely import its food and by a navy (Athens) which could only sail around a land mass (Peloponnesus) and effect minor skirmishes. Through it all the tragic and comic theater continued, men came and went at Athens, the damage seems in some ways more psychological than real. One sees that particularly in the fantasy plays of Aristophanes. In 425 and 424 he presented the *Acharnians* and the *Knights.* Both are strong, intelligent, political statements, attacks on policy, attacks on the political maturity of the assembly, both suited to a critical time when wits need to be sharp to confront the horrendous problems of the day. But in 423 when the battle of Amphipolis carried off Kleon and the Spartan general Brasidas, Aristophanes presented a parody of the Sophists in the *Clouds.* In the *Peace* of 421 he did deal with the peace of Nikias, which was concluded that year, but it was such an unsatisfactory political arrangement that war began almost immediately, and yet Aristophanes did not play to that failure. Was it too delicate a matter? Or was he too tired? Analogies with the frothy movies put on in the Great Depression will not work, because Aristophanes' art form was a serious form of social criticism, whereas these movies never pretended even at their most pretentious to be more than entertainment. In 414 when the smell of disaster was everywhere, and the Athenians were facing defeat in Sicily, he put on the *Birds,* his most delightful fantasy, in which an Athenian decides to flee, to join the birds, to build a city in the clouds. By 405, the year of the disastrous battle of Aegospotami, the end of the Athenian hopes, he produced the *Frogs,* which is marvelous literary analysis but ends on that desperate note of wanting Aeschylus back for the right kind of indoctrination. One hears the totalitarian ring.

More harrowing than any event of the actual war was the plague that came in 430 and carried off Pericles in 429. It decimated the population already crowded into the city because of the siege condition brought on by the Spartan invasion. Thucydides describes the plague in his history (2.74ff.); elsewhere almost no mention is made of it. This is strange. Here is an event that should have played upon the latent guilt that the entire enterprise of empire must have engendered. The Greek had a horror of the consequences of going too far. These middle decades were a time of real change in Athenian philosophy. Empire was not in the Athenian tradition; it was alien to Greek thinking in any case. One would imagine that the plague provoked overt responses to the imperial adventure that had been latent or at least muted. Yet Athenians had built up an extraordinary self-justification on their heroism at Marathon and Salamis. Patriotism had marvelous powers of self-delusion. It is tantalizing to read into the theater of the time, but dating of the extant plays is sometimes hazardous. We can date all of Aristophanes, all of Aeschylus save the *Prometheus,* about half of Euripides' plays, and only the *Philoctetes* and the *Oedipus at Colonus* of Sophocles. Even relating a play to a more general movement or point of view is often dubious. *Oedipus Tyrannus,* for instance, is thought to have been produced about 430 because of the plague motif and because Oedipus and Jocasta seem to be shown as the kind of rationalist, energetic overachievers that we presume Pericles and his extra-legal consort Aspasia were, and yet who knows?

Alcestis is Euripides' first extant play, produced in 438, although it is recorded that he competed for the first time in 455. The *Hippolytus* came in 428, the year after Pericles died and the year before Gorgias arrived to dazzle Athenian audiences with his verbal pyrotechnics. In the *Hippolytus* we seem to see the definite impress of sophistic teaching. Phaedra dying of love for her stepson, Hippolytus, represses this emotion, true to her instincts of decorum. But she confesses the situation to her old nurse and confidante, whose reaction is done brilliantly by Euripides. At first she is shocked, horrified, acting upon the same premises that led Phaedra to be silent. She goes off, but then returns to say (435f.): "Second thoughts are sometimes best." That in itself is interesting, for Phaedra has acted out of right instinct, that code of behavior inculcated in the aristocracy that passes for natural. When the nurse returns with changed mind, she poses alternatives, allowing for rational rather than instinctual reactions to the situation. Her speech which follows is the sort of thing one gets in sex hygiene classes today: sex is natural, it is good for the body, its positive aspects far outweigh ethical or moral considerations which are in any case conventional rather than natural. The arguments are what we find written in the fragments of a fifth-century Athenian Sophist named Antiphon. Man, said Antiphon, is subject to natural law. The law of nature is that man seeks life and avoids death. Man-made law coerces and therefore is opposed to natural law. We must disregard man-made law as far as we can in pursuing each of us our own needs. Euripides furthermore shows sophistic coloration by posing Aphrodite and Artemis as the two symbolic poles in the play, allegorizing them into Sexuality and Abstinence, making Hippolytus a study in repression.

Next to the plague the other catastrophic event of the war was the Athenian expedition against Sicily in 415, which began in such high hopes and ended so disastrously for the Athenians with the battle in the harbor of Syracuse in 413, as we can read in the very detailed and very moving account by Thucydides. Euripides' *Trojan Women* was produced in 415, the same year as the sailing out, the year after the Athenians had brutally forced the citizens of the island of Melos into submission, killing and enslaving the population. The uneasy and foreboding emotions that both the sack of Melos and sailing must have produced are something that cannot really be openly talked about in time of war; once the decisions are made there can no longer be regrets uttered aloud. The power therefore of the tragic theater, its social value, is clearly shown when a production like the *Trojan Women*, which is about both massacre and high hopes dashed, can imply what is felt but cannot be said. We must remember that the publication or the public reading of Herodotus' *Histories* came about somewhere in the 420s. It shows that the paranoia induced by pride and success which is so evident in Aeschylus for instance and is probably a marked feature of the late archaic age is still very much a part of the society's thinking. If not the plague then certainly the disastrous Sicilian expedition must be the jealousy of the gods striking at Athenian pretensions. Among the charges brought against Socrates in 399 was that he was guilty of impiety because he introduced new gods. Socrates' enemies fastened upon the general uneasiness that Athens' catastrophic defeat produced to touch latent religious anxieties to ensure a conviction. Once before in 450, Pericles' teacher and friend, Anaxagoras from Klazomenae, was tried for impiety because he taught naturalistic interpretations for meteorological phenomena, a practice calculated to put seers and soothsayers out of business.

The Sophists' teachings did not destroy the traditional religion as much as the failure of the city-state and the increasingly inherent improbability of there being religious inspiration in so thoroughly anthropomorphized beings. The gods of the state, the Olympian Pantheon that was a metaphor for the *polis,* faded with the state, could not survive in any effective form other than a point of reference in poetry and prose. The failure of the city-state was more a loss of faith. At the same time almost a century after it was begun Kleisthenes' political experiment was severely shaken. The Athenian loss in Sicily, which Thucydides describes so majestically and mournfully, was a catastrophe at Athens. Suspicions and hatreds were everywhere. Fear of the Persians, always latent, became overt. Athenian allies revolted. Easy and quick solutions were sought: Alcibiades alone could save Athens, a new constitution promised strength. In 411 in January Aristophanes presented the *Lysistrata,* a brilliant comedy of sexual politics; in March he presented the *Thesmophoriazusae,* a satire on women, homosexual men and literature. But the political atmosphere was tensing up as conservatives at Athens tested their strength in the absence of the fleet at the island of Samos. By May a provisional government took over, charged with establishing a body of four hundred men who would choose a group of five thousand to replace the unstable, unreliable assembly. Pay for public offices was abolished to remove the poor. This oligarchic government would not yield to any power (always a problem for oligarchies and aristocracies) so that the council of four hundred and the assembly of five thousand were also executive bodies; as such they were impossibly unwieldy. The revolt of Euboea in September alarmed the city, and when the fleet won two signal victories, the traditional constitution was restored. But the illusions and the enthusiasm were gone. As Athens settled into a kind of torpor in the fourth century the reality could not vie with the legend. Plato for instance looked to an ideal city and turned his back on the actual. He foreshadowed, however, the destiny of Athens. The city was to enter the mythology of history, to become the symbol of ancient Greece. For many observers mankind's finest hour was lived in the fifth-century B.C. city of Athens. It is a place we can never enter or know. As Thucydides said (Book 1, Chapter 10), ". . . if the city of the Lacedaimonians were deserted and there were left out their temples and the foundations of the buildings, I imagine that after the passage of time there would be considerable doubt by successive centuries as to their greatness relative to their fame, . . . whereas if Athens suffered the same fate, one would consider their power to be double what it is on the basis of the sight of the city." Even then he foresaw that Athens had at her command money, talent, cultural vitality and, if we can believe Pericles' funeral oration ("Athens is the teacher of all Greece"), a sense of her place in history if she chose to put herself in it, which made of the city and her achievements already a myth in the heroic tradition from which her culture had sprung.

CHAPTER SIX
THE BEGINNINGS OF PROSE

It is Hekataios of Miletus who tells this tale. I am writing what follows as it seems true to me. For the stories of the Greeks are both inconsistent and laughable, or so it seems to me.

Hekataios

Goddamn an eyewitness anyway. He always spoils a good story.

Colonel Crisp as quoted by Harry S Truman

Epic poetry did not survive the invention and spread of writing, but its ethos did. Since it remained the staple of Greek culture, memorized by youngsters, epic poetry's influence did not diminish. Its vision of life became transformed into the two major verbal art forms of the fifth century, tragedy and historiography. Both are responses to the needs formerly filled by epic, each in a way peculiar to it. Tragedy mythologizes saga or epic action, history endows it with details, space and time. Still neither departs completely from the rich epic source from which it sprang.

Greek history writing was in prose. Prose writing betokens literacy. Even when meant to be recited prose is different from poetry. Its successful production in a society still not much used to literacy marks a real revolution. Early practitioners of prose are pioneers whose voyages through to the completion of a written text are daring experiments. All sorts of changes and new discoveries are made en route.

Long prose pieces are all the more titanic efforts. To criticize them requires a feeling for the hazards and unknowns, for the peculiar aesthetic weightlessness that the absence of a tradition or recognized standard induced. In a period of time when two verbal systems, the epic and tragedy, were functioning (although the former was not a vehicle for anything new), it is remarkable that the very conservative Greeks brought forth such an innovation. What needs did history meet?

The first major specimens of prose come from what we call historians, that is, Herodotus' account of Persia and its empire, culminating in the war with Greece, and Thucydides' narration of the events of the war between Athens and the major Dorian city-states. Both present numerous problems of interpretation. Partly these stem from the commonly held notion that Herodotus and Thucydides are historians in our sense of the term, and that what they have given us are a history of the Persian War and a history of the Peloponnesian War. The words "historian" and "history" inevitably prejudice our understanding of these authors. Then too, it is almost irresistible, although it is misleading, to compare the two figures, since they were almost contemporaries, seemingly writing in the same genre. Furthermore, we who are heirs to a rich and established prose tradition perhaps cannot notice or appreciate the experimental and tentative nature of the prose Herodotus and Thucydides essayed, each in his own distinctive manner.

Even if the words "history" and "historian" impose too much on our imagination there was a change in the purpose and assumptions of narrative (as we can dimly perceive this change) from Homer's day to the time when Herodotus commenced to write. Whatever it was, Herodotus and Thucydides were doing something new and they understood this.

Myth and saga poetry portray a never-changing, inevitable world that is only tenuously, if at all, related to the time in which we, the auditors, dwell. Myth particularly belongs to spans and spaces inaccessible to temporal delineation. *Once upon a time*, we say, events occurred; even their occurrence has only a spurious and scanty chronological scheme. In myth what happens is inevitable; sequence of action, therefore, does not have to be emphasized. Partly this inevitability derives from constant retelling and rehearing these stories, having them as familiar furniture of the mind. Anyone who has ever spent evenings telling children stories will remember how this audience will not tolerate the slightest variation in the narration, for they, who are preliterate, have a certain fixed version in their *memory*. So it is that these oft told, oft heard myths had for the auditor an inevitability. When for example in the *Iliad* Hector says to Andromache, "I know in my heart that someday sacred Ilion will perish" and when he then returns to the battle, this is neither stupid heroism nor stiff-upper-lip courage. Hector plays out his part in a saga many times rehearsed. What he does needs no justification or explanation; there are no alternatives.

Inevitability is reinforced also by the repeated structure of stories. Consider, for instance, the following three mythical stories reduced to one-sentence summaries so as to get at their structure.

Actaeon inadvertently sees Artemis nude and his dogs kill him (because they are attracted by a fawn skin he is wearing, or because she drives them mad or because she turns him into a stag—there are several versions).

Anchises after being seduced by Aphrodite is crippled by Zeus' thunderbolt.

Adonis, who is loved by Aphrodite, is killed by a boar.

The essence of these three stories is that a human male without design has a sexual or quasi-sexual encounter with a female deity, for which he suffers. To put it still more sharply, the sexual encounter between human male and female goddess is destructive to him.

Ignoring the psychological and theological ramifications of this notion we may notice rather that the components of these myths are autonomous. One person or event does not cause or affect another. The storytellers or poets, however, will sometimes introduce details, naturally, to suggest some sort of linkage. Artemis in anger at Actaeon's seeing her nude maddens the dogs; Zeus because of Anchises' public boasting of his sexual exploit strikes him; Adonis is killed by one of Aphrodite's jealous divine consorts. But because there are so many stories on this pattern, it is the pattern rather than the details of any particular story that governs our perception of the whole. The pattern presents persons and events without justification, inevitable participants and acts. One might say that the pattern justifies the actions.

But how to bring myth or saga into the sequence of time? Oral cultures have only their sagas for communal recollection. To use saga and folk tale as the source for your past is to insist that they are true. This is less easy when the bridge is weak between the sacral past, where saga action lies, and the contemporary culture. Homer does very little to relate his story to his auditors' time other than to say once or twice that men of his time could not lift the stones that Ajax flings so easily. Yet in similes he introduces details from the homely, humble agrarian life of his own time, and describes contemporary weapons and implements made of iron while consistently in the narrative outside of similes he has his heroes using bronze, true to the history of metallurgy's evolution. When he describes (*Iliad* 12.8) how the wall the Achaians put up to defend their ships is demolished by the gods when the war is over, is he perhaps apologizing for its absence at the site of Troy or its absence from the general tradition? Homer is playing true to the facts, we might say, giving a hint at least of different periods of time, thereby betraying antiquarian tendencies.

His near contemporary, Hesiod, is also not content with repeating the traditional story of man's evolution or regression through the ages of metals (*Works and Days* 109ff.). He has to account for Homer's heroic world. The traditional Age of Bronze, it seems, was peopled by ferocious, giant men who destroyed each other. Hesiod, who is acquainted with the far more human personages of the heroic age as they are presented in the oral poetic tradition, therefore makes another age, one of hero men, a more humane age, to go between Bronze and Iron. Hesiod, too, is playing true to the facts, so to speak, and at roughly the same time the Trojan stories were set in sequence, starting with creation stories, then the war and its aftermath, going beyond the *Odyssey*, to the story of Odysseus' death. In this way all the motifs and actions of saga tradition, which hitherto were autonomous, deriving from a fundamentally episodic narrative art, came to be ordered in time, relative time at least.

When Hesiod's Muses tell him (*Theogony* 26ff.) that they know how to tell lies as though they were true, the peculiar relation of verbal narrative to reality is broached, fact and fiction are distinguished (although neither is preferred) and saga begins to lose its quasi-historical authority, although for centuries Homer's poems continue to be considered historic documents. Once the alternative potentials for fact and fiction are made explicit, the saga tradition can be analyzed, sieved and mined for its so-called truth. Epic catalogues represent bodies of data; epic genealogies are the first ordering of things into a time sequence. The *Theogony,* that vast repertoire of both catalogues and genealogies, represents the ordering of data in relative time. At about the same time the places encountered in sailing about the Aegean were listed in a work called a *Periplous, The Sailing Around* [the coast]. Some scholars believe that Odysseus' narrative of his travel adventures grew out of some kind of early, hexametric *Periplous.* Names, places and to a lesser extent events began to be ordered, and moreover to be analyzed. Such was the work of the early prose writer Hekataios of Miletos. Xenophanes, the philosopher-poet, like Hekataios a man of the sixth century, declared that no one could accept the poetic-mythic accounts of the gods since their behavior was corrupt by commonplace standards of morality. Xenophanes too is analyzing the epic tradition for truth and fiction. Although we perceive this very dimly, the oral saga tradition seems to have been scrutinized, criticized and consciously reworked. The mythic assumptions of this body of commingled fact and fiction were being set aside so that new questions could be asked of tradition, and new ways devised for preserving the truth in a temporal perspective. These preoccupations are everywhere in the works of Herodotus and Thucydides.

Herodotus since Cicero has been styled "the Father of History"; Thucydides, on the other hand, has been taken to be the first "true" historian, at least in nineteenth- and twentieth-century terms of historiography. The tidy habits of the ancient literary taste-makers have left us only these two; there were many more, although perhaps very few who were earlier than Herodotus. The fragments that survive of the other historians throughout antiquity reinforce the taste-makers' decision: Herodotus and Thucydides seem to be the best.

Put side by side in our tradition, they are often compared. Comparison fails, however, because these two authors are not doing the same thing. Thucydides invites the comparison by indicating how he will differ from his predecessor. "Perhaps the absence of storytelling will be displeasing," he remarks (1.22) in a frosty, condescending manner that may have helped to motivate successive ages to consider Herodotus garrulous, lightweight and, as a narrator, definitely self-indulgent. Although strangely enough Thucydides is not mentioned by many of his immediate successors, such as Plato, who surely should have known him and read his work (as the parody in the *Menexenus* implies), in later centuries he has been preferred as the more sober, the more "scientific" historian. His reputation has grown very great in the last 150 years. Now, however, Herodotus is often said to be the superior historian, because what was once called garrulity, that irresistible and self-indulgent need to give every anecdote and fact that came his way, is now valued as the historian's obligation to lay all his sources before the reader. On the other hand, Thucydides, who was hitherto praised for the control of his narrative, the absence of that luxuriant subjectivity that marks Herodotus at every turn, is now felt to have concealed so much of what went into his research that we have no way of knowing whether he tells the truth. Thucydides searched hard, got what he felt was the truth and told it. Late-twentieth-century historiography, however, will allow no such confidence and demands to see the methods of research behind the narration. He who thinks himself objective is only naïve, and therefore Thucydides seems somehow faulted.

It is idle to compare two such disparate figures. Moreover, how are we to judge them against contemporary standards of historiography? Why indeed call them historians? Historians, as we know them, are professionals who possess a technique, who know a body of rules and standards, who are judged and may assess themselves against the performance of their colleagues. This begins to be true even in the fourth century B.C. and more so in the self-conscious and academic Alexandrian Age that followed. What Herodotus and Thucydides were doing, each of them, was altogether innovative; their objectives often realize themselves in the writing. They follow no rules, meet no standards, but rather create them. More important, to call them historians is immediately to introduce a profound separation between their writing, their style and their material. Expository prose has, for better or for worse, been consciously reduced over a long period of experimentation to the barest, minimal communicative experience. It often seems sterile when it is trying to be neutral. Someday perhaps it will be simplified enough for computers to read. But none of this has to do with what Herodotus and Thucydides were doing. They wrote with remarkably personal styles, styles hard to achieve which reveal amazing artistry and mastery. The narration is often the master of the event that is narrated. Therefore the question of how they said what they said is central for contemporary historians as well as literary critics.

Now that we have established what perils lie in the use of the words "history" and "historian," let us make bold to use them at every turn.

Certain facets of ancient Greek culture impose themselves on Herodotus and Thucydides which they assume, unawares, at the deepest level, and these are the very opposite of contemporary assumptions about the writing of history. Epic poetry was the major antecedent model for the earliest historians. As we have seen, a distinctive feature of oral epic is typicality—the typical hero, the typical action, the typical phrase. We find this again in tragedy although contemporary critics more often speak of the archetypal figure, an archetypal situation and tragic diction where the language and thought are idealized and generalized. The typical phrase of epic is equivalent to the aphoristic statement in Hesiod; they appear in combination in the maxim poetry of Theognis and to a large extent in Solon's elegiacs. Pindar, too, generalizes after the fashion of Homer and Hesiod.

The impulse to generalize and to typify all action is very strong in both Herodotus and Thucydides, whereas contemporary historians believe first of all that every action, moment and situation are unique, and that history does not repeat itself. Pericles, for instance, typifies for Thucydides a certain state of mind in Athens at a certain time; more than being a unique individual, however, Pericles is a manifestation, a principle. Isolated actions of warfare immediately bring forth in Thucydides generalities about the nature of human behavior, rather than being seen simply as composite details of the war. Herodotus even more obviously hews to this epic view of things. Croesus, for example, becomes a type when he is the paradigm behind the portrait of Xerxes. Herodotus often enters his narrative to point out that what he is narrating is typical action. The Greeks had little love for the uniqueness of things.

There is also a strong bias against change in epic. The bias is reflected in the historians, who write as though what they narrate is characteristic for all times. There is no sense of change or progress. Human action is not ongoing in any significant sense. Thus, while there may be some movement and change within the frame of their narration, there is not

—nor is there in the Homeric poems—a sense of the absolute passage of time, the evolution of men and events.

This pervasive mood is closely linked to what is surely from the modern's point of view the most bizarre feature about Herodotus, especially, and Thucydides too, if not of all the Greeks of this period, and that is their lack of any strong time sense. As we sit amid our many clocks and calendars with electronic devices everywhere to reinforce always the passage of time, it is difficult to realize that for the Greeks of the fifth century B.C. a strict chronology was not available. They did not count the passing days. There was no reasonable calendar. The lunar calendar which all city-states used was 354 days. At random intervals an intercalary month of 30 days was inserted; not only was this not rigorously scheduled, it was not done universally at the same time in all the city-states. In addition, in Athens, for instance, the *boule* operated on a solar calendar when apportioning the year into *prytanies,* whereas the older magistracies were held for the period of the lunar year, so city government was often very much out of synchronization. (See the complaints in Aristophanes' *Peace* [406–15] and the *Clouds* [615–26].)

How do Herodotus and Thucydides handle this? The former tries to make do with very little chronology. Certainly he does order events of the Persian War into some sort of chronological schema, but of absolute chronology he has no notion. Once he mentions an Athenian archon (8.51.1), who, since he gave his name to his year of office, makes that year in a certain sense an identifiable moment in the sweep of time. But there is nothing more in Herodotus, and one often has the impression, common in epic, that these events took place *once upon a time.*

Thucydides on the contrary struggles mightily with chronology. Certain lists had been verified and published by the chroniclers, lists of priestesses, of Athenian public officials and Spartan public officials, of lists of victors, establishing the date of their tenure or victory. These Thucydides uses to identify a moment in time. Since fighting began in the spring and ended in the autumn, he often indicates in a general way the point of time in the solar calendar. He tries hard as we can see (for example, 2.2.1; 4.133.2–3; 5.19.1) and he is aware of the problems (5.20).

HERODOTUS

Herodotus, it is commonly remarked, had an epic poet's sense of size. Plato called him very much like Homer. Consider the grand overview; all the land of Persia's dominions, all the time in the passage of almost a century, names and places and events spill out to give everywhere a sense of vastness. Then too, Herodotus digresses like an epic poet. His narrative moves, but moves like a glacier, assuming everything from its path. It is recorded that he was closely related to Panyassis, who was the last epic poet working in the remains of the oral tradition, now, of course, gone literary. That is the kind of biographical detail the ancients seized upon to underscore what they recognized as Herodotus' epic propensities.

Herodotus is like an epic poet, too, in the distance that lies between him and his subject. He records events of fifty to one hundred years earlier. He must have been a boy at the time of the Persian War, which is the climax of his work. He deals with strange peoples and remote places. What marks the distance is that he, the most allusive and anecdotal of writers, does not allude to contemporary events, as if he were contriving by design to keep the events of his history in another temporal setting, akin to the never-never land of epic saga. His opening sentence has intimations again of the epic poetic world: "I am writing so that the amazing feats of both the Greeks and the non-Greek peoples* shall not lack their fame . . ." One is reminded of Homer, of the epic poet's belief that his natural subject matter is the famous deeds of men. Twice in the Homeric poems occur a motive and justification of epic poetry, and of epic action as well. As Helen says to Hector (*Iliad* 6.357f.), "Maybe the gods set this doom upon us so that we could become the subject of song for later generations of men." We must also remember that Herodotus lived at a time when oral culture was very likely in the process of slowly disappearing, not simply epic poetry, but legend, folk tale and the like. So it is quite

* The Greek is *barbaroi,* which is generally translated "barbarian" (from the Greek word). It is onomatopoetic and simply and naïvely means those people who make unintelligible sounds like var-var-var instead of speaking Greek. Its pejorative sense grew slowly; we can see its start in Herodotus.

possible that Herodotus aspires consciously to replace the oral tradition, not simply the epic tradition, but the story-telling tradition of the villages. Nonetheless he has real affinities with epic style, in the generic thrust of his narration, and also in the details, as for instance, the catalogue of soldiery (7.61ff.), which reminds one of the beginning to a Homeric *androktasia*.

The word Herodotus uses for his particular intellectual activity is *historia,* which is akin to our idea of research. *Histor* in the *Iliad* means a judge, but the root is the same as that for "to see" and in that sense "to know," so perhaps a judge in the sense of someone who has sorted things out; perhaps then *historia* means coming to know things through analysis, the technique of sorting things out. A great deal of Herodotus' source material was presumably what we would categorize as legend, folk tale, tradition and gossip. Certainly none of this is to be despised, since even for our present-day sociological purposes this material forms a cultural ambience every bit as valid and authentic as independently verifiable data, facts and events are. The celebrated travels of Herodotus and his predecessor, Hekataios, are impressive attempts on the part of both to impose themselves upon this cultural surround, to insinuate themselves into it and make it theirs. Here we can see a profound difference between the epic poet and Herodotus, for the former accepts his material and to an unknown degree his poetry as a thing apart; he calls upon the Muse to bestow it. The *historia* of Herodotus, on the other hand, is in pursuit of fact and explanation, the energy to understand what has transpired. For example when Herodotus wants to ascertain certain facts commonly told about the Egyptian worship of the god Hercules, he, as he tells us (2.44), "sailed to Tyre in Phoenicia to a very old temple there, because I wanted to get some clear information on these matters." Herodotus is the father of history in that he created a mode of awareness about past events, the acknowledgment that these events are juxtaposed in time in a manner that makes sense, or better still that it is possible to make a sensible juxtaposition, and more particularly that this arrangement is relevant to the contemporary reader.

Herodotus is wise, however, not to allude to his contemporary world. The stuff of his research is from one or another kind of oral tradition. This material is true in a certain way that contemporary fact is not. The latter is fully verifiable by first- or second-hand sensory experience. The former is true to certain notions a people entertain of themselves and others. For an example from twentieth-century American culture, it is now a documented fact that the great blues singer Bessie Smith was not refused admittance to an exclusively white hospital in Mississippi and thus tragically, ironically unnecessarily bled to death before its doors. Rather she was fatally injured in the crash and was heroically if vainly aided during her last moments by a white doctor. The true version, however, does nothing to satisfy our vision of the American South in the first half of the twentieth century, nor does it sustain the Good-Evil dichotomy, neither does it enhance the conception of the powerful black woman as doomed; moreover we want our blues singers to live out and die their blues (cf. Billie Holiday). Therefore on every count the earlier, untrue version is "truer"; Edward Albee's *The Death of Bessie Smith* is the expression of this. We live in an age when almost anything can be finally accepted or discarded as absolutely true or false. Herodotus lived in a different age when anything beyond the sensory experience reposed in the culture's memory and became authenticated by satisfying the culture's needs. Very likely Herodotus' instinct keeps him from introducing material from his contemporary world, material so alien in tone. Certainly this makes for a significant distinction between Herodotus and Thucydides.

Those who applaud Herodotus for introducing material that he himself believes to be incredible do so on the ground that he thus objectively makes his evidence available to us. But they misunderstand what he is about. Certainly Herodotus does not have to believe a story to introduce it, but because it *is* already true in another sense, true to the culture. It is a *donnée* of the tradition, a legitimate datum, no less. As Herodotus remarks more than once (e.g. 7.152.3), "My job is to write what has been said, but I do not have to believe it." Here he seems to be rather boldly and clearly setting out the two levels of reality, or the two natures of cultural fact with which he is dealing. When he says (2.123), "As to what the Egyptians say, let him believe it who finds it believable," he means to say that this oral tradition is what defines Egyptian culture; in that sense it is true. Whether the stories told are objectively true or are literally believable is something each man must decide for himself. Indeed Herodotus says elsewhere, when discussing a goddess (9.65), "I should imagine, if one must take a stand concerning things divine . . ." which is to say, mysteries are mysteries, what can we do?

In his introduction (1.1), he wishes to sustain the memory of great and fantastic deeds. Often enough it seems as if the remarkable, the fantastic are narrated for that reason alone. He dwells lovingly and long on fantastic customs and, where he finds it, fantastic natural history as well (3.98–109). He is particularly keen on the madness of Cambyses; the narration (2.27–37) is one of his best. And the long account of the self-mutilation of Zapyrus (3.154–60), so horrible, so extraordinary, is in the book because it, too, is so fantastic. Throughout the work one gains the impression that the Greeks are beyond or devoid of the exuberance, wildness, madness, if you will, of these cultures to their east. As has recently been remarked, the Greeks seem to have managed to impose their rational faculties so early and so long upon their mythic tradition that what we have left is a body of myth shorn of fantasy. Perhaps the same could have been said of the folk tales and oral popular history. Herodotus shows us from the East a living tradition of quasi-history filled with the bizarre and the perverse. More than cataloguing the fantastic, it seems to be part of his purpose to show the extraordinary range and diversity of human and other natural beings.

That is why he does not hesitate (4.30) to disgress upon an amazing fact that does not seem to be immediately pertinent to the narrative. Amazing things *per se* are valuable. Hence we find him (4.144) narrating a completely irrelevant remark of Megabazos' which is however *amazingly* or *remarkably* apt, hence marvelous. The instinct for such anecdotes is intensely humanistic. Small-town gossip, when it is not being malicious and self-destructive, is otherwise reinforcing; anthropocentric, it encourages the group's love of humanity, rehearsing man's outrageous and extraordinary deeds, setting out for examination what it is to be human and affirming the value of it. Notice that even when chronicling Persia's imperial expansion Herodotus can select the data for inclusion on the same basis ("Most of his [Cyrus'] minor conquests I shall say nothing about, but mention only those of his campaign which gave him the greatest trouble and are in themselves the most interesting" [1.177]). Much of Herodotus' narrative comes across like village folklore and traditional gossip. One senses at times that Herodotus is keeping the family album, as, for instance, when he refers (5.95) to Alcaeus' poem about losing his shield in battle, an instance totally irrelevant to any of the issues or the outcome of the fighting. But Herodotus is using a document handed down from that time.

One must take care, however, not to overlook other significances which lie in what may seem to be a chance and random anecdote. Often enough they are simply throwaway stories, such as Herodotus' description (9.83) of the fabulous human remains, giant-size, not conforming to normal biological expectations, which seems to be absolutely gratuitous, grist for his never-ceasing, ever-curious mill. But equally often we can find some that on the surface seem inconsequential, yet are very much to the point, such as for instance the following story (7.190). Herodotus has just mentioned a large and calamitous shipwreck, the loss of much life and treasure; he continues by saying: "This wreck turned out to be a good thing for a certain Magnesian, named Aeminocles, the son of Cretines . . . for he picked up on shore [various valuables are here listed]. This made him a very rich man, though in other respects he proved less fortunate; for, in spite of his luck with the treasure, he came to grief over some distressing affair connected with the murder of his son." These words function very much like the Homeric simile. The anecdote gives scale to the immensity of the gold and the calamity of the shipwreck—the man on the beach who grows rich from the spoils. Then the allusion to Aeminocles' later misfortunes underscores the ebb and flow of man's affairs, their chanciness, which of course returns us to what the shipwreck of treasure is.

Herodotus justifies a long discussion of the island of Samos when he says (3.60), "I have said more about Samos because of three great works [of engineering] there." Yet none of the anecdotal remarks he makes about Samos relates to these works. Certainly he is on solider ground when he says at the beginning of his long discourse on Egypt (2.35), "I shall say more about Egypt because there are more extraordinary things there and monuments beyond description are everywhere." What follows is a truly dazzling assemblage of lore, fact and speculation about an area Herodotus clearly studied well.

From the modern point of view Herodotus' rather impulsive willingness to halt the narrative for observations on still one more fantastic person, thing or event seems self-indulgent or naïve. Perhaps we fail to consider sufficiently to what extent the piece is affected by the oral mentality. We do not know how Herodotus composed (or few other of the ancients for that matter); there is evidence in the text of habits of mind peculiar to someone composing straight off, with minimal premeditation and revising; this is very much the oral manner. We cannot easily imagine doing so because we are in bondage to the printed word, to the principles of outlines, preliminary essays and revisions. But Herodotus did not have available to him any of the writing materials modern authors take for granted, materials that make revision especially a very simple matter—no good paper, erasers, scissors, glue, for instance. His papyrus was, for all practical purposes, continuous. How could he easily find places he wished to reread and revise, how was he to insert new material at its so-called proper place? Coupled with this are certain obvious evidences of his having composed without stopping to rewrite, to place matters in their proper sequence. For instance, in the marvelous story (3.68ff.) of Phaidime, who discovers that the man with whom she is sleeping is not the man he claims to be, Herodotus tells it true to the technique of recounting such stories even into our own time, that is, the denouement or punch line occurs the third time around. Phaidime's father tries three times through three messages to devise some way that she may identify the man with whom she is sleeping. In the third message he says, "Check to see if he has ears. If not, you will be sleeping with Smerdis the Magus, not Smerdis son of Cyrus." At which point quite anti-climactically and false to the whole rhythm of this sort of narration, Herodotus breaks in to say, "I should mention here that when Cyrus was on the throne he had the ears of Smerdis the Magus cut off for some sort of punishment." Here is information that any thoroughly literate person, used to the techniques of writing, would have put in somewhat earlier, whether at the initial writing or in the revision. Herodotus, whatever his method of composition, is not embarrassed to add the fact at the very moment when it occurs to him, when indeed it is relevant, if awkward to the raconteur. In the first book Herodotus says (1.6) that Croesus was the first foreigner to have dealings hostile or friendly with the Greeks, but only a few sections later he corrects himself to say that Gyges, earlier by seven generations, was the first. But he does not erase, cross out or cut out his previous misstatement. This is the oral mentality; it implies that Herodotus set to and composed his book without stopping from beginning to end.

In any case it is fair to assume that Herodotus wrote with an eye to reading his piece aloud, that is, he was writing down words intended to be spoken, so that all the normal practices of the oral performance would come naturally to his printed page. We can see the reverse of this today in the academic world where scholars consistently deliver from the platform lectures which they might as well hand around in printed form since they are meant to be taken into the mind through reading rather than through hearing.

Herodotus' style also reflects an oral mentality. Called *lexis eiromene,* speech strung together (like beads on a string), the style is paratactic in its construction. It is not unlike the appositional style found in the epics, where an idea is defined and redefined and expanded through the accretion of words, phrases and clauses in apposition. *Lexis eiromene* eschews subordination, the hierarchy or organization of ideas through syntaxis. The sentence does not withhold meaning until the last word is in place as does the periodic sentence.

This style, characteristic of early prose, shows the impress of the demands of an oral culture. This prose is meant to be heard rather than read. The complexities and economics of a syntactic style demand, in varying degrees, naturally, slow reading, whereas the open, extended style, with ideas juxtaposed but not conjoined or subordinated, can much more easily be assimilated through hearing. The celebrated opening lines of Herodotus' work are characteristic of the paratactic style. Here they are literally translated, which makes a somewhat incoherent effect however accurate.

Of Herodotus, the Halicarnassian, of his history this is the setting forth so that neither the things which have come about from men in the course of time shall be obscured nor the deeds both great and fantastic, on the one hand, among the Hellenes, on the other, among the barbarians, having been set forth, shall become lacking in fame, and various other things and on account of what reason they went to war with each other.

Of the Persians now then the reports say the Phoenicians themselves are responsible for the dispute. For these from the sea called Eruthes coming to this sea [Mediterranean] and dwelling in that land where even now they dwell, suddenly with great sailings set out, leading Egyptian and Assyrian goods to many another country they came and also especially to Argos.

Herodotus is also able to achieve some telling effects with periodic sentences where meaning awaits the last word. Consider the close of that moving anecdote about Adrastos, who unwittingly kills the son of Croesus, who had so generously befriended him after he had earlier inadvertently killed his brother. Notice the juxtaposition with the short sentence.

"So Croesus buried in a fitting way his own son. But Adrastos, the son of Gordias, the son of Midas, this man as we know, having become the murderer of his own brother, now a murderer to the man who had purified him, when the calm of men came about at the tomb site, coming to know himself to be of men whom he knew the most unfortunate killed upon the tomb himself" (1.45). (Herodotus underscores the solemnity and finality of this realization with one six-syllable ["coming to know himself"] and one seven-syllable ["most unfortunate"] word.)

Another sentence fittingly captures the change from exaltation to despair that Xerxes experiences shortly before crossing the Hellespont.

"When the time came that the entire Hellespont was by ships covered over, all the heights and the plains of Abydos filled with men, then Xerxes called himself blessed, but after that he burst into tears" (7.45).

Critics regard this style as the revelation of the kind of mind that strings together one element or episode to another, giving little thought to the architectonics of the whole. This is like the epic way of doing things. It is not hard to imagine that Herodotus may simply have begun from the beginning with his notes and whatever materials his researches had provided him, and continued stringing one piece to another until he had used them all.

For modern critics the work presents problems of unity,

or, at least, as with so many ancient works, raises the question of what constitutes the unity of the piece. Many will take refuge in the surmise that the work is unfinished. This assumption arises from the very anticlimactic ending to the whole work. Still, ancient literature is not noted for ultimate crescendi. We may compare the *Iliad*'s "and thus they buried horse-taming Hector," or the quiet ending of the *Symposium*.

Herodotus' *Histories* is divided into nine books. It commences with a description of Lydia and her last independent king, Croesus (1.1–94), then proceeds to a description of Lydia's captor, Cyrus, his kingdom and its people, the Persians (1.95–140). Thereafter Herodotus describes in an extremely diverse and extended narrative the imperial encroachments of the Persians under their kings, Cyrus, Cambyses and Darius (1.178–5.27). This allows for lengthy accounts of Egypt (almost the whole second book), Scythia (4.1–144), Thrace (5.1–27) and Libya (4.145–205). The focus then becomes more precise with the narration of the hostility between Persia and mainland Greece beginning with the revolt of Ionia (5.28–38; 5.97–6.42) and the invasion at Marathon (6.94–120) together with the background information on Athens and Sparta. In books 7, 8 and 9 Herodotus narrates in greater detail Xerxes' plans for the invasion of Greece and the invasion itself, containing the famous accounts of the battle of Thermopylae, fatal to the Greeks (7.196–239) and their brilliant victory at Salamis (8.40–112) and finally the decisive Greek land victory at Plataea (9.1–89) and sea victory at Mycale (9.90–106).

The contents seem lopsided. The focus of the first book is the elegant and self-contained narrative of Croesus, which, however, ends in the 92nd section of a total of 216 sections. The entire piece has to do with the reign and campaign of Cyrus, which leads us naturally to the second book, where we find a lengthy description of Egypt, which Cambyses, the son of Cyrus, planned to conquer. It seems that Herodotus has established three ways to continuity and coherence here. Perhaps unity is a term that must be confined to definitely literary texts where premeditation is obviously possible. The three motives with which Herodotus works are: the Croesus story, especially the philosophy it reveals, which comes back after the manner of epic rehearsal and reiteration in the narrative of Xerxes' exploits in the latter part of the work;

the relative chronology achieved through organizing events in the successive reigns of Persian kings—the discussion of Egypt follows that of the Massagytae and Babylonia just as Cambyses succeeds his father; and the geographic and chronological facts of Persian world domination ("The course of my story now leads me to Cyrus: who was this man who destroyed the empire of Croesus and how did the Persians win their predominant position in Asia?" [1.95]).

Still one must admit that the nature of the narrative of Croesus and of Xerxes' invasion of Greece is markedly different from the material in the central portion of the work. The dramatic narrative, by turns heroic and philosophic, that characterizes book 1.1–92 and books 7–9 is absent from the rest; instead Herodotus presents an excellent and far-ranging ethnographic review of a number of people, the whole or even its parts somewhat vitiated by the minimal organization the *lexis eiromene* demands, allows or encourages. The middle section just falls short of being a miscellany.

Point of view, some previously thought-out attitude, is, perhaps, not quite an informing principle in his anthropological miscellany, but rather his material is obedient to his curiosity. We might call this the research of culture except that Herodotus' curiosity seems instinctual, and this central portion of the work less deliberate. Herodotus seems to have understood, though not to have phrased, the idea of culture as being inherent in the natural order. He can speak of the flow of the Nile, certainly a complex kind of natural hydraulics, and he can detail the burial customs, the marriage customs of a people in a way that makes them an arrangement analogous to things in nature. Culture is the human response to being just as the flow of the Nile is water's response to being. At one point in his extraordinarily rich offering of the myriad exotic details of social behavior he pauses to quote and agree with a line from the poet Pindar, to the effect that custom is master of us all. This notion sums up what he is in fact showing us, to wit, in the midst of the remarkable diversity of human responses there persists organized, systematic human behavior, which is culture.

Herodotus' interest in culture or cultures would be natural to him, born as he was in a community in the land of the Persians, a community originally Doric-speaking which the associated itself with the Ionic culture in Asia Minor. Further more he traveled in Egypt, the Levant and southern Italy. and he spent time in Athens. From his earliest years he must have had a naturally cosmopolitan outlook far different from the narrow Athenians, who only began to discover cultural relativism in the fifth century.

Athenian mercantile adventures overseas in the sixth century began to awake the people a little bit to the fact that alternative ways of life, equally authentic, existed throughout the Mediterranean. Previously small-town parochialism coupled with the traditional aristocratic belief in inborn virtue had led the mainland Greeks to overemphasize, as all unsophisticated people do, human nature (*physis*). One can see clearly enough in the Homeric poems how Odysseus is a maverick among the other heroes because he can think of and often act out alternative forms of behavior. Diomedes and Achilles, particularly, are examples of the aristocrat whose self-confidence and pride derive from the simplistic notion that right behavior is inevitable (unless one's wits are betrayed by external supernatural forces). So Achilles can disapprove of Odysseus (*Iliad* 9.312ff.), saying "hateful to me . . . is the man who can say one thing and hide another in his heart."

But as acquaintance with the broader world showed the Greeks how other men did things otherwise, there came the notion that custom (*nomos*) was somehow an alternative to human nature. Much of the intellectual energy in Athens in the fifth century went into weighing the claims and value of the one or the other of these two forces in human life. Yet Herodotus instead of debating the question shows by his truly exhaustive survey of the societies then known that culture (*nomos*) is a manifestation of human nature (*physis*) by the very fact of its being natural. He might have left it at that, but instead of reposing in a neutral cultural relativism he goes on toward the close of the work to imply that the Greek way of life is ultimately superior, certainly in the sense of being more successful—witness the Persian defeats at Marathon, Salamis, Plataea and Mycale. Here began the tradition of the East and the West and the abyss between them.

The implication of Greek cultural superiority comes through a number of anecdotes interspersed throughout the narration of the Persian invasion of Greece. These combine with another concern in the earlier ethnographic, anthropological books. Herodotus' penchant for exhibiting some of the more bizarre and perverse doings of mankind is marked throughout this part. It is more than just quirk or whim. Such stories combine eventually to give a sense of the excessive and fabulous to the whole of the Eastern world Herodotus has been describing. No such terrible and wonderful anecdotes attach to the Greeks, so that the contrast grows. Finally during the course of describing the Persian invasion of Greece, one story after another reinforces this, for instance, how the Persians bury people alive (7.114), how Xerxes commanded Pythius' son to be split in two (7.39), how a man was forced to castrate his own sons (8.106) and how a father gouged out his six sons' eyes for disobedience (8.116). In this later part these anecdotes commence to be answered with some of the Greek customs. There is the occasion when the Persians see the Spartans stripped for exercise and combing their hair which inspires Demaratus to discourse on Spartan virtue (7.208f.), there is Xerxes' wonder at hearing that Greeks compete for nonmaterial rewards (8.26) and there are speeches in praise of Greek liberty (8.142ff.) and Greek poverty (9.80ff.). The contrast that emerges in these two sets of anecdotes is finally verbalized by a king of Sparta, who has been encouraged to insult the corpse of the Persian Mardonius as revenge. "No, no," he says (9.79), "that is much more in the style of the barbarian way of doing things than the Greek, and even them we fault for doing such things."

When Xerxes appears in the story he seems to embody all that excessive and mad energy that characterizes the anecdotes of the middle books. His challenge to the Hellespont, his violent rages and cruel punishments, his sudden tears, his colossal army, his pompous progress through to Greece are manifestations of that way of life. Herodotus returns to Xerxes at the very close of his work when he recalls Cyrus' advice to the Persians to stay lean, hard and poor, for Xerxes in luxury and triumph and then in defeat stands as proof. Athens and Sparta victorious in their simplicity and poverty are also proof. One wonders whether Herodotus saw here an oblique warning to Athenian imperialistic pretensions of the second half of the fifth century. Nothing is more curious than the way Athens in those later years played out a drama for which Herodotus could have written the scenario.

The warning, if indeed it is there and intended, comes itself from Herodotus' conviction of the chanciness of human affairs, expressed at the very beginning of the work (1.7): "I'll go along telling the story of great cities and small. Most of those great were once small and vice versa—it makes no difference whether the city I write about is great or small, since in this world nobody remains prosperous very long." The elucidation of this sentiment is perhaps the most important feature of the central books aside from the sheer massing of facts. The reiteration of examples of this truth gives this part its coherence. In turn it is only here that we have Herodotus in his own words framing the philosophical justification of events which elsewhere so frequently appears in the mouths of his history's major figures. At 4.205 he describes the cruel death of a cruel woman and proceeds to say: "Thus this daughter of Battus by the nature and severity of her punishment of the Barcaeans showed how true it is that all excess in such things makes gods vehemently jealous and begrudging to men."

Nonetheless the last three books and the Croesus episode in the first book show a style and a control lacking elsewhere. They are highly polished narration; they are philosophical and dramatic just as the other parts are factual and expository. The difference is probably due to the fact that Xerxes and Croesus suffered tremendous reversals in their lives. This excites dramatic narration, something that an assemblage of facts, even when presided over by a Cambyses, does not do. The ethnographic parts lack a hero. It is questionable whether Herodotus or any other author at this time could manage the organization and the necessary overview of his material without using a hero. This is the legacy of epic. Therefore the very materials as they were set forth by Herodotus motivated very different techniques of exposition.

On the other hand, one can easily imagine the young Herodotus, endowed with strong curiosity, poking immediately into the diversity of customs which surrounded him, and finding that kind of investigation congenial to him, practiced it until, a body of material having been assembled, he began to question its ultimate significance, and having been himself reared with the heroic epic poems as his aesthetic and philosophic staple, looked to struggle, contest, war and ambition as the touchstones whereby human action could be judged, and found his own answer in the tradition of the

Persian Wars, which event brought together in collision two peoples, whose mores he had known since youth to be in opposition, thereby providing for his researched material a frame of action, action to which quite naturally philosophic speculation would attach after the manner of epic's Nestor or early tragic choruses. (The preceding sentence is an example of *lexis eiromene* in our own tongue.)

Herodotus clearly intends to do more than give facts. In the last part of his introductory statement he says, "My aim is . . . to show what kind of cause it was that made these people war with one another." Immediately thereafter Herodotus begins a great display of claims and counterclaims of the parties to this dispute. The stories of Io, Medea and Helen are stripped bare of all charm; instead of the abstracted and idealized mythic loves of Zeus, Jason and Paris, the three women are analyzed as being abducted by anonymous sailors or other adventurers or otherwise sluts who went off of their own accord. Although Herodotus makes nothing of this material, except to dismiss it and make a fresh start (". . . this is what the Greeks say; I for my own part shall go on with what I know to be so . . ." [1.5]), he has in fact shown his audience with those busy, pointless paragraphs that he well knows the principles of rationalizing the myths and legends of his tradition. Thucydides takes over this technique of introduction, advertising his acumen and talents before he gets to the business of his narration.

Historical speculation grows out of epic. A part of this is setting the legends straight, making them conform to temporal realities, to physical realities and to psychological realities. Pindar among the poets does the same, insisting upon variant, "cleaner" versions of myth. In his First Olympic Ode for instance, as we have seen (p. 126ff.), he rejects the traditional story of Demeter's absent-minded eating of Pelops' shoulder, because gods are not cannibals. Hekataios had begun the rationalizing of myth. Hellanikos, the contemporary of Herodotus, also rationalized the myths, an example of which is his statement (fragment 28) that the fight between Achilles and the river god in the *Iliad* really describes a spring flood in the river fed by melting mountain snow. The banal rationalization of myth is almost a constant until the time when the Stoics began to allegorize. Herodotus is more skillful at it. A cleft in the mountain, he says (7.129), is not, as the natives claim, Poseidon's handiwork, but was caused by an earthquake. How could Hercules, he asks (2.45), being no more than a man, as they say, have the natural endowments to kill tens of thousands of people? Sometimes Herodotus wants it both ways. He gives the fantastic version of the miraculous founding of the oracles of Ammon in Libya and Dodona in Greece. Then he offers a rationalized account (2.54ff.), which he says was given him by the keepers of the temple at Egyptian Thebes. But the account bears all the traces of the Greek habit of rationalizing; it is not likely to be an Egyptian priestly idea. Perhaps Herodotus made it up, trying in this way to preserve the sanctity of the oracles while demolishing the miracle.

He also analyzes and clarifies more contemporary events. For instance, he gives and then debunks the evidently famous story of Xerxes' nearly disastrous sailing back to Persia across the Aegean (8.119). Herodotus is very severe here, in contrast to what appears to be elsewhere a tolerance or nonchalance toward untrue or unlikely stories. This story, however, since it is illustrative of nothing, can be demolished, whereas most of the stories whose truth Herodotus doubts nonetheless reveal the "truth" of folklore, which is to say, of culture.

For a great many critics Herodotus' singular achievement has been to order narrative in terms of the principles of cause and effect, as he promises to do in his introductory statement and in the subsequent *tour de force* of rationalized myth. Indeed he then goes on to bring in contemporary causes, naming Croesus and Gyges as responsible for the conflict. One cause after another is presented. Herodotus is looking for first causes, that is, he is taking the overview of the entire conflict between East and West. This is far removed from the static action of epic (". . . and the will of Zeus was accomplished" [*Iliad* 1.8]). Herodotean cause and effect, therefore, seems to be the true sign of the beginnings of history.

But let us examine Herodotean causes more thoroughly. His history presents the story of Persian imperial expansion; yet we are very much kept in the dark as to the reasons for this expansion. Herodotus gives us only the mechanics of this imperial rise, although that in itself is a triumphant accomplishment of fact. Still, like every Greek, he must ask himself why, or if not why exactly, he must try to generalize the events. This again must be the influence of epic narrative, which is human experience distilled into the typical, the general and the abstract. Tragedy, since skeletal myth was its substance, assimilated this life view very easily from epic; proto-history, however, had for its natural subject a mass of detail, far more resistant to this treatment. Herodotus seems to be asking and answering the "why," so far as it goes, in his initial paragraphs in the résumé of traditional accounts from saga and myth, the stories of Io, Medea and Helen. These do not satisfy; he turns to narrate thereafter *how* Gyges, then Croesus, Cyrus and the others proceeded to subjugate peoples and lands. But he does not again address himself in so many words to the "why."

Nonetheless a great part of the histories is given over to a kind of explanation of the events, to answering the "why." To do this Herodotus uses his most overtly storytelling technique when describing the imperialistic designs of Croesus and Xerxes. One may examine these narratives for their philosophy; but they are interesting also in what they reveal of the mental habit of assigning cause and effect.

A cursory reading of the work would perhaps lead one to say that Herodotus has come up with a philosophy no more complicated than "pride goeth before a fall" and "God punishes sinners." Before proceeding to assay the subtler aspects of Herodotean thinking, we can pause to acknowledge that these two maxims are in fact about as basic and serious as any that attempt to characterize human experience. They have indeed withstood the test of human experience over several millennia—although it is not impossible that man has ordered his experience to conform to the expectations these maxims excite. In human beings the lust for life, the joy of life, the exhilaration of being a sentient human being—states of being that are expanded, euphoric, as *pride* is—precede their deaths, the absolute reduction of *fall*. Furthermore people conceive of evil as being self-destructive or socially destructive and that is painful, and that nexus between pain and evil is located in the expression "God punishes." Simplistic, perhaps, but most thinking is and ought to be so.

Interesting extensions of these maxims are contained in two very memorable vignettes of unfortunate men, one Adrastos, the description of whose sorry suicide we previously quoted (p. 200), and the other Polycrates, the tyrant of Samos (3.39–43). In microcosm they reveal ideas about evil and suffering in man's life that permeate the entire work. These are emphatic passages; although smallish, these episodes are narrated with such skill, are so complete in themselves, set within the larger narrative, that they remain with the reader of Herodotus as do certain other extremely moving, even smaller scenes—Croesus' son regaining his voice, Harpagos gathering the pieces of his children, Xerxes crying at Abydos and so on. Certainly the great speeches of Solon and Artabanus are memorable and offer the reader the intellectual or philosophical context for the narrative of action, but these two small episodes manage better to convey the tone of the action.

Polycrates, tyrant of Samos, was blessed with such prosperity and happiness, such power and successful dealings, that his good friend, Amasis, king of Egypt, grew uneasy. He wrote to Polycrates to encourage him to do something to break the continued run of good luck. Throw away, he counseled, whatever you value most. Polycrates approved the idea, considered, then chose a great emerald signet ring, which he took aboard ship and when far from shore flung into the sea.

A few days later a Samian fisherman who had caught an extraordinarily large fish decided to present it to Polycrates. Polycrates handed the fish to his servants to prepare, and when they cut it open they found his signet ring, which the fish had swallowed. Polycrates, says Herodotus, saw that something divine and supernatural had come into his life, and he wrote what had happened to Amasis, who immediately broke off his diplomatic pact and friendship with Polycrates so that when some calamity fell upon Polycrates, he might avoid the distress he would have otherwise felt, had Polycrates remained his friend.

And sure enough Polycrates was subsequently lured to his death and his corpse was hung on a cross (3.120–25).

We cannot say that Polycrates brought upon himself that ugly, sorry end. Certainly we cannot call it punishment since he had done no wrong. In fact he had quite earnestly tried to avoid anything that might lead to misfortune. There is no moral cause and effect in this story. Was Polycrates' prosperity the cause of his downfall? Herodotus does really nothing more than to suggest that these things are concomitants. Had he been poor, we say, this would not have happened. The statement as a condition contrary to fact derives from a world view dependent upon cause and effect. Remove the cause and you will get a different effect. But we cannot here remove the so-called cause, namely Polycrates' prosperity. He himself tries, as Herodotus describes, but it returns to him because it is part of him. He was destined to fall, we say. But Herodotus does not make that claim at all, he merely notes that with the return of the ring, Polycrates senses something other than normal or governable at work. Herodotus makes very little of destiny here.

Polycrates is one of those people, like Paris who was born more handsome than normal, who cannot shed their endowments. For Polycrates it is prosperity—and his subsequent death. "Subsequent" is a temporal description and wrong; the doom was inherent in the prosperity, and the prosperity, as the story of the ring and the fish shows, was not alienable, not a thing apart from Polycrates. In turn, the prosperity was a symptom of the frailty of Polycrates' life.

The story of Adrastos (1.34–45) is more complex since others, Croesus and Croesus' son, Atys, share in the misfortune. Adrastos had inadvertently killed his brother and so became a taboo figure. No matter that he was not guilty, again we are away from cause and effect, he was a fratricide and therefore taboo. When he came to Croesus' court, that noble and generous king purified him by the necessary ritual designed to remove the taboo, and kept Adrastos by him at the court. Now Croesus had once dreamt that his son, Atys, would be killed by a blow from an iron weapon, so he removed all metal weapons from the men's quarters. After some time and when the young man was newly married, a petition came to Croesus for help against a great boar marauding in the neighboring farm lands. Croesus was at first willing to send out a body of men without his son in command, but then the youth proceeded to argue with him, saying that a boar had no metal weapons, but tusks. After a lengthy argument Croesus relented ("You have vanquished me, my son, with your argument, and since I am defeated . . ."—the irony in this resignation, maybe even half-comprehended by Croesus, is altogether tragic). As a precaution he summoned Adrastos and asked him to go as a kind of protector of Atys. Adrastos was unwilling, saying that it was not right for someone so unfortunate as he was to consort with one who was by contrast blessed with youth, marriage and royal station. But Croesus works on him as Atys had worked on Croesus; Adrastos relents, is persuaded to go in return for the great kindness Croesus has done him. Irony, irony, irony.

In the fight against the boar Adrastos hurls his spear, misses the animal and—naturally—kills Croesus' son. "Naturally" is our most important reaction to the events presented in the narrative. What happens is inevitable, not because, as Herodotus announces, this is god's punishment for Croesus' pretensions to be considered the happiest man alive. Of course, once introduced, that does become the formal cause, at least for the effect worked upon Croesus, his newly found sorrow, which makes him mourn Atys for two years. Atys, we might say, is little more than god's victim, the necessary agent to produce a reversal for Croesus. Yet the story contains one ingredient that makes Atys' doom less something sent by god and more something inherent in himself, that is, his recent marriage. Folk tale often describes a young bridegroom who is subsequently killed. There is a close and natural relationship in stories between new love or new marriage and death. Such a detail in this context (think also of his insisting to go, the sense of doom in it) makes Atys a candidate for death. There is no cause and effect, there are only concomitant states or actions.

In this story however, it is Adrastos who is most important. He is very fully described upon his first appearance and when he kills himself upon Atys' grave, Herodotus delivers the full and sonorous sentence quoted earlier (p. 195). Adrastos kills two men inadvertently, unwittingly. Causes are irrelevant, he is taboo. When he is purified, it lifts the taboo formally, but Adrastos continues to see himself as a creature apart, perhaps a fundamental murderer. So it is that when he accompanies young Atys, all unwilling, as he was indeed when he slew his brother, his fatal talent for murdering those close to him quite naturally comes out.

Adrastos is like Polycrates; they are doomed, perhaps one can say. But there is no way to find a cause for this. It is in the nature of things; we and they are born to it. Doom itself is not a cause.

In the beginning when Herodotus talks of the reversal in prosperity of the cities in the Mediterranean world he makes it an observable fact that is in the nature of things. His narrative is there to show how these reversals occur. When briefly he explains *why* they occur, then he is assigning causes. But one never has the feeling that the cause is absolute; indeed it is almost random. For instance, Herodotus says, "since things were bound to go wrong for him" (4.79) or "the Pythia [the prophetess at Delphi] said that Miltiades was bound to end up unhappily" (6.135) or, as he reports from a message, "there never was and never will be a man who was not born with a good chance of misfortune—the greater the man, the greater the misfortune . . . Xerxes is human and is sure therefore to be disappointed in what he hoped for" (7.203). Rather than real causes Herodotus speaks to the dicey nature of human existence.

Destiny and free will are and always will be troublesome concepts since most people cannot live believing that all things are destined, and yet as they find themselves wherever they happen to have arrived in life it is easy to imagine that destiny propelled them there, if for no other reason than that one cannot forever endure to bear all the responsibility for one's failings and failures. Free will is the view from which we advance to the doing of anything, destiny is how we see it in hindsight. But just as women after bearing a child are said to forget the awful pain of childbirth so that they can go on to having more children, so we forget destiny and seemingly freely and willingly advance on subsequent action. Epic poets who must look at the whole with hindsight—after all, they are narrating what came before—and yet present their heroes as in some sense free to act, steer clear from any absolute stand. But they are poets and not philosophers. A prose writer such as Herodotus who accepts so much of the epic scheme of narrative handles the conflict between free will and destiny rather lightly. Despite the fact that he alludes often to destiny, he shows people acting freely. Or is he determinist like twentieth-century Marxist and Freudian historians? Adrastos and Polycrates, for instance, act freely, yet their actions create a pattern that Herodotus makes us feel was there all the time.

When Croesus ultimately finds himself upon the pyre and all is lost, we can conclude with Herodotus that the Lydian king's downfall came about: because the family of Gyges was doomed since first he slew Candaules; because an oracle prophesied disaster if he, Croesus, attempted to take on Persia (only Croesus misunderstood the oracle); and because Croesus was guilty of excessive pride (*hybris*) and brought down upon his head divine punishment (*nemesis*). Herodotus presents all these explanations as true, for they represent three ways of looking at the same series of action. The first is the product of hindsight when we can see destiny's hand; the second is free will, based upon miscalculation, although with that special and tantalizing element always attendant upon Delphic oracular utterance that we must somehow inevitably miscalculate if we are not free to escape the prophesied future. Yet the miscalculation is free; we could as well have understood, lent our necks to the blade of fate and have been done with it. The third, phrased here as it is generally, seems like a Christian way of stating the situation with its "guilty" and its "punishment," that is, a free act of disobedience to divine laws. Yet those words probably conjure up a facile analogy that is not at all there.

Pride is very important to Herodotus; one of his best-contrived personages, the Greek sage Solon, is made to talk at length of pride (1.32f.). Herodotus has defined a field of action where more than normal prosperity, that is, the absence of some periods of misfortune, has a special psychic aura to it. The context for this unremitting prosperity must be agrarian in origin. Farmers who every day face the prospect of out-of-season frost, flash floods, hail, drought, the sudden ravages of invading insects and every other calamity we can imagine understand how frail our survival is, and because they are used to the rhythm of some natural catastrophes interspersed in the growing process, their absence is a cause of real concern. If the rhythm gets distorted, if too many days of perfect weather succeed each other, must it not follow that the missing random bad days will come some time all at once, bringing an unparalleled devastation of fields? Farmers are always waiting for this. Farmers generally are paranoid, ancient farmers—who endowed natural forces with personalities, made them divinities—especially so.

Unremitting prosperity is therefore dangerous in the thinking Herodotus represents. There is, however, another side to it, namely that because it is so rare, and at the same time so liberating, it induces psychological reactions like spiritual and moral giddiness, where one is vulnerable to all kinds of instincts and desires. This also is not a relationship of cause and effect. The prosperity is like getting drunk, it makes you feel good, it makes you feel secure, more like your real self, able to act out the true you in otherwise generally repressed dimensions; it also makes you giddy. Your success makes you successful. The Greeks talked of prosperity (*olbia*) or satiety (*koros*) when one's person was expanded, his being was so high, that the natural limits of his personality and intuition were not there; this is his pride (*hybris*). At this point the intoxication is fatal, every stimulus is a seduction (*ate*). Underneath it all we must remember that prosperity is frightening. The flushed prosperous, prideful man thinks to commit himself on the inflated terms of his successful self, he misjudges (*hamartia*), misses the mark as the Greek word implies, and is engulfed in catastrophe (*nemesis*).

Croesus, as Herodotus portrays him, is an obvious paradigm of this course of action: wealthy beyond calculation, he thinks himself the happiest man alive. He proceeds to act out his greatness and prosperity by invading Persia; the intoxication, seduction and miscalculation are all there in his sending for and then misunderstanding the oracles. So he finds himself at last a prisoner of war upon a pyre. Herodotus shows that all these things are inherent in the prosperous man; prosperity is not the cause therefore, but only the outward symptom of a doomed man. Prosperity, euphoria, miscalculation are all aspects of the same state, as in a less obvious way is catastrophe or divine retribution or however we wish to style *nemesis*. The entire play of this moral or psychic situation bears a resemblance to clinical descriptions of manic-depressive attitudes or behavior, the euphoria, the overstriving, the upswing as prelude to the swing down and depression. In our own time manic-depressive states are the most commonly observed departure from the so-called normal. If its frequency were also true in ancient Greece, it would help to explain why the Greeks concentrated so on the nexus of prosperity, overweening pride, seduction, miscalculation, error and downfall.

Herodotus seems to want the Croesus story to be a general explanation of human action. It is placed as an introduction to his history after the fashion of the first book of the *Iliad* and to a lesser extent the *Odyssey,* where many of the issues upon which the action turns, many of the motives which define and illuminate the action, are laid out. The figure of Solon is very important to Herodotus because he is the means to presenting an abstracted explanation of events. So important is Solon, this legendary wise man, that either Herodotus willfully falsifies, knowing very well that Croesus and Solon did not grow to adulthood at the same time and therefore could not have met as he shows them, or the mechanics of Greek folklore had already seen how very natural such an encounter would be. They are indeed the perfect complements. Solon is a kind of Euripidean Sophist, or a tragic choral counterpoint, objectifying Croesus' actions. The convention of presenting serious ideas in dialogue, already well established in epic, is taken up by Herodotus. He is self-conscious about this, unsure; elsewhere he feels he has to apologize when he introduces three Persian speakers who most improbably discourse on political theory ("words which to some Greeks seem incredible, yet they were said [3.80]").

Solon talks not only of the chanciness of life, but also of god's envy of man's prosperity. Herodotus seems to be invoking a cosmic principle, rather than referring to an anthropomorphized, jealous god. "The jealousy or the begrudging of the divine [thing]" is how we may translate *phthonos tou theiou*. Notice that Herodotus does not name one of the anthropomorphized deities of myth, nor does he say the jealousy of *the* god. "The divine thing" is more like the principle of divinity.

Phthonos tou theiou perhaps means the cosmic sense of proportion. A man's extraordinary actions are begrudged, not because he apes god, nothing so anthropomorphized. It has rather to do with taking on too much. There is some kind of limit; but such is the variety of life that who truly can know the limit except when he has gone too far? The idea of *phthonos* is born out of folk wisdom, partly in the idea that we can all spot losers, born losers (true at least in cultures with strong contest systems). To the extent that our instincts in this are often guided by the jealousy and fear we experience upon contemplating someone doing something beyond the limits that we, for the equilibrium of our psyche, have deemed prudent for our own behavior, we are indeed ourselves here on earth the *phthonos tou theiou*.

The narrative of Xerxes' invasion of Greece has numerous similarities with the story of Croesus. The similarity suggests that here we can find Herodotus' conception of the meaning of past events, but, more important, the similarity seems to show, however dimly, the way at which Herodotus arrives at meaning in narration. It is one thing to state a fact or say a truth, it is another to say it in such a way as to make its meaning clear for the auditor or reader. There are, however, many possibilities of interpretation in various elements of this part of the narration.

Xerxes' two advisers are analogous to the Delphic oracle and to Solon in Croesus' life. The adviser is a common feature of folk tale, common in Greek literature as well, as Poulydamas, for example, in the *Iliad*, who several times over advises Hector, each time rightly as it turns out, including the last and fatal time when Hector spurns the advice. Similarly Croesus rejects Solon's advice, and he misunderstands the oracle, which is rejection of a sort. Whereas Solon offers wisdom, the "truths" of the situation, the oracle is an instigator or motivator to action. It is the nature of the answers the Pythia gives to Croesus' questions. By foretelling the future the oracle brings on the future, and so brings Croesus to the future; in that way it motivates. Solon's wisdom is static, true for all times. Croesus' appetite for gain is whetted by the oracle, so we may say he is seduced by the oracle, although the seduction derives altogether from misunderstanding the oracle. This experience is part of the general psychology of euphoria and exaltation of which prosperity is the material outward sign. Croesus' enlarged or heightened sense of things makes him particularly vulnerable to or prone to that kind of misinterpretation. For instance, the oracle Herodotus paraphrases (1.53.3, the first line of which Aristotle quotes directly [*Rhetorica* 3.5]), if Croesus attacks the Persians a great empire will be destroyed, is immediately and exuberantly misunderstood in the context of the emotions we have described.

The oracle comes ultimately from Apollo, so the ambiguity, the seduction, is god's doing. Polycrates, we remember, when the ring came back, realized that something divine was entering the human scheme of things. There *is*, Herodotus points out from time to time, some intrusion into human affairs from the divine plane. The oracle and the miraculously returned ring seem not to be the same kind of divine intrusion. Compared to the ring the oracle is static; when we say that the oracle is seductive it is to see it from Croesus' vantage point. It, like the ring, poses limits and Croesus misunderstands the limits.

Of Xerxes' two advisers Artabanus offers common-sense advice and Mardonios inflammatory, seductive advice. Mardonios, says Herodotus (7.5), was the kind of man who was ever searching after new things. Ambitious and seeking, we would say, and perhaps we could call him a projection of the manic mood. He exalts Xerxes, who is already on the edge of excessive self-exaltation ("I have been pondering how to avoid falling short of the honor achieved by the previous kings . . . I've found a way to get equal honor for myself" [7.8]), when he says (7.9), "O Lord, not only are you best of all the Persians presently alive, but of all those who are yet to be born, and everything you say is true and excellent . . ." It is Mardonios who urges the fatal invasion of Greece. Artabanus, on the other side, urges caution. It is he who repeats the philosophy of Solon, the dangers of excess which bring on the *phthonos tou theiou* ("God is always ready to cut down to size all things which grow too big" [7.10]), the chancy nature of human affairs. The distinction between Mardonios and Artabanus seems at first to possess that characteristic symmetry in antithesis, altogether Greek, true to the law courts, true to tragedy (as Artabanus says [7.16.1], "the one point of view encouraging your arrogance [*hybris*], the other diminishing it"). What we now expect is that Xerxes will decide to invade Greece, will accept Mardonios' advice, a freewill act, although tragically, ironically already understood or accepted as being inherent in the king's prideful and glorious position.

Instead Xerxes chooses Artabanus' moderation and caution, only to find it denied him by a succession of nighttime demon dreams. Here Xerxes is more like Polycrates the victim than Croesus the actor. But Herodotus is playing with so many possibilities in his narrative that there is no simple explanation of events. When he described Croesus' fall, Herodotus outlined after the fashion of one, two, three the presumed causes, whereas here he formulates a succession of ways of viewing the events.

What are these dreams? Artabanus has (7.16.2) a very sophistic, up-to-date psychological explanation. "They are not, my child, of divine origin . . . most of all the dream apparitions which are wont to come out are the things about which one is thinking during the day . . ." But shortly thereafter he himself is assaulted by a violent apparition who says to him (7.17), "Are you the one who is trying to keep Xerxes from the invasion . . . ? You cannot stop either now or later that *which must be.*"

To this point in his narrative Herodotus has shown us a prideful, successful king, ripe for the experiences that confronted Croesus, then quite the other coin, a prudent man who would listen to reason, and further a man beset by dreams of obvious wish fulfillment, dreams of glory and grandeur, and finally a man who like Polycrates is the victim of his situation. Thereafter Herodotus describes with great skill the steady increase in power, pretension and expectation until we more than anything else see Xerxes as a latter-day Croesus. His exaltation and pride reach a marvelous peak as he punishes the Hellespont (an act which Herodotus points out [7.35] as being both foolish and not Greek) for allowing the storm upon its water to destroy his bridge. This strong and detailed scene is set square between Xerxes' reception by Pythius, who offers him in abject Persian devotion all of his fabled wealth, and Xerxes' arrogant and wrathful decision to cut one of Pythius' sons in two in anger at his host, who had asked that his sons be excused from the army. The narrative here is frenetic and extravagant. It leads to the moment on the hill at Abydos overlooking the plain and the water when Xerxes bursts into tears. Xerxes' collapse is again true to the manic-depressive cycle, therefore "true to life," even as the observation Xerxes makes after his tears is so true to the Greek view of things. Asked why he cried, Xerxes replies (7.46), "It came to me as I was contemplating a great feeling of pity at how short all of man's life is, how none of these men present here will be around a hundred years from now."

The subsequent narration of the encounter between the Greeks and the Persians in battle is informed by these scenes to the very end of the work. The Greek victories over the Persians were very much unsuspected, they were amazing. Herodotus, however, does not really pose the wars as a Greek success story. Certainly he offers occasional observations on Greek mores that imply their superiority, but the story of the Persian Wars is far more Xerxes' failure than Greek triumph. This, too, is characteristic of the prevailing Athenian view of life, the tragic sense of life that dominated most of fifth-century Athens. An explanation can be found in defeat but not in victory.

For Herodotus the workings of history are the re-enactment, the reiteration, the rehearsal of action. The facts of Xerxes' invasion of Greece are given validity or meaning when they are given a pattern or shape as they re-create the Croesus story. It is a mind habituated to the mythic mode

that will realize in *fact* a story structure, a mind that instinctively knows that nothing can be said for the first time
or for the last time, a mind that fights the particularity and
uniqueness of every historical event. History for Herodotus
is the emergence of a pattern or shape or outline. The
anecdotes give the sense of story motifs imposing themselves on some more or less factual material. On a grander
scale Herodotus has given us the story of a king's fall in
brief (Croesus) and then imposed that narrative on the mas-
sively detailed and seemingly uncontrollable adventures of
the Persians in their invasion of Greece. And through the
storyteller's art he has made sense.

THUCYDIDES

In contrast to Herodotus Thucydides at the very first (1.22)
emphatically announces the absence of the storyteller's art in
his own narrative. However, he is not writing a simple exposition of surface fact for he immediately impresses his
reader by the dense and complex nature of his prose. Although he must have been two or three decades younger
than Herodotus, he was his contemporary. Yet the writing he
has left us is far away in mood, tone and purpose. One
wants to emphasize the highly idiosyncratic quality of his
prose, although we do not have a large number of examples
of other prose as a basis for the observation. What we do
have, however, shows a general prose style that is considerably more lucid. Thucydides is hard to read (although
translations that are instinctively cosmetic cannot or will
not easily indicate this). If we were to establish some artificial
continuum of prose style from Herodotus to Plato and the
other fourth-century prose writers, in order to show a general style, Thucydides' writing would appear peculiar and
personal. Yet, before the time of general publication, before
the time when there existed a repertoire of printed texts of
prose, the potential for idiosyncrasy was far greater. Therefore it may not be highly significant, this strange diction.

Some critics like to see the Thucydidean style as a feature
of the evolution toward the developed prose style of the
fourth century and beyond. On the contrary, what Thucydides was trying to do was very special and did not really
have lasting influence, at least among the Greeks. In the
Roman era, however, for reasons peculiar to their need to

assimilate Greek culture, we find a historian such as Sallust self-consciously imitating the manner of Thucydides.

In the latter part of the fifth century prose gradually became a developed art as poetry had been since the time of Homer. The influence of the Sophists and the demands of the law courts helped to formulate recognized prose techniques. They in turn much influenced the dialogue of tragedy. Polarity is always a feature of tragic drama; in the later fifth century analytical argumentation becomes the manner in which this is expressed, very much in the fashion of a legal brief (Euripides' *Medea,* the debate particularly between Medea and Jason, is an especially good example of this). To what extent was Thucydides a part of this intellectual development? He was in exile from Athens from 424 for almost twenty years. Whether or not he did his writing during this time or thereafter—a subject much disputed—he was nonetheless isolated during a long period when his intellectual habits, his reflections on contemporary events would be developing without the stimulus or restriction of the Athenian intellectual climate. Idiosyncrasy flourishes in isolation. Likewise the pervasive verbal, quasi-intellectual experience during the first part of Thucydides' life must have been contained in tragic drama. During his exile the habits of mind tragedy imposed upon him in his youth may well have grown strong in the absence of alternatives. We can expect its influence in his work.

Thucydides composed toward the close of a centuries-long period in which oral communication was predominant. Even that which was written was meant to be read aloud. It is arguable that the extremely complex, dense, often barely manageable style that Thucydides contrives at his most serious moments represents the first really liberated *writer.* That is, Thucydides chose to write to be *read,* natural enough for a man alone in exile who would not have an audience available to read to. Simplicity of one sort or another is the hallmark of Greek verbal constructs in this oral period, whether achieved through formulae, clichés, reiteration, block imagery or whatever. Perhaps the most experimental feature of Thucydides' prose is that he felt free to compose the kind of convoluted, structured, tiered sentences and ideas that had to be worked out through *close reading.*

The celebrated chapter (1.22) where Thucydides discusses his method shows a high degree of self-consciousness. Self-consciousness over matters of diction, style and meaning in prose was a product of the new intellectualism. For example, the exaggerated antitheses in the speech at 1.70.2ff. are part of this, or the very rhetorical speech at 1.120ff., or the verbal parallels between Pericles' speech at 2.60 and Kleon's speech at 3.37ff., all are testimony probably to Thucydides' participation in the general enthusiasm and concern for what language can do. The arrival of Gorgias in Athens in 427 and his speechmaking there were said to have dazzled the Athenians and brought on a new and furious exaggeration of rhetorical technique. Thucydides had already begun his work by then presumably, and was soon to leave in exile.

Perhaps more than anything else Thucydides should be considered self-consciously experimental. This would account for his being so uneven, for the unique phenomenon of the Melian dialogue, for instance, or the absence of speeches in books 5 and 8, or for that matter, the cluster of speeches in the first half of the work—two thirds of the forty speeches are in the first four books—or the general triviality of much of the battle narrative, the peculiarly dramatic description of the sailing for Sicily and so on. The first book confirms this view, for Thucydides tries out a number of styles in order to show some of the possibilities of narrative with which he is grappling. There are many other thoroughly contrived passages in the work but none so sustained as a whole book nor any other that seems to be principally demonstrating style and technique.

It is ingenious the way that the first book is an introduction both to the technique and to the subject. Thucydides does manage to establish his principal ideas on war, political power, naval power, Sparta and Athens while at the same time thoroughly revealing how he proposes to narrate his material.

He begins by arguing that the war with which he will be dealing in this work is the single most important event or the greatest war in Greek history. It seems a naïve point of departure. Some critics insist that he simply wishes to demonstrate the greater importance therefore of his own work over that of his predecessor. What he does, however, with his argument seems infinitely more impressive than the argument itself and that is perhaps the real meaning of sections 1 through 21, a display of technique.

He recounts the emergence of the Greek people as a political entity from the earliest recorded times down to the onset of the war between Athens and the Lacedaimonian confederacy. This material survives largely as recorded oral history. The earliest episodes, in fact, derive from saga. Here Thucydides shows his mastery of sober analysis, his ability at summation. Unlike Herodotus, he does not narrate events, and the difference between the two is striking. He means it to be so from the first. He means to set this closely reasoned analysis against Herodotus' opening passage, the by comparison banal and naïve rationalization of the myths of Io, Helen and Medea.

With cool logic Thucydides in turn analyzes the myths relating to Agamemnon and the Homeric account of the Trojan War to show the nature of early Greek imperial power. He shows a marvelous capacity for isolating truths and generalizing from the frail evidence early stories provide. Notice, for instance, his very intelligent observation about the hazards of determining the prosperity and power of earlier societies on the basis of their material remains (10). He justly points to sea power as being the fundamental fact of Aegean empire building, again working very intelligently, partly with myth, partly with saga or other obviously oral accounts. Everything he says in this section is a masterful analytical synopsis of a great period of time, from which he has distilled its most important truths. Nothing could be further from the story narration of events. Herodotus can discuss the flow of the Nile in this fashion, but not human happenings, because human action releases in him the instinct for dramatic narrative.

Thucydides begins the conclusion to this portion (1.20) remarking on how uncritically most men accept and hold to the oral tradition. Men cherish legends, they uncritically accept and pass on misinformation about contemporary affairs that investigation would dispel. Again he seems to be opposing what in Herodotus we have been calling "cultural truths" in distinction to verifiable fact. "On the whole," he says, "he who accepts my analysis on the basis of the inferences which I have made will not be led astray. He will not have to put his faith in the poets who are more concerned with art nor in the storytellers who are more interested in audience response than in purveying truth." The control in this early section reveals already the author's sense of authority, an authority so powerful that, as many have remarked, he has forced upon us, often unwitting, but often unwilling, a view of the war that we cannot test, change or gainsay. He has done this most of all by a display of intelligence, the sober use of logic, the ability to grasp the essentials, to abstract from the abundance of uneven oral saga materials. And this surely has been his primary concern, to create an advertisement for himself.

He turns now to contemporary events over which another kind of control must be exercised. But the point has been made that his habits of mind offer the surest proof of the authenticity of his material. He therefore proceeds first to analyze the methods he has employed to gather, check and select contemporary information. It is further evidence of his interest in technique and style, this self-conscious revelation of his intellectual manner.

What each party said both before and during the war, both I and my various informants had difficulty maintaining an accurate rendition of the actual words. Therefore I created the speeches by keeping as closely as possible to the general tenor and sentiment of the actual remarks but also on the basis of what each party would necessarily in each one of these situations be bound to say. As to the tangible facts of warfare I did not think it right to base my account on whatever any informant who happened along said, but rather, on the basis of the evidence offered me by others as well as by virtue of the fact that I myself was party to many events, I have gone through a point by point analysis as carefully as possible. My results did not come easily since the various eyewitnesses did not all say the same thing, either because of varying capacities of memory or because they were moved by prejudice.

In this passage Thucydides poses a dichotomy between words and deeds. He proposes to allow a contrivance, an idealization, a hypotheticality to the speeches that he will not allow for the deeds of war. What this implies he proceeds to clarify in the later sections of this first book. The dichotomy itself between words and deeds is very traditional in Greek thinking. In one sense the distinction here very likely reflects contemporary tragic practice. One senses it in two ways in tragic performance. It is the contrast between choral ode and dialogue in a great many plays, where the action as it were is the dialogue, or posed in the dialogue, and apart from this or complementary to it are the choral odes, which verbalize an abstraction of reality or are reality at a greater remove, we might say. Or the dichotomy can be sensed between the action in a tragic drama and the verbal response to that action. The latter is really a definition of the play as acted, since both the dialogues and odes take up, discuss and reflect upon the minimal essential action that constitutes the core of the play, as for instance sibling reunion and matricide in the *Choephoroi*, suicide in the *Ajax* or going to the mountain in the *Bacchae*.

Thereafter Thucydides settles into the narration proper of the earliest, provocative events that brought war. Here as elsewhere Thucydides omits to mention the Athenian decrees barring Megarian trading throughout the Athenian Empire, a provocative and warlike act. Thucydides' silence shows naïveté according to some critics, calculated misrepresentation according to others. Perhaps neither explains. Instead one might say that the inclusion of the affair of Epidamnus and the affair of Potidaia, together with Thucydides' silence on the economic attacks made on Megara, is fundamentally random, that the episodes are there *not* as final statements on the causes of the war, but as display pieces of tactical narrative. They are in short illustrations of what he had defined previously (1.22) as the "tangible facts" as opposed to the speeches. Certainly the Megarian economic war would have been considerably harder to narrate; perhaps he did not have the diction, the way of phrasing for such a narrative. In fact Thucydides may have boxed himself in when he emphasized the distinction between words and deeds, a distinction in its most traditional and narrow sense as old as Homer. For the deeds were traditionally deeds of combat, then deeds of war more generally, but always actions in one way or another calculated to produce physical mayhem. The conflict and the strategies of economic warfare, while they may be perfectly well understood (when Aristophanes alludes to the Megarian decrees we may assume that there was some popular understanding of what was going on), are in fact neither words nor deeds in the traditional sense, and therefore they are perhaps unmanageable.

The speeches subsequent to the narration of these two military events reinforce the impression that Thucydides is contriving a display of techniques he has analyzed earlier.

For here we have specimens of speeches set after the specimens of tactical narration. This is the only occasion when Thucydides gives four speeches in debate, as though at the beginning for purposes of exposition he wanted to try out the potential of the speech as a device in his narrative. These speeches are unusually abstract; they offer a perfect introduction to the personalities and problems that were determining factors in the ensuing war.

How true are these speeches? What kind of accuracy does Thucydides have in mind? According to Thucydides the Athenians were in Sparta, heard the speeches or heard of them, and addressed the assembly there themselves. Some Athenians, therefore, could have reported back to Thucydides. But what? Exact words? An outline? The gist of them? The mood? Or merely the fact of the assemblage and the talks? There is no way of knowing and it is one educated guess against another. Thoroughly literate persons must always bear in mind that members of a partially or predominately oral culture are able to remember things verbatim in a way that literate people can scarcely imagine.

Thucydides has said that he tried to create the speeches partly on the basis of what each party would necessarily say in each situation. The situation here described is a gathering of allies faced with the prospect of the eruption of a large-scale and presumably protracted war. Hence the speeches are naturally introductory; there is the mood of commencement and prelude. Yet it is remarkable how free of passion or shortsighted urgency the speeches are. The long view prevails; there is the sensation of reading introductory chapters, the masterly summation of the substantive ramifications of events. One is hard put not to assume that Thucydides took the occasion for what it was and created speeches that were a suitable introduction to his entire work (however long he may have conceived that to be when he was at this point).

Like the opening sections of the work these speeches are analytical. Otherwise the style is very different. They are contrived, highly rhetorical, often exceptionally epigrammatic. The Corinthians, who are the first to be *quoted* by Thucydides, speak of the personalities of Athens and Sparta in phrases that isolate and abstract in an elegantly economical and thus memorable fashion certain psychological characteristics, for instance:

"Beyond power they dare, beyond common sense they gamble, in disaster sanguine, whereas your way is to do things not taxing either power or sense, never trusting in your security, but thinking disaster cannot be escaped" (1.70).

The Athenians follow with what is an apologia for their imperialistic tendencies, but what is as well a historical explanation of the psychological characteristics with which the Corinthians had endowed them. The Spartan king Archidamas follows with an analysis of naval warfare, a speech that grows out of both those preceding (Athens' naval empire means a naval war; Sparta's strength lies in her anti-democratic, anti-intellectual, slow-moving, conservative spirit). The last speech by a Spartan ephor is different; it is an appeal to the emotions. Most of all it seems to arise naturally from the occasion, and indeed returns us to the realities of an assembly of men on the verge of war. For this reason, set as it is against the other dispassionate, abstracted speeches, it, too, seems to be the product of art, rather than simple recorded fact.

The speeches concluded, a vote is taken, and the treaty between the Lacedaimonians and the Athenians is declared to be broken. War comes a little closer. Thucydides very neatly brings together the end of the exposition of this method with the end to the period of cooperation and truce between the main peoples of Hellas.

Before continuing, however, he introduces a curious statement, which seems to stand as summation. The Spartans, Thucydides says, finally voted to break the truce because of their fear of the Athenians. Thucydides has given this explanation before as a prelude to this section (1.23.6), a bit of ring composition that all the more apparently outlines this section. Some critics see Spartan fear as peculiarly irrelevant to the speeches of this section. Corinthian fear, yes. The Spartans, on the contrary, come across as conservative, cautious, inward-looking, really turtle-like. As an isolated land power they are indifferent, we might say, to what must have been Corinth's sources of anxiety: the Athenian navy, commerce and empire. And certainly there is nothing in Spartan history that allows us to believe that they were moved by compassion at the sight of injustice (the ephor's speech seems false in that respect).

What Thucydides has done, however, is to capture a mood here as he will again elsewhere. Everything said by the

Corinthians and the Athenians shows us what a formidable abyss lay between the Spartan and Athenian mentalities. Archidamas' speech, which is a justification of the Spartan way of doing things ("we are too ignorant to despise the laws, too self-controlled to disobey them, and unconcerned with useless matters" [1.84]), is coupled with the ephor's, full of rage, frustration and impotence. Together they show the churning emotions in Sparta confronted by the abyss; it is the classic portrait of the reaction of the ensconced toward the *arriviste*. While all the details Thucydides introduces in the speeches are invaluable and illuminating in many different ways, what does finally surface as the most profound cause of the war is exactly that mood he labels Spartan fear. The conflict is emotional, personal, indeed, one of personalities. The conflict between Athens and Corinth would be economic, otherwise their outlook would be much the same; therefore one cannot develop the conflict of personalities, which is Thucydides' legacy from heroic saga.

The rest of the first book, while made up of passages markedly different in intention and in the manner of their execution, has been made whole by cunning cross-weaving. We have a chronicle of the fifty years' interval between the Persian and the Peloponnesian wars, another speech of the Corinthians (1.120), biographical anecdotes about Themistocles and Pausanias, and a speech of Pericles'. Notice, however, that prior to the formal beginning of the description of those fifty years Thucydides recounts the anecdote of Themistocles and the rebuilding of Athens' walls. In the course of the story he also mentions Pausanias, so that here again he has a device to make transitions. Most importantly we might notice that the description of those fifty years is in the chronicle style of Hellanikos. At least Thucydides apologizes for his description, saying that Hellanikos' account was too brief and too confusing in its chronology. Thucydides, however, seems to be equally brief, even if he has cleared up the chronology. In any case, he recounts facts in the chronicler's manner. This part is not at all like the opening analysis of prehistory, nor the detailed close-up of the Epidamnian and Potidaian adventures. It is another style or another intellectual manner. It is preceded by the anecdote of Themistocles and the rebuilding of the walls, followed by the speech of the Corinthians, as though Thucydides were indicating that the anecdote style belongs to the Persian

War period (Herodotus), the chronicle to the mid-fifth century (Hellanikos et al.) and the speech technique to the period of the Peloponnesian War (to wit, his own invention, or the mark of his historiographical style). The continuity the anecdotes of Themistocles and Pausanias provide is achieved again by the way in which the final element in the book, the speech of Pericles, is made to reflect back on the previous narration. For it answers point by point the second speech of the Corinthians. In this way Thucydides had managed to weave together what might otherwise have been unbearably diverse and episodic material. His continuity comes from the exposition of style and not the chronological narrative.

Critics point up the irrelevance of the descriptions of Themistocles and Pausanias, but they are again illustrations of a style. The style is that of Herodotus and it is to be associated in time with that period after myth and saga, a period that was for Thucydides' contemporaries not at all as accessible naturally as current events. The anecdote style and all that it implies were more suitable to the Persian War period, as Thucydides manages to demonstrate with this section.

In the fifth century there arose alongside the narratives of Herodotus and Thucydides the beginnings of a school or tradition of chronicling local events by years. Hellanikos composed among other things just such a chronicle, known as *Atthis* (it survives only in fragments), which is the history of Attica from the earliest times to his own. Historical reportage of this sort is not the same as the Herodotean ecumenical view, or the analytical summatory writing of the opening passages of Thucydides, or his speeches, or his narrowed subject matter. In short, it represents another view, another narrative. Thucydides chooses to develop the facts behind the Athenian apologia for a naval empire and the Spartan fear and he does so in the factual annual local account, which Hellanikos might have written, certainly another example of experiment in style.

Finally Thucydides points up the artificiality of his speeches, underscores their conventional nature (after all, can everyone have spoken in that same contrived, tight, complex way?) by posing Pericles' speech as a thorough rebuttal to a speech that surely Pericles never heard and of which he very likely had only, if at all, the merest notion. Thucydides by having created this very unnatural and unlikely relationship between the two speeches is thereby insisting that they serve some further purpose in his narrative than the exposition of pure fact.

For all his self-consciousness Thucydides keeps himself out of his narrative rather thoroughly in contrast to Herodotus, whose style next to Thucydides' seems downright conversational. Thucydides' modest reference to himself (4.104.4) as a participant in a battle is self-effacing. It reflects an important side of Thucydides, the writer as observer. In the fifth century, apart from tragic drama, apart from these attempts at history, the best-developed verbal method of organizing reality lay with the medical men. We have from this time a body of prose thought in antiquity to be from the hand of the celebrated Hippocrates or those close to him; whatever its source this medical literature is contemporary with Thucydides, and one can see its influence on him. The most obvious instance is his masterful description of the plague at Athens; what is more he demonstrates his closeness to the medical literature by using technical terms that do not occur in general prose. Medical reporting at the time was a dispassionate account of the progress of a disease through a description of the successive symptoms. It was dispassionate in the sense of accepting the fatal course of the disease rather than trying for or thinking of cure. Thucydides scarcely remarks on the origins and causes of the plague more than to dismiss that line of inquiry. Catastrophes such as plagues are, of course, hard to get at, yet one could expect some discussion. Instead the emphasis is upon the symptoms so that, as Thucydides says (2.48), the plague might be *recognized* if it came again. Recognized, not cured.

The concern of ancient medicine was prognosis, which is true to ancient Greek culture, characteristically disinclined to thoughts of change, progress or alteration. Thucydides transfers the Hippocratic method of describing symptoms to the world of political behavior and implies that he sees human nature, like the body, to be immutable. In his clinical description of the details of the revolution in Corcyra, which reads like the presentation of symptoms, he says (3.82), "Horrible things . . . happened and will always happen as long as human nature stays the same . . ." Cure or correction is beyond discussion. Recognition is all-important, akin to the tragic *anagnorisis*. But tragedy makes us sage;

in Thucydides recognition more often than not becomes cynicism.

The plague and the revolution at Corcyra are inherently exciting, momentous human dramas. But Thucydides has chosen this same method of description for narrating military matters and then it becomes trivial. The contrast between the Thucydidean speeches and tactical narration is astounding; the former are always thoughtful, the latter inevitably banal. What is worse, the authority of Thucydides is strong enough to have made detailed, minutely detailed, descriptions of battle a staple of historiography. While one can understand, say, for example, a relatively thorough discussion of the British victory on the Plains of Abraham at Quebec since it involved a novel military tactic, it is sad that Thucydides' influence should lead knowledgeable historians on the one hand to devote pages to the minutiae of the battle of Marathon, in which one cares only for the outcome, and on the other to condense Athenian cultural history to a matter of sweeping generalities.

One must wonder at Thucydides' disinclination to discuss strategy. He describes one military engagement after another, but never tells us why. Those who insist that there must be some meaning to his lengthy description of the Athenian occupation at Pylos (4.3ff.) quite miss the point. He was well supplied with details concerning this event. Since the details severally are significant in the Hippocratic medical view and since Thucydides seems to have chosen that manner of writing for his narration, he conscientiously introduces as complete an assemblage of these details as possible. It is the theory of prognosis at work again. Compare this to the very unusual speech delivered by Alcibiades before the Spartan assembly when he is advocating among other things that they establish a permanent presence in Attica (6.89ff.). Whatever he suggests he relates to strategic value. Succinct, systematic, he shows high military intelligence. There is, of course, the difference that Alcibiades is in a sense anticipating action, analyzing hypothetical action, which always seems to make the Greeks more thoughtful than when they are treating with reality. Thucydides, however, is always recounting that which has already taken place, and therefore he has to be true to the principles of symptomology. But why the difference? It is tantalizing to consider. Was Thucydides perhaps a poor strategist? He was not a military success himself.

Was he deep down uninterested in war as war? His military narration seems to show that. Alcibiades was supposed to have been very sharp, and this speech may reflect this, may be his own words, or very close to them, somehow come into the possession of Thucydides. Or then again perhaps in the later stages of the writing Thucydides grew to realize that speeches could be used to indicate strategy, which is in a way the philosophy of war, just as he has used speeches for philosophizing about human existence.

Thucydides puts his intellect to understanding power, which he believes is the most important aspect of human existence. From the very first, in his analysis of the earliest Greeks, and thereafter Thucydides measures peoples and persons in terms of strength and weakness. One rather peculiar feature to notice is that Thucydides nowhere acknowledges the immense cultural, artistic creativity in Athens of the fifth century. Nothing about the architecture, the drama or the vases, to name but a few areas of Athenian excellence. When Pericles says in the funeral speech "we are the teachers of all Greece," that does not mean what we moderns generally take it to mean. For we think of Athens as the primal mother of our own cultural tradition. Pericles seems rather to have meant that Athens shows the way politically and socially. This relates more directly to her power, it relates to the struggle between oligarchic and democratic factions in the city-states, to the differences between Athens and Sparta and the quasi-ideological underpinnings to Athenian claims to hegemony.

War and politics for Thucydides are the outward manifestations of power. Empire is the furthest extension of power. Athenian and Spartan military activity are therefore the details of power and politics. Each act is relevant as a manifestation of power. As a sign or index the military activity assumes a legitimacy in description that the events of the plague have. Does Thucydides subscribe to the belief that might makes right? Certainly one gets enough of it in the speeches, especially those of the Athenians. There is nothing to show that this is an article of faith with Thucydides, but plenty to show that he acknowledges as a fact that the strong dominate the weak. There is nothing to show that Thucydides believes in the right, whatever that is. Dominance is power. Perhaps Thucydides would say that might makes things as they are and let it go at that. But then it is very difficult to extract any great ideas from the military narration.

The speeches, on the contrary, are alive with ideas, too much so, in fact, if we are to believe that they represent something actually delivered orally. In the mouths of all speakers and for all occasions the diction remains the same; contrary to normal usage in oral communication what is said is unusually dense and complex, even given the considerable sophistication and intelligence of the ancient Athenian general populace. Like tragic stichomythy much is platitudinous and epigrammatic, not so persuasive as clever, something to be read again and to be savored, for instance:

"The only sure basis of an alliance is for each party to be equally afraid of the other" (3.11.1).

"Man hopes for what he longs for, but rationalizes away what he does not want" (4.108.4).

Thucydides' speeches are marked by antithetical structures.

A marked feature of early Athenian rhetoric is a much expanded use of antithesis. The Greeks were by nature antithetical thinkers; as we have discussed (pp. 28f.), their language at its most basic in parataxis is structured by oppositions on the one hand, and on the other, a continuing rhythm throughout Greek culture. One thinks of Aristotle's law of the excluded middle, of post and beam architecture, of tragic conflict—particularly, that favorite of Hegel's, the *Antigone*. Like alliteration for the early Latins antithesis is an easy device ready to hand for an "artistic" effect in prose. But it also has a great effect on intellectual habits. Dionysios of Halicarnassus, the first-century B.C. author and literary critic, complains that Thucydides gets carried away with antithesis. True, his speeches have a good deal, but in Thucydides' case, one is ready to argue that the antithesis is fundamental to his view of things, or that this war very sharply brought out antitheses, whether it be Athens and Sparta or the generals Alcibiades and Nikias.

Antithesis must be the essential Thucydidean view since throughout the work he seems deliberately to have set up so many polarities. The contrasts are sometimes artificially juxtaposed to a degree that shows Thucydides, the manipulator, the artist at work, rather than what we would call a historian. Athens and Sparta, for instance, seem an inevitable antithesis on the surface of things, but why not Athens and Corinth, the two great seagoing trading powers of the time? Certainly they were the real rivals, the real antagonists. Yet we have very little on Corinth from Thucydides; he mentions no Corinthian by name, he does not go into the role we may imagine Corinthian money and ships must have played throughout those years. Is this because Athens and Sparta are a far more significant—artistically, philosophically —and true antithesis? The presentation of the differences in the Athenian and Spartan outlook and way of life in the first book gives a special, serious perspective to the conflict. It is the collision of two conceptions of human existence, really quite metaphysical (a text often replayed or alluded to in the Cold War of the mid-twentieth century). None of this, we can assume, could have been achieved from setting out Athens and Corinth in conflict.

Thucydides is able to personalize Athens and Sparta in a way he could not personalize Corinth. It is the legacy from heroic saga which dictates that the history shall be seen in individualized human terms. The conflict between Athens and Corinth would be economic, not a conflict of personalities, nothing emotional or personal. The Corinthians, again we can only assume, being citizens of a coastal sea power, a trading city, intent on financial gain and growth, must have had a point of view and a way of life much like that of the Athenians. Therefore the immediate antithetical quality is missing. Still Thucydides missed the truly important antithesis in Athens and Corinth, that is, their great similarity, yet one producing a great culture and the other only going beyond the nondescript.

Some critics think Thucydides naïve for creating personalities for his city-states, as, for instance, when he says (1.25.3) that the Corinthians "hated" the Corcyraeans for their indifference (like the jilted lover), as though that were suitable only in public speeches, as, for instance, when the Corinthians put on wounded parental dignity (1.38.1ff.). The issues seem to be obscured when human psychology is made the major motive and political and economic aspects are set aside. Thucydides says, for instance (1.103.4), that the Corinthians hated the Athenians for fortifying Megara. He makes it seem an affront to the Corinthians' dignity rather than an assault on their trading position that would produce something other than hatred; for Thucydides makes everything a problem of a wounded ego. But perhaps there is something more than heroic tradition behind this. Thucydides confers personalities upon city-states perhaps because he thinks of them in terms of their assemblies, particularly the Athenian assembly, where issues, especially those involving other cities, would often be argued emotionally. We moderns think of the reaction of bureaucrats, special-interest groups, the power elite. These are the so-called important reactions, since they derive from the persons able to effect change. Usually such persons because they are quite knowledgeable react quite coolly. The same cannot be said of an open assembly, which is addressed by one after another speaker who wishes to sway their opinion. Since in Athens at least the people had such constant and direct power there is the possibility it was this that unconsciously moved Thucydides to talk in terms of city-state personalities.

When, on the other hand, he has the Corinthian delegation speak of Spartan sluggishness, timidity and caution as though these were genuine quirks of personality, he misses by not mentioning the cause of these, that is, Sparta's great and continuing problem of repressing the enormous slave population, which in decades past had risen up more than once. Spartan fear of their slaves made them cautious and slow to act; it was not a character trait.

One of the best-contrived features of the Athens-Sparta antithesis in the first book is the way that Thucydides dramatizes it in the stories of Themistocles and Pausanias. First he poses the antithesis in the speeches at the Spartan assembly, then later come the anecdotes of these two men, Themistocles, ambitious, clever, cool, Pausanias, made crazy when once he got beyond his native provincialism, the Good Hellene and the Bad Hellene. Here the personalities Thucydides has created for Athens and for Sparta are revealed in two men, as projections of the two states.

The most notable antithesis of men is Pericles and Kleon, who seem to stand for Thucydides as manifestations of all that was good and all that was bad about the Athenian city-state personality. Pericles is Thucydides' ideal statesman; therefore Kleon is made to appear as the absolute opposite. We have no evidence, however, that Kleon was corrupt, only that he was loud, vulgar, flamboyant; he was not at all an aristocrat as was the elegant Pericles. Kleon had extravagant schemes of exploiting Athens' so-called allies. Still Pericles had exploited the allies, using their tribute money to build fine public architecture in Athens. But

Thucydides leaves this out and concentrates instead upon the repressive plans of Kleon. The evidence does not suggest that Kleon was much of a good thing, but it is Thucydides' antithetical sensibilities that cast him as a villain to Pericles' white knight. The other human antithesis is between Alcibiades and Nikias; the former is young, ambitious and unscrupulous, the other is old, cautious and decent. Although Alcibiades seems to have been very intelligent, Thucydides emphasizes his frivolousness and ambition. He is like Athens setting out to conquer Sicily. Nikias is old and decent, that is what Thucydides concentrates upon. But perhaps he was also rather lacking in judgment, if not stupid. That is ignored for the sake of the contrast. One could imagine many another antithesis of personalities, but Thucydides names remarkably few persons in his history. Perhaps only the Spartan Brasidas is introduced with anywhere near the same amount of attention as these four.

The antithesis to the plague is Pericles' funeral oration, which directly precedes it (2.35ff.). The plague seems to be echoed in the description of the Corcyraean revolution; one senses in their parallels that Thucydides is transferring the idea of sickness to the body politic. Sickness is so common a metaphor in tragedy for spiritual or moral failing that it would be natural for Thucydides to do so. But the plague and the funeral oration provide something more in contrast; they are portraits of Athens at its zenith and in its decline. The plague, of course, happened at a moment in time that could not be altered; it must appear inexorably placed in the narrative. But Pericles more likely than not delivered various funeral orations over the war dead, so that Thucydides' decision to precede the plague with this full encomium of Athens has aesthetic and philosophical motives. And the antithesis says so many things: the chanciness of life, of war, against which neither logic nor hope offers any recourse; pride and exaltation followed by abject despair, the wild swing from high to low, that Greek manic-depressive vision; that equally common Greek tendency to look back to what is irretrievably lost; man as he can be, the good society, the good citizen against man as he must be, the corrupt and fearful animal; Pericles and the Periclean golden days against the somber and hallucinatory vision of the post-Periclean years, the time of debacle. Thucydides is so restrained, so objective that he insists upon nothing; yet the contrast is very powerful and works upon the reader's historical imagination. It is the grouping of these two events that more than anything else in the work seems to argue for the idea that Thucydides composed the whole or did much revising after the war, since this antithesis seems to be a statement of the entire war.

There are many other minor antitheses in the work. Partly the antithesis is Thucydides' natural way of organizing the flow of his material and because it is so common here, and in Greek intellectual patterns as well, one must not over-emphasize it, nor try to assign it too much special meaning. Yet, it raises the question of symmetry; very likely episodes or people of relatively secondary importance might from time to time have to be given considerably greater prominence in order to balance whatever is their artistic or logical antithesis. Perhaps the Melian episode and particularly the dialogue has grown as large as it is in the narrative to complement and oppose both the funeral oration early on and more particularly the longish description of the Athenian fleet's departure for Sicily.

These are all isolated antitheses. There is one, however, that runs fairly consistently throughout the entire work, and that is the conflict between hope—always simply named— and what we can call realism or cynicism or awareness. These two views, the one idealistic and sentimental, the other realistic (or whatever we wish to say), seem to have been quite commonly juxtaposed in late-fifth-century Athens. One sees them everywhere in the tragedies. Consider the reactions of Phaedra's nurse to the disclosure that her mistress lusts after her stepson, at first horror and shock, then a sympathetic speech on the psychological health of yielding to one's sexual appetites. Consider Tyndareus' attack on his grandson's defense of matricide in the *Orestes,* or Pheres' condemnation of his son for allowing his wife to die for him in the *Alcestis.* Each time the traditional position is set forth, noble and ideal, and then is cast down before some harder, sterner, more realistic view.

It would be tedious to go through every instance of the juxtaposition of what, for brevity, I shall crudely label cynicism and hope. Athens' initial arguments for her supremacy stem from an idealization of her role (the savior of Greece from the Persian menace). Pericles' funeral oration maintains the same tone. They both differ with Pericles' speech to the Athenians when they have begun to tire of the war (2.60ff.), when he explains to them how Athens is an imperial tyranny and there is no quick or easy way out once you have begun to exploit and enslave people. Kleon says the same thing still much more bluntly in the debate over Mitylene. The way in which Thucydides has Kleon's speech echo verbally that of Pericles gives the sense of a bad dream come true. Throughout the work in speech after speech human motives and actions are divorced from the traditional Greek ethical context, that is, the heroic-aristocratic, and a very new and quite cynical interpretation is put upon human affairs. One cannot help believing that Thucydides purposely emphasizes this antithesis because he is able to use it with great irony in the latter part of the history when Athens, cool and wise, becomes victim of her own hot delusion.

The Melian Dialogue is the ironic crystallization of this conflict. The conference on the island of Melos between its inhabitants and the Athenian army who have come to offer them the choice of abandoning neutrality or being overcome, killed or enslaved is generally known as the Melian Dialogue. It is the only occasion for the dialogue form in the entire work. Frequently Thucydides' speeches answer each other closely point for point so to that extent they resemble the two parties to a dialogue, but it is only here that one side answers the other immediately after each point is made. Some believe that the Melian Dialogue was not finished, that it represents the way in which Thucydides initially thought out his speeches, that after he had worked out the verbal possibilities in countering or exposing arguments in sequence, he then took the two sets of responses and made them into integral speeches. It is, however, more likely that the dialogue form here underscores and emphasizes, raises to the crisis, makes all the more antithetical, the conflict between hope and cynicism. For the Melians, who do not at all have the military might to withstand the Athenians, resist, and base their resistance upon a certain ethical stance. They cannot do otherwise because they believe themselves to be right, and they have to believe, as they say, that rightness will prevail. The Athenians for their part very cynically or realistically—cynicism being a pejorative word—analyze their motives and the Melian prospects. Here is *Realpolitik* of the coldest, boldest sort. The Athenian delegation particularly fasten on Melian expectations, their hopes, to deride persons who will put their trust in hope (5.103). Athenian rationalism, the hallmark of every speech in this work, of Thucydides himself, has never been so chillingly displayed. If the Corinthians in the first book had managed to portray in unforgettable terms two ways of life, two personalities, the Spartan and the Athenian, here the Melians and the Athenians dramatize in classic fashion two justifications for existence, two ways of getting on with the world. And the Melians subsequently are destroyed.

The antithesis to this vision of the triumph of cynicism or realism is the Athenian sailing for Sicily. Thucydides dwells on the Sicilian campaign; he describes the departure for Sicily fully. This is preceded by a description of the vote in the assembly for the expedition. He describes what expectations move the assembly, their wild enthusiasm and eagerness (6.25). The event of departure is described with the details Herodotus would use. The sense of adventure, extravagance and enthusiasm has been well captured. But what, of course, marks the whole is the Athenian dependence upon hope, so ironic after the immediately preceding narrative.

When at Syracuse all begins to go so badly for the Athenians that all they can any longer rely upon is hope, Nikias must say (7.61.3), ". . . my life has been one of devotion toward the gods, there has been much justice, I have not offended against other men. Therefore I have a strong hope for the future . . ." It is weakness at the end, tired, used-up Nikias, falling back on hope, Athens losing her nerve, ironically looking to hope, but another kind than that which moved the Melians. The Melians relied on a moral order, the Athenians in essence are hoping for *good luck*. Again Thucydides has found antitheses and within them still other antitheses. It is complex, subtle and tragically ironic; it begins in fact with the description of the Athenians by the Corinthians, for what they are describing is the personality of the entrepreneur, which feeds on expectations more than anything else, pretending to be shrewd, but looking to the future with hope.

Perhaps we would do better to say that Thucydides has arranged his events, has introduced his emphases with an eye to creating what we might call a tragic nexus of events. Consider the initial Corinthian estimation of the Athenians, how it emphasizes their intelligence, their quick, sure way of solving problems. Parenthetically think of Sophocles' conception of Oedipus; how like to this description of Athens he is. Pericles' funeral oration further elaborates and defines what we would call the Athenian genius. From these two passages and elsewhere there appears a society at the pinnacle of its powers, prestige and talents. If Athens is indeed more than a little tyrannical, nonetheless the tone is essentially praise and respect. This is a great and good city and as we know by the end of the Sicilian campaign (still more by the end of the war, which point Thucydides does not reach in his writing) a city brought down in crashing defeat. Thucydides has concentrated upon a period of time that shows particularly an extraordinary political reversal; it is also a tragic reversal.

The Corinthian estimation and the funeral oration show excessive prosperity, which in early tragedy is the first condition of catastrophe. Thucydides shows this great and good city blinded by, puffed up by pride; this is how one can analyze the Melian Dialogue and justify the importance Thucydides assigns to a minor historical event. He shows the Athenians in their pride being led on, seduced by the glittering, corrupt Alcibiades. Notice here how Thucydides chooses to pass over Alcibiades' dubious character when he first appears in the narrative (5.43.2) but waits until such a revelation will have more point (6.15.2–4). This may be unconscious, yet it is true to the manner of tragic exposition, which requires a denouement. It is also false to the narration of fact, which ought not to hold back, to keep its audience in bondage or suspense.

After the pride and the seduction there comes the gross miscalculation, the *hamartia*, the invasion of Sicily. Thucydides makes it epic-like and mighty. There is the exalted moment of sailing, there is before the last battle (7.57) a catalogue such as we find in Homer and Herodotus, an unexpected touch of grandeur. Readers can argue, of course, that one of the curious facts of this very curious century is that Athens' rise and fall, so to speak, resembled generally and often in detail the *metabole* of a tragic hero. Eventually one wonders to what extent a society, very much in the spell of tragic drama, quite unconsciously shaped events and verbal constructs on some sort of tragic model. Or to what extent those who recorded or depicted this society did so again on some sort of tragic model. Consciously or unconsciously?

Thucydides appeals very much to the modern mind. He is

stern, elegant. He takes a dim view of existence. "All things," he says (2.64.3), "are born to diminish." He believes that war and power are the measure of man. He is sparse and grim, like tragedy. Tragedy's grimness, however, its mournfulness and pessimism are always redeemed by the tragic hero. Perhaps Thucydides personalizes Athens so much so as to make the city-state his hero. Unconsciously, of course. Thucydides did not imagine that he was writing tragedy. Out of the personalized Athens, then, he can draw for the changes of mood the resolute, sensible, intelligent Pericles, the flamboyant, crude, tough Kleon, the unbalanced, glittering, manic Alcibiades and the tired, depressed Nikias. The story is sad, but not tragic. Thucydides like his Athenians who rebuke the Melians for their beliefs cannot believe, and therefore he has given us an account that is better called gloomy.

CHAPTER SEVEN
THE CRITICISM OF TRAGEDY

> Art is not an imitation of nature, but a metaphysical complement to it—something created with the express purpose of dominating it.
>
> Nietzsche, *The Birth of Tragedy*

> Greek tragedy, my dear, decorum: the ultimate gesture is performed offstage.
>
> Genet, *The Blacks*

Ancient Greek drama is strange. We know that, but forget it. Strange, apart from us, in one sense long gone in time, tragedy has at times become ours to interpret as we will. Like Melina Mercouri's character in *Never on Sunday*, whose personal conception of ancient Greek tragic resolution made her insist that "they all went to the seashore," most of us can find in the plays whatever we need.

To sit in the ruins of the Theater of Dionysus at Athens brings home with a shock how remote, mysterious and unknown the tragic drama of the ancient Athenians must be for us; only the words of the dramas remain. Words only, yet words with extraordinary power. For ancient tragedy even in this much reduced state has so survived and thrived in the European tradition of the last two millennia that the personages and actions of at least a dozen players have become as much staples of modern culture as elements of the Judaeo-Christian mythologies. Thus what was Sophocles' conception of Oedipus has become very much *our* Oedipus, not at all an antiquarian's curiosity piece to be viewed with amusement or condescension or awe over the vast abyss of time.

But when in fact we set the idea of "Sophocles' conception" against *"our* Oedipus" we come to a crux in criticism. We may indeed ask to what extent is it legitimate to speak of "Sophocles' creation"; for how long-lasting, how strong is the force of the original creation? Sophocles and his world are long gone; only a printed text remains, which only we can bring to life. Sophocles and the other tragedians when they presented plays spoke to their contemporaries out of a profound awareness of their common past and present. We can surely never recover the deep, special awareness of the tragedians, but probably not even that of their contemporary audiences. Their past and present will always be shrouded for us.

Therefore, in seeking to develop an intelligent criticism of ancient literature, but most particularly ancient drama, we are caught between two objectives. The one, the more immediate, obvious and natural is to consider and refine what each play seems to be saying to us directly. Here we can ignore the fact that we and the ancient Greeks inhabit two very different worlds.

Greek tragedy has in part survived because persons, actions and motives are presented in clear, bold outlines which are able to evoke empathetic responses century after century. Very few of the extant tragedies are so obscure that one finds his responses impossibly ambiguous. While there are many unsettling reactions, still a critical opinion can be formed.

It is, however, the other objective in forming critical judgments that is hard, that is, to set the plays as well as possible back into their historical context, to try to come to grips with whatever psychological or sociological nuances exist in each play that derive from the facts of the period in which the plays were created. The distance in time is so vast, our evidence is so fragmentary, that the task can never be done really well. Yet to dismiss this background leaves one with either a solipsistic appreciation of the plays, or, what is more common, produces a surface understanding where each play divorced from the detailed mosaic of its context, existing in its lineaments only, takes on a symbolic function. Think of Shelley and *Prometheus Unbound* or most contemporary stagings of ancient theater.

Most people encounter ancient tragedy only in the printed word; therefore, for them to keep in mind that it was and is theater takes an effort of imagination.

How do we come to criticize or appreciate ancient Greek tragedy? It is difficult. Tragedy is "theater" or "drama," words that have very peculiar associations for late-twentieth-century ears. These associations hinder our understanding of ancient tragedy because the conditions of production and the expectations of the audiences are so different.

First, theater in our time is very special. Most people watch television or film. Only a very special and dedicated group goes to the theater. In America the theater of Broadway provides mindless entertainment for a segment of New York and its visiting tourists who either enjoy curiosity pieces or still associate theater with status; Off-Broadway mounts a variety of new pieces aimed at extremely special sensibilities; and provincial repertory, often in the care of amateurs, pursues the illusory task of maintaining "culture." All this activity takes place in an environment indifferent or often openly hostile to it. Commercial television, which might be thought to be the real alternative to this, is not. Commercial television provides only the most simplistic, commercialized entertainment, innocuous, idiot-simpering in the form of drama that is reminiscent of the vulgar Roman pantomime, which sought to compete with dancing bears and jugglers in the ancient city of Rome.

In our time for most people the central analogous cultural experience is the film, and many unconsciously take the aesthetics of this medium to apply to ancient tragedy. But intimacy is the essence of the film-viewing experience. Consider the darkened auditorium, which eliminates our sense of the other spectators, the large vision on the screen, which overwhelms and demands total submission and complete absorption from the viewer. Then too, the viewer has thrust at him from the screen the smallest details. In reading tragedy one's imagination projects a detailed, refined and intimate stage scene. This, however, surely had nothing to do with ancient theatrical practice.

Tragedy was a *public* event. At Athens the Theater of Dionysus built against the steeply rising east slope of the Acropolis was large enough to accomodate fourteen to seventeen thousand. The sense of the group, of community, was moreover enhanced by the fact that the audience sat

ogether on stone benches without seat division so that arms,
egs and haunches could touch, and emotions could race
through the audience, physically making them over into one
common response.

Viewing tragedy in the theater of fifth-century antiquity
was quite the opposite experience of film viewing. Per-
ormances were out of doors, in daylight, continuously, start-
g at dawn in a large arena, where there must have been
constant movement, as at present-day sporting events. People
eaving to relieve themselves, people going home to eat,
hawkers selling food, these were moving elements of the
panorama as much as actors and chorus. To make an out-
ight and provocative disturbance during the performance
became a capital offense.

A large crowd is characteristically animal; the atmosphere
s charged with passion and a tension that betrays the crowd's
volatile nature. Large crowds are not at all primarily rational
and theater was in any case an emotional experience.

The focus of the audience was directed to the flat area
before the rise of benches known as the "dancing place"
(orchestra in Greek, which is the reason for the present-day
practice of calling the ground floor in our theater the orchestra). Here the chorus performed. Behind them was the
area in which the actors performed. They were probably
almost on a level with the orchestra of the chorus; the raised
stage came later.

Behind them was a building known in Greek as the skene,
which has become our word "scene." Originally the skene
meant "tent"; the tent was a simple place for actors to
change masks and costumes, and when the script called for
it, a place into which to withdraw. And then it became
elaborated into a two-story building forming a rudimentary
backdrop and sounding board. Numbers of Greek tragedies
take place before a royal palace probably because the skene
would naturally serve for this. It had doors into which actors
could go, and windows from which one could speak. Furthermore it gave the support for the machine that conveyed aloft
actors representing divine figures, from which comes the
expression deus ex machina (a Latin translation of the
Greek theos apo mechanes, "god from the machine"). This
machine was perhaps suspended over the side of the building
like a crane and ran on a track on the roof. Nothing we
know about the means for creating settings suggests any-

thing elaborate or any great concern for realism. Sophocles' *Philoctetes* needs a cave and the *skene* serves for this. Probably the notorious tendency to maintain the same scene throughout the play ("unity of place") derives from the psychological difficulty of change when the *skene* provides a fixed locus (although Shakespeare's theater was not so inhibited). Perhaps the confinement also suggests a reason for the convention of narrating scenes of disaster and physical mayhem in the conventional messenger's speech rather than portraying them. Such scenes need more movement, a larger field of action and often they take place in more than one setting. All this is so difficult physically that verbal description is considerably simpler.

But in turn we may relate this to a more profound turn of the Greek mind, that is, their tendency to abstract all reality, most often through words. Of course, words particularly are what survives from antiquity. Nonetheless one can see it in the Homeric poems, the extraordinary preponderance of dialogue in place of descriptive narrative: what happens is not so important as a person's narrative of what happened or more particularly someone's commentary or analysis of what happened. Most episodes in the *Iliad* reveal this, it is a major theme of the *Odyssey*. In tragedy one finds minimal action and maximum verbal realization of this action. The historians in turn rely upon monologues or dialogues in the place of simple third-person description, and Plato's use of the dialogue shows the tradition persisting. In this sense the stage setting was symbolic and cerebral, in keeping with the nature of ancient tragedy.

The abstract quality of ancient tragedy is also implied by the very size of the theater. The distance from the middle of the tiers of seats to the middle of the orchestra, not to consider the extremes, was in most theaters considerable. Given the fact of uncorrected myopia in the ancient audience the spectacle must have been abstracted, not detailed. Consider too the complete absence of mechanical aids toward creating a focus: no darkened auditorium, no lighted stage, no proscenium arch, only the seating set in semicircle. The enormity of the area makes any analogy with open-air Shakespearean theater unlikely.

Finally there is a common feature to ancient theater architecture that needs comment. That is the generally splendid and compelling view that lay beyond the *skene*. Concentration must have always been a problem and yet the spectator seats look out to hypnotic vistas, at Delphi a marvelous valley, at Pergamon a breathtaking and vertiginous drop to a far-off valley, at Taormina the rugged coast, at Segesta distant valleys between mountains. Partially this derives from the necessity of carving the seats of the *theatron* into a hillside, from which generally there will be a view. But a slightly different siting in most instances would have severely limited the panoramic sweep. In some way ancient theater seems to have been conceived as part of a process rather than an end, and the lack of focus is therefore natural.

We have mentioned before the public nature of tragedy, contrasting it with the elitist theater of the twentieth century. Its closest corollary in this instance is television or the movies of the thirties, although both of these media are commercial enterprises in a monopolistic, capitalist society imposed upon the people. They generate a bastard culture rather than articulating or abstracting through imagery and symbol the culture that is native to the people. They only peripherally touch on the wants, needs and interests of the people. They pose an alien culture, one deriving from New York or Beverly Hills, neither of which cities relates to the broad general culture of America in any way like the city culture of ancient Athens related to the life of rural Attica. Tragedy was part of the ancient public domain.

The public quality of ancient tragedy means that tragedy was part of the public process, rather than something special. This corresponds to the physical setting for presenting tragedy discussed above. When Aeschylus asked to have inscribed in his tombstone only the legend "He fought at Marathon" he was not being precious but simply assigning priorities. He was also signifying that he was not an intellectual nor belonged to a coterie. He was simply part of the public, as his plays were part of the public experience. Euripides, on the contrary, perhaps felt himself to belong to a somewhat special category; through Aristophanes' depiction of him we sense that he is perhaps what we would call an intellectual and probably thought of himself as one. Aeschylus and Sophocles, however, were temperamentally if not literally members of the aristocracy, and Euripides' intellectual status in the late-fifth-century bourgeois society was perhaps something similar.

The days of performance were community events. All

citizens were there in a community small enough to sustain wide acquaintance. The producers, the *choregoi,* were men of the community distinguished for their wealth and thus certainly known to many. The chorus was made up of talented men of the community. Not only would many know some of the participants but many more may have participated.

Tragic performances were a staple of the festival in Athens that we call the City Dionysia or Greater Dionysia, a festival that was older than tragedy itself. In the second half of the fifth century another city festival of tragedy appeared; dramatic festivals were so popular that from time to time they were held in the countryside of Attica, and, of course, the custom spread to most other cities in the Greek-speaking world. The City Dionysia took place in late March shortly before the April period of harvest. This may tantalize those who see tragedy as specifically celebrating the death of the year god, presumably a feature of agrarian religion. But more likely the date for the festival derives from the fact that by late March the winter storms that make the Aegean sea a menace are over and rain is little likely to ruin this outdoor festival. The cessation of winter storms meant the arrival of foreigners who had business in Athens whether diplomatic or commercial. The Greater Dionysia was open to all Greeks everywhere; it was probably initiated by the tyrant Peisistratos, who in many other ways as well tried to establish Athens' cultural superiority among the city-states of the Greek-speaking world. The presentation of the tragedies was bound up in civil and international affairs in this festival. Before the day's performance the children of those who died in Athens' service were paraded, honors to outstanding citizens were proclaimed, ambassadors were publicly received. More than a religious event, it was a state holiday; even the prisoners were released from jail for the festivities.

The festival also made a place for comedy, a feature established somewhat later than the presentations of tragedy. There were also dithyrambs, choruses of young men and boys singing lyrics not unlike the extant choruses of tragedy although initially the dithyrambic choruses were much more given over to narrative; later the words were overwhelmed by the music (paralleling a growing interest in the musicality of choruses on the part of Euripides). Tragedy was in any case only a part of the festival.

The festival was a public competition. Each playwright who presented himself for the competition offered three tragedies and a satyr play. The three tragedies on the same theme are called a trilogy. The only surviving one is Aeschylus' *Oresteia* (*Agamemnon, Libation Bearers* and *Eumenides*). Only Aeschylus wrote trilogies where there is demonstrable continuity in the action and idea. But the titles of lost plays suggest that maybe a connection of some sort existed between plays. We must therefore be cautious when interpreting a tragedy, for we do not know how it was meant to play against the other two. And we may not ignore this on the grounds that the plays were discrete structures. Tragedies were short—about one and a quarter hours' playing time—and played without much interval and that in itself is continuity of sorts.

The arrangement of performance changed during the fifth century. The three playwrights were chosen to present their work. This they did on three successive mornings, the tragedies followed by the satyr play. Initially there were three comedies presented one each on these three afternoons. Later when the number increased to five they were all presented on a day subsequent to the tragic days. In the earlier period the festival gave five days to performances, three for tragedies and comedies, the last two for dithyrambs.

Ceremonies began at dawn; the tragedies were presented without any real break, so that the satyr play which followed was a psychological device to modify the extreme intensity tragedy engenders. The dithyrambs also demanded less of the audience, being narration in the third person or even more simply rhythmic and musical events with words.

The audience arrived for the plays with little anticipation. That is to say, there were no advertisements, no critical reviews and no friends and acquaintances who had previously seen the plays. New plays were put on each year; revivals were not common until the fourth century (although some plays of Aeschylus may have been revived toward the close of the fifth). Considerable cooperation was therefore demanded of the audience. They had to respond, to get into the train of thought of the play. This must be borne in mind when watching or reading the tragedies, for the landmarks and signposts as the plot develops are exceedingly sparse. What may have helped to prepare the audience was the custom on the day prior to the beginning of the festival of bringing playwrights and actors before the public to announce the general subjects of the plays. But the arena where this was done was small. Here we may perhaps see a practical reason for the tendency upon the part of the trage-dians to confine their plots to certain well-known stories. The ancients had a vast fund of myth and legend. While a simple announcement was enough to stir the memory, it would be of great value to limit the variety of stories. Eu-ripides, who often prefers unusual stories, ensures compre-hension by outlining the action of the plot in some detail in the prologue. Simplicity and familiarity were probably de-sirable virtues much appreciated; indeed, Euripides, who in-dulged in more complicated stories, did win fewer firsts in the competition than Sophocles and Aeschylus.

The tragedians competed for first, second and third place. This is not surprising considering how competitive the an-cient Greeks were. First prize was a gold crown. The way in which the public at large gave acceptance or appreciation of the tragedies reminds us too how very political and social ancient theater was.

The choice of the three poets who were to present plays was up to the archon eponymous. This archon, we must re-member, was simply an official in the Athenian system of government, a kind of alderman chosen by lot, rather than by popular election. Apart from whatever characteristics of personality he possessed he may stand for Everyman, in any case certainly not a drama critic or a theatrical producer. (One archon, for example, is known to have refused Soph-ocles.) Nothing makes clearer that ancient tragedy was not the manifestation of an elite or a class (excepting of course the fact that free-born adult males *do* constitute a class and not the populace). How the archon came to pick the three tragedians among those who wished to present plays is unclear; perhaps passages were read or acted out for him. But we have no way of knowing what criteria he fostered.

The judges who awarded the prizes were not better quali-fied in literary or cultural matters than the archon who initially selected the competitors. To begin, names were drawn up from each tribe by the council, which was free to choose persons formerly connected with the theater: actors *choregoi,* playwrights. At this point considerable effort was made by the producers of the tragedies to get friends and adherents on the lists. These names were then placed in ten urns, one for each tribe; the urns were then sealed and stored until the day of performance. On that day one name was chosen from each urn. These ten judges made lists of their preferences. From these ten lists five lists were chosen at random and on the basis of these five the victor was determined. Such a system makes victory a random matter but frequent victories assume a good deal of significance. The considerable number of victories assigned to Aeschylus and Sophocles represents therefore an astounding unanimity of community approval of their plays.

Public reaction was strong. There was a custom that on the day following the Dionysia a meeting of the *ekklesia* was held to determine if any impropriety had occurred during the festival, and upon this occasion the judges who awarded the prizes could be attacked for faulty judgment. The audience reacted vigorously throughout the performances, the judges had continual index to community sentiment toward what was being presented. If we can believe our rather flimsy evidence Euripides presented an original version of the Hippolytus-Phaedra story in which the lovesick queen propositioned her stepson. Such a sight repulsed the audience and they rejected the play. His second version used the device of the nurse, thereby weakening the dramatic strength of the story, but sparing the public from scandal.

What did the public want in the plays? Aristophanes' *Frogs* is evidence of critical intelligence in the audience. Furthermore, the *Frogs* shows that the audience had a latent knowledge of the actual lines of a number of plays, some of which may not have been produced for a long period of time. Since social communication still depended upon memory, memories remained incredibly acute. An Athenian therefore must have been able to view a tragedy, to empathize with it while simultaneously it was reflected in his mind against the frame of reference of the dozens of tragedies he had previously witnessed. This would be true for plots, language, nuance, special effects. Furthermore if an Athenian remembered in detail the language of tragedy, a style and diction used for the most serious topics, it is reasonable to imagine that whenever his mind turned to such topics the tragic language and manner may have seemed the natural vehicle for his speculations. The Athenians may thus have been self-consciously immediately involved in tragic style.

The Athenian audience probably approached tragedy with moral seriousness. Criticism of tragedy has to take this utter seriousness into account, the sense of social need, the recognized communal nature of tragedy. Frequently the tragedies present attitudes and actions that are unspeakable although not at all unthinkable. In this way they provide in a socially acceptable way, a communal way, a chance to give vent to feelings individuals must repress as too socially destructive. Dramas of parental cannibalism (the banquet of Thyestes), incest (Oedipus), matricide (Orestes), suicide (Ajax) and so on allow the human being to identify in a safe way with all sorts of impulses within himself. Or tragedies can articulate certain common fears, as for instance underlying hostility between the sexes (Clytemnestra, Dejaneira, Medea, Agamemnon, Hercules and Jason). Then too, dramas set up models of behavior, suggesting alternative ways to confront situations that are in some ways common to us all, as for instance in the *Antigone* or the *Bacchae*. Philosophers might say that tragedies are verbal constructs of the reality that surrounds mankind, that through empathetic response with successive characters the audience is led through modes of reasoning, made to abstract after a fashion in a time when the apparatus of logical inquiry and formulation was not yet well enough developed for any kind of self-conscious use of it.

The structure of tragedy remained constant in the fifth century. Generally a *prologos* appears to give some start to the dramatic proceedings, either by setting the mood, as the watchman does in the *Agamemnon*, or delineating the problem, as Antigone and her sister Ismene do in the *Antigone*, or by outlining the subsequent events, as the goddess Aphrodite does in the *Hippolytus*. There follows the entrance of the chorus, the *parodos*, characteristically entering on anapests ($\smile\smile-$), a marching rhythm. Subsequent to these there are a series of dialogue passages, episodes, arranged between the choral odes. The last choral utterance accompanies their departure from the scene and is known as the *exodos*. Do the dialogue passages advance the plot while the choral odes are a pause in this movement? Or are the choral odes lyrical restatements of what the dialogue developed in the episodes? Or reactions to it? The choral odes prompt a variety of questions. The extant tragedies reveal a variety of relationships existing between episode and episode—not all of them cohere so as simply to advance the plot—and between episode and choral ode and between choral ode and choral ode.

The poetic structure of the parts of tragedy also remained constant. The choral ode is divided into strophes and anti-strophes, the latter of which is a passage that answers exactly to the meter of the strophe. Sometimes the two are combined in a triadic structure with what is called the epode, an equally sized passage of lyrics that are metrically akin to the preceding strophe and antistrophe. The meters of the choral passage are widely various and schematizing them without the music that accompanied them is one of the more ambitious and vain scholarly enterprises.

The dialogue by contrast was in iambic trimeters, that is, $\smile-\smile-/\smile-\smile-/\smile-\smile-/$, thought to be the closest stylized approximation to human speech. The Greek language had a characteristically high number of short vowels in its early period. Thus the epic dactyl $-\smile\smile$ may not have been far off the vernacular. Gradually these vowels combined, contracted, but the language naturally still had some shorts, hence, the iamb $\smile-$, whereas English, for example, is generally considered to be by nature a spondaic language, i.e. $--$.

Dialogue normally consists of a longish passage of these iambic lines to which another actor responds in an equally longish passage. Often there appears something more abrupt, more in keeping with conversation, known as stichomythy (speech in rows), which is a line by line exchange between two characters. But the syllabic parallelism introduces a certain singsong quality which encourages a certain what we might call singsong mentality whereby the lines become highly epigrammatic, aphoristic, self-contained. Unlike responsive human speech, the lines of stichomythy are aggressive and competitive; this may, of course, reflect in an abstracted way that characteristic Greek turn of mind.

Occasionally actors, usually one, however, and the chorus will have an exchange, generally altogether in lyrical rhythms, and the moment is one of deep emotion, corresponding perhaps to showcase moments such as the sextet from *Lucia di Lammermoor*. The long prayer to the dead Agamemnon sung by Electra, Orestes and the chorus (*Libation Bearers* 306ff.) is particularly operatic in our terms.

Initially the poet acted in his own plays, later the state paid for the services of three professionals, one assigned to each tragedian, awarded by lot. How they recruited their other actors is unknown. All parts were played by males. These actors were not professional by our standards; there was not enough theater to make a profession of acting, although revivals in the outlying districts occurred and actors might have played the circuit in other Greek cities. We may assume they were men talented enough to command pay for their services. The job was indeed hard, that is, playing the protagonist role in all three tragedies and the satyr play. This would mean switching from Clytemnestra in the *Agamemnon* to Orestes in the *Libation Bearers,* for instance. For a modern actor who was trying to "get into the character" this would be singularly hard. It should help to show us the surface nature of ancient acting, which relates immediately to the limited sense of character in the plays. Nonetheless the actors were important. As the fifth century progressed the audience grew more and more attentive to the quality of the acting; actors became celebrated, by what criterion it is not clear, but very likely for the sheer technical skill of projecting.

Apart from the chorus there were never more than three actors in a play, which means that no more than three speaking parts come together at one time, although we know of up to eleven roles in one play. Sometimes lightning changes of mask and costume must have been necessary to get an actor back on as another character. In Sophocles' *Antigone,* for instance, the actor playing Creon goes out at 1114 and returns as Eurydice at 1180, departs at 1234, then returns as Creon at 1255. In the *Trachiniae,* it seems that the same actor played Hercules and Dejaneira. Theseus may have been played by three different men in the *Oedipus at Colonus.* The many examples of this kind suggest that the audience was not looking for subtleties of characterization. Costume and mask were evidently the necessary surface. The rationale for the limitations on the number of speaking parts eludes us. Three, of course, is a number of many metaphysical attributes. It is the perfect expression of the family particularly as seen through the eyes of a child or as a grown person will remember his family situation. It is also the neatest expression of the group (two's company, three's a crowd). It has been suggested that three actors reflect the Indo-European structuring of person into I, thou, he (we, you, they). Others imagine the use of three to reflect a tendency to limit the number because of the problem of finding persons able to measure up to the feat of throwing the voice such a distance combined with the ancient Greeks' natural conservatism (once a limit of three, always a limit of three). Symmetry and conservatism are very likely to be significant causes. Then too, the essential antithetical nature of ancient tragedy prohibits conversation (compare a Shakespearean play, where there is immediately a sense of the *group* which does not exist in Greek tragedy except in the chorus, and there in a very different way). Two characters have a dialogue, a third listens then offers an alternative antithesis, as for instance the scene in Euripides' *Bacchae* when Tiresias and Cadmus try to reason with the agitated Pentheus, and they take turns offering him different ideas antithetical to his position. If the antithesis is not there the third character has no reason to speak. Cassandra has rightly nothing to say as she observes the famous psychic duel between Agamemnon and Clytemnestra; furthermore her silence suggests the finality and inevitability of the events in the play. When later she commences to hallucinate all the events of the House of Atreus come together as though at one moment in time. Her silent, knowing presence is the silent universe pregnant with events past, present and future, known and necessary.

The actors were particularly noted for their voices, for having strong voices able to project a great distance (150 feet at Epidaurus from center orchestra to top row) in an open-air auditorium which brought no sound back, against clothing which deadens sound and against the sound of movement and muffled conversation in the vast outdoor audience. Furthermore the actors were projecting their voices through masks. Clarity was praised, volume with lack of strain, tone quality, the ability to change it for the mood of the character —these are the matters ancient critics bring up. Masks made facial expression unnecessary; gesture and body movement we know next to nothing about although it is assumed that movement was stylized. This may derive from the innumerable vase paintings, which naturally catch scenes and freeze them, rendering in us a certain notion of austerity not unlike the effect bare whitened marble has. Certainly gestures had to be large, simple and broad in order to be seen and comprehended in so vast an auditorium. They may well have been more or less symbolic again to make them more readily understood.

The mask was a constant feature of ancient tragedy. While

(in later antiquity) the masks became standardized in order to represent a range of conventional expressions, in the fifth century they were individual. Masks are a common feature in primitive religion. They are a means whereby the worshiper may assume his god; by puttting on the mask he puts on god. In transferring this idea to the theater the actors were able very simply to reinforce their roles, here by "putting on" the character. As a practical matter, of course, masks with exaggerated features would help to demonstrate at a great distance the visages. Masks would contribute to the surface sense projected in so many other ways. Unconsciously an audience knows that actors are portraying persons and thus there is no true bond, union, relationship between the physical being observed and the character developed. But ancient theatrical convention perhaps insisted more upon the artifice so that one saw the dramatization of representation. The nature and degree of ancient theatrical artificiality is important in trying to gauge the nature and degree of empathetic response from the audience.

What response the chorus achieved is still more difficult to imagine because we know next to nothing of their dance and of their music. Both these elements worked with the words, but only the words remain. Sometimes choral lyrics seem so superficial or banal that we assume the playwright was more interested in the music. Clarity is always a problem for a group of singers, and a number of choruses are so complicated in terms of imagery and development that they must have demanded acute attention. The convention of repeating exactly the meter of the strophe in the antistrophe (that is, the meter of the first stanza, so to speak, is reproduced in the second) may in part represent an effort toward clarity, easier for the chorus singing unison a second time in the metrical pattern, easier for the audience to follow. Evidently the music became more exotic, rhythms more complicated and forced. Aristophanes' parodies of Euripides show that the tragedian was interested in musical effects such as trilling. Here we see the gradual ascendancy of music over the choral words; the evidence also suggests the growing dramatic awkwardness of the chorus and finally its disappearance in fourth-century tragedies.

In some way the choral passages must have been an intrusion upon the episodes because the chorus members had to group to dance, so that greater physical movement commenced where none had been before. Perhaps this explains the very common practice of having the final remarks preceding a choral ode be of an extraordinary banality, on the theory that the audience observing the chorus preparing for movement sympathetically rearranged themselves in their seats. Thus these insignificant lines were to be thrown away in the attendant noise and distraction. Compare this with Shakespeare's custom of situating a few rhymed lines as a coda to a scene. They are often simplistic but the rhyme scheme makes them cunning, and brings one's attention up sharp to the end. Their simplicity, however, allows for reduced concentration.

How the chorus moved is almost completely uncertain. Vase paintings suggest some things, but, of course, there is no actual movement in the painting. They moved in generally rectangular formation, five rows three deep. Phrynichus and Aeschylus were said to have invented many dance schemes, and the normally conservative Athenians possibly made these into the conventional choreographic patterns. Vase paintings show more concentration on hand gesture; perhaps there was little movement from place to place. These hand gestures may have been some sort of pantomime.

While the origins of tragedy are very obscure, the chorus was an original element. In the archaic period the dithyramb, a song in honor of Dionysus, was sung by a chorus. The dithyramb was essentially narrative; the choral divisions, antiphonally responsive to each other, create a kind of rudimentary dialogue. If the chorus leader sang alone he was a kind of individualized actor. The *Iliad* and *Odyssey* provide excellent models of the kind of dialogue that in fact appears in developed tragedy. It is not impossible to find elements in their separate state that may have gone into the formation of tragedy.

It is customary to say that the chorus diminished in importance in the course of the fifth century. In Aeschylus' plays the chorus is well delineated and very much enters and affects the action, for instance the hysterical women of the *Seven Against Thebes* who so upset Eteocles or the Erinyes who pursue Orestes in the *Eumenides*. In Euripides' plays, however, they often seem to stand about. Tragic convention had the chorus present throughout the action with few exceptions; thus when they were no longer delineated, no longer made to participate, they simply existed to sing odes. Indeed they seem to be an embarrassment, an irrelevancy in the tragic action. Yet, on the other hand, Sophocles' *Philoctetes* and Euripides' *Bacchae,* two of the very last extant plays written and produced, show amazingly powerful choral roles. The isolation and desolation of Philoctetes is no better demonstrated than by the choral remarks on the loneliness of Lemnos, more specifically by the chorus lying to him, becoming in that moment the fundamental hostility of his human environment as opposed to his integration into his natural environment. The Maenads in the *Bacchae* exhibit in the human psyche all the calm, the gentleness and the hysterical, cruel passion that the religion of Dionysus develops; they show the mood of the women in the hills and the psychic dilemma of Pentheus and the others in Thebes. Throughout the play they relate to Dionysus as a participating actor. On the basis of the extant plays we may say that compared to the Aeschylean use of the chorus as actor later plays often show a disregard for their dramatic potential. To go further than that is hazard although perhaps we may cite a trend in noticing that Agathon, Euripides' counterpart according to Aristotle, started the practice of writing choral passages that could be transferred from play to play. Thus we have the chorus become mere entr'acte. In any criticism of tragedy it is central to try to ascertain the presence of this tendency in individual plays.

The production of the tragedies was an obligation, a kind of income tax, laid upon Athens' wealthier citizens, who considered it an honor and an occasion for finding glory. The aristocracy's traditional penchant for display, for advertising their quality through material displays whether architecture or poetry readings, found an outlet in the democracy with state-imposed conspicuous financial obligations whereby the rich could content themselves with something like building a bridge or a warship. Mounting a tragedy must have been an exquisite joy. The tragic poet might act in his plays, or direct them, but the cost of the production was borne by the *choregos* ("he who leads the chorus"). Costumes for the chorus, training the chorus, their salaries, their trainer, the flautist, these were the responsibilities of the *choregos*. Each playwright had his *choregos* so that competition appears here as well to see who could mount the most brilliant production. Since the *choregoi* were wealthy they must have had some power. One wonders if, as powerful men, they attempted to influence the playwright. We know that they tried to influence the judges, but that would be for reasons of prestige. Did they take an interest in the plays? Did they ever find them morally offensive? Did they try to introduce political ideas and ideologies into the plays?

Athenian playwrights were composing pieces for an audience that participated in the fullest sense in their city government just as they participated in choruses. They were aware and *engagé* to an extraordinary degree: issues, values, theories, we may assume, were the subject of daily debate or conversation. It is important to remember this because since ancient tragedy has remained with us in an important way for two and a half millennia and its original historical setting has receded from our ken the tendency to look for the most abstracted universals in tragedy becomes a natural critical approach. One wonders, however, if the original audience were not too involved in social and political life to be content with such universals.

We are not sure of the degree of political reference in the plays. Aeschylus' *Eumenides* seems to be a celebration of the Athenian legal process as an alternative to traditional justice, and its date of performance relates to a period of changes in the Athenian system where the Areopagus court dominated by the aristocracy lost ground to the popularly controlled juries. The *Oresteia* celebrates among other things the transference of justice from family to city, a corollary to the decrease in aristocratic power. To take a somewhat more subtle example, if in Sophocles' *Oedipus the King* Oedipus and Jocasta summoned up to the Athenian mind their most prominent general, Pericles, and his common-law wife, Aspasia, then the sufferings of Oedipus in the play must have a political meaning that otherwise would not be there. Or in Sophocles' *Oedipus at Colonus* how may we relate Theseus' goodness, Creon's malevolence, the bitter historical hostility of Athens toward Thebes (of which place Creon is the legendary king), the choral ode in praise of Attic olive trees, the fact that successive Spartan invasions had destroyed the olive trees? Is the fundamental goodness of Athens relative to the other Greek city-states to be seen in Theseus? Is Athens' failure and sick fatigue in these last days of the Peloponnesian War to be seen in Oedipus' cursing his son, in a sense cursing the future, which the old who are defeated tend to do? It is as though it were the revenge of a failed society. And is Oedipus' apotheosis at the play's end meant to suggest the transcendence and survival of the legendary and ideal (of Athens perhaps) over the ephemeral and terrestrial, much as the choral song imposes the continued vision of the olive trees of Attica even when they are gone? In varying degrees, often in details, political references may exist which we cannot control.

Consider, for instance, Sophocles' *Philoctetes*. Among other things it has to do with society's rejection of an individual man and its subsequent exploitation of him despite his personal feelings. Or consider Sophocles' *Ajax*, which toward the close has to do with the public rehabilitation of a man who has acted against the group's leaders, hence against the group. One should see these plays against the law of ostracism. Now, the ostracism law was infrequently invoked. Yet it remained a feature of the political life, operative on men's expectations. Moreover in moments of crisis ostracized men could be recalled due to the desperate need of their qualities of leadership. One such was Cimon, a leading figure of old-fashioned views, exiled in 461, recalled some five or six years later. His story must have been part of the city lore. His treatment is very much the story of the *Ajax* or the *Philoctetes* more especially as well as other tragedies. Certainly the audience must have thought of the tensions in their own political system when they saw these plays rather than thinking only in such abstract terms as rejection and exploitation.

Balanced against this, however, is the absence of specific allusions. This together with the emphasis upon a kind of stark portrayal of action shows another dimension to tragedy. The critical problem is to balance these two elements. Naturally enough tragedy will mean something to us in our time that very likely will be at some remove from the ancient Athenian understanding. But insofar as we are able it is worth the effort to try to understand the circumstances that surrounded their understanding because it allows for a fuller appreciation of the ancient plays.

Another crucial factor in the ancient perception of tragedy is the common culture. Particularly in secular pluralistic America, where mass education has introduced a variety of classes and groups to a smattering of learning reduced for easy comprehension, and specialization is a matter of course for anyone with pretensions to education, there can be no such thing as a common culture except on the simplest, crudest level. And the same is beginning to be true in Europe. The Athenians, at least the adult free-born male Athenians, were educated little but alike, that is, they got their sense of history, mythology, philosophy, ethics, literary style and so on from memorizing the *Iliad* and the *Odyssey* and the poems of Solon through the early years of schooling. The Homeric epics portray an aristocratic culture and the Athens of the seventh and sixth centuries was itself an aristocratic culture which only began to change in the democratic fifth century. The emergent bourgeoisie, the mercantile group, never thought of themselves as a separate class with separate values and aspirations as was the case in Rome and, of course, in modern European history. One common culture was accepted by all to which the playwrights could speak easily and generally. Therefore the frequent aphorisms for which ancient tragedy is famous are really part of the common consciousness, allusions to a stable and complete view of life possessed by the entire audience. That, too, must be considered in trying to criticize the plays.

Over the last two millennia the critical approach to tragedy has changed many times. Perhaps the most common critical starting point to tragedy is a discussion of the hero.

Fifth-century tragedy shows a development of the individualized hero and the dialogue with a concomitant diminution of the role of the chorus. In political terms this can be considered a movement away from the aristocratic concentration upon the group, where the physical, social and sensual values of music and dance are emphasized, toward the bourgeois concentration upon the individual and a verbal intellectualist structuring of reality. The increasingly resolute despair of the tragic experience may as well reflect the individual's emergence from a society made up of extended families, the *oikos*, which has a continued existence, to the isolated world where each of us in dying individually faces total extinction.

The Greek conception of the hero is also often taken as a point of contrast with cultures of the East. For the Greeks, it seems, exalted the ego, an exaltation that has remained a distinctive point of the Western experience since. On the other hand, it is much more debated to what extent the Greeks in their drama created fully rounded characters with personalities, distinct, unique personages. When the Greek tragedians are compared with Shakespeare's plays, for instance, the Greek tragic heroes at once seem far more two-dimensional, much more type figures or archetypal figures than individuals. But to define these tragic heroes is to see the image the fifth-century Athenians projected of man and hence of themselves as well as to face a conception of the human dilemma that has informed Western tradition to our own day.

The centrality of the hero in our critical sight has, however, been challenged on the view that Aristotle's keen emphasis upon action in tragedy in the *Poetics* points to the fact that the drama is best understood as a structure of events, a frame of action. The characters are not, of course, simply incidental to the action, but they are not on the contrary the reason for the action. Action has a value and an existence independent of the characters. Critical emphasis upon the action has opened up tragedy to structural interpretations, that is, to breaking down the action into its essential elements. This has led to associating the action of the drama ever more closely with the myth from which it is drawn. Often this can be confusing since the dramatic presentation and the myth are not at all the same thing.

Structural ideas have led to a renewed interest in the archetypal nature of the characters and the action, or if not archetypal in the Jungian sense, then the typicality of characters and action. Again the nature of myth is important because myth is often considered to be action, pure action, distilled from contexts and personalities.

In the same way critics look into the tragedies for acts and attitudes that seem to have the same abstracted quality. Or critics consider how tragedies, in fact, create acts and attitudes that become abstractions, capable of separate existence in our minds, having a myth-like quality. One thinks, for instance, particularly of the speakers' *agon* whether it be Menelaus arguing with Odysseus over Ajax's honors, or Admetus arguing with Pheres over Alcestis' death. To study this phenomenon, however, is to look more at culture than at the tragic art.

Certainly an enduring fact of ancient Greek tragedy is its extraordinary universality. The fact of tragedy can be manipulated and distorted to accommodate differing value systems, as for instance the way Seneca's Stoic re-creations of the Greek tragedies paved the way to Christian tragedy. Still there remains a basic structure which speaks to human beings at all times. Perhaps, in fact, one could say that the tragic heroes, that all of us, are going finally to the seashore, freely and sometimes joyfully. It is the *hamartia*, the human frailty or failure, the *metabole*, the reversal, and the *anagnorisis*, the realization, that provide the succession of tragic events. That, it seems, is death and our knowledge of it, or our eventual realization of it. And this is true to the fact that man is the only animal who realizes that he is doomed. Human existence is the travail of coming to know this. But tragedy is not pessimistic, as some would maintain, or gloomy, for the concentration is not on the *metabole*, but on the glorious, hard-won, hard-to-hold *anagnorisis*. It is this act of unblinking clarity that justified man to himself, and always shall, in a world of puny gods and senseless fate.

CHAPTER EIGHT
MYTH AND TRAGEDY

The harder they come, the harder they fall, one and all.

Jimmy Cliff

The dice of Zeus are always loaded.

Sophocles, fragment

The tragedians avoided original plots. They did not invent their stories but found them in the rich saga tradition of the oral period. Euripides' strange play *Alcestis* has a plot that probably comes from fairy tale, and that is unusual. Fairy tale has to do with rags-to-riches, materially as in the case of Cinderella or emotionally as in the case of Sleeping Beauty. This movement is antithetical to the rhythm of tragedy, which in Aristotle's words shows a better than average man going from a better to a worse situation. That bare formula gives the underlying action of tragedy regardless of the more fully devised surface plot. It is a celebration of death, better yet a rehearsal of death, the rite of death. Tragic theater, like so much else in what is crudely termed "the humanities," prepares us to die just as science helps us to live, a distinction noted over half a century ago by Unamuno. The sagas from which the plots came grew fewer, concentrated upon the doings of certain illustrious families. We have extant several plays dealing with events in the royal family of Atreus, Aeschylus' *Oresteia*, Sophocles' *Electra*, Euripides' *Electra* and *Orestes*, *Iphigenia in Tauris* and *Iphigenia at Aulis;* the House of Labdacus is celebrated in Aeschylus' *Seven Against Thebes,* Sophocles' *Antigone, Oedipus the King* and *Oedipus at Colonus* and Euripides' *Phoinissai.* Curiously enough the Athenians had little local mythology so that the action is rarely laid at Athens in tragedy.

The saga world was not thought to be reality but on the other hand it was not fiction. The ancients understood saga's essential untruth and thereby allowed their poets to alter and shape the stories to serve other than narrative ends; at the same time the *traditional* nature of saga, its evident mirroring of real events, its coloring of history, gave inevitability and solidity to the things there related, a solidity that outright fiction could not possess; after all, the oral poetic tradition constituted the Greeks' cultural heritage, their only history handed down from the prehistorical period. There was a world, then, inhabited by figures acting out events who not only resided in the people's cultural consciousness but who appeared enough times from drama to drama to acquire some kind of substance. Creon, for instance, brother to Jocasta, uncle of Antigone, appears in three of Sophocles' extant plays (as well as Euripides' *Phoinissai*) which span almost thirty years of playwriting. In a sense Creon, too, has life and his existence has dimension. This is not true of those ephemeral beings, whether Caliban or Nora Helmer or Blanche Du Bois, who are the creatures of an author's mind summoned forth into an existence solely of his making. The figures of saga lived in a world of their own that no single author could control.

Occasionally poets tried stories based on actual events. The late-sixth-century Athenian tragedian Phrynichus dramatized the fall of Miletus and after bringing it before an Athenian audience he was fined for his pains because of the grief the audience felt at reliving this disaster. This anecdote is instructive because it implies that there were qualitative distinctions to the emotions to be engendered by the dramas. Aristotle makes the well-known but hard to understand reference to the purgation of pity and fear. We may suppose pity to be the product of the empathetic response ("there but for the grace of God . . .") just as we cry at funerals principally for ourselves; fear, however, derives from the dramatization of the horrible fact of death. Phrynichus' play aroused these emotions too much or in the wrong way. When the events

were real, the audience related to them so directly that there
was no stance they could take before them, no way to get a
purchase on them, to maintain that measure of objectivity
that keeps us knowing when it is life and when it is art.
Ancient tragedy is obvious artifice, there is no sustained attempt at realism; true plots are therefore antipathetic to this
mood.

Aeschylus tried what seems a more successful dramatization of true events, the *Persians,* which is instructive of the
way Athenian audiences perhaps wanted action. The play has
to do with the aftermath of the battle at Salamis, where
Athens won an extraordinary naval victory and significantly
destroyed the Persian fleet and moreover Xerxes' dreams of
Persian control of Greece. The play was perhaps produced
for some kind of Athenian victory celebration, and obviously
there was no mood of sorrow to be touched, a difference in
circumstance from that which Phrynichus confronted. Aeschylus, however, has contrived a play that is altogether remote from the immediate Athenian interest. The action takes
place in innermost Persia. The characters have strange-sound-
ing ("foreign") Persian names, no individual Greek is mentioned; in sum, the particularities of the event of September
480 B.C. in the gulf between the western coast of Attica
and the island of Salamis are avoided or omitted although
they form the necessary background and cause for the actions
of the play. The central concern in the play is Xerxes'
expectations in mounting this expedition and how his defeat
relates to these. In this way Aeschylus has transcended the
historical facts, found a stance from which he and the audience may view them, and more withdrawn, more objectively
proceeds to look at the workings of pride and its delusion.
This becomes the "truth" of these real events. Aeschylus'
Persians is not *verité,* not documentary, but instead seems as
universal and inevitable as the action of myth and saga, which
is located midway between historical fact and fantasy.

The tragedians did not generally take episodes from the
Homeric poems and turn them into tragedy, although
Aeschylus referred to his pieces as "slices from the banquet
of Homer." Aeschylus had a strong sense of the style of epic.
One thinks of that ornate, majestic and—for theater—very
slow descriptive recital of the warriors who wait to fight at
the city's gate in the *Seven Against Thebes* (375ff.). Sophocles
mounted characters who derived their ethos from a Homeric

heroic temper, an Ajax or a Philoctetes. Euripides appreciated the symbolic value of the Homeric figures whom tradition and education had so thoroughly realized in his contemporaries' minds, and he used many of them. Still none of them reworked any of Homer's story. Perhaps this is so, partly, because of the way in which the poet of the *Iliad* poses Achilles' tragic dilemma. Although done with great economy, it nevertheless requires the several thousand lines of books 1, 9, and 18–24 to work out. Tragic drama turns on the barest skeletal acts and the Homeric narration has given Achilles' story a great flesh of complexity.

This is the problem with using Homer. The poems are complete statements that leave nothing to be said. Likewise they do not advertise where any part might be to advantage removed. The context and the act are inextricably linked. Tragedy, which does not need details, locale or context, looked then perhaps to saga stories that survived in versions more like chronicles without the richness of a Homeric treatment, where the actions alone stood forth.

The subject matter of tragedy, however, is something different from saga. Saga, quasi-historical, traditional and presumed to be true, is narrative that tells a story where there is interaction between people, places and events. Tragedy is something other. It is often distilled saga.

The structure of the subject matter of tragedy is called myth, but no two critics can agree on what is meant by the term. It is used by psychologists, anthropologists and literary critics among others. Each group refuses to relinquish the term as a part of its jargon. Myth comes from the Greek *mythos*, story; our word "myth" means story, too, with special emphasis on the action. Myth is the narration of acts. Character, personality, locale, prior events, none of these factors that normally influence and qualify action in a story are essential to myth. It is action undiluted, distilled from antecedents, coincidents and posterity.

Psychologists like to talk of archetypal acts and anthropologists speak of the ritual behind myth. Both groups are talking of abstracted action; that is central to myth. One can see this in, for instance, the Homeric Hymn to Aphrodite, which recounts how that goddess was stricken with love for the fair young shepherd Anchises, a mortal (see pp. 96f.). One need not strip this story down far beneath the brief description of physical beauty and Aphrodite's journeying to Anchises' tent to get to the often encountered story of a goddess seducing a young man whereby he is destroyed. It is the basic story of the Earth and the Season who fertilizes her and then wanes. Added here is the fairy-tale element of the prohibition to Anchises against revealing the identity of his love partner and his subsequent catastrophic disobedience. It is Cinderella's being told to get home by midnight, or Bluebeard's injunction not to open one door in his castle.

Similar action without context can be found in the Hymn to Demeter where Demeter loses her daughter Persephone, who is snatched away by Hades, the god of the Underworld. While tearfully wandering the world in search of her daughter, Demeter in disguise acts as nursemaid to a young princeling Demophoön, whom she nightly lays in the fire's flames to ensure his immortality. She is discovered by the baby's mother, the charm is broken, Demeter drops the disguise and tells the mother how close the boy came to being immortal. Likewise when Zeus negotiates with Hades the return of Persephone the Underworld god gives her a pomegranate to eat, which it turns out (like fairy-tale foods) will prevent her from remaining forever with her mother. Thus every year when Persephone departs her mother will grieve, crops will not grow. Both events repeat the truth of the baby Demophoön's close brush with immortality.

The archetypal act or the ritual act is constant. Myth, too, in its storymaking has this quality. The action described in myth is eternal, either because it will be repeated in this or some other guise forever or because it has no real subsequent action to blot it out. Actions such as an overpowering goddess seducing and destroying her young male paramour are incessant and inevitable; even as crops come and go Demeter will lose, seek and find her daughter; as death follows life and always as a surprise, so Demeter will always try to bestow immortality and the charm will be broken.

The stories most commonly used by the tragedians satisfied their audiences because they articulated deep-seated, difficult-to-express urges or tendencies individually or culturally felt. The main tragedies portray familial situations. While the family is a good metaphor for the body politic or the commonweal, it is more precisely the primary arena for interpersonal relationships. The extant tragedies present in various external dress certain key relationships: husband-wife, brother-sister, father-son and so on.

The very common relationship is a destructive conjugal one: Clytemnestra-Agamemnon in Aeschylus' *Agamemnon*, Dejaneira-Hercules in Sophocles' *Trachiniae*, Medea-Jason in Euripides' *Medea* are principal examples, although others could be added. The relationship of Phaedra to Hippolytus in Euripides' *Hippolytus*, although actually stepmother and stepson, is remarkably similar as is in certain respects the Alcestis-Admetus relationship of Euripides' *Alcestis*. In each instance the male rejects or resists the woman and she retaliates overtly or unconsciously to this. Agamemnon kills Clytemnestra's daughter, abandons the mother and in the course of the play resists stepping on the ceremonial carpet and entering the house (a situation with sexual implications), Hercules resists returning to his wife's embrace as he returns with a new concubine, Jason plans to abandon Medea and marry anew, Hippolytus rejects Phaedra's advances and Admetus is willing to see his wife die in his place. Clytemnestra plots to cut her husband down, Medea kills Jason's children, Phaedra lies about Hippolytus to his doom, whereas Dejaneira innocently kills her husband with a love potion and Alcestis piously imposes upon Admetus a lifelong obligation to mourn her. That Agamemnon is a tired, somewhat failed general or Jason a heartless opportunist or Admetus a pompous egotist or Hercules an old-fashioned, highhearted hero who never thought of a woman's feelings or that Hippolytus is a prude and a prig is beside the point; the circumstances do not extenuate.

It is better to think of roles. Contemporary criticism emphasizes action over character in Greek tragedy. Agamemnon, for instance, is general, king, head of the house and father. The collision in Aeschylus' *Agamemnon* comes in acting out these roles; Agamemnon, then, is not a personality, a character making a personal choice, when he does what he does. One can extend this range in order to get at the richness of suggestion in tragic "thinking," which might equally be called creative ambiguity. Agamemnon is also a sacrificial victim, a year god, an embodiment of excessive pride and a wayfarer just as Clytemnestra is a victor, a high priestess, emblem of the Great Mother Goddess, the embodiment of divine seduction and a welcoming host in the house. Above all they are man and wife, battling for their place in the house. Neither is a realized personality. One cannot imagine them in the routine of their life away from these moments in the stage drama.

The lists of titles of the plays performed in fifth-century Athens indicate that the same stories were often used although very few extant plays tell the same story.

Sometimes, however, a playwright's interest in a theme spans a generation; there are extant three plays of Sophocles dealing with the House of Labdacus at Thebes: the *Antigone,* probably produced in 441; the *Oedipus Tyrannus,* probably soon after 430; and *Oedipus at Colonus,* posthumously brought out in 401. Antigone and Creon appear in all three, Oedipus in two. A common critical error is the tendency to take these plays as some kind of trilogy. Of course, they are not, not at all. Then, sometimes it seems easy to imagine the playwright living with these figures in his mind. It is crucial to decide this point because characterization in tragedy is notoriously minimal, which argues that the figures are types or symbols and/or the emphasis is always fully on the action, hence the dramatis personae are nothing more than actors or doers. If, however, some strong consistency or continuity in characterization seems to exist, it can be argued that neither playwright nor audience needed extensive characterization, that the actions were natural and complex individual extensions of fully realized characters that peopled the minds of every member of the culture.

The character of Oedipus is so central to the story that he naturally displays certain common features in both *Oedipus Tyrannus* and *Oedipus at Colonus.* The man in ignorance has done things that make him upon his discovery of them a taboo figure. He has been reviled and exiled, he had in fact unwittingly decreed himself excommunicant in the land of Thebes. These events cause anguish, a tortured personality—this comes out in the *Oedipus at Colonus.* He is struck with his own undeserved misfortune, and sees himself in his uncommon suffering as elevated or isolated from mankind's common experience. So his suffering, however awful, is the lever to his veritable apotheosis. His existence, he himself, are awful in the two senses of the word. The dazzling energy of the king of Thebes, energy that turns to relentless inquiry and finally to grim ferocity as the lineaments of the awful truth become more obvious, is akin to the strength of his anguish in the latter play. Oedipus in his suspicions of Creon and Tiresias, Oedipus determined to torture the aged shepherd to

get him to acknowledge what Oedipus now dimly knows will
be his own destruction—this is the same man who savagely
curses his own son, grimly willing the young man's death,
just before he himself in thunder and lightning disappears
from this earth.

Sophocles' realization of Creon, however, is more instructive because he is central only in the *Antigone,* and therefore
the story's events do not so much create him. Brother to
Jocasta, he is not meant to rule, but to remain instead no
more than a prince of the household. This is the role and
personality Sophocles gives him in the *Oedipus Tyrannus,*
where he delivers (583ff.) a long, characterizing speech describing the pleasures of royalty, which are his free of all
monarchical responsiblity. The speech is meant as proof of
his assertion that he would never seek Oedipus' throne.
Sophocles has contrived in Creon a contrast to the driving,
energetic, insecure Oedipus. Creon is amiable, pleasure-lov-
ing, passive. Another facet to his character, an aristocratic
trait, is his sense of privacy. He twice urges that action or
talk take place within the palace away from the eyes and
ears of the people. Oedipus, on the contrary, is a public
man, as evidenced from his initial speech in *Oedipus Tyrannus,* which despite the exigencies of tragedy's form and
style comes something as self-advertisement (. . . "I have
come, I whom all men call Oedipus, the famed"). Creon's
measured calm remains even after Oedipus has put out his
eyes and Jocasta kills herself, leaving Creon to the throne.
We have it in the colloquy between Oedipus and Creon at the
play's very end; Oedipus still impetuous, still commanding
("send me from Thebes," "lead me away," "don't take the
children"), Creon platitudinous and passive ("everything in
due season," "make that request of the god," "don't try to
control everything").

Creon in the *Antigone* is Sophocles' earliest preserved conception of that figure. The perspective is inevitably different
since here Creon is established king at Thebes pitted against
Antigone, who has committed crimes against the state, which
Creon takes to be embodied in himself and thus they are
acts hostile to him personally. The part is large, Creon has
much to say on the nature of freedom and obedience, the
state and the individual, and he is made to suffer in the latter part of the play as he learns that Antigone, his son
Haimon and his wife Eurydice have all taken their lives partly

in protest against his policy, partly because they cannot endure the world he wants, the situation he has created and insists upon maintaining.

In contrast to the deliberate inaction of the Creon of the *Oedipus Tyrannus,* a Creon who elaborates the virtues of being a spectator, this Creon believes in action and responsibility. "One cannot know a man," he says (175ff.), "his personality, his mind, his ideas, until you see him holding responsibility functioning in the laws and customs of the city." On the one hand, this remark in reference to himself derives from a sense of identification almost akin to that implicit in *l'état, c'est moi;* on the other hand it reflects, although in exaggerated form, the dominant philosophy of the city-state (best expressed in Plato's *Crito*) that every man finds his fullest identity and expression as he functions within and as realization of his *polis.* The collision between Antigone and Creon is tragic; as Hegel pointed out, the rights and obligations of the individual and of the state are inevitably antithetical, and for Sophocles they remain tragically irreconcilable. As the play progresses and Creon speaks more and more of law and order (473ff., 659ff.), of hierarchies (762ff.), Antigone first ("I wasn't born to join in hating, but in loving," 523), then Haimon (683ff.) and finally the chorus (782ff.) speak of love. The latter concept is probably the best expression of the individual personality as law, order and hierarchy are of the social organism. Creon is misguided, grown tyrannical in his desperation, but he is never really malicious.

To these two portraits we may contrast the Creon of the *Oedipus at Colonus.* Here is a monster of a man, a liar, sanctimonious, alternately brazen and wheedling, who will use any ruse, lie or show of force to get Oedipus back to Thebes. He is here the natural foil to Theseus, ruler of Athens, and as the commentators point out Athens and Thebes were bitter enemies at the time of the play's production. Perhaps that dictated his characterization, or perhaps Sophocles wished to show off in this way the directness of Oedipus. In any case here as in the *Oedipus Tyrannus* considerations within the play, namely, the effect of contrast, call forth the characterization. There seems, therefore, to be no consistent conception of Creon that is carried over through all three plays. Certainly it is hard to imagine the Creon of *Antigone* evolving into the Creon of the *Oedipus Tyrannus.*

Unlike the several figures who reappear in different plays

there is only one example of the repetition of the same story. Three dramatic versions of the Orestes-Electra story are extant and they are instructive in showing how the playwrights used myth in creating a plot. The result is different from fiction because of what is familiar and what is assumed. The Electra-Orestes dramas also reveal exactly how saga was distilled into myth and what the poets could do with it. Aeschylus brought out his *Oresteia* in 456, the second play of which is called the *Choephoroi* (*Libation Bearers*), dealing with Electra, Orestes and the slaying of Clytemnestra. Sophocles and Euripides each brought out a play entitled *Electra*. Euripides' version came in 413. One of the more tantalizing scholarly games is dating Sophocles' version. It is thought to be roughly contemporaneous but the question of priority is interesting, for to some minds it is a corrective to Euripides' conception, whereas to others Euripides' play is a parody of Sophocles' *Electra*.

The legend of the House of Atreus presents certain elements with which the dramatist must work and some that he may or may not include. The part of the legend relative to Orestes and Electra in bare outline goes as follows:

Agamemnon, chosen as overlord of the expedition against Troy, faces military disaster when the fleet is becalmed in Aulis harbor. Winds are promised if he will sacrifice his daughter Iphigenia. This he does, and the fleet departs. His wife Clytemnestra, in grief at her daughter's death (real or feigned motive), takes a lover, Aigisthos (her husband's cousin), and plots Agamemnon's death. Upon his return, caught by deceit, he is struck down. Clytemnestra and Aigisthos now rule openly, casting from their rightful position Agamemnon's daughters, the royal princesses Electra and Chrysothemis. All of this is much to the distress of Electra, who continually laments her father's death and prays for the return of her brother. Their brother Orestes, sent away by sympathetic hands at the time of Agamemnon's death, grows to manhood, an exile in a foreign land.

Finally Orestes returns at the behest of Apollo to his native land to exact vengeance from his mother for his father's death. Since he has been gone from infancy he is unrecognizable. His return leads to a joyful recognition scene between brother and sister, plans are laid for killing the mother, and there is in turn a tearful and hideous recognition scene between son and mother. When she and her paramour have been killed Orestes is subject to a very strong adverse reaction, from either religious or psychological causes. The events of this paragraph contain Electra's and Orestes' story proper, but the playwrights assume knowledge of the preceding details.

The essence of the story is the son slaying his mother; closely related to this is the dejection, bitterness and yearning for revenge of the sister, and perhaps equal to that in importance is the recognition of the brother and sister. Psychologists have dealt with this story; some find it analogous to the Oedipal situation save that a tendency to euphemism translates the incestuous intercourse of the son with his mother into the less taboo matricide. Note, however, that his "punishment" is harsher. Pausanias records (8.34.1–2) that after killing his mother Orestes bit off his thumb, which has been interpreted as a form of castration, more obvious than Oedipus' putting out his eyes. Some social psychologists, however, see this as only another instance of the general fear of parents (which indeed underlies the banquet of Thyestes). That is to say, Atreus dismembers and cooks children, Thyestes eats children (albeit unwillingly), Agamemnon kills his daughter, Clytemnestra spurns Electra and wishes Orestes dead.

The constantly expressed fear of Orestes by Clytemnestra is similar to that in the Oedipus myth; that of the son who will come back to destroy his father. Here, Orestes, who has been sent away, will someday return with fatal results. Clearly enough details differ, motives are not the same, but the skeletal outline remains the same, as though there were indeed certain human acts that are basic, and so repeat themselves from legend to legend. This consideration is most important in analyzing Greek tragedy, for it becomes the sameness that is important, the *rehearsal* of events.

A number of familiar human feelings are evoked in this story beyond that of the potentially malevolent mother-son relationship. There is, for one, the closeness of the sibling relationship at times bordering on incest. Most pervasive is the phenomenon of recognition. The brother returns and recognizes his native land (in the Sophoclean version Orestes' traveling companion, his aged tutor, points out all the local sites, dramatically emphasizing the recognition). Orestes and Electra are reunited through a celebrated scene of recognition tokens. Clytemnestra recognizes her son. In one version

Aigisthos suddenly recognizes the corpse of Clytemnestra, which hitherto he had imagined to be that of Orestes. Another element that strikes at hearts in common is the sight of the outcast girl bereft of father and brother, disowned by her mother. In a society where the family provided the only social security this situation must of course have been considerably more poignant. Add to this the girl's virginity, a reminder of the female sex's absolute dependency upon the male in ancient Greece. Electra is the *soror dolorosa*.

What the playwright has to work with are: the return of the brother; the disguise of the brother; the oracle of Apollo; lamentation of the sister; recognition of brother and sister; confrontation of son and mother (deception, recognition, defense of action, matricide); and the son's reaction. The playwright is free to find his own emphasis. In this story one point of view never tried but certainly possible (one would think) is Clytemnestra's defense of her action stemming from her position as an outsider, a victim crushed by the fateful forces of the House of Atreus. There is a hint of the inherent attraction of this interpretation in the tired reasonableness with which she confronts her hotheaded, absolutist, quite puritanical offspring, especially in the Euripidean version.

Minor variations in the story are unimportant and do not constitute commentaries upon the story itself. They merely change the focus slightly. For instance, Euripides has Electra remark that Clytemnestra had children by Aigisthos (62). This is a "normal" domestic detail in an intensely domestic play, but it withdraws a great deal of tension from the stark household of Clytemnestra, her paramour and her disowned daughter. The rejection is no longer active and positive, rather carnal and negligent, natural to a woman starting another family. Instead of the significant willful rejection common to the other plays, there is more the sense that Electra is absent-mindedly abandoned.

The story of Orestes appears prominently in the *Odyssey*, for Orestes is the natural *paradeigma* or example for Telemachus, who must face the suspicion that his mother will marry one of her suitors and do him out of his inheritance. The situation is enough analogous to use Orestes' story almost as a leitmotif. The Homeric version is simple: Orestes does his duty by throne and family in dispatching Aigisthos, who had murdered his father and seduced his mother. It is implied that he kills Clytemnestra too, although after the fashion of Homer's allusion there are only hints as to her complicity in the death of Agamemnon and her ultimate fate (cf. *Odyssey* 3.310). The oracle, Orestes' ultimate reaction and Electra's part in the events are all absent from the Homeric account; thus there was room neither for the famous recognition scene nor for Orestes' moral dilemma.

The recognition scene, however, seems to be a traditional part of the story. It has the hallmark of fairy tale. One thinks, for instance, of fitting the glass slipper on Cinderella's foot or the kiss that roused Sleeping Beauty. The second is more likely since Electra has been slumbering in a numbing mood of bitter, resentful impotence until her brother arrives to bring her hatred awake.

Aeschylus' treatment of Orestes and Electra is different because their story is part of a larger whole, a trilogy that manages in the grandiose Aeschylean manner to move from the very beginnings of the family's doom, through the better-known events of Agamemnon's death and his wife's triumph on through Clytemnestra's death until finally we are given Orestes being tried for matricide before a court. The action moves from the period of sacral history familiar in myth and saga to a time and context akin to the political and social situation the audience themselves experienced. This grand sweep occurs on levels other than the story or the allusion to events antecedent to the story. Images, for instance, taken from the natural world show a coherence or thematic change through all three plays of the trilogy. Orestes and Electra are much more symbolic figures caught up in the universe's rhythm of crime and retribution, which like the tide ceaselessly figures and organizes the affairs of men, so that Clytemnestra's revenge upon her daughter's father becomes a crime against her husband and her son's revenge upon his father's murderer becomes in turn hideous matricide. Still we can take the single play the *Choephoroi* out of the trilogy and set it beside Sophocles' and Euripides' telling of the story.

Aeschylus presents the *Choephoroi* as Orestes' story. Electra exits for the last time at line 584 (in a 1076-line play). This is so, first, because Aeschylus chooses to focus on the act and Orestes does the killing; then too, the third play, the *Eumenides,* makes explicit an underlying tension between the sexes that pervades the entire trilogy. Consider, for instance, the "man-thinking" wife Clytemnestra cosily greeting her cuckold husband, who in turn is the husband who

killed their child, his wife's *raison d'être,* making her in turn
his victim, so it is better for the male Orestes to come alone
to seek his father's revenge against the woman, wife and
mother. The *Choephoroi* is not a simple play, but the action
is relatively slight. The brother arrives, meets his sister, they
both lament and pray to their dead father in the kommos,
he seeks out his mother in disguise, kills her, and is pursued
by the Furies. The kommos, the confrontation between
mother and son and his subsequent pollution constitute the
major dramatic movement of the play. The action in a sense
repeats that of the *Agamemnon;* after a lengthy lyrical passage recalling some grim past history (in the *Agamemnon*
the context of Iphigenia's death, here Agamemnon's death)
a traveler (ironically returned here, in the *Agamemnon*
openly so) is offered the hospitality of the house. In the
Choephoroi the man who arrives is malevolent, in the *Agamemnon* the malevolent one is she who offers the hospitality.

Electra is central to the long kommos. She is the incarnation of suffering, hers is the misery and hopelessness of the
situation in the royal palace. While Sophocles' Electra goes
on for one hundred lines in joy at seeing her brother, ten
lines suffice for Aeschylus' grimmer Electra. But then she is
not so much characterized in Aeschylus' play; she seems
undifferentiated from the women of the chorus. In fact she
reflects everyone's misery, Clytemnestra's as well, in this
miserable palace.

The poet speaks much about justice in the *Choephoroi,* as
in the *Agamemnon* which precedes it and the *Eumenides*
which follows it. Orestes is an instrument of justice come
from God, as it were, here, being motivated by the oracle
of Apollo. He is nemesis visited upon Clytemnestra, who
had in her turn brought retribution upon Agamemnon. For
Orestes himself, however, the perspective is different. He is
led along, seduced into this action by Apollo, who is thus
functioning as *ate,* a kind of divine delusion, as by turn
Clytemnestra did before in the *Agamemnon,* wheedling and
commanding the exhausted Agamemnon to step upon the
carpet. And Orestes obeys the god, kills his mother, a mis-
adventure—although commanded by a god (these things
are always complex). He too therefore faces nemesis; it
comes in the form of the pursuing Furies, who drive him
mad.

It is Orestes' play but set against the greater scale, the

universe wherein these rhythms of justice, of give-and-take, are played out. The chorus often reminds us of the larger perspective in speaking of the abstract quality of justice. This is a religious play. The force and presence of the god is achieved in the manner of using the character Pylades, who is silent throughout the play except for one line, spoken out of his silence, pregnant like an omen or oracle. As Orestes pushes forward in his resolve, loyal to his father, obedient to the god, he grows suddenly hesitant as son regards mother, who bares her breast and reminds him by this gesture that he, like all men, owes his life to his mother. He turns to Pylades, who has silently accompanied him, and asks, "Pylades, what shall I do? Should shame and awe stop me from killing my mother?" And Pylades replies, "What then will come of Apollo's oracles? Or of oaths sworn in trust? Consider the gods closer to you than any man." It is as though Apollo has spoken again.

In addition to the voice of a god Orestes is also moved by moral concerns. He speaks of the punishments for those who fail to avenge their fathers. "He who does not avenge his father's death is cast adrift" (291f.), the state in fact in which Orestes and Electra find themselves, exiled, bereft, cast down (cf. "wanderers," 132, "exiles from home," 254). Revenge alone can give some ethical basis and form to his existence. The play moves to the killing of Clytemnestra as the cleansing act. For Orestes and Electra personally, however, there is no resolution; at the end they are still wanderers, still alienated (cf. 1042–43, where Orestes speaks of going out again in exile), destroyed people.

Electra comes on in this play as almost like the personification of grief, especially familial grief. The chorus describe her sorrow (17f.) with a word of many meanings: "in her harsh grief she is conspicuous/outstanding/fitting." The chorus themselves abstractly express lamentation and Electra is a part of them, slightly individualized to express the further dimension of family in her woe and her love. The often expressed idea in the kommos that Agamemnon was denied the true honor of burial is an expression of a family destroyed, roles forgotten. Electra keens as a daughter for her dead father just as it is Orestes, the son, who kills for his father. His tragedy is that the victim must be his *mother* (just as his mother had to kill her *husband,* and Agamemnon his *daughter*).

The reunion between Electra and Orestes is quick and matter-of-fact. There are tokens of recognition (matching strands of hair, matching footprints); the identification is a moment of joy, simple, not developed dramatically, set in the midst of the lengthy expression of grief from the chorus and Electra. Because there is little emotion and no personality in this recognition one has more the sense of the event than its effect upon the participants; it is more a key being turned, a piece of a puzzle falling into place, the sense of fate manifesting itself. The quality of inevitability reinforces the idea that the events of the human scene are symbolic of some divine rhythm.

In Sophocles' *Electra* Orestes appears very little, the recognition scene is delayed until the last part of the play, Clytemnestra is killed first before Aigisthos and the oracle of Apollo is scarcely mentioned. It is the same story, to be sure, but these details change materially the idea the story evokes. This play is not part of a trilogy, it is self-contained and does not look beyond for actual or emotional solutions to the issues created within. The reversal in the order of Clytemnestra's and Aigisthos' deaths seems to be contrived with this in mind. The matricide in some way will provoke, if not revulsion, then uneasiness. For Aeschylus a large part of the *Eumenides* goes to working out the dilemma. Sophocles, who wishes to avoid that focus, neatly shifts the death, thereby allowing the joy or gratification one feels at the death of Aigisthos, a demonstrably evil figure, to obscure the prior feelings evoked by Clytemnestra's death. We are not left at the play's close with the spectacle of Clytemnestra's death.

The moral issue of the matricide is less important because Orestes' actions are less important. Electra is central here, and she is not affected by Apollo's oracles or disguises or moral confusion. She laments her dead father, hates her living mother and prays for Clytemnestra's death. That is the action of this play. Such is the artistry of Sophocles that he manages in this very long lyrical expression of grief, so static, so one-dimensional, to introduce a thrilling moment of action: that is the two-hundred-line (679ff.) false account of Orestes' death in a chariot race. It is dramatic, evoking strong visual images, but it nonetheless comes and goes, exciting only in the moment of its delivery, effective otherwise only in amplifying Electra's sorrow. Sophocles moves along

very smoothly from the opening speech of Orestes' old companion and tutor, who remarks on the local sights at Argos,
at the same time weaving in details of Orestes' background.
To this Orestes replies with a eulogy of his old friend, then
passes on to details of Apollo's oracle, then a stratagem
for the old man and one for himself. Very briskly and
formally Sophocles rids the play of suspense and potentials
for alternative action. Everything is settled and known (80f.).
Very early on Orestes poses the prospect of meeting Electra
and the old man vetoes it. Sophocles thereby openly reminds
us of one of the staples of the plot and then indicates that
the emotions and dramatics inherent in the recognition scene
and the inevitable subsequent action, that is, the revenge, are
to be ignored. So in a kind of program note to the audience's
subconscious the playwright indicates that he will linger at
the fourth step in the story's progress. The story as a story is
laid to rest, and the playwright may concentrate upon something else, and that is the person of Electra, and specifically
the quality of her grief.

Electra is first heard crying in her chamber; she then
comes on grieving aloud before the chorus. She calls upon
the sun and sky to bear witness to her woe (86ff.), she vows
to cry as long as she can see the night and day (103ff.);
throughout is the idea of bearing witness. Electra in her
mourning is testament to her father's murder, as the meteorological phenomena are testament to the universe and the
order of things. Thus, the plan to imprison Electra underground out of sight and hearing is a response to her emblem-
atic role (cf. 108–9: "before the doors of my father's house I
weep"). To the chorus' remonstrance that impotent grief
might as well be abandoned, that life has more dimension
than the expression of sorrow, Electra compares herself to
the nightingale (the bird of mourning) and to the mourning
Niobe turned to rock; in short, her grief has an existence
of its own, it is not part of her, but all of her, natural as the
instinctive animal response, permanent as the petrified Niobe,
regular as the sun and stars.

The chorus in their usual fashion are reasonable, talking
of moderation, proportion, change, healing, acceptance.
Electra opposes all of this with her own desperate logic, she
will not accept or wait for the passage of time that brings
change to all things. She fights against the seasons to make
her grief complete and natural. As she says (189), she is a

foreigner in her father's house; she is the anomaly. The chorus warn her of forever creating new ugliness in her tortured soul (215ff.); she asks where is the end of evil (236). There is no rational approach, no accommodation, no way to make death fit, for the loss goes on. Indeed, she can argue (245ff.) that if in truth the dead are dead and nothing more, then the religious awe surrounding death, based on a belief in the "realness" of the dead person, would be nothing.

The lyrical exchange between Electra and the chorus is over two hundred lines long; her character such as it is for this play is established and at the last here she sums herself up in these pitiful lines (303–4, 308–9): "While I wait for Orestes/I myself am being destroyed . . . When one is set in evil circumstances/There is strong pressure to practice evil too."

Grief-stricken Electra is juxtaposed to the chorus, Chryso-themis and Clytemnestra, all of whom seem better by com-parison. Then too, Electra does some mean things, as for instance, ordering Aigisthos' corpse to be thrown to the dogs (a hideous idea to the ancients). That is not a mark of an ugly character but rather an indication of the extreme to which her mood of grief and the attendant morbidities of resentment, bitterness and vengeance have brought her. In the stichomythy of 1014ff. Chrysothemis appears to be sensi-ble and Electra is raging, the natural result of her psychology, as is her assumption (1033–34) that Chrysothemis will be-tray her. Chrysothemis points out how far gone into para-noia Electra is by denying any such intention, saying, "I, at any rate, do not hold that kind of hatred for you" (1034).

Clytemnestra appears very strong and positive in the play, reminding us again that every participant in a story taken from ancient myth can be vulnerable or defensible depending upon the author's perspective, and his perspective can shift. Christian criticism has a strong Manichaean streak in it, and we seek the evil forces, the villains, into which category Clytemnestra is almost inevitably put. Here she seems eminently cool (514ff.): "with Aegisthus gone, you wander about, pay no heed to me—although you tell every-one I control you brutally . . . I have no malice, but I'm certainly ready to give back to you what you say to me . . ."; and reasonable (547ff.): . . . "that's how I see it even if you don't agree"; "therefore what has since happened has not broken me down"; and civilized (556ff.): "of course, I'll let you speak. If only you had always entered into conversation with me in this way [Electra asked if she could speak the truth] you would not have been so impossible to listen to"; and feeling (766ff., 770f.): "It's awful to save one's life by the misfortunes of one's very self" (meaning her son, whom she has feared, and now believes to be dead). Clytemnestra is in command here, not running scared as Electra had indicated earlier (254ff.). Again the paranoia, Electra's determination to seek revenge have increased her sense of Clytemnestra's guilt, imagistically conceived in her fear.

Electra's character is a portrait of the typical fifth-century female just as her brother Orestes is the typical male. She is housebound and emotionally bound to her family, an impotent, sulking person. He is free, a man on the move, a decisive figure, who acts, whereas Electra can only suffer. As Chrysothemis says to her (997), "Don't you see? You were born a woman not a man."

Recognition is not used in this play to fashion an episode of action in the drama. Lamentation is all, once in the play's beginning, once at the messenger's speech, once over the urn, and nothing thereafter cancels it out.

Recognition and reunion, which are basic themes of this story, appear ironically in this drama. Orestes does not wait at the beginning of the play for Electra to come out, Electra believes in the false tale of Orestes' death, greets the false urn of ashes, denies the authority of the true tokens reported by Chrysothemis, and Orestes when he meets Electra fails to recognize her, to which Aigisthos' false identification of Clytemnestra's corpse is chilling counterpoint. Electra remains in the grip of her solipsistic grief, everything else is adrift.

The grief of Sophocles' heroine appears in Euripides' play but with a peculiar change. Instead of an emotion that is made to be a total psychic state, a spiritual condition, the Electra of Euripides is given a stage situation that reveals her misery. She is in rags, living in a rustic hut, and most extraordinary, married to a simple farmer. Now, it is very hard for a modern critic to read this play, so much time has elapsed. Euripides is a very intelligent playwright, although sometimes sloppy and indifferent to tragic proprieties. But nearly everything he does he does on purpose.

Electra's initial appearance comes as a shock and surely a calculated one. The farmer acts as *prologos;* his speech is in the Aeschylean manner of exaltation. It moves from the glory of the Trojan War, down the passage of time through the high heroics of the doom of the House of Atreus, their murders and sorrows, to the particulars of Aigisthos' attempts to keep Electra a virgin, down to a thump in line 34: "Electra he gave to me," says the farmer. It is shocking certainly, and possibly comic.

Electra's entrance comes shortly thereafter. She is the farm girl. The contrast of Electra, daughter of Agamemnon, and Electra, wife to the farmer, already played out in the movement of the *prologos'* speech, is reaffirmed in her opening words: "O black night, nurse to the golden stars," she begins in an elevated diction common to tragic figures, but follows this in another vein: ". . . in which I go about with this jug set upon my head, carrying water from the spring." Again unsettling and possibly comic. The conventions are being violated, or seem to be.

Still and all, one can say easily enough that Euripides (although supposedly he created this play almost exactly contemporaneously with Sophocles' version) is speaking to a different audience, or really to different concerns in the same audience; that he is addressing their bourgeois sensibilities wherein alienation and woe are conceived socially (a bad marriage) and materially (a hovel, patched clothes).

Thus when here again in this play we find the chorus (167ff.) offering cheer and common sense, indeed exuding good will like an Ismene or Chrysothemis, they conceive Electra's rehabilitation in terms of new clothes and finery. And she rejects the chorus in those terms. When she speaks to Orestes about her suffering material deprivation is paramount (cf. 305ff.).

The same dimension of the human condition is reflected in the initial exchange between Electra and her farmer husband. They talk of the barnyard and housework. This is not tragic convention. Tragic heroes do not, however, talk of domestic details nor do they mouth the kind of platitudinous remarks Electra's husband is fond of putting in her direction, for instance, ". . . it's a disgrace for a girl to stand around talking to young men" (343f.), or "if a woman puts her mind to it she can always find something to set on the table" (422f.).

This last must help to bring to mind a picture of the erst-while Princess Electra now coping with pots and pans, her celebrated grief hitherto so lyrical and tragic now turned more to a snivel. That sort of picture is reinforced by Orestes' distaste at entering the farmer's shack (391ff., esp. 397) after having praised the nobility of his soul. Nobility of soul is all very well, but the smells of the barnyard shack are greater. So, too, Electra's grief loses some of its heroic and tragic quality so strangely set in these gross surroundings. If Euripides is playing this straight, it's a rather mean little play.

Well, then, is Euripides being comic? And indeed overtly funny? Who can tell the temper of his original audience, whether in a series of plays traditionally given to solemn, elevated themes calculated to produce something like "pity and fear" they were able or ready to find one humorous? The concluding satyr play, after all, was there to release the store of pent-up laughter that unrelieved tragedy often produces. Whether within the series there was room for humor is impossible to know. The situation of the play is unsettling; it makes one rethink the nature of tragic action viewed from this very difficult perspective. Laughter is often said to be the product of a confrontation with the unknown or unusual so that perhaps here laughter came involuntarily, making the audience still more confused. One thinks of the brother/nar-rator and his biting sarcasm in Tennessee Williams' *Glass Menagerie*, which is all at once comic and horrible.

There are interesting moments of conventional tragic dramaturgy in this play which set off still more sharply the unusual nature of Electra's situation. The farmer/*prologos* touches most of the obvious clichés in rehearsing Electra's background, but this seems in part calculated for its juxtapo-sition to her present state of ignominy. Electra's initial lyri-cal lamentation (112ff.) is conventional; there are the ex-pression of grief, the apostrophe to her father, the allusion to his murder, all the things one expects in Electra's view. While it is a traditional poetic incarnation of suffering there comes through considerably more personal anguish than in the Sophoclean version so that rather than suffering becom-ing the central object it is Electra herself. Then too, the diction is considerably more exotic because the word order is more complicated. Euripides was remembered for his experimental and exciting music; this song is a bravura piece as well as the exposition of high emotion.

When the traditional tokens of recognition are introduced Euripides plays with them for what must have been at least a mildly amusing if not downright hilarious effect. Electra's old servant announces to her excitedly (518ff.) that someone has visited her father's grave and left a lock of hair just like hers. Could it be Orestes'? Nonsense, says Electra. Orestes would not sneak into the country, and furthermore how can one match hair? The old man persists, speaks of footprints. Electra sniffs; the ground is too rocky for footprints and furthermore how could siblings of such different sizes have similar footprints? The old man falters; would you believe a piece of clothing? Electra coolly reminds him that Orestes could hardly still be able to fit into his baby clothes. It is a long scene, all the elements of recognition are touched on. Why, we may ask, does Euripides play so importantly with the recognition? It is said to be criticism of the Aeschylean version; notice how it is followed by the introduction of a believable token of recognition, a scar on Orestes' brow (558ff.), as though in contrast. The scene in the *Electra*, however, is no aside; it seems to be a dramatization of a new sensibility rather than simply criticism of Aeschylus; at this length in fact it would be stupid. Aeschylus, clearly an intelligent dramatist, is not interested in portraying the realities of recognition on something other than the surface level, therefore realistic detail and setting do not matter. Aeschylus offers us the basic fact of recognition divorced from the realistic details of the method so that the audience concentrates on the fact, not distracted by the cunning inherent in the manner. For obviously it is silly for persons to take such flimsy evidence unhesitatingly and uncritically. Euripides surely understood this. Euripides presents this scene instead to show how the nature of myth conflicts with the contemporary needs of drama, storytelling and character.

Drama, the "thing done," is human action, which when it is unpredictable is suspenseful. Suspense in many forms of theater is a chief ingredient but not so in that of the ancient Greeks. The instinct for suspense even in earlier narrative is not strong. If the action of myth, the stuff of ancient narrative, is truly ritualistic or archetypal, then suspense is impossible for the action proceeds from the known to the known; in the telling all is anticipated.

Suspense is inherently antithetical to the tragic mood or to tragic irony. Yet, while it is inevitability that has tragedy in it some kind of will gives dignity, without which human existence would be such a nullity as to be, if not psychologically unbearable, then aesthetically repellent. The idea of *hamartia* derives from an instinct for endowing human nothingness with proportion. With will man contrives his death. It is not thrust upon him as though he were a steer mindlessly meeting the mallet stroke in an abattoir. This need for dignity in free will was reinforced throughout the fifth century by the increasing emphasis upon the rational process. Problems could be identified, solutions could be found, again the manifestation of something like free will. This is reflected in Euripides' handling of the recognition scene. First he denies its inevitability, secondly he shows a free human intellect dealing with the given, then other possibilities of thought and action are suggested, the moment is fluid and variable. It is not in the least tragic.

The Euripidean sense of character is another force at work in changing the nature of this recognition scene. The fifth century was a period of a growing sense of individualism. Peculiarity is the essence of individuality and this in turn is the antithesis of the typical character. While early narrative is peopled with types, typical characters are not common in Euripides. He often investigates what kind of person lies behind the figure of the myth. A marvelous brief instance of this in the *Electra* is the superb description of the real Aigisthos drunk at the grave of Agamemnon, his age-old hatred impotent with its object gone (326ff.). So here we begin to see Electra as a character; she acts from personality, the events do not create her. At this moment it is Electra who controls the recognition scene rather than the other way around.

The notion that this version of the recognition scene may have provoked laughter derives from the sense that late-fifth-century audiences were becoming self-conscious, as were the poets who created for them. The forces that led the ancient Greeks to their rigid concentration on convention and repetition in literature obviously encouraged comparison, allusion and imitation. These were the beginnings of a literary sensibility. Euripides often seems to be asking his audience to understand what they see and hear in terms of another work—particularly the Homeric epics. Sophocles is able to use this consciousness to great effect in the *Philoctetes* when he introduces Neoptolemos, Achilles' son, as a reminder of the play's Homeric counterpart, the embassy to Achilles in the ninth book of the *Iliad*. Aristophanes is able to build several plays upon his audience's literary sensibilities, notably the *Frogs*, produced in 405, eight years after Euripides' *Electra*. Creating action in the frame of reference of other theater or other literature calls for a kind of intellectual response that is not conducive to generating empathy. The audience and the playwright are too aware, the drama grows more objective, more immediately philosophical, no longer really a thing done, but a thing said. In this play even the chorus have doubts, they sing of Thyestes seducing Atreus' wife (699ff.), how Zeus therefore changed the course of the sun, an event which they admit (737ff.) is highly unlikely. But, they continue (743ff.), "frightening stories have the benefit of encouraging mortal man in the worship of the gods," which seems to mean that the myths while not true lead one to a better way of life. Questioning makes the myth weaker and theater of this sort becomes weaker with it.

Euripides' *Electra* effectively dramatizes the essential paradox of appearance and reality by presenting the myth somewhat askew, neither participants nor events quite conforming to expectations yet always manifestations of the traditional story. Appearance and reality form the major intellectual consideration of the play as well, coming in the recurring discussions of true goodness. Orestes first develops this idea (367ff.) in discussing Electra's lowly husband, offering the conventional suggestion that nobility lies within; the farmer indeed turns out to be one of the few figures of the play displaying kindly motives (although he seems—quite by design surely—to be tediously platitudinous, as for instance at 80–81, 343–44, 422–23).

Euripides has the farmer answer Orestes' speech in a monologue where he stresses that material comfort, a full belly, really is the source of man's character: "I think of the power money has, money to entertain with, money to pay the doctor bills; a little bit will buy the food and a man with a full belly is the same whether rich or poor" (426–31).

The farmer's speech reinforces the materialistic, bourgeois, domestic element of this drama which we have noticed before. He and Orestes are getting values from very different sources. Yet Euripides comically shows Orestes offended by the "good" farmer's poverty while preparing grimly to accept his hospitality, then later provides a contrast full of ambiguity when the messenger describes (774ff.) the lordly and gracious manner in which the play's villain Aigisthos invites the disguised Orestes to join in sacrifice. Ironically later Aigisthos will be the sacrificial animal and in his hospitality he is momentarily sympathetic. Where, indeed, and what is goodness?

Ambiguity comes again in the juxtaposition of Electra and Clytemnestra. Electra's suffering is dramatized longest and strongest as she exults if not gloats over the corpse of Aigisthos. Everything is there; her rather prurient observations on the royal adulterers' sexual life (918–24, 945–51) recall the references to her own ripeness at the play's beginning ("Electra's flowering" [15]; "when youth's flowering time took hold of her suitors swarmed around [20–21]; cf. 343–44, her husband's admonition: "nice young girls don't stand around talking with young men, it's disgusting") and her awareness of her mother's sexual satisfaction compared to her own neglect ("breeding children in Aigisthos' bed" [62]; "mother in bed with another man" [211]; "women love their men, not their children" [265]; the farmer's mentioning that out of respect he has left his wife a virgin [40–53]). She speaks of money, again, of Aigisthos' comfort and her own privations (938–44). All is a marvelous outpouring of hatred; afterward Clytemnestra appears.

Clytemnestra is tired, she is monomaniacal on the subject of Iphigenia, a woman's rights and sex. One has the feeling that she has had to defend these positions too often. For the traditional Clytemnestra in the traditional story these are indeed her standard verbal props and these come from her mechanically. Euripides, however, combines sensitivity and rationality, which combination suddenly projects a personality from out of the well-rehearsed positions of Wronged Wife and Mother ("don't hate until you know what you are hating" [1015–17]; "There is a fool thing in women and when their men cheat on them they'll go right out in imitation and get a friend for themselves" [1035–38]; "My child, you were born to love your father; that's just the way it is. Some love their father more, some their mothers. I quite understand and sympathize with you" [1102–5]). At the end she seems to show boredom (1109–10): "O me and my strivings and schemes—perhaps my hate against my husband was too much."

Electra's reply (1060ff.) shows the other side of Clytemnestra, not a very pretty side. Her words do not reverse the situation but they show how complicated the affair is, reinforcing a mood of ambiguity rather than moving to a solution; this is the feeling at the play's very end. The Dioscuri arriving *ex machina* give an ending, but Orestes' and Electra's desolation show that the ending is imposed, not evolved out of the action: at the end (1292ff.) we see two human beings having acted out something somehow not their fault, but the work of Apollo and of fate. At the same time neither is a hero who enlists our sympathies; Electra and Orestes are just as ugly people as Clytemnestra and Aigisthos. What Euripides has done is to build characters. Electra, the force of grief, the eternal nightingale, emblem of her family's destruction, becomes the depressed, emotionally starved and angry person that such concentration on grief can suggest. Orestes, less thoroughly realized, becomes a guilty killer. The myth, the traditional story, the conventional actions— these are fate and Apollo, and they have demanded these characters, Orestes and Electra.

This is the thrust of a great deal of Euripides' theater. In his remarkable play *Orestes* he presents the consequences of this tendency, dramatizing them rather than simply giving criticism. At the same time the intellectualist dramatization of a critical stance hints at why the art of tragedy lost its strength roughly around the end of the fifth century. The *Orestes* was produced in 408. Its plot according to the ancients was Euripides' invention, in itself an unusual dramaturgical move, in this case an imaginative development of the affairs of Electra and Orestes after they have killed Aigisthos and Clytemnestra. In modern times the play has aroused considerable hostility because when viewed through the filter of the aesthetics of realism it appears ludicrous. The ending especially offends, when Apollo, the *deus ex machina*, brings solutions boldly and jarringly at variance with what receded. More recent criticism, perhaps sensible to notions of the importance of the absurd and at least less dependent upon realism, has been more sympathetic. Aristotelian emphasis upon resolution may be true to structure but it is less relevant to the play's idea, and may be misleading. Euripidean theater particularly as a theater of ideas may take up and open up problems but not resolve them. The *Orestes*, however, presents an irreconcilable problem so strongly, so finally that the very strong sense of no solution is itself adequate resolution. A statement has been made.

The familiar brother and sister appear again in this play, yet much changed. He has gone mad and she is burned out, as though dead. His madness does not come from the pursuing Erinyes of Aeschylus. Orestes thinks he sees them, but we know and Electra knows that they are phantoms of his psychosis. The externalized reaction of a shame culture has been internalized to guilt. "What is your sickness?" his uncle asks him and he replies, "My awareness, that I am conscious of having done dreadful things" (395–96). It is still more, however, a disease of the soul coming from a way of life and associations rather than just what he did, and at one point he warns Pylades that it is catching (793). The advice is not needed for Pylades is equally affected, has been all along.

At the beginning Orestes has an attack of madness. When it subsides he is rational again. "Now once again," he says (279), "here's the calm after the storm." His words refer beyond this moment to the madness of the matricide; he has done that huge and frenzied act, it is over, and this is now the Orestes of this play. He speaks of his weariness (301ff.), his depression and loneliness (296ff.) and his despair (281ff., 288ff.). These spiritual elements Euripides adds to his traditional weakness, his natural impotence (in the *Choephoroi* he is a creature of the god Apollo and Pylades in a sense gives the command [900f.], in Sophocles' play he is no more than the flesh and blood manifestation of Electra's resolve; here again [1105] it is Pylades who finally speaks decisively). This Orestes is very much a flawed person, much like Hamlet, here more so than in the earlier versions, deceit and disguise having turned to confusion and madness, impotence and irresolution to guilt and despair.

Electra is a destroyed person. "You are among the dead," she says to the memory of her mother (201ff.), "and I pas my time in groaning and crying, tears all night long, unmarried, barren . . ." A living death is what she describes, one to balance her mother's. The heroic resolve of the Sophoclean Electra, whose grief and sacrifice of self are constant testimony to the outrage her mother and Aigisthos have committed, makes no sense after Clytemnestra's death. Electra has moved into *history*, into the aftermath, where she is a burned-out shell. Myth, on the contrary, like art, has no aftermath. Euripides has made the tension of the *Orestes* derive from the collision of intellectual attitudes toward the close of the fifth century and suggests that myth is obsolete.

Myth is cyclic, the action, whether understood to be ritual, formulaic or archetypal, is essentially repetitive. As we have seen in the case of Aphrodite and Demeter their actions are not lodged in time but they do have beginnings and ends to which points everything proceeds by the same route again and again. A mother will always lose her daughter; a great female deity will always have intercourse with mortal man. This mythic sense of time and activity is in conflict with historical vision, for history is linear and progressive; it continually moves along a time span, never repeats, never goes back, always evolving. In the late fifth century historiography shows an alternative manner of working out a temporal and narrative scheme although tragedy clearly influenced even so enthusiastically historical a mind as Thucydides.

Myth's suggestiveness also clashed with the prevailing intellectual temper. As we have seen, myth allows for illogicalities to be resolved in a way impossible to the intellectual mind. Hesiod's conception of work as punishment and virtue at the same time is an example. Aeschylus' creation of Prometheus is another; the bound god in his relations with Zeus is somehow all at once man freeing himself from god, an aristocracy repressed by a harsh tyrant, and a generation of deity grown harsh and absolute in Zeus' new dispensation. The fifth century saw Athens move to the very edge of a rational society where the exercise of logic made the use of the symbols inherent in the stories of myth more orderly, more specific; the movement was toward allegory. There was a tendency to re-examine traditional stories to redefine their meaning, which can be seen on its more naïve level in Herodotus' attempts at rationalizing myths and legends.

The point of view toward the participants in the stories also changed during this time as there emerged a greater emphasis upon the personality and upon the validity of the individual person while at the same time the traditional aristocratic emphasis on family and group, wherein human action is seen as universal and normative, came to mean far less. Action and character in tragedy became less the definitions of universals, and instead there appeared dramatic personalities. Not coincidentally, at roughly the same time the men who played the major roles in the tragedies grew to excite far more interest in their audiences, an interest that hitherto had been bestowed only on the play and playwright.

Euripides from the evidence of even his first extant play (the *Alcestis,* performed in 438) shows an interest in playing with the personalities which are potential in the action. This play has to do with death and salvation on the mythic level (we can compare it to the story of Orpheus and Eurydice or to the theme of the stealing of the virgin out of the Underworld, generally known as the rape of the *kore*); it has the fairy-tale motif of doing a good turn for the miraculous stranger; it shows traces of the mentality of submerging a wife's identity completely into that of her husband's, best known through the Indian custom of suttee. For Euripides it becomes a black comedy of manners in which we see the kind of selfishness, the motives for revenge, the need for a public face that animate Alcestis and Admetus. Euripides has created two individual personalities who would do the kind of things that the story has them doing. In a sense he has carried the story to its logical conclusion; that can often be fatal, and his *Orestes* is a calculated exhibition of that.

The collision of myth and history is most clearly expressed in the words (491ff.) of Tyndareus, grandfather of Orestes and Electra. As so often Euripides wants almost a straightforward prose exposition of his dramatic idea, the intellectual struggling with the dramatist. (Or perhaps one might say the dramatist yielding to an untheatrical convention of his time, the rhetorical *agon,* here between Tyndareus and Orestes.) One of Euripides' favorite agents for exposition of this kind is a stern old-timer who tells some home truths. Pheres in the *Alcestis* is another example, as is the nurse in the *Hippolytus,* or Hecuba in the *Trojan Women* and in the *Hecuba.*

Tyndareus begins by pointing out to Orestes very simply that there are courts of law for redress in such situations; it was therefore senseless for Orestes to kill his mother. The effect is shattering because the mythic story has been brought into history, particularly the point of view of the late fifth century, and what emerges as its core, valid in history as in myth, is that Orestes is a murderer. Furthermore the story is denied its symbolic or archetypal functions; it cannot exist as a piece of action independent of time whose

meaning and implications reside in and are forced out from
the action itself. Lodged in history the story must have consequences; its "problems" demand solutions. Tyndareus goes
on to say (507ff.) that since murder begets murder some
solution must be imposed. The essence of the mythic and
ritual mind is exactly this revolution of action, the same
action played out cyclically, eternally in a variety of contexts,
in this story Thyestes seducing Atreus' wife, Aigisthos seducing Agamemnon's wife, Atreus the host destroying (in a
sense) Thyestes at table, Clytemnestra the hostess welcoming
her husband with murderous intent, Electra welcoming her
mother in the same way, Clytemnestra getting revenge, Orestes getting revenge. The events of this house have an unmistakable organization and rhythm, always returning to the
beginning which in turn is the end.

There was more to the story of Orestes than the matricide,
although that was all Homer seems to have known, and indeed that act forms a sensible focus that needs nothing more.
Some immediately post-Homeric poet dealt with the details of Orestes' purification for the murder. This necessarily
involved the source of his affliction, the pursuing Furies,
known to the ancients as the Erinyes. What we have therefore is another focus, another story, the Affliction, Wandering
and Salvation of Orestes, a story that is independent of what
precedes, does not indeed need those antecedents. Sartre's
play *The Flies* shows the strength of this story existing by itself. When we speak of Euripides bringing the matricide into
history, illuminating its aftermath, we refer to something
very different, for the focus is still on the matricide; it alone
determines the state of the characters.

It is instructive, however, to notice how Aeschylus dealt
with the later events in Orestes' life. The *Eumenides,* the
third play in the *Oresteia* trilogy, covers the time after
Clytemnestra's death until Orestes is purified and freed of the
religious pollution matricide conferred upon him. The event is
brought into history in the sense that Orestes and the Erinyes
argue their positions, which are traditional and derived from
the myth, before an idealized Athenian jury. Orestes is finally
acquitted when a hung jury is righted by the goddess Athena,
casting the decisive vote. This does not make Orestes "innocent," but it contrives an end to the system of justice by
vendetta murder; since the entire play turns on the themes of
justice and murder this is an intelligent finale. Although

Aeschylus has advanced the action into a historical after-math one has no more sense of history here than in his *Persians*. He mythifies history by making the real acts general, giving the arguments and the jury decision the sense of being inevitable, by making the Erinyes the central character. It is still tendentious, allusive and particular; in this sense Euripides and Aeschylus often resemble each other. None-theless Aeschylus has transferred the Athenian jury system and the philosophy that lies behind it to the timeless plane of myth, whereas Euripides in the *Orestes* allows myth to disintegrate in the forces of history.

"I shall," declares Tyndareus (523ff.), "defend the law as far as I am able, and put down this brute savagery and murderousness which ever destroys land and cities. As a mat-ter of fact what in the world kind of mind could you possibly possess when there was your mother beseeching you, show-ing you her breast? . . ." Again the old man goes to a central fact of Greek myth, its familial nature. Much of Greek mythology turns on family relationship. These familial crises —incest, infanticide, matricide, sibling rivalry and killing—reflect many of the deep-seated unspoken psychological at-titudes of them. The family also serves immediately as a convenient symbol for the integrated social and spiritual life of the free-born men of the early *polis*. Thus, this system of myth was extremely productive in a prerational period. But in analysis when the facts of these myths are isolated and in-spected, when the immunity that time and the need for sym-bols confer is withdrawn, there is left the residue of what is often no more than sordid criminal behavior. Orestes did in fact come back to Argos and in a kind of unblinking way kill his mother, while his sister cheered him on from the side. Not nice people. Not nice myths, repositories of "brute sav-agery," which is in effect an animal quality, the opposite of the rational process. Tyndareus opposes this to law.

In origin Clytemnestra, Orestes, all the figures of myth are distillations of society, symbols of humankind, but they are never part of society. Historically they reflect an aristocratic class organized in the lines of class which did not acknowledge society as such. In fact one cannot really speak of society be-fore the advent of the consolidated city-state after the time of Kleisthenes. Members of aristocratic families did not reckon the effect of their actions on persons outside their family. In myth this is reflected in the narrow, inner forces of these figures; the emphasis on closeness is everywhere. In this particular myth the almost incestuous relationship of Orestes and Electra (see her speech 307ff.) is an expression of this general attitude; they are indeed not part of society. In this play that position is challenged by the ever present threat of the people of Argos. Euripides has chosen to demonstrate another inadequacy of the mythic vision by revealing the impossibility of Orestes' and Electra's almost solipsistic position. In fact Euripides implies that every figure in the story is vulnerable. Helen herself must sneak through the streets of Argos, and Menelaus is quite wary throughout. Orestes must defend himself and Electra before the city. This is the dramatist's conscious reformation of the educational and communicative roles of myth. Orestes has always acted as example through the myth, he is a paradigm. Now he goes to speak analytically, rhetorically, logically; the ideas he advances are to no avail. The people condemn him and at the same time, Euripides seems to be saying, they are condemning the very function of myth.

Tyndareus has opposed irrationality with law. When law becomes the articulation of an increasingly rational society then Orestes' archetypal act is reduced to murder because law defines the needs and dilemmas of society, it robs from traditional literature its symbolic potential. The stories are thereby reduced to their crudest, simplest truth, and often, as here, this truth is repellent.

Who, then, is to blame for what has happened? Is it indeed blame that is to be attached? "Apollo," says Orestes (596), "went astray, not I. What was I to do?" Yet there is moral confusion for as Tyndareus remarks (531), Orestes is hated by the gods for what he did. Apollo or no, he stands somehow condemned. Orestes' remark about conscience shows that he in fact has a more personal, individual understanding of what he has done. He begins to know that the fault is not in the stars but in himself; he discovers that he is responsible for his action by acting out the character the myth has given him, first as a violent madman, then as a murderous delinquent advancing on his aunt and cousin.

The plotting to kill Helen (1105ff.) parallels the traditional killing of Clytemnestra. This attack upon Helen seems to be Euripides' own invention. Here in the suspenseful land of absolute fiction where at last Orestes and Electra are *free* they can do nothing other than act out the ritual of vengeance, the ritual of a son's attack upon his mother, all out of context. To underscore this Euripides has shown Helen to be no noble victim as Clytemnestra always is. Helen is catty ("still a virgin, dear"), vain ("only cut the tips of her hair"), overelegant (Trojan slaves) and vulgarly proprietary (1108, the vision of her putting owner's signs on the furnishings). The act thus isolated is made foul.

Toward the play's end the moral and theological ambiguity is resolved in the invocation to Agamemnon (1225ff.) where the blame is placed on the dead king ("it is because of you that I suffer," [1227]; "I offer up to you my tears . . . and my lamentation," [1239]). But Euripides is not launching an attack on Apollo or Agamemnon or any other single element within the story. The call to Agamemnon, himself conspicuously a victim, and remote as a source of his children's immediate woe, summons the entire story to mind. The myth itself becomes the agent of this grief, a grief that has been both the prop and stay of their life and the cause of their annihilation. In a sense Orestes and Electra are victims of their story. While this is a truism applicable to all, and we know that history in retrospect is as inevitable as the inexorable nexus of events in their lives, the retelling of myths, their traditional nature, gives an irony, the sense of foreknowledge that "real life" lacks. Hence a story's participants appear doomed; they can appear to be victims, crushed by the relentless logic of the story.

The finale of this play is particularly brilliant because again Euripides has succeeded in dramatizing an idea. The murderous trio—Pylades in his bravado, Orestes in his meanness and Electra in her bloodthirstiness, being second-millennium precursors to America's folk-heroic trio Bonnie and Clyde and C. J. Moss—having been egged on cheerfully if mindlessly by the chorus (1353ff.), turn their attentions to burning the palace.

Throughout the play there have been references to this building, as a dwelling, as the seat of the family of Atreus (see particularly the choral ode at 807ff.). Physically it is the House of Atreus, the family so celebrated in myth as a family, interreacting inmates of a house. Historically aristocratic families occupied grand houses that set before the populace, like this stage palace before the audience, a continuous spectacle and example of living. Orestes' defense before the people of Argos turns on the symbolic value of his

act (cf. 565ff.), really his worth as living theater and symbol.
His very act of defense is indeed theater. Pylades' arguments for murdering Helen (1132ff.)—"we'll punish her in
the name of Hellas," "you won't have the title of matricide
but killer of Helen"—reinforce the idea of Orestes as em-
blematic. And ironically as we have remarked before, Orestes
is the first significant paradigmatic figure in extant Greek
literature.

Allied to the idea of the *house* are ideas of family and inheritance which also come up often in the play. These ideas
are inseparable and they constitute the matrix of the myth,
almost of in fact, myths generally. Electra's first speech is
a typical rehearsal of the mythic history of the House of
Atreus. What she says seems so commonplace and yet Euripides has contrived an unsettling mood. Electra is strangely
halting as she speaks, unsure or weary or both. She lists it
all in an odd way:

Tantalos, known as the lucky one—and I am not being
ironic or bitter—born of Zeus, or so they say . . .
paid the penalty, as they tell it . . .
why should I list all these unspeakable things . . .
Atreus? . . . well, I'll pass over his fate . . .
then that famous, if indeed he was famous, Agamemnon . . .

The story is told, but the reluctance in the telling is unmistakable. Electra's aversion to her story, to her family is an
obvious and natural psychological fact but Euripides invests
it with new significance. In the course of the drama myth
itself appears faulted, the aversion can thus be generalized.
So it is toward the close of the play, having acted out the
murderous natures given them in the story, they turn on
the house, the incarnation of the myth of the House of Atreus
more still the symbol of the myth, to destroy it.

The destruction is reinforced in the peculiarly absurd directions of Apollo, the *deus ex machina*. This scene has
caused untold confusion among the scholarly critics because
it is so outrageous, so incongruent with what precedes. Yet
that exactly again portrays the inadequacy of myth. The
cyclic nature of myth is reflected in the neat and arbitrary
way in which events and persons are arranged in violation of
the dynamics engendered in the preceding scenes. For instance, what is more marvelously ridiculous than Apollo's

saying, "Hermione there at whose throat you have your knife is destined to be your bride"? Cyclic action is static but Euripides has allowed these characters to evolve. The collision between myth and history could not be greater. Myth is shown to be irrelevant.

Euripides' most telling dramatic device is the Phrygian eunuch who appears toward the close of the play, surely the most curious figure ever in ancient theater. The slave's speech is a messenger speech of sorts, so that he stands before us as the very representation of tragic convention, as he tells of the horrendous events going on within the palace. The slave's way of mangling the language is completely shocking. It is important that we realize he is trying for tragic diction. He manages a number of literary or mythical allusions (e.g. "bull-horned Ocean," 1376), he extends himself ornamentally in the common epic convention (1577–79). The chorus has to ask him to speak more clearly (1393); he agrees to give each detail but then can't resist the imagistic (1400–1) "All right ladies, if you want the details, then came in this pride of lions [Orestes and Pylades]."

The words of the Phrygian eunuch are perhaps the most shocking element of the play. We have the language of confusion, of ignorance. This language figures the *reality* of this state of mind rather than a coherent, articulated, hence abstracted depiction of the state as is customary in ancient theater. At the same time the eunuch's poetic tag lines caught up in broken Greek seem to make a mockery of the stilted and elevated diction peculiar to tragedy. As he has called in history to challenge the myth he summons reality, her counterpart, to suggest the irrelevance or absurdity of the tragic-lyric linguistic convention. Art is denied for truth.

CHAPTER NINE
THE VARIETY OF TRAGIC EXPERIENCE

Nothing too much
Know thyself
E

inscribed on the temple of Apollo at Delphi

The impulse to generalize about ancient Greek tragedy is irresistible. The religious occasion of its presentation, the unchanging structure of tragedy, the abstracted nature of the drama are motives to believing that tragedy can be refined, distilled to an essence that will be the key to unlocking the secret of ancient Greece. For the ancient Greeks remain a puzzle, always will, hiding behind their works and fame, the enigmatic smile to be found on archaic statues emblem of their ambiguity.

The tragedies lose their distinction when they are rigidly categorized. There is no tragedy, but rather tragedies, presented over a period of more than seventy-five years, which are each idiosyncratic, a product of a certain mind speaking to a certain moment in time. They have only the Dionysiac Festival in common; unlike the Christian Mass with which they are often and unwisely compared, the script changed at every performance. They offer immensely varied insights into the sensibilities of the people of Athens. To read them all is to penetrate into the deepest concerns and convictions of a profound people.

Ignorance of ancient tragedy is an important consideration in our criticism of it, although this is too often passed over.

We have a limited amount of data for the production of tragedy even in the fifth century, which causes embarrassments. A famous example is the dating of the performance of Aeschylus' *Suppliants*. Scholars and critics have made chronological schemata for the ancient plays in order to chart what is presumed to be the progress of development of the playwright's technique. Until recently the date of the *Suppliants* was unknown. The play, however, has traditionally been thought to be the earliest extant tragedy, because the dramatic role of the chorus is large, the choral odes are immense and advance the action of the play and the roles of single characters are small. There is the theory that tragedy developed out of choral pieces and in addition there is the observation that during the course of the fifth century the role of the chorus consistently diminished in extant tragedy. Furthermore the fifty daughters meant a chorus of fifty equivalent to the fifty-member dithyramb chorus from which tragedy is thought to have evolved. So the *Suppliants* has been a comfortable example of "earliest tragedy." Here we are deep in the awful thicket of surmise and assumption.

The *Suppliants* is taken from the story of the fifty daughters of Danaus, fugitives from Egypt, pursued by their male cousins, who seek asylum in Greece. The play turns on the crisis caused by their petition. The chorus of Danaians take the major part of the play, singing in long lyric choral odes the miseries of their position and their hopes for the future. The girls completely overwhelm the two actors who appear as their father, Danaus, and as Pelasgos, the Greek king before whom they plead to stay.

The greatest anguish resides in Pelasgos' bosom, for he must face the crisis of war if he admits the girls. He is damned if he does, damned if he does not, which is probably an accurate approximation of Aeschylus' tragic vision. It is also the fate of Eteocles, Clytemnestra, Agamemnon and Orestes, which makes Pelasgos an Aeschylean tragic hero of sorts. Still, however much we may agonize with Pelasgos he is not present long enough nor does he say enough to take our attention away from the girls. The *Suppliants* emphatically belongs to the chorus, which is not true of any other extant tragedy. We certainly seem to be in possession of the earliest tragedy.

Some twenty-five years ago, however, a newly discovered papyrus fragment suggests that the *Suppliants* was brought out in the decade of the 460s, in any case after the *Persians*, which shows a so-called "later" style or technique of dramaturgy, and is known to have been performed in 472. Suddenly the *Suppliants* becomes an anachronism. What are we to make of this? Either Aeschylus wrote the *Suppliants* early and brought it out later unrevised or he archaized or he was indifferent to stylistic evolution or he transcended it. Or better still, stylistic evolution is not so rigid or so sure a principle. It will not in fact work for the *Suppliants*. If the story is to be presented from the girls' point of view then their multitude is a constant dramatic fact. An enlarged part for the chorus is obvious. It is the subject that demands the form.

Discussing the surviving play in a trilogy is equally hazardous. Aeschylus' *Prometheus* seems to be an indictment of tyranny, especially divine tyranny. Prometheus is portrayed as a victim, moreover an innocent and righteous victim. Yet many think that in the final play there comes a reconciliation between Zeus and Prometheus in which Prometheus acknowledges Zeus' kingdom and powers as the highest good. This was the conventional wisdom. Hesiod's *Theogony* shows Zeus to be the evolved, permanent major deity, a moral god, almost a god of righteousness. Since Aeschylus generally seems bent on reaffirming the Hesiodic wisdom it is most likely that the *Prometheus* trilogy closes with Zeus' hegemony acknowledged, ratified and supported. We must therefore be prepared to look more closely at our *Prometheus* to see where some alternatives to the simplistic notion of Zeus tyrant, Prometheus victim are presented. For it is unlikely that the final play presented a denouement entirely unexpected; that is not consistent with the Greek practice of story narration, which abhors suspense or surprise. Therefore knowing what we do of the Aeschylean *Prometheus* trilogy we must be cautious in situations where we know far less.

One crucial factor in the analysis of the tragedies is the degree to which critics may safely abstract and generalize. Bad enough that most critics speak of "ancient Greek tragedy" when in fact they can only mean "the extant plays of three Athenian playwrights of the fifth century." We know that there existed other playwrights, other plays by the famous three, productions in other cities, in other centuries, but still we continue to speak simply of "ancient Greek tragedy."

It is most difficult of all, however, to refrain from generalizing about the plays of Aeschylus, Sophocles and Euripides. We have seven plays of Aeschylus, who is known to have composed between seventy and eighty. Sophocles is thought to have composed a hundred and twenty-three plays, of which we have but seven; Euripides composed between eighty and ninety plays, of which we have nineteen. Even adding the great number of fragments of other tragedies, the sample for generalizing is very small indeed; then too, works of art even by the same person are always in some way unique.

The history of the surviving Euripidean plays shows still further the hazards of generalizing. The *Alcestis, Medea, Hippolytus, Andromache, Hecuba, Troades, Orestes, Bacchae* and *Rhesus* were preserved as an anthology in the schools in use around A.D. 200, whereas the others are from a surviving part of the alphabetized collection of Euripides' plays made in Alexandrian times. Hence the second category of plays is a random sample and infinitely more valuable for assessing the totality of the playwright's work. It is surmised that the seven extant Aeschylean plays and seven Sophoclean plays represent an anthology of the Roman period. In addition we have manuscripts of the Byzantine period with the Aeschylean *Prometheus, Persians,* and *Seven Against Thebes* which represent a further reduced anthology. The anthologizing represents a great threat to sensible generalizing about the tragedies of the tragedians, for our sample is created by an intelligence with a point of view and one that is not at all necessarily that of the playwrights. What we are getting is a man's or an age's concept of a playwright. We are perhaps therefore only able to generalize about the generalization the anthology happens to be. In the case of Euripides, however, the larger selection of his plays and the contrast between the two groups perhaps does truly demonstrate the range of his creativity. Then too, the exclusion from the anthology of plays that demonstrate several other tendencies in Euripides' dramaturgy, notably plays one might call creatively untragic or anti-tragic, shows concretely the existence of, if not the nature of, the bias of the anthologizer.

Then too, formulae for long-term change or trends in tragic viewpoint are arbitrary; one notices that some Euripidean plays pose situations very much as Aeschylean plays did. Hippolytus, for instance, clings to his chastity in an obstinate and prideful way that reminds one of Aeschylean *hybris*.

Hippolytus is punished for this starkly and simply in the old-fashioned manner. The chorus of the *Bacchae* might as well be an Aeschylean chorus. The *Eumenides* is talky in just as simple-minded a way as a number of Euripidean plays. Sophocles' *Oedipus at Colonus* is structurally very much like the *Prometheus*, where in each play the hero who is static not active, not a mover, awaits his visitors, culminating in his person past and future, suffering finally a catastrophic or cataclysmic change. Ultimately then, each tragedy stands alone and the more one resists placing it into a scheme the better will be the understanding of it.

The tragedies were prepared for presentation at an annual event that must, after the passage of time, have aroused certain expectations. It is remarkable therefore how diverse the extant tragedies are. The tragic form, the succession of odes and episodes, the tragic diction, these remain constant throughout the fifth century. But the uses to which these were put were many and make it less likely that tragedy was formed in some kind of religious ritual, the Dionysia. The rehearsal or restatement or recommitment or ritual as we see it, for instance, in the Christian Mass is not found in tragedy. Aristotle talks of *peripateia* (reversal) and *anagnorisis* (recognition or denouement) as though they were constants in tragedy. Yet even our sketchy evidence refutes this generality. The *Trojan Women,* for instance, does not turn on a *peripateia* nor does the play bring on an awareness that is not there at the start. Still it is more often than not true that the tragic hero ultimately finds himself in a position where he can exclaim "Now at last I understand" and true also that the hero's situation has changed for the worse in the drama. Yet there is nothing rigid or formulaic in the particulars.

The rhythm of action in tragedy is the same from play to play. In our theater the crisis occurs in the very last moments, bringing with it an instant resolution or projecting a resolution assumed and imagined. Crisis occurs much earlier in ancient drama; the *peripateia* and *anagnorisis* occupy the second third of the play. Agamemnon is stabbed 1343 lines into the 1673-line play. Oedipus rushes out knowing all at line 1185 in that 1530-line play. Suspense was distasteful to the ancients, therefore the playwright did not fashion his action to create a final explosion of revelation. Then too, the implications of the violent reversal and revelation needed working out. Oedipus returns blinded, we learn of Jocasta's death, the ruined king plans his future with Creon, the regent, Theseus discovers how dreadfully Hippolytus has been used and so on. The line of dramatic action moves invariably toward some kind of revelation, from ignorance on the part of some, if not all, characters toward a new understanding and thereafter toward some kind of accommodation to this newly found knowledge.

There is only one extant play that radically departs from a simple story line. It is Euripides' *Phoenician Women,* a very ambitious experiment at episodic, saga-like drama, much more Shakespearean in effect. Here the poet tries to encompass the entire story of the family of Oedipus, which other playwrights dealt with severally. Later hands probably added still more, we are not sure. It stands as a very long play, over 1700 lines, full of killings and changes of scene. There is also a subplot, the sacrificial death of Menoeceus, the son of Creon, who shows himself to be gallant where his cousins, Eteocles and Polyneices, are by turns rabid and petty. There are far more characters in this play; Oedipus and Jocasta remain alive as their sons war with each other. By the end, however, Jocasta is dead, the sons are dead and Antigone is preparing to go with Oedipus into Attica. Whatever his fancies, Euripides has put all the pieces back in place at the end.

While most plays have a simple plot structure, there are among the extant plays significant variants that test the common sense of critics who compulsively search for unity, whatever that is. Sophocles' *Ajax,* for instance, often worries critics because its hero commits suicide, thereby resolving his personal predicament by line 870 in a 1420-line play. He precedes this fatal act with a marvelous speech that shows how well he understands that he is an anachronism. For the *Ajax* hints at being a tragedy of history, an idea Sophocles develops more fully in the *Philoctetes.* Ajax's intransigence, his heroic largeness, is out of place in the group-oriented society that makes up the play, mirroring the *polis* world of the fifth century. The poet dramatizes this when the maddened Ajax rushes upon the army cattle, thinking he is revenging himself upon his brother officers, then again later in the moving speech on yielding (644ff.) in which he ironically acknowledges how he must cede to the changes and new environment in which he does not belong. Ajax's drama is played out emphatically early on in the play.

We are left with more than five hundred lines that do not seem to relate to this when the Greek chiefs argue over whether or not to accord Ajax a hero's burial. Some critics like to call the play a "diptych," the passion of Ajax being one panel, I suppose, and something akin to the deposition being the other. The humiliation of Ajax, however, with which the play begins locates the action in the heroic concern for public esteem, calling up the Homeric world of shame and honor, and the play ends with the same theme as the chiefs argue over the public funeral of Ajax, which will be the kind of communal rehabilitation a hero requires. The marked division in the play, Ajax alive, Ajax dead, reveals two facets of a heroic person. Alive, Ajax when lost and disgraced acts and retrieves himself through suicide, whereas when dead the continuing presence of the man, a corpse before us, but like all heroes a strong unseen but felt force, redeems Ajax when the funeral is planned. Odysseus moves through the play in counterpoint, unwilling to gloat at Athena's side over Ajax's madness (121ff.), for he knows the humility a god can never know, arguing finally for his late rival's honor, because, as he says, "I hated when it was all right to hate" (1347); "enemy, yes, but he was a noble man" (1355); "I am not one to praise a rigid mind" (1361). Odysseus yields, is resilient, as the ever obdurate Ajax could not be. Odysseus survives into the new age, Ajax goes, yet the heroic legacy stays on to fill the latter part of the play.

Sophocles' *Trachinian Women* poses two major figures in conflict, Dejaneira, the loving, dependent, jealous wife who unwittingly kills her husband while trying to regain his love, and Hercules, the conquering hero, the erotic victor as well, who arrives home with his latest amatory conquest only to die at his wife's hands. Sophocles arranges the action so that the two never meet: Dejaneira leaves at 812, Hercules appears for the first time already mortally wounded at 965. The same actor, in fact, played the two roles. One may speculate whether the play gained anything by this, the conversion or transformation, as it were, of Dejaneira into Hercules. It is as if the play showed the obverse and reverse of the conjugal coin, the female effectively vengeful, although rage is repressed, the male, suspicious and quick to judge.

Euripides has two plays extant that break down into very separate actions. In his *Hecuba* the old queen at first learns that her daughter Polyxena is to be sacrificed at Achilles' tomb. In a very moving speech (251) of great dignity she pleads with Odysseus for her daughter's life only to be denied in an ugly, cold and rational speech. Polyxena then accepts her death in a speech of such nobility and dignity that it fortifies Hecuba for the emotional ordeal she must suffer. The girl dies, the funeral preparations begin, Hecuba departs (628). Shortly thereafter the corpse of her son, Polydoros, is brought in, killed treacherously by the queen's former ally and friend, Polymestor. In a rich deepening of character Hecuba goes mad with rage. It is the straw that breaks. In a speech to Agamemnon that structurally parallels the earlier one to Odysseus she begs for the right to avenge Polydoros' death. When Agamemnon agrees, the old queen finds in her pent-up hate all the reserves of energy needed to carry out dreadful murders and maiming. The deaths of Hecuba's two children have nothing to do with one another except in their effect upon the queen. In the two symmetrical speeches as Hecuba pleads for Polyxena's life and Polymestor's death Euripides has depicted two emotional states of a victimized and brutalized human being, exploring the sources and limits of love and of hate.

In his *Hercules* Euripides presents the hero as a savior when he returns to save his wife, children and aged father from death in a political vendetta. Thereupon (814) madness seizes Hercules and he kills his family. The two actions stand distinct; nothing in the first prepares one for the second. Savior and destroyer in one, Hercules says at the bloody end (1279): "I have suffered and endured and this is my last trial and labor." And endure he will. "Now, as it seems," he says (1357), "I must become Necessity's slave." It is not the gods who have designed this. Hercules denies (1341ff.) that they would devise so cruel an act. "These are poets' ugly stories" (1346). The heroic extreme and resolve that carried Hercules through so many labors, made him triumph, has at last brought him triumphant, huge and overwhelming to his home, destroyer of his family, by necessity. Abruptly the heroic persona is replaced in this catastrophe by the human one. Hercules stands revealed.

Both plays are structured on antitheses so absolute, so sharp that they are immediately symmetrical, providing what was for the ancients the most abiding kind of unity. Moreover the antitheses pose the hidden but immanent facets or elements in situations or persons. So it is that the perplexing, meaningless as it seems turns of events are again a thrust toward revelation.

Aristotle although being descriptive is usually taken as being prescriptive. What is more he seems oddly enough to be generalizing largely on the basis of Sophocles' *Oedipus Tyrannus*. As a consequence this play has come to mean the perfect tragedy in our Western tradition. But in fact it is only one kind of tragic experience; the extraordinarily successful way in which the play becomes that experience is, on the other hand, remarkable, for more than in most plays we exist with the play, experience with the play, find total empathy, never self-consciously getting distance on the play so that it becomes objective. Perhaps what is so successful in this play, why we always return to it, is the fact of *experiencing* the play, rather than having an idea emerge from it. Thus we cannot think this play at all. More than most tragedies the *Oedipus* resists being *philosophized*, although it has more than most been the object of such efforts. Let us consider the perils.

At the outset we must dismiss the tendency forged in the West's Judaeo-Christian ethos to see the play in terms of crime and punishment. Sin, which is at the core and is the very definition of post-classical Western man, is absent from classical Greek thinking. The tension between good and evil in the Orphic cults, for instance, is not part of the mainstream of thought, not the communal belief, as is obvious in any descriptions of common woe following military defeat. There is no cry analogous to "Forgive us, O Father, for we have sinned." Sin, taint, these are concepts bound up in a belief in the vitality of evil, of inevitable, primordial evil. We sin because we are by nature prone to it; sin, moreover, is the positive, knowing transgression of god's law. Shakespeare's Iago is an example of the creatively evil or sinful man; such a conception does not appear in pagan antiquity.

The Athenians did not use sin or evil to account for the world's misery and suffering. When Socrates insisted that man by nature will always choose the better course of action he is reflecting the attitude of his countrymen. To be sure the Greeks recognized the dark side of life. There was little sweetness and light in their perspective. They imagined their gods, for instance, to be an ever present source of woe, often inexplicable if not overtly irrational. But their culture was so competitive that the idea of a flawed person, the idea of sin being a natural component of mankind would be difficult to sustain. Instead they believed in failure and error and their moral life took its form from ideas of strength, weakness, success and failure. When we read the *Oedipus,* therefore, we may stop looking for the impulse to sin, the will to punishment. Dostoievsky's Raskolnikov is the perfect antithesis to the Greek tragic hero.

The *Oedipus* poses for us the very real critical problem of getting at the prejudices of the Athenian audience. With what sense of Oedipus did they enter the theater? And to what extent does their prior knowledge act upon their reaction to the Sophoclean play as it is presented? We can never know the answers to these questions and they are crucial for many plays. In this one, for instance, we must try to get at the importance of the oracle. It is sometimes argued, for instance, that Oedipus was in grave error killing a man and marrying a woman both demonstrably older than himself when he had just learned that he was fated to kill his father and marry his mother. His was really an act of impiety and this is underscored by his and Jocasta's talking against oracles in the play. In the same way his determination to stay out of Corinth suggests a prideful and delusive belief that he can evade oracular inevitability. So he is punished and Jocasta is first a provocation and then a kind of accessory victim in the god's machinations, not unlike Euripides' Phaedra.

Such a line of interpretation is philosophical and analytical of the whole story, and it immediately leads to hair splitting. For one must ask perhaps simplistically whether in antiquity a man's mother, who was perhaps thirty-six or thirty-seven when he was twenty, looked all that much older. More importantly one must ask how Oedipus is punished. By his own act of putting out his eyes? By the woe attendant upon his discovery of what he has done? By his public disgrace? But these are all consequences, in fact part of his doom, prophesied by the oracle, a doom that is his simply by existing and hence hardly punishment. To argue that nonetheless a mood of crime and punishment settles over the events demands that the audience accept subconsciously an unsettling construction of the action. What *did* Oedipus do wrong? Or should we say that he sinned in order to meet the misery that was fated to be his? Furthermore his occasional explosions of temper are not a flaw in character of sufficient proportion to justify the turn of events. Are we to imagine that his celebrated anger, which perhaps caused him to kill his father, thereby was the cause for his later punishment, namely being found out as incestuous? This makes the anger an agent force equivalent to the oracle. Every way we *ponder* the play generates new uncertainties, and these are not the productive ambiguities that can indeed be found in other plays.

Our tendency to emphasize the oracle derives from our knowledge of the myth as a whole. In the myth it is fundamental that Oedipus is fated to do as he did. Yet in fact the myth here and in every other instance is *not* the play. The play as produced, the succession of events dramatized, must cancel out the myth, for it is that much more immediate and compelling. Familiarity with the myth perhaps should not imply more than eliminating the need for plot exposition. The events of this play actually correspond very little to the main events of the myth. Everything in the myth, the foundling, the oracle, the patricide, the riddle of the Sphinx, the marriage, everything, up to the last moments before Oedipus blinds himself, is prior to the dramatic action and little happens following the catastrophe. The play is the story of a man trying to learn something, it is a drama of inquiry. The compelling and awesome quality of this play lies partly in the fact that here the conventional manner of tragic exposition is made tragic, hence the normal course of events becomes tragic. The *Oedipus* shows life's rhythm, existence, as being tragic without extenuating circumstances; questions and answers produce woe. Oedipus does not *do* anything in this play. Instead he simply becomes through self-realization a tragic figure. This is existential woe beyond choice, beyond cause and effect. It is woe that is there, is in place, has always been. One becomes aware and realizes his woe, one lives therefore and is woeful.

The particular details of Oedipus' career are secondary. The universality of this play lies in the unimportance of these details. Aeschylus' Clytemnestra, on the other hand, is bound to her daughter's death and her husband's departure. Only the investigation and analysis of Oedipus' life matter. Sophocles presents this with great psychological insight and clarity.

Oedipus is optimistic, a problem solver; as such he is ambitious and aggressive. He solved the problem at the cross-roads, killed Laius and drove through, he solved the riddle of the Sphinx, took the throne, and now he will solve the problem of Thebes' pollution.

Oedipus' aggression and ambition show an effort of will that is dramatically revealed in his extraordinary determination to torture a man so that he will admit to a truth that will destroy Oedipus, which Oedipus already senses. It is further enforced by being contrasted to Creon's self-proclaimed belief in acquiescence and withdrawal and to Jocasta's desire to cover up whatever is unpalatable. Almost allegorically they offer alternative intellectual styles, to wit indifference and evasion. The bigger contrast, however, is the blind Tiresias, whose blindness is a kind of knowledge beyond intellect (eyes) that Sophocles uses as the cohering theme of his play.

As Oedipus moves forward toward the fatal self-realization he is several times baffled by his intellect, which formulates the facts falsely; first when he accuses Creon of political intrigue and last when he assumes that Jocasta's sudden desperate desire to avoid the truth stems from her fears that he will prove to be slave-born. Sophocles in portraying the sudden suspicion of Oedipus that Tiresias and Creon plot against him primarily shows Oedipus using his intelligence to *avoid* the truth; Tiresias says enough for any rational man to understand if he wanted to. Secondarily Sophocles portrays Oedipus as somewhat paranoid. Both elements return in his speech at 1062ff., when he suddenly fancies himself slave-born. To the universal psychological characteristic of being creatively resistant to facing impossible truths Sophocles has added a touch of personal characteristic. Oedipus in his own and everyone's eyes is not the legitimate ruler of Thebes, he is not the son of the late king; he arrived a stranger and lives with Jocasta, Creon and Tiresias, all part of the established power. As such he shows himself suspicious and alien from time to time. His temper, too, seems a Sophoclean expression of his aggression, ambition and insecurity.

The play has to do with inquiry and learning; it is also a dramatization of irony. Jocasta's logical analysis of the impotence of oracles (707ff.), while meant to be helpful, lets clues fall in place; the messenger who is pleased to be able to tell Oedipus that Polybus of Corinth was not his real father ("Why should I not free you from this fear, my lord, since I have come to you in all good will" [1002–3]) ironically moves Oedipus closer to truth and to destruction. Matched to this are the desperately joyful outbursts of the increasingly cornered Oedipus as he finds loopholes, the one when he learns that his presumed father died in his bed, a speech of hysterical triumph, the other just before he learns the truth when he is still caught up in the fantasy of his birth.

"I am really a child of Fortune," he says.

The months, his brothers, were the seasons who saw him on Mount Cithaeron first; and before he was the child of Jocasta and Laius he was the creation of Fortune. Our authenticity, our being is a random, fateful fact and each must come to know this special self. Oedipus is a monster. The shape of his peculiarity is outrageous and vivid enough to make him an excellent projection of the act and effort of self-knowledge.

In this play, nothing the chorus says, nothing Oedipus says after his discovery go to suggest that Sophocles wants to offer an idea, a moral to his story. The first choral ode is a lyrical description of and an acting out of the misery the priest was describing at the beginning of the play; the second reflects the anxiety derived from attacking the institutions of religion. Jocasta has been disproving oracles (707ff. and 849ff.); her last remark on the subject is vehement. The choral ode reflects on pride and daring haughtiness and finally insists there must be some natural order and it must be reflected in the oracles. Their deep concern is in response to Jocasta's disproval of the oracle; at the same time they seem to be revealing her own thoughts for she returns to the scene with garlands and incense to propitiate the gods, particularly Apollo, the god of prophecy. The third choral ode, directly following Oedipus' discovery and his departure, is again a direct expression of the situation. Oedipus is destroyed, he who won so much now turns out to have more misery than glory; everything comes out in the end—all unassailable platitudinous remarks.

The last portion of the play shows us the man, taboo, the marked man, the *discovered* man. Oedipus again is presented as a public spectacle, but his lamentation throughout comes from his discovery of himself. To the end he who goes forth to exile is the commanding, problem-solving person; he makes the decisions for his exile, even after the revelation he remains strong. The play is an optimistic affirmative view of man's capacity to accept the horror of human existence, not just accept, but more to go forth, to demand from nature the truth of this horror. Oedipus is a strong man, a courageous man who will not allow himself to be life's victim. Instead he goes to the truth, unmasks it himself, makes it his own rather than letting it be imposed upon him.

But we have not yet got to the essence of the audience's experience in watching and participating in this play. It is the irony in the experience that works upon them. Oedipus seeks to learn, moves to learn what is already known to them. Thus one has more than in most other plays the sense that this has always been so, that he (we) move to realize what is *fait accompli*. The *Oedipus* reveals perfectly and clearly a common mode of Greek perception; it is the point where destiny and free will merge. Free will and destiny are, we may say, different aspects of the same action, the former looking into the future and the latter being hindsight. We move freely to what will happen but when it has occurred then we see that it *had* to be that way. There are no alternatives. Every line of the play lives for the audience in what is a double temporal field. Oedipus when he formally declares the unknown killer of Laius to be a taboo figure in Theban lands is showing the free and rigorous exercise of kingly power but in fact he is describing himself as he shall be at the end of the play, and the audience knows this, so it is in a sense already true; for he is indeed already a taboo figure, a patricide, and incestuous. Sophocles manages a brilliant stroke when Jocasta comes upon the quarreling brothers-in-law, Oedipus and Creon, and scolds them like a mother. She intervenes compassionately as a wife and sister would, yet we know in fact that she is a mother in this scene, and her behavior becomes a revelation of what his deed has been.

The *Oedipus* does not impose an "idea" on the audience as we sometimes can notice is done in other plays. The audience instead participates in a vigorous and increasingly desperate search for knowledge or truth which does not come to exist but has always been there. To be sure, this is the nature of most truths, but nonetheless man's imperfect means of knowing, his tendencies to ignorance make the moment of realization momentous. "Now I know, now I understand" is that rare moment when the generally hidden outlines and dimensions of our world become apparent and we see that we are not alone, free and moving, but in place. It is frightening but those who have the courage and energy to force themselves to this understanding are heroic. Such is Oedipus.

Euripides' *Trojan Women* is similar in the sense that once the audience has made the identification, then the emotion of the experience passes to them and they have it vicariously. Again there is no idea. The *Trojan Women* is even more simply a state of being. The play is a threnody, a long, operatic expression of grief, a verbal description of suffering. The movement in the play is minimal and mostly peripheral. Passage of time is important only in the fact of the Greeks' future shipwreck and sufferings at sea, coloring the Greek triumph and the Trojan dejection, giving dramatic substance to Hecuba's often repeated theme of her changed condition from queen to abject slave. The uncertainty in human affairs which must keep us from exulting overmuch in good fortune, very much a commonplace of Greek thought, is the moral philosophical field in which this passionate drama of suffering unfolds. Euripides seems clearly enough intent on maximizing the audience's participation in the dramatic distress, for the play is near to what we would call a tear-jerker. This is not to say that a young girl slain in cold blood, a young wife and mother led off as concubine, her husband dead, her son to be killed, a young boy thrown to his death from the city's walls and an old queen groveling in the dust are not all legitimately hideous aspects of warfare. But Euripides makes them tearful rather than horrible. One sees this especially in Andromache's departure from Hecuba and then in Talthybios' description of Astyanax's death and in the old queen's lamentation over the dead boy's corpse. What movement or development there is in the *Trojan Women* comes in the crescendo of grief at this point. This is like the moment in Sophocles' (panoramic and static) *Oedipus at Colonus* when Oedipus curses his son Polyneices, creating an intensity of emotion that gives some kind of direction to the play, for it moves us in its intensity toward the greater moment of Oedipus' departure from the human scene and away from the feeble and impotent old man of the opening scene.

It is customary to say that the *Trojan Women* represents Euripides' public demonstration against the Athenian slaughter of the Melians in 416–15, against Athenian military policy in general, indeed against war itself. It is less topical than that, however. It is a profound anti-war play without slogan or program, simply by locating the grief in the destruction of innocents. Polyxena, Cassandra and Astyanax, virgins and children, the ancient world's emblems of innocence, are killed or violated. Beside the death of individuals Euripides gives equal claim to the death of a city; it is the main theme of the chorus, particularly of the odes at 511ff. and 1060ff., and the play ends with the burning city as the focus of all grief. The city's death, an abstraction covering all individuals, is greater, the destruction of civilization. Andromache and Hecuba, through whom the poet of the *Iliad* was able to convey the way of life and values that Hector defended, appear here as the mutilated remnants of the same values and social relations. Particularly Andromache's speculation on forgetting Hector when she goes to bed with her captor Neoptolemos reflects the collapse of all human order, of civilization, for Andromache is the paradigm of a wife in Greek culture.

Sophocles' *Electra* is likewise the portrait of an emotion. The playwright deliberately omits emphasis upon the action elements of the story, the reunion, the plotting, the killing (cf. 273ff.), so that what emerges instead is Electra in her grief. She verbalizes only the quality of sorrow; her personality remains undeveloped.

These plays have in common the absence of conflict, I mean, central conflict. Electra's hostility to Clytemnestra is not matched by her mother's emotions, nor do Chrysothemis and Electra manage to establish a vital antithesis. In the two Oedipus plays and the *Trojan Women* the conflicts between Oedipus and Creon, Creon and Theseus and Helen and Hecuba are all secondary. What we might call an idea is absent from these plays. Therefore, positions are not taken, compared, contrasted and hence explored so as to offer the dimensions or shape of an idea or ideology.

Some plays, however, are intellectualist, centered upon ideas, made of dialogue that explores the ranges of the competing positions. Aeschylus' *Eumenides* might seem to be an early example of this as the competing claims for Orestes, Clytemnestra, Apollo and the Erinyes are argued over in court, but instead the emphasis is upon the dramatic fact of the conflict and its resolution and not upon the verbal details, contentions and proofs. Euripides often poses arguments as though they were lawyer's briefs, as for instance when Helen and Hecuba argue before Menelaus in the *Trojan Women;* or he will put into a character's mouth the sort of speech that resembles a learned aside, as the nurse's speech in the *Hippolytus,* which resembles nothing so much as the doctrinaire speech of a contemporary sex hygienist; or he underscores the irony of intellectualism in late-fifth-century Athens by putting a very professorial discourse on myth symbolism in the mouth of the seer, Tiresias in the *Bacchae.*

But in the *Medea* he has created a white paper as it were on the indignity of the position of contemporary Athenian women. The *Medea* is a startling and moving account of a woman's exploitation and her retaliatory rage. Nothing is more powerful dramatically than Medea's struggle to suppress her rage as she offers the complacent Jason presents for his new bride, or her tortured resolve to murder her children. The real strength or character of the drama, however, lies in the arguments between Jason and Medea on their roles and obligations. Medea is a foreigner, alien, dependent upon Jason, a woman who has killed her brother and thereby destroyed all ties with her own family. All of which sums up the nature of the Athenian bride, who must leave her family and go in submission and dependence into her husband's family. Even the servants in this play are wordy and wise. The tutor is cynical ("Don't you realize we love ourselves more than our neighbors?" [85–86]), the nurse a veritable treasury of platitudes. Her speeches at 115ff. and 184ff. sound more like choral passages than actor's dialogue as she rings the changes on the dangers inherent in greatness in temper and in station or the inadequacy of song at stemming grief. But this frigid rationalizing is only preparation for Jason and Medea.

Medea's first speech (214–67) is an exposition on the dilemma of being a foreigner, then of being a woman. The two ideas are well juxtaposed to bring out the idea of woman as an alien thing, the woman as nigger, in fact, in fifth-century Athens. The speech is so strong, so bold in its contention that we hunger to know the Athenian reaction. Did Euripides palliate the bitter truth with the fact that Medea was a foreigner and a sorceress? Greeks were chauvinists, Medea was a non-Greek. Were the males in the audience able to turn back the criticism because they could reject the dangerous, strange and non-Greek Medea? Euripides, however, keeps the attack on men general. "Women," snarls Medea sarcastically (407–8), "who are helpless at doing good, are the smartest authors of every ill," echoing a commonplace of Greek literature from the early archaic period onward. Medea has determined to kill her husband, his new bride and her father; still the chorus remains sympathetic. "Let the water of the sacred river run backward," they sing (409ff.), "let justice turn around. Men's plans are corrupt, men's oaths sworn before gods no longer trustworthy. Town talk will give me good repute, honor will come to the female race." Faithful to the choral injunction Euripides has fashioned a denunciation of self-seeking, indifferent males and a sympathetic insight into the burden of womanhood. The climax comes in the bitter, brutal, intelligent exchange between Jason and Medea (446–627) where he outlines all the practical advantages to the scheme—upward mobility, security—and she rehearses what he owes her and talks again of her dependency. As a historical document these speeches in the *Medea* give an index of how far Athenian society had moved in the direction of the so-called nuclear family. Here in this play two egos howl at one another. Again and again she calls him a coward; he strikes back where presumably both have hurt each other:

You wouldn't think my plan so bad, if your empty bed
  weren't grating on you.
You women—if everything is OK in bed, you think the whole
  world's rosy,
But let a little trouble come about in bed,
And you grow hostile to the best and finest things. (560ff.)

They part in anger and Medea proceeds to act out her anger and impotence, killing, destroying, mean and hateful. The traditional story has been thoroughly colored by the ideology of the first part of the play. Medea is no exotic sorceress, inhumane enough to kill her brother and now her children, Jason is no hero, misguided enough to get ensnared by this cold magician. On the contrary, Medea is a hysterical, repressed, rage-filled wife and mother and Jason is her unfeeling oppressor. It is an amazing play which complements a number of other Euripidean insights into women's condition in late-fifth-century Athens. But one is struck more by the ideas and the exposition than swayed by the emotion of Medea's predicament.

Often ideas occur in an ambiguity that allows for an illogical presentation, for the juxtaposition and combination of inherently contradictory notions. The *Prometheus Bound* is a good example of this, although again we must beware of overinterpretation, too positive interpretation when we lack the other plays of the trilogy. Hesiod's *Works and Days* and *Theogony* imply that the Prometheus story in outline was well known. It is the Greek version of man's attempt to justify the continuing presence of suffering in his life. Here indeed is a story of crime and punishment. The *Prometheus Bound* has to do with the punishment of Prometheus but that is only the surface, just as the play only seems to be static. It is hard to stage, it is lyrical rather than dramatic; the very long speeches do not work as dialogue. It is formal; the motionless Titan is approached by the Oceanids, Oceanus, Io and Hermes. They all reflect him, and in that manner explain him, but only the Oceanids suffer with him; except for Oceanus no one offers alternatives, and even he does so only superficially. There is conventional action only at the very beginning and very end of the play when first Prometheus is nailed to the rock and finally he falls into Tartarus. But within what is really a pageant—the passion of Prometheus, so to speak—the poet has fashioned a sense of action, first, through the arrival and departure of the several other characters, then by the vast range of space evoked in the numerous geographical references in the play, but most of all through Prometheus' prophecies and recollections, which move back and forth in a great passage of time. This is, indeed, a *big* play, and it is made lively by the tension in the paradoxes that lie in it.

Hesiod's *Theogony*, where we find the Prometheus story recounted (as well as in his *Works and Days*), has to do with the generations of gods. Two elements of that tradition are particularly evident in the Aeschylean story: the violence in the divine family and the overthrow of absolute authority. As Hesiod tells us, Ouranos is cast out by his son Kronos, who is in turn overwhelmed by Zeus. The violence leads, as Aeschylus continually notices, to roughness in the new authority; the *Theogony* shows the older generations of god to be rough, brutish, and the fight of Zeus against the Titans is seen as the progress to a new moral order. In this story god is presented as carrying the seeds of his own destruction. It is in Freudian terms a very Oedipal story. Zeus, according to Hesiod, escapes being overthrown by swallowing the consort he impregnated, foetus and all. Since absolutism and eternity are essential components of any profound notion of god this primitive act of Zeus is theologically very sophisticated. These elements bear on the drama in that Zeus is the new order, Prometheus is the older generation of god, a Titan (who, however, chose to side with Zeus in battle against his fellow Titans); furthermore the issue of Zeus' survival lies unspoken just behind what is said. For Zeus is fated to sire a son by the goddess Thetis who will overthrow him. This is what Prometheus knows (167ff.) and what Zeus must find out.

We are not sure that Aeschylus wrote this play. Whoever did boldly introduces ambiguities, for instance, the relationship between fate, the omnipotent and omniscient Zeus and Prometheus, who sees all the future. The resulting contradictions well reflect any open-eyed contemplation of the workings of the universe (cf. 515ff.). Zeus, who knows all things, whom Might at the play's beginning fears may be watching, who when Prometheus alludes to his doom immediately sends Hermes to get the secret from Prometheus, does not paradoxically know the secret himself; before that he did not even know that Prometheus was intent on stealing fire. Prometheus in turn, who knows all the future (cf. 97ff.), chose to serve Zeus even though he knew what ill treatment lay in store for him (224ff.), yet elsewhere (267ff.) he seems not to have realized what suffering lay ahead. This state of mind is reflected in Io, for when Prometheus has revealed her pain-filled future and she says (750) that suicide is her only alternative, she nonetheless goes out and on into that grim future. Io shows persistence, survival; she is the dramatic realization of the quality of hope which Prometheus gave to man. He himself possesses it (cf. 187ff.), hence his suffering.

Another paradox in this play resides in the sympathetic portrayal of Prometheus and the hostile conception of Zeus. Zeus is almost wicked, almost a villain in contrast to the good, victimized Prometheus. Other Aeschylean plays as well as the quasi-philosophical, theological tradition found in Hesiod and Solon among others show that the common conception of Zeus is as the guardian if not creator of moral order. The *Prometheus Bound* therefore offers a far more complicated conception of Zeus.

The play unfolds on several levels of meaning. References to tyranny would have been somewhat topical to an Athenian audience. The Greek mainland had witnessed the arbitrary establishment of one-man rule, sometimes benign, often cruel, in opposition to the hereditary aristocratic control in many cities; in the fifth century the brilliant cities of Sicily were ruled by tyrants. When the chorus express their horror at Io's plight (88ff.) it is first in terms of a girl who has been destroyed by getting mixed up with people too powerful for her. Oceanus comes on as an old-fashioned aristocrat who has learned to yield quietly to the new violent power (311–12, 329) and Hermes is the tyrant's lackey (941ff.). Athens particularly had a horror of rule by power. The whole trend of the establishment of democratic institutions of the fifth century is to eliminate individual power. The arbitrary harsh, tyrannical rule of Zeus would, we may assume, have been very antipathetic to the audience.

The *Prometheus* also poses a conflict between god and man. Prometheus is man's protector; more than that, as he suffers through his love or care for man, he stands more to the side of man than god. He suffers for man and has chosen to identify with man. As Io is a human victim of god so the divine Prometheus too is a human victim. Likewise he resembles man in his intelligence and his optimism. Prometheus, as he says, gave mankind hope and skill. Ironically these are his own particular endowments. Man ameliorates his lot with skill and intellect and he confronts doom with the hope that it will not be so. Science and technology, the pursuit of the better life, are optimistic and betoken an enterprise actuated by hope. Prometheus, who succeeds through craft and guile (intelligence and skill), allies himself with Zeus, whose victories as Prometheus foresees will come to him through intelligence (cf. Themis' prophecy 214ff.). Now as he suffers, a victim of Zeus, once his colleague, he survives on the empty (as the audience well knows) hope that he will see Zeus overthrown, an empty hope that he surely senses as empty. Is hope, however, in any case vain, still necessary?

Prometheus and Zeus, man and god, one might say. It is a symbiotic relationship. What distinguishes man from god? First, the gods are immortal, then, each has some mark, quality, attribute, some role that makes him an essential part of the universe. Man, in the Greek theology, is coeval with the gods, not god's creation. Yet man at creation has no particular attribute; he is helpless. Prometheus bestowed upon man technical skill and hope, which help him to survive; they are to him what immortality is to the gods. And Prometheus himself, become in this play all of man's striving and suffering, reveals the power he has over Zeus, which by extension is the power man has over god: the secret of god's overthrow. Zeus needs Prometheus, needs Prometheus' secret. God needs man for the same reason. The idea is made comic in Aristophanes' *Birds* when it is proposed to block the passage of smoke from sacrifice on earth as it goes heavenward to the gods. Gods exist in man's image, Xenophanes had said a century earlier. The *Prometheus* reveals the mutual dependency of man and god.

But there is still another obvious facet to the tension between Zeus and Prometheus. Because Zeus is presented so unsympathetically in this play it may be forgotten that conventionally he is thought to have ushered in a new moral order. Progress is on Zeus' side; Prometheus is of the old order and the trilogy as a whole surely must have been consistent with the general philosophical position of Hesiod's *Theogony*, where the victories of Zeus imply the evolution of god toward a better universal order. Then too, man's position is severely limited by some moral absolute, else moral anarchy will ensue. The common metaphor of this play is that of disease. Disease is a form of anarchy. Disease was thought to be the imbalance of the body's humors, and balance is everywhere in this play: tyranny and victimization on the historical level; Promethean insolence and daring; Zeus' harsh, overweening authority; man's presumptions. Ultimately the balance, we may assume, comes through the reconciliation of Prometheus and Zeus.

Balance and harmony will not, however, deny the many tensions Aeschylus has brought to the drama. The greatness of this play lies partly in the poetic reconciliation of elements, which no prose statement of theological doctrine could achieve. Prometheus as victim of tyranny, as the old divine order that must pass, as symbol of man, as the sufferer who drinks of hope; Zeus as harsh tyrant, arrogant god, herald of a new moral order; the Oceanids as martyrs to Prometheus' intransigence, their father's accommodation, his wisdom, their folly; Io's wanderings, sufferings, victimization, hope and delusion. One could go on. It is a mysterious play that has often suffered from those who see Prometheus as a kind of Christ. But there is a brooding bitterness in the play as well as a delicate balance of frailty and power in Prometheus which make the play uniquely mysterious.

By contrast the *Oresteia* trilogy is instructive because here Aeschylus orders a number of ideas through symbols that seem to avoid the ambiguities of the *Prometheus*. It seems a different kind of poetic style. The plays, particularly the *Agamemnon,* however, sometimes suffer from neat interpretation. For there is great passion in these plays which the traditional interpretation tends to pass by. It is customary to talk about the historical fact of the evolution of Greek social and political life from family to state as being an important theme of the plays. Blood feuds give way to courts. The crimes of the House of Atreus are finally settled, resolved in an Athenian court of law. Then too, the moral vision Herodotus displays in the Croesus story is said to be dramatized by Aeschylus. Prideful Agamemnon goes too far, is seduced and cut down by Clytemnestra, who in turn seduced by Aigisthos has gone too far and is cut down by Orestes.

One cannot deny the importance of both these ideas. There is political significance in the *Eumenides* when the Erinyes, who are ancient, irrational, avenging forces of the family, are made to surrender to the rationalism of the city courts. Politics is already apparent in the *Agamemnon.* The chorus of old men who wait behind in Argos describe the catastrophes of Iphigenia's death, Paris' seduction of Helen, the measures for war, all those glory-seeking, destructive acts of the aristocracy, and then they tell of how the citizens mutter in rage against the destruction of the war (437ff.). This very long choral passage begins (40ff.) in a vision of the glorious generalship of Menelaus and Agamemnon; the heroic vision ends with the political reality. Similarly when Clytemnestra comes forth with the corpse of Agamemnon, prepared to justify his murder, the play becomes once again political; indeed the drama ends with an angry confrontation between Aigisthos, who is contemptuous and arrogant before the people, and the citizens, who will not accept Agamemnon's death. For Clytemnestra defends her action in familial, personal terms whereas they are not satisfied that his death was a *political* necessity.

Then too, Aeschylus has mounted the action very deliberately in terms of pride and ruin. Agamemnon in the very zenith of glory and power prepares to sail for Troy. When becalmed at Aulis an omen compels him to sacrifice his daughter Iphigenia so as to get the sailing winds they need. He chooses to sail and therefore to sacrifice Iphigenia; when he returns Clytemnestra meets him and in one of the best-known scenes from Greek tragedy persuades him to enter the palace walking upon a purple carpet as a conquering hero. It is the paradigm exposition of this conception of pride. Agamemnon, prosperous in war (*olbos*), is seduced by Clytemnestra (*ate*) to commit the prideful act (*hybris*), which he does mistakenly (*hamartia*), and is thus destroyed by her (*nemesis*). She demands this walk of him so that he will commit in her presence an act symbolic of his killing Iphigenia ten years ago. When Orestes stands before Clytemnestra sword in hand, he hesitates at matricide, until his friend Pylades reminds him of Apollo's mandate. Apollo is the seductive destruction (*ate*) of Orestes as Artemis was of Agamemnon. The healing force of this harsh and ugly divine force is always mysterious. The chorus of the *Agamemnon* say (176–83):

> Zeus shows man the way to think,
> setting understanding securely in the midst of suffering.
> In the heart there drips instead of sleep
> a labor of sorrowing memory; and there comes
> to us all unwilling prudent measured thought;
> the grace of gods who sit on holy thrones
> somehow comes with force and violence.

The price to know what is immanent in things is very high, and there is no choice, but, as ever in Greek culture, awareness is all. "To suffer" also means in Greek "to experience." The heroes of Aeschylean drama act out what they must, they are wise, aware. Not so the chorus. As Cassandra hallucinates before the terrified chorus, describing to them the awful horrors of the House of Atreus, past and present, visitations convened into one moment of time, they do not understand. While Clytemnestra plans her husband's death, the chorus nervously hope that their current uneasiness will somehow dissipate. When that dreadful cry comes from the palace, "I have been struck," the chorus twitter like a flock of chickens, impotent, confused and unknowing. As always, the greatness of the tragic heroes makes the chorus impotent in their misery puny.

Critics of the *Oresteia* overlook the powerful expression of sexual attitudes and familial roles in this trilogy which is the source of so much passion. The final play portrays the transformation of the dread Erinyes into the beneficent Eumenides. These figures, the incarnation of curses, closely associated with the earth and with Demeter in cult, are vengeful, irrational, unceasing in their pursuit and punishment, most particularly of crimes in the family. They are an expression of the hatreds, feuds and vendettas, gruesome, cruel and tenacious, that spring up and flourish in the hothouse atmosphere, enclosed and incestuous, of the extended family. The women of the family, introverted upon the family as they are isolated from the outside world, creators from their bodies of the family, are the most vehement in their protection of the family on the elemental level, most insistent in feud and punishment. The women of the family are indeed its Erinyes. The *Eumenides* dramatizes the transference of power from the family to the *polis*, from the woman-centered arena to man's social construct, the state. In this transformation the Erinyes become superfluous; justice and social stability become the affair of men and the Erinyes become kindhearted ladies.

The debate of the *Eumenides* contests the superiority of men and women, more particularly the role of each sex in the reproductive process. Are we children of the father or the mother? Must Orestes avenge his father or no? Was he killing his true parent when Clytemnestra died? The argument seems flimsy to us, especially since the biological facts of reproduction are incontrovertible today. But the issue of the courtroom scene is more about the roles of each sex in the family and the value of each sex within the family. This conflict animates the entire trilogy.

At the beginning of the *Agamemnon* the chorus sing of the events that led up to the Trojan War, of Agamemnon and Menelaus as proud avenging eagles, of the pregnant hare whose unborn young is destroyed by the eagles of Zeus, of Iphigenia led to the altar and slaughtered by her father, of Helen, sensuous seductress who brought ruin on the men of

Greece and Troy and destroyed the kingdom of Priam. All the while Clytemnestra silently moves about to the altars with thanksgiving offerings at the news of Agamemnon's victory. The mother moves across the story of her daughter's slaughter, acting out the vision of the eagles destroying the fetus in the pregnant hare. Agamemnon's decision to sacrifice his daughter to save the fleet is not only the betrayal of the mother, but her very denial since a woman of that period was in fact defined by her childbearing role. Moreover it is a male's outside interests and ambitions in fatal conflict with his familial obligations within the home. Then too, Agamemnon as male war lord kills what woman creates. The antagonism, competition and aggression are immense. "Man-thinking," the watchman calls Clytemnestra (11); she counters masculine suspicions elsewhere with some nice sarcasm. Are you certain the war is over? the old men of the chorus ask. Do you think you are dealing with a simple little girl? (277) she replies. And later (348), these are the things you learn from me, just a woman, of course, to which the old men shortly respond (351): "Madam, you speak very well, like an intelligent man." Throughout the *Agamemnon* and the *Choephoroi* Clytemnestra's ambition and aggression remain something to which every character returns. The proud, sad queen is in fact an unusual figure in this story; she is essentially a victim of the House of Atreus and its horrible, oppressive, never-ending fate. She has married into the family, now become subject to it, to which she can only respond by monumental self-assertion.

Agamemnon has also betrayed her by deserting her bed for ten years. In her welcoming speech Clytemnestra describes the worry and anxiety, the loneliness of the woman left behind. ("Gentlemen, . . . I am not embarrassed to mention my love for my man before you. Modesty passes with time; that's only human" [855–58]). The longing for Agamemnon has become the lust for revenge and she describes its satisfaction in marvelously sexual lines. She tells of stabbing him dead and what is really the final, most satisfying orgasm for which she has waited so long.

He gave birth to a sharp stream of blood,
hit me with black drops of dead man's blood,
and I rejoiced no less than the corn does
at god-given rain's sparkle in the birthtime of buds. (1389–92)

When Clytemnestra awaits Agamemnon at the palace door the carpet is rolled out, deep purple, a stream of blood to engulf him and destroy him. She tempts him to walk upon the carpet, she demands that he walk upon the carpet. It is an astounding scene calculated to produce the maximum horror, at least in men. There is the age-old fear of woman's power over man acted out, man approaches at woman's command, makes entry and is cut down. Intimations of the Great Mother Goddess and the dying male god are in the scene. There are hints of the *vagina dentata* in the knives that lurk in the warm, moist bath beyond the door. Agamemnon is so listless, so ready a victim that in turn the scene becomes very like a bullfight arena as the bull slowly turns upon the outpoised sword in the hand of the matador.

The moment is repeated in the *Choephoroi* when the son who will avenge his father and at the same time succeed to his father's place as man of the family approaches the same door to confront the same woman. As the *Agamemnon* was the family drama of husband and wife, this play is the drama of parent and child. The chorus admonish Orestes (826ff.):

> Take courage when your part in the action comes,
> as she shouts "Son"
> at you, shout back "Father,"
> and do it,
> murder her without blame.

But Orestes, like his father, hesitates before the door before his mother's bared breast demanding the son's obligation to a mother. But he will kill her for betraying his father, principally for her adultery. Perhaps on another level of consciousness the play acts out the Oedipal fantasy whereby the father is overcome and the son succeeds to his father's bed. Matricide, say some psychiatrists, is euphemism for the greater family crime of incest. Orestes murders, penetrates his mother's body in one way or another and goes mad, hounded by the vengeance of family and women, the Erinyes, destroyed as his father was before him by a woman.

While Clytemnestra strives to get Agamemnon onto the carpet, Cassandra is a silent spectator to the scene. Aeschylus, as in the case of Clytemnestra's opening scene, uses silence in a telling dramatic way in Cassandra's appearance. The duel between Agamemnon and Clytemnestra is between a mother betrayed and a father who killed his child. Cassandra, the slave and concubine and female victim of Agamemnon, changes the terms of the confrontation, that is, the sexual weapons in the royal couple's relationship are brought forth. Clytemnestra begins the play as a mother betrayed and is revealed as an adulteress who betrayed her husband. Each of them has offered to the other the final insult: Agamemnon kills Clytemnestra's daughter, and she takes another man into his bed. The shift in Clytemnestra in the *Agamemnon* is paralleled by Orestes in the *Choephoroi,* who changes from an avenger of his father into the murderer of his mother just as finally the Erinyes are transformed into the Eumenides. Cassandra's hallucinatory speech in the *Agamemnon* (1072ff.) shows that the actions of the House of Atreus are forever present, adultery and the killing of children are implicit in everything done. In the great conflict then between man and woman the wife who grieves for her lost child is already betraying her husband with another man, the son who will redeem his father must inevitably destroy (rape) his mother. Only the horrible, tenacious vendetta sprung from family crime can be changed, truly transformed as human relationships are ordered in the man-dominated city.

Perhaps ancient Greek tragedy was supposed to ventilate the feelings, and then return the audience to some sort of composure. While we cannot tell what was the ending of the Promethean trilogy, there are other tragedies that do show an opening to many meanings and then a kind of resolution, for instance Sophocles' *Antigone* and Euripides' *Bacchae.*

The most obvious, most celebrated movement in the *Antigone* is the conflict between niece and uncle where she advances the claims of religion against his insistence that the state has prior claims on our loyalties. State, religion, those are elements of the culture, and both Creon and Antigone eloquently defend their position several times over. Creon's is the more reasoned, analytical speech (162ff.), perhaps befitting the more intellectualist underpinnings of the state, whereas Antigone's (450ff.) is more emotional. It is possible to believe here that as he advances the claims of the state the original audience may have sensed if not realized that they were part of a bewildering historical process whereby the state was indeed supplanting the family as the source of spiritual, cultural and economic life. Indeed in the historical transition from family to state tragedy was one means of transition, for it dealt often with political problems in familial terms.

But pulling against this another way were the counterclaims of individual and group; here Antigone is the very manifestation of individual behavior, whereas Creon insists upon the group. In the few extant plays of Sophocles we find this collision in three: in the *Ajax* and in the *Philoctetes,* as well as here. What we know of fifth-century Athenian life shows a marked development through the century of the status and prerogatives of the individual. This is curious in that Sophocles is often considered to be looking back for he has created a kind hero seemingly on the model of Homer's Achilles. Such a hero is highly individualistic, isolated, egoistic.

And yet where Achilles becomes wise and yields in Homer's *Iliad,* Sophocles' more intransigent heroes, Ajax and Antigone for instance, simply force their deaths, which arbitrarily resolves all conflicts, but does not demand any change of heart. So here Sophocles has taken the old insight, the willful, withdrawn Achilles—inherently tragic but made more so by the dramatist—and it supplies the perfect projection of a tendency in contemporary society. Therefore as Antigone argues for the old she stands as an individual defiant of the group.

The expression of her individuality is very well captured in Sophocles' delineation of her nasty personality. Heroes are of course never sweet; they pursue their line grim-faced, tight-lipped. Sophocles, however, emphasizes this by juxtaposing Antigone to her sister Ismene. Antigone becomes in part the study of a female out of control but more an individual energized by demon qualities in pursuit of what she must have. The poet is able to bring several of the themes of this play together, that is, family ties, state obligations, authority within the family, the societal role of individualism in Creon's speech at 640ff., especially the latter half ("If I allow disorder in my house things will certainly get out of hand in the city . . ." [659ff.]).

The initial scene, which functions really as the common Euripidean prologue in setting up the situation, also establishes the considerable difference in the characters of the two girls. Ismene has the viewpoint and reasonableness so often found in the tragic chorus. She begins by pointing out all the misfortunes that have destroyed the House of Labdacus and thus indicating that the two sisters have the power to end it with them. She talks of the frailty of their sex, talks of obedience, rejects futile action. But Antigone will have none of it: "I shall bury him and when I have done that, death is best" (71–72). Ismene urges passive goodness: "I'll do nothing evil but I wasn't born to stand against the people's will" (78–79). Antigone eventually explodes: "Oh hell, denounce me. If you're so lily-livered as to keep silent on my behalf I shall despise you all the more" (85–86), to which Ismene makes a memorable reply: "You have a hot mind over chilly things" (88). Later when Ismene repents of her prudence and wishes to share Antigone's punishment, Antigone shuts her out: "You didn't want to be part of this and I didn't give you any part" (539). And Ismene is tender when she asks Creon: "You mean you'd kill the bride of your own son?" (568). But Antigone is hard although she laments the fact that she will die a virgin. Even when she is sealed in the tomb she is relentless, will not be passive. She will not starve to death, let death come to her, but reaches for it, kills herself.

Antigone seems the dramatic working out of Heidegger's interpretation of the very famous second choral ode of the play (332ff.): "Many are the wonders of this world but nothing that lives is stranger than man." For the ode has to do with man's relentless impulse to reshape nature. As Heidegger points out, the creativity implicit in this demands the destruction of what was before. Man thus is destroyer and no one is more so than Antigone. Granted that the conflict between herself and Creon is in the nature of human relationships, Sophocles nevertheless by emphasizing her hardness has shown her to be irresistibly drawn to destroying whatever equilibriums might be achieved. Creon is static, mouthing his position, while she comes at him. In fact, the peculiarly ambiguous double burial of Polyneices also underscores her ferocious tenacity. She does have a hot mind over chilly things.

When Ismene argues against action because they are women another tension is introduced to which Creon sometimes alludes. This is a conflict between a mere slip of a *girl* and an important *man*. "She will be the man instead of me, if she wins, and gets away with it," says Creon (483f.), and later on, "I must not be beaten by a woman, if defeat ever comes at least let it be a man who brings it. I will not be pointed out as someone who is weaker than women"

(680ff.). These sentiments play on two very powerful tendencies in fifth-century Athenian society: misogyny and intense competitive spirit between males. Sophocles widens the scope of the conflict by introducing male supremacy. And only a mention would be enough to make conscious what must have lain somewhere in the minds of all those male spectators. Sophocles as a dramatist in this way widens his play so as to avoid the simplicities of the monolithic antithesis that has so often been read into this play. It is, indeed, far more complicated here by the fact that Sophocles has made Antigone's situation sympathetic enough that the natural misogynist juices rise in confusion.

What in turn ironically encases the whole action is the family, that bond Antigone lives for and Creon denies. As in so many plays the female is of the family, the male ranges outside. One thinks of Electra at home, Orestes in exile, Clytemnestra brooding on her daughter, Agamemnon marshaling the forces at Troy, Hecuba sorrowing for her family, many more. So Antigone must bury her brother, but to do so she defies her uncle, sets up a chain of events that ultimately destroy her cousin, who is also her intended husband, and her aunt. The family is destroyed in this play, ironic because it is Creon's family; in the end he suffers at its going, he who had before insisted on the state. More ironic is Creon's speech to Haimon when the boy offers loyalty to his father: "A marriage could never mean for me what your benevolent paternal authority does" (637f.). Creon in answering him stresses loyalty in the family, which of course he has opposed in Antigone's actions, but there of course the loyalty he wants is a son's toward his father. Sibling loyalty is perhaps beyond a parent's ken. In any case the conflicts are unsettling.

Then finally this hard girl talks of love: "I cannot deal in hatred but in love" (523). Of course, it was love that brought her to bury Polyneices. It is love at this very moment that sends Ismene out of the palace to join Antigone's fate (*Philadelpha*, says the chorus, "Sister-loving" [528]). Haimon loves his father so that he tries to criticize his authority (683ff.) only to get his father's sarcastic assumption that Haimon speaks as a lovesick groom ("You woman's slave" [756]). Eurydice, we may assume, dies of a broken heart.

The tragedy in this play lies in the fact that the fabric of human events and associations must inevitably be rent beyond repair. In his few extant plays Sophocles often celebrates the insoluble. The threatening instability of human affairs is laid bare. The drive toward destruction and extinction is made evident. The poet has opened up the play by exposing all the tensions and countertensions that fray and tear human existence. They are destructively contradictory; that is tragic.

Nothing is really resolved in the play. Sophocles introduces three conclusive situations that together bring the play to a close. We are exhausted finally, we yield to the situation, but afterward the problems and conflicts remain. The first of these three conclusive episodes is Antigone's departure for the cave to her death. This moment marks the culmination of her fury and staunch resolve which have been her very being since the play began. Heroes of her stamp must go positively to their deaths so as to provide a moral aesthetic. It is like artists who must work within the frame of their canvas or photographers who crop their pictures. There must be nothing incidental, no falling away in the letdown of aftermath. Only death can arrest Antigone's career at its fullest moment. So she goes to die; death measures her conviction and makes it profound.

Tiresias enters thereafter to announce the gods' displeasure. The timing is essential. Had he come earlier Antigone's stance would have been diminished by his advocacy. Sophocles does not seem to be encouraging the notion of "Oh, what a pity! If only we'd known earlier . . ." Not at all. Antigone's actions have been bold and articulate throughout the play; nothing can touch them. Now Tiresias is here to introduce the overriding norm: the dead must be buried; it is age-old custom and the will of the gods.

The final moments in which Creon comes to grief at the suicides of his son and wife recast the action in another dimension. Creon, who had insisted upon the primacy of the state over the family, finally must stand alone, his family dead. He must see the corpses of three persons who died for love, love of one sort or another, but love in the family; Creon, who has insisted upon authority, must now confront within his family a hideously successful rebellion against his authority. And a play that began as a public conflict, an argument in patriotism, closes in the ruin of the family. Here again the poet has proposed an important and unsettling point of view, that even as the city is some kind of family writ large so within the family there exists a kind of politics.

The *Bacchae* in turn is an unsettling play because different contrary moods and expectations are continually merging. The shape of a part of the action resembles, so far as we can tell, the ritual of the Dionysiac cult. It is not clear whether at the end of the fifth century when the play was presented these rituals still were practiced, but the memory must have persisted. At least the central features of the ritual must have been apparent in the play. The idea of the holy scapegoat who is hunted, the putting on of the god by ·putting on animal skins, or the rending to pieces of the animal the god has entered, for instance, must have made the scene where Pentheus departs dressed as a woman and bewigged, the subsequent description of his death and his mother's appearance with the dead man's head peculiarly awesome.

The final appearance of Pentheus is one of the most frightening scenes in ancient tragedy. He is hallucinating to begin with. Then he has been seduced by the god, not physically but in some nearly sexual way. We remember his constant prurience, his grim belief that all kinds of sexual doings are going on among the women in the hills, his peculiar enchantment with the looks and physical presence of the god, his overt physical contact with the stranger when he cuts his hair, takes his thyrsus. And indeed the god has got him to go to see the bands of women by playing on his most secret desires; when Pentheus in anger goes to leave the scene (810) Dionysus calls him back: "Wait. Would you like to *see* them sitting around altogether on the mountain?" Which goes to the heart of the matter. The repressed soul who lives far more constantly and closely with whatever he is furiously denying himself is always therefore in wait of it. One brief invitation and the walls come tumbling down.

Repression, of course, is a very contemporary term. Would the ancients have seen this in the play? Euripides' *Hippolytus* is explicit enough about repression to imply that the psychological phenomenon was known. Hippolytus, who refuses to honor Aphrodite, is more than an unwilling religious devotee; he is rigidly intent upon his personal chastity. His entering speech describing the untouched meadow is a powerful evocation of the psychological state of repressed sexuality.

The theme is opened up in the lovesick Phaedra's attempts to repress her strong desires for Hippolytus and the nurse's sophistic discussion of the pros and cons of repression.

The idea of repression is best conveyed in the *Bacchae* through the imprisonment of the disguised Dionysus and his subsequent escape during an earthquake. The walls *do* come tumbling down, an irrepressible power is released. Nothing so strong can be contained.

What is important in the *Bacchae* is the naturalness, the expected quality, the *necessary* quality of the skeletalized ritual portrayed. We must consider the choral odes in this play as projective or supporting this mood or feeling. Incongruent as it must have seemed in the late fifth century to have a human victim scapegoat, nonetheless we must ask ourselves whether the elements of the ritual were in themselves strong enough, supported by the choral odes, to achieve an empathy, an acceptance, from the audience that allowed them to become altogether part of the play.

The audience will join with the chorus in their beatitudes, accept with Dionysus the rightness of his cause, rejoice with him in his escape from the confines and bonds, mock with him the hysterical Pentheus. And the young Pentheus? He participates as well in Dionysus' design.

For Pentheus, of course, also serves the god—by his hysterical, mad attempts to stamp out his worship, to deny him. Like his prurience these strenuous efforts bring him closer and closer to the god until finally indeed the god visits him. For contrast the poet shows alternative service; a kind of mock service, as Tiresias and Cadmus enter dressed in the worshiper's costume. Their defence of Dionysus, the one based on expedience, the other on the rationalization of myth are the kinds of denial of god that cannot harm. Old Tiresias and Cadmus only serve to make the passion of Pentheus a more serious enthrallment.

The chorus in this play have a strong personality, a well-defined group of worshipers, their strength unusual for a play so late. They offer throughout the play a consistent encouragement to the worship of Dionysus by proclaiming the spiritual, the psychic blessings of the state of the devotee. One cannot escape the effect of this chorus. Beginning with a processional ("Clear the streets, make way for the god" [68–69]), continuing with the Bacchic beatitudes (72ff.), straight through the play they invoke the joy, the peace, the creative serenity of participation in the Dionysiac world. Thus when they at last enthusiastically think (78ff.) on Pentheus' cruel death and his mother's deluded assist at it, they still seem to be right, for as they go on to say (997–1000):

> He goes with lawless mind and perverse rage
> against your Bacchic rites, your mother's
> rites, he moves with madness
> and wits diseased,
> madly assaulting the mysteries of god
> profaning the rites of the mother of god.

Behind the continuing invocation of peace lie wellsprings of madness or at least frenzy. The women of Thebes *are* racing over the mountains, the chorus talks peace and spits hate (877ff.):

> What is wisdom? What more beautiful honor
> comes from god to mortals
> than to push one's hand down
> powerful over the heads of enemies?
> That is beautiful and precious forever.

And in a long, curious ode (977ff.) they sing of the killing of Pentheus in thoroughly bloodthirsty terms, then pause to remind us that death returns mortals to a sense of proportion; they excoriate wisdom and seek instead holiness and purity, and close with an invocation to Dionysus to destroy Pentheus, "falling under the feet of the Maenads" (1022–23).

The play, however, ends in horror, which is foreseen in Pentheus' last appearance (918–70). The audience is immersed in the flow of the action of this play because it follows so closely religious sensations or experiences with which they are familiar. But when Pentheus enters, hallucinating, dressed as a woman, acting coquettish, he is mad, isolated from all reality, a sacrificial victim utterly alone upon the altar. Then Pentheus' great vulnerability, his humanity begin to work on us, producing true pity and fear. This moment is the turning point in our feelings. The audience is taken through extraordinary changes of mood in this play. At first we were with the chorus accepting the sweet ecstasy of yielding to the god, marking the hysterical Pentheus as a fool; then we

were with Dionysus in the exultation of breaking forth
from prison, at the same time mocking Pentheus, who almost
like a comedy figure could not keep his prisoner down;
then finally when we learn of Pentheus' hideous death and
watch Agave's return, we are at once murderer and victim,
mutilator and mutilated, all passion spent.

At the close of the play Cadmus remonstrates with Dionysus (1344ff.):

CADMUS: Dionysus, we beseech you; we have done wrong.
DIONYSUS: You have understood too late; and when you
    should have, you did not know.
CADMUS: Yes, now we have learned; but you attack us
    too hard.
DIONYSUS: But I who am born a god have been ill-used
    by you.
CADMUS: It's not right that a god's temper should be like
    a human's.

Nothing is more tragic than that naïve assumption that
the gods care for man when in fact they do not. The mighty
power of Dionysus has swept across Thebes, ruining the
royal family. What the women of Thebes were caught in
cannot be rationalized, nor made human. It is a power
before which humans can only submit; acceptance, which
brings exultation, exhilaration, peace and revulsion, is like
the mood the Dionysiac ritual on the island of Tenedos
ritualized.

At last there is calm if not peace. The play closes with
the chorus saying:

> Gods are here in many shapes,
> gods bring to pass the unforeseen;
> what we anticipate comes to naught;
> for the unexpected god finds a way,
> and so it happened in this play.

This is a truth that Odysseus knew and tried to tell the
suitors (p. 161), a truth that lies behind the eloquence of Ajax
when he says (Sophocles, *Ajax* 643ff.):

> Strangely the long and countless drift of time
> Brings all things forth from darkness into light,

Then covers them once more. Nothing so marvelous
That man can say it surely will not be—
Strong oath and iron intent come crashing down.
My mood which just before was strong and rigid,
No dipped sword more so, now has lost its edge—

. . . .

              Winter's hard-packed snow
Cedes to the fruitful summer; stubborn night
At last removes, for day's white steeds to shine.
The dread blast of the gale slackens and gives
Peace to the sounding sea; and Sleep, strong jailer,
In time yields up his captive. Shall not I
Learn place and wisdom? . . .

                    (translated by John Moore)

CHAPTER TEN
THE COMIC VISION

A certain story came to mind, vulgar, a real pigsty
of a story.

fragment of a comedy by Cratinus

A hard man is good to find.

New York subway graffito, 1973

It is most difficult to achieve empathy with Athenian
comedy of the fifth century both because it is amorphous
and because over the centuries people's funny bones shift
location. Ancient comedy just does not seem all that funny.
But recently we have had a close analogy to it that should
help us to appreciate its qualities. That is the great rock
musical *Hair*. The name itself is similar since it picks up a
feature of the action that becomes a symbol of everything
the play wants to say. *Hair* is spectacle rather than drama.
The actors casually move into scenes that only very loosely
pursue a plot. There is constant interaction with the audience, ending in a typically Aristophanic joyous celebration
where the audience is invited to dance with the cast. There
are political songs, satirical songs, great moving, lyrical songs,
such as "Let the Sunshine In," and for puritan America
there was the enormous fact of the nudity at the close of the
first act. All in all quite Aristophanic; not really so funny as it
was good-natured, not so much structured as it was simply
shape or presence, that is, organic commotion.

With *Hair,* of course, we know the music and the dancing.

We have very little to go on when it comes to talking about
the fifth-century comedy, especially that which preceded
Aristophanes.

The festival of Dionysus, the Greater Dionysia, as it is
called, was expanded during the time of Peisistratos in the
second half of the sixth century, around 535. Thespis was
said to have performed the first tragedy in the city; it was
for this festival. At the turn of the century, the custom was
fixed of adding a satyr play to each set of tragedies. The
satyr play is little known to us; only one has survived complete, Euripides' *Cyclops* (the subject is the well-known
meeting between Odysseus and the Cyclops). This one is
typical to the extent that the major thrust of the satyr play
was a gross distortion of a mythological story or mythological persons, or simply a parody of myth or saga, always
with a satyr chorus and often with a monster. The relationship between the satyr plays and the tragedies is obvious
enough. As one ancient critic said, satyr plays are tragedy
at play or tragedy making jokes. The formality of tragedy,
the skeletal nature of its action, all combine to demand
the greatest, as it is always called, "suspension of disbelief."
Clearly enough the process of action in tragedy was not
meant to simulate reality, but its inevitable relation to real
things and persons makes its departure from realism a thing
sensed if not acknowledged. The satyr play gave the opportunity to acknowledge this. The formalism of tragedy,
the shallow dimension of the characters were always just
the safe side of caricature. The satyr play's distortions of
themes often met with in tragedy gave expression to the
potential for caricature in the tragedies just seen. As altar
boys who must suppress their giggles burst into whoops of
laughter once back in the sacristy so the Athenian audience
must have found the satyr plays wildly funny.

In Sicily in the first quarter of the fifth century a certain
Epicharmos wrote plays that were more complicated and
serious than satyr plays (we have only the barest fragments),
but which were also parodies or burlesques of mythologies
and saga themes. Epicharmos' work springs from the same
psychological needs and responses that animate the satyr
plays. The great influence and continuing presence of the
epic saga tradition and the far-ranging system of myth were
ripe for parody. Parody was the means to get a purchase on
an extended and complex vision of the world, to take a

stance apart from saga and myth, which permeated one's very being, carried in memory, therefore latent and inaccessible.

Parody and burlesque form one of the principal forms of ancient Greek humor. The *Battle Between the Frogs and Mice,* an early fifth-century parody of Homeric battle narrative mostly, is an amusing distortion of the heroic perspective, as though the characters of *The Wind in the Willows* were to take on the major roles of the *Iliad.* The often mentioned *Margites,* which has not survived, probably had definite affinities with *Don Quixote,* for it was said to be an epic adventure story in which the hero was a fool or simpleton. The *Margites* certainly could have been very amusing; epic figures take themselves so seriously, particularly in the *Iliad* (another reason why Longinus was right to assign it to Homer's youth), that in certain perspectives they come across sufficiently wooden to make of them noble fools. Homer himself may be exploiting that sensation in the scenes where he portrays the gods so amusingly. Like a lightning rod that attracts the electricity and leads it safely into the earth, these scenes take the need for laughing at the enormously serious mortal heroes and channel it into the sight of Zeus and Hera quarreling, the god of war falling on his ass or Hera beating Artemis over the head with her arrows.

It is not clear what made the ancients laugh. The following exchange from the very somber *Trojan Women* (1049f.) shows how immense the gulf may be between our own and Athenian sensibilities. Hecuba does not want Menelaus to succumb once again to Helen's charms and says: "Do not let her go aboard the same ship with you," to which Menelaus responds (doltishly? playfully? or just plain straight?), "Why not? Is she heavier than she used to be?" The idea of comedy or comic comes from either the Greek root *komos* or *kome.* The first means a celebration that was drunken, jolly merrymaking, the second means village. *Komodia,* comedy, is therefore perhaps some rustic festival event full of high spirits. The derived word *komikos,* comic, is used more technically. It is used, for instance, to differentiate the *Odyssey* from the *Iliad.* Elsewhere we find the scholarly opinion that Euripides' *Alcestis* and *Orestes* are more comic. That means presumably that they have more or less happy endings however much it seems a misreading of both plays.

Or it may refer to the roles of Hercules in the *Alcestis* and the Phrygian slave in the *Orestes*. What is clear enough at least is that comedy does not demand *laughter*. In fact, satyr plays and the sort of thing Epicharmos did were probably intrinsically much funnier than Aristophanic comedy. Comedy may be fundamentally the portrayal of a sense of well-being. There is a phrase in epic poetry that suggests this. At moments of exuberance, joy, delight or beauty, there often appears the epic phrase "the whole earth laughed." That is the laugh of joy, the laugh of well-being, the shiver of bone-deep contentment, but it is not outright humor.

By the time of the Persian War Athens had voted to include "comedy," whatever it was, alongside tragedy, satyr plays and dithyrambic choruses (which had been imported from the Doric world by the last decade of the sixth century). The institution of *komodia* with state support certainly supposes something more serious and socially valuable than entertainment. We have no complete examples of the comic theater of fifth-century Athens other than eleven of Aristophanes' plays (from some forty or more), the first of which (*Acharnians*) was produced in 425 and the last (*Plutus* [Wealth]) in 388. If these are any kind of reliable index, the comic theater of the fifth century was an important vehicle for social thought. Although we have only fragments of other comic playwrights, their work seems to be substantially the same. Aristophanes is ever fond of remarking through the person of his choruses how superior he is to his comic competitors, especially the notable Cratinus and Eupolis. Cratinus may have tended more to mythological travesties in the tradition of Epicharmos but he seems just the same to have been political and allusive like Aristophanes. There certainly seems to have been a competition to be topical. Like the constantly similar cover stories of *Time* and *Newsweek* there are interestingly coincidental themes in comedies. Philosophers, for instance, were the subject for both Aristophanes (*Clouds*) and one of his competitors in 423, tragic poets engrossed Aristophanes (*Frogs*) and Phrynichus in 405. The latter date was just after the death of Euripides and Sophocles, so tragedy's future and past must have been very much on the minds of the Athenians. The fact that two poets chose this theme also points up that such a subject should not be considered as apolitical, hence escapist. Indeed the political question of Alcibiades' return is debated in the *Frogs*. Tragedy was a thoroughly political institution; the death of its two greatest practitioners coming at a time when the future of the city-state itself was being tested could inspire plays of dramatic criticism which are in fact microcosm reviews of the city itself. Shortly after this, comedy itself seems to have changed. At least Aristophanes' last two surviving plays, which come after the turn of the century, are different. Especially the last, *Wealth,* is a divertissement, an entertainment, with languid attempts at an idea (proceeding from the hackneyed notion that wealth is blind). Neither this kind of comedy nor the earlier sort is riotously funny, mindlessly, outrageously funny. Even allowing for the enormous passage of time and change of feeling we cannot get stitches in our sides or tears in our eyes from Aristophanes' comedies. In fact in translation Aristophanes most often comes across as arch. One imagines himself to be back at comedy night at camp or with the school humorist at the class picnic of the high school graduating class. The fault very probably lies in American English and the twentieth century. The quality of vulgarity lays a heavy restriction on American English. It is hard to get away from being refined and still to come across honestly, impulsively, directly from the id. Vulgarity waits there to snatch the unwary.

As the *polis* superseded the family and became in fact the great extended family that embraced all Athenians through their interlocking tribes, brotherhoods, clans, religious ceremonies and so on, the theater became the gathering place of the family, the tragic drama became the focusing element of the *polis* family, a place where family behavior could be translated to *polis* scale, where family life became the metaphor for *polis* life. *Polis* action and family action became the same. The politics of the family revealed the politics of the city. It is clear why, as Aristotle notes, the subject matter of tragedy becomes increasingly narrowed to the histories of certain dynastic families, the House of Atreus, or the House of Labdacus. The members of the successive generations of those legendary families become the projected *polis* family, the conformation of the state, the inner family, the religious family.

Comedy instituted by the state became the other aspect of the *polis* family, that is, the externalized family experience, the social experience, the political experience. Aristophanes often plays to the idea of the organic union of spectators and actors when he includes the former in the action. In the *Clouds*, for instance, there is a search for "elastic assholes" (1096ff.) that puts the audience into the dramatic perspective.

"Do you see any elastic assholes among the spectators?"

"Yup."

"What? Really?"

"By god, almost all of them are elastic assholes. This one, for starters; and that one I recognize; and that one with the hair."

Comedy's customary large-scale central choral passage with its political and theatrical antagonisms, the hero with his fantasy stratagems re-create the *ekklesia* and its major motivating figures, not in specifics but in general psychological tendencies. Aristophanic comedy is often termed political comedy; critics scan his sententious remarks to discover his platform. They note his attacks upon Kleon and imagine what activist role his theater had in guiding Athens. But this is to misconstrue the force of state comedy. Although it was part of the festival to see prominent persons ridiculed, as with tragedy so with comedy, city officials chose dramatic pieces that were consonant with public sentiment. Aristophanes and his colleagues survived Kleon, his successors and two political revolutions. Politically effective, which is to say, politically powerful theater, does not survive in that kind of environment. Furthermore the idea of political power in comedy goes against the strong hostility toward all power bases in the Athenian democracy.

Aristophanes' most politically topical play is the *Knights*, produced in 424. It is on one level a violent attack upon Kleon, and contemporary critics praise Aristophanes for his courage in the attack. But the play is actually a rather funny statement about the body politic in a democratic society. The people in the character of Demos is the central figure; two leading contemporary generals, Nikias and Demosthenes, both of them well-born, are this sluggish dolt's slaves. The backstairs slave household has been augmented by a crude Paphlagonian tanner (Kleon) who will later be ousted by a sausage maker. The play turns on the efforts of these two to compete for mastery of the household and the master. The play is an account of the enslavement of the generals to the people and the nature of their servitude. It is true to the underlying fact of Athenian political life that the *ekklesia* never surrenders its sovereignty. "Just keep serving them sausages . . . use that coarse voice of yours," says Demosthenes to the sausage maker (213ff.). The year before (425) Kleon had won an incredible victory over Spartan forces at Sphacteria on their own land, and was now at the height of his popularity. The truth of the matter is that in a society where so much emphasis was placed upon public honor Kleon had to pander to the *ekklesia* to receive it; his achievements such as this chance and totally unlikely military victory were so many tasty tidbits which he fed to the people. The *Knights* is first of all a comic vision of the political and social system where popular esteem requires slavery, where masters are in fact slaves, where slaves are masters, where glory requires pandering, where class distinctions make for angry accusations. The young well-born men of the chorus are in particular viciously hostile to Kleon; many of their complaints turn on misused money. What it means is that the moneyed classes are hostile to the average citizens, who benefit financially from empire, rather than that Kleon is a crook. The angry censure of the chorus is another of the burdens that anyone in public life must assume.

The play does not seem to be meant principally as an attack upon Kleon, because Aristophanes seems to ally himself with the slaves of Demos when he speaks (503ff.) about the problems of being a comic playwright. He speaks through the leader of the chorus in a speech (502ff.) addressed to "those who delve into all kinds of poetry." He says that at first he mounted his plays under a pseudonym, but now he reveals himself, and seeks the audience's favor. Aristophanes knows, says the leader (517–18) that the audience is changeable by nature and betrays its earlier poets when they grow old. The audience and their wayward ways, their cast-off favorites seem to be a restatement of sluggish Demos and his slave generals. It seems simplistic to see the play just as an attack on Kleon, especially considering that he was a favorite, and that the *Knights* was chosen by a public official and won first prize from the judges. That the play emphasizes the tendency of the generals to pander to the public out of their own self-interest is true. But this is a universal truth. The marvelous quality of mind that gave the ancient Athenian freedom to look at such things is remarkable. But we need not accommodate the play to our own need for public hypocrisy and convert the *Knights* into a political vendetta. The ridicule was clever, cruel, but not devastating.

Comedy offered another perspective on Athenian social and political life. By making consequences absurd, grotesque or fantastic comedy nullified the authority of change. To that extent comedy was conformist. Aristophanic comedy relies heavily upon burlesque, parody and travesty, displacing the balances of the known world, the recognizable world, releasing the spectator from the gravitational forces of common sense and prejudice so that he may float by and around familiar objects. They are rendered harmless in the new perspective, his commonplace perceptions are neutralized. The extant plays mock war, peace, intellectualism, avantgarde dramaturgy, sexual roles, philosophical conservatism, the assembly and the jury system. Each of these is frightening to most people to some degree or another. That is to say, one has unresolved feelings about matters that shore up the foundations of his self-esteem, identity or sense of stability.

Consider the inherent viciousness of thwarted idealists whose capacity for change or new thought is stuck in the rusty machinery of their minds. Such are the chorus of old men in the *Wasps*, who describe themselves aptly as wasps endowed with stingers. Or consider the caricature of Agathon, effeminate, exquisite, sweet and yet complicated, the very avant-garde of theater, who introduced a new tone and a new ethos into tragedy, which was so serious a popular medium of community expression and communication that the change was threatening. Figures such as these are both demonstrably real and grotesquely perverse in Aristophanes' creation. The reality forms a true emotional response in the spectator, the deformity nullifies its issue. One eats his cake and has it, too. Likewise smaller moments show a similar combination of opposites. Dicaiopolis in the *Acharnians*, for instance, who at the beginning of the play is found gazing out at his beloved farm land, now lost to him and damaged, presents a truly pathetic figure; the sorrow is genuine. At this moment Aristophanes dispels the authority of his emotion by reminding us of his frailty and triviality when Dicaiopolis talks about his farting. Again in the *Lysistrata* when the heroine voices a considered yet emotional plea for the end to war, bringing up the ugly truth

of bloodshed between Greek-speaking peoples, the men before her are utterly consumed with their passion for the
naked goddess of peace, which makes them most vocal about
the pain of their prolonged erections. The tragic dilemma of
internecine war is lost when its fomenters are portrayed as
unbearably horny men.

Although Lysistrata's plea is overshadowed by the men,
there may be another side to this scene which shows the
complexity of comic criticism. Here are Lysistrata, the naked
goddess and the lusting men. There is real pathos in Lysistrata's sincere and telling plea for peace. She is a woman
and women must see their children die in battle. That is
even said by the chorus in this play. Opposite her and
Peace—a female figure—are the men, who make war, who
kill, who at this moment cannot heed or even consider
Lysistrata's call, they are so preoccupied with their erections.
The scene is a profound statement about sexual roles, about
the eroticism in sexual roles. But Athenian comic theater is
hard to understand because it was so topical yet so subtly
allusive. We need to know so much more about public opinion
than in fact we do know. For instance, Lysistrata's lament
about the stupidity of the war seems so true to us but then
we are not in the midst of that war, where a populace is
immersed in its inevitable justification. The male-female confrontation and, more to the point, contrast seem more boldly
delineated, but did the Athenians have enough sense of
women as people to listen to them speaking seriously? The
plays of Euripides, in which women appear so prominently
to protest their lot, imply that the outlines of the contemporary Athenian woman's life were becoming better
known. Yet we must not discount the enormous machinery
of repression rendering women negligible. The audience may
only have laughed at the men hungry for their sex object,
who was by contrast (and thus humorously) trying to speak
as a person.

Then too, Aristophanic comedy is full of fantastic schemes
and stratagems. Fantasy action is the very reverse, the mirror
image of political action, where pragmatism dictates the vote.
Nonetheless Athenian political action in the late fifth century
grows to have a substantial element of fantasy in it. The
decisions to launch an expedition against Sicily in 415, for
instance, is almost called fantasy by Thucydides: "A lust to
set sail fell on everyone alike" (6.24.3). Later on in 411, 410

and 406 extraordinary Athenian victories at sea caused the
Spartans to seek peace; each time the Athenians rebuffed
them although their own position remained entirely precari-
ous. There was fantasy in the air at the *ekklesia*. These were
the years of the *Birds* (414), the *Lysistrata* (411), the *Thesmophoriazusae* (411) and the *Frogs* (405). The manic exhilaration of the Athenian *polis* is perhaps reflected by the
comic fantasy. The *Birds* is Aristophanes' most thoroughly
realized fantasy play. The stratagem of creating a new *polis*,
its inhabitants birds, the subsequent idea of conquering the
Olympian deities are all well worked out. The play looks to
the heavens away from this earth of failure, it rejects Athens
and humans and envisions a new start in Cloudcuckooland;
furthermore, it rejects history by subverting the religious
system in which the universe has arrived at its present moment. This play is renowned for its brilliant lyric poetry,
among the very best in the Greek language (for example,
209ff. are beautiful lyrics in the nightingale's song). The poet
keeps fantasy to the fore everywhere (see, for instance,
123–42, where he lists the dream wishes we want from life).
Most notable of all are the many references to happiness
throughout the *Birds,* for happiness is not a notion with
which the Greeks concern themselves much. It is in fact the
very idea of happiness in the *Birds* that is the most outrageous
fantasy of them all.

The city's capacity for self-deception is caricatured in
Aristophanes' hilarious account of the causes of the war
(*Acharnians* 515ff.), which sounds like the same mythopoetic
propaganda that forms the substance of Herodotus' stories
as he dissects the causes of the Persian War at the beginning
of his work. Yet Aristophanes' audience was evidently able
to take some harsh truths. Charges against the jury system
(*Wasps* 650ff.) are given seriously, almost prosaically; its
parasitic function in Athens' parasite empire is particularly
emphasized. The Athenians were evidently able to look at
things without blinking. Elsewhere the reality is extrava-
gantly, hyperbolically arranged, as, for instance, in the scene
(*Acharnians* 729ff.) when the starving Megarian comes to
Athens to sell his daughter. It is illegal because he is a
Megarian. It is a portrayal of the effects of the Athenian
edict against Megarian products and markets. The scene is
farcical and cruel at the same time. It is silly and cruel on
another level as well; sows, says the Megarian, is what he's

selling. In Greek "sows" is also the equivalent of our slang word "pussy." The same is true of the brief description of the misery of old age (*Wasps* 356ff.). There are no shadows, no gradations, no pathos. It is stark like the humor of Groucho Marx.

Generalizing about Aristophanic comedy is hard; the sample is small, the variety great. The structure of Aristophanic comedies is loose, but one sees the shape of tragedy in most of the plays. Tragedy's stark formality demands the utmost simplicity and clarity in the delineation of time and space, for instance. Aristophanic comedy, on the other hand, races from scene to scene, lurches through time. The poet demands every kind of act of imagination from his audience. Vignettes succeed each other like a contemporary light show. There is a prologue which limns the basic givens of the plot. It is here that the comic hero is struck with the mad idea or stratagem he pursues throughout the play. Because the plots of comedy are fiction the prologue is important. During his career Aristophanes moved from monologue to dialogue exposition to a fully dramatic prologue in the *Lysistrata, Thesmophoriazusae* and *Frogs*. This parallels the increasing subtlety in the structure of his plays. The chorus arrive (*parodos*), in opposition to the hero; the atmosphere of conflict and hostility is characteristic of Aristophanic comedy. It is the comic counterpart of the tragic *agon*. Moreover it goes to the sense of contest or antithesis that is at the heart of Greek culture. Comedy, however, is more aggressive, more strident, even violent in tone. The language is abrasive, even the farts sometimes seem part of an artillery attack.

After jousting with the chorus the hero often departs the scene and there follows what is technically known as the *parabasis*. The chorus and more specifically the leader of the chorus address the audience on a variety of subjects. Often the dramatic character the chorus initially assume in the play slips away and the author himself appears speaking through them. So Aristophanes complains about the lot of the comic playwright in the *Knights,* defends his political position in the *Acharnians,* pleads for political amnesty in the harshly polarized atmosphere of the last decade of the fifth century in the *Frogs*. Sometimes the choral *parabasis* remains an integral part of the play, as in the very musical *Birds* when the birds sing of Procne, recount the early history of the world from the birds' view and tell the reasons why men

worship birds. The musicality of the birds is enhanced by
bird calls interspersed throughout (see pp. 143f.). This followed by their singing of the superiorities of the life of birds
and the advantages of having wings. Paraphrase, of course,
cannot get at the extraordinary delicacy, as well as the exotic
sound of this *parabasis.*

Following the *parabasis* the drama resumes more or less,
although the form of comedy is always loose. Sometimes, for
instance, there will be a second *parabasis* as in the *Peace*
(1127ff.). The latter portion of the play is generally episodic
as the hero proceeds to act out the bizarre idea or fantasy
that has come to him earlier on. In the course of this action
he meets a variety of characters who respond differently and
characteristically to his ideas. In the *Frogs,* however, the
latter part of the play is taken up by the celebrated debate
or *agon* between Euripides and Aeschylus over the merit of
their respective works. This passage is subtle, demands
great attention; each poet makes telling criticisms of the
limitations of the other's art. While the entire passage is remarkable it fits very poorly with the announced intention of
Dionysus' trip to the Underworld, that is, to fetch up Euripides. Still more the god's ultimate decision to return with
Aeschylus because he improves the state is a surprise (that
in itself is a surprise in ancient theater) since the god
initially went for Euripides because as he says, "I've got a
yearning for Euripides that's devouring me" (66), and a
little later says that Euripides' tragic style absolutely drives
him mad (103). Dionysus is like any fatty sneaking out to the
refrigerator in the dead of night. The change from self-
indulgence to a puritan sense of self-improvement is not
impossible but unlikely. It sat well with his audience, however, since Aristophanes won first prize at the Lenaea festival
with the *Frogs,* and he received the unique honor of a revival.

While the *Frogs* ends with Dionysus returning to earth
with Aeschylus, most of the plays end with a celebration of
food, drink and sex. This is what remains for many persons
the distinguishing feature of comedy. It is an affirmation of
life as we live it, moreover of the life force that creates
us and nurtures us. It is why Odysseus can be called a
comic hero, a man who counsels Achilles to eat before he
fights (*Iliad* 19.221ff.), who remains resolutely intent upon
going home wherever he is, whose home is his wife and his

bed, whose journey is the exploration of many women. Odysseus is the man who turns down Calypso's offer of immortality for the pleasures or challenge of this life. So they who go to bed or banquet rather than to ponder the limits of their humanity are yielding to life rather than to death. One is timid at making these assertions because the colossal and pervasive symmetry and antithesis of ancient Greek culture seems sometimes too neat. There is the *Iliad*, there is the *Odyssey;* there is tragedy, there is comedy. The patterns lie so near the surface that one is again reminded that much of our knowledge of antiquity comes from the dogmatic selection and formulation of materials for teaching from presumably the third century B.C. on. Could the celebrated Greek humanistic tradition be in fact a gigantic easy teaching syllabus or anthology created by centuries of teachers whose interest was pedagogical method and efficiency rather than purveying the whole truth, complicated and ambiguous as it must have been?

Most of all the triumphant hero departs from the view of man that tragedy offers. Both tragic and comic heroes share in being autonomous, self-sufficient creators of action, doers. But for the comic hero there is no revelation of the abyss, of the flaw in things, of the inherent frailty and failure of hope and ambition. In short, the comic hero does not face death, but he goes to his own peculiar comic doom, which is a banquet or marriage, full belly and exhausted loins. The triumph of will that he displays in conceiving his fantasies and imposing them upon the chorus does not desert him at the end. He goes out drunk and bellicose as the old father Philocleon in the *Wasps,* or with a girl on each arm as Dicaiopolis in the *Acharnians,* burning down the Sophists' lair as Strepsiades in the *Clouds* or marrying the girl as Trygaeus in the *Peace* and Pisthetaerus in the *Birds.* The energy of the hero is constant throughout the plays as he hurls insults to all and sundry, defending himself from any attack or even advance. The most memorable Aristophanic hero is a man of years; he creaks, groans, laments the passage of time, contemplates his youth with nostalgia. But he is comfortable in his age. Tragic heroes by contrast are at the same time youthful and ageless, that is, no emphasis at all is put on their age, no details given to establish it while at the same time the remnants of a Homeric heroic outlook which cling to them stamp them as young. Again the dichotomy of young/old: tragedy/comedy which is implicit in the *Iliad* and *Odyssey* is present here, corresponding to a basic fact of change in outlook in the human psyche over the years. Yet the Oedipus of Sophocles' *Oedipus at Colonus* is akin to these comic heroes: old, intransigent, violently cursing his son, on the defensive, he finally departs the scene in triumph and glory.

Not all Aristophanes' plays have such a hero. Dionysus in the *Frogs* is a sentimental, vague and confused person of great good will; Mnesilochos in the *Thesmophoriazusae* is nervous and gossipy, actually a man very little characterized. The hero, however, who most of all makes a fitting contrast to the tragic hero, who complements the tragic hero, is Dicaiopolis in the *Acharnians*. A country man, simple, direct, honest, without pretension. These men do not like the city much. Strepsiades in the *Clouds* has married a city woman and he laments her attitude and values. The son in fact has been ruined by them. The rustic sensibilities of the Aristophanic hero have strong political and ethical overtones. The farm, the land were the center of Greek culture until the end of the Persian War. The agricultural society of the earlier Athens was dominated by the aristocracy: loyal to the family, free of empire, indifferent to shipping and trading, simple in expectation, pious in practice. The rustic man, therefore, in the folklore of the time was a *good* man, as the distinction between Strepsiades and his extravagant and pretentious wife and mindless son makes clear.

The love of the country appears at times to be almost the beginnings of the pastoral sensibility. At least there are feelings about the countryside that are new or unusual. The Greeks are notorious for their indifference to nature. Homer, for instance, has no descriptions of natural settings as such except for the gardens that surround Calypso's cave in the fifth book of the *Odyssey*. His similes come generally from the animal kingdom or from farm life except for the rather common theme of the story. The epithets he uses to describe places are always the vaguest and most general. That indifference to nature persists in the literature (except for Hesiod, who alternates between positive dislike and grudging acknowledgment of some of its beauties). It was true to life. When Socrates walks with Phaedrus outside of the city walls of Athens to lie in the grass and talk it is a *rare* occasion. The concept of organized greenery or greenery to be enjoyed was foreign to the Greeks. The Greek word for garden or park is *paradeisos,* a Persian word brought to Greek by Xenophon, Plato's contemporary. But the lyrical bird calls of Aristophanes' *Birds* are a verbal *paradeisos;* the joys of country life are celebrated or mentioned in almost every play. The description of the rural world in the *Peace* (566–600) and the contrast with the city (602ff.) are pastoral in mood. The sentiment parallels that of Euripides' character Ion, the sweet, simple temple boy whose pleasure in working close to nature and away from the city is the principal feature of his personality (*Ion* 82–183, 585–647). The *Ion* is thought to have been produced in the decade of 420–10 when the cramped living quarters of the city after ten or more years of war must have become exceedingly oppressive, especially with the memory of the claustrophobic plague still everywhere. Aristophanes' rustic heroes play not only to nostalgia but to contemporary longing.

More than the country lies the moment of Marathon as a rallying point or focus for the men of Aristophanes' comedies. Marathonioi, the men of Marathon, they are often called, like the American Legion's 40 and 8 group, dedicated to a moment sacred to them and their country expressive of whatever ideals they believe the country possesses. The chorus in the *Wasps* are Marathonioi. Their song (1061–1121) relives the glorious moment when they killed and repulsed the Persian invader, their strength and ferocity now metamorphosed into wasps' stingers, that is, irascibility, petty nastiness, grumbling. Anyone who thinks Aristophanes defends the views of the conservatives of Athens, let him reread this speech. It is a brilliant portrait of the way in which unswerving allegiance to a former moment of military might becomes decadent. Yet it too is achieved with affection and understanding. Aristophanes does not really ever take sides except when he makes Strepsiades burn Socrates' "Thinkery" down. Here is the unconscious hostility of the artist sensing his own devastation as he will be superseded in time by the unpoetic, non-imagistic, analytic prose technique. Aristophanes' swan song is given him, and beautifully too, by Plato in the *Symposium* where he makes not only an amusing but a very telling and poignant comment on love with the memorable image of humans trying to rejoin their severed halves. Plato, who is always so ambivalent about the rival claims of prose and poetry, gives to poetry a triumphant final statement in a prose dialogue that is a kind of comedy ending with the drunken Alcibiades in search of love.

The Marathonioi and every other stout old man of Aristophanes' plays match the vigor of their enthusiasm and their successful stratagems by the conviction of their ideas. It is part of their success, of course, and why they can march off resolutely to their weddings and banquets. For they have earned them. Again Aristophanes may seem to be glorifying overly much one point of view, but he makes the men ludicrous as well as charming. That is the glory of Aristophanes' art, also no doubt the reason why his heroes are sometimes distinctly older men. Fifth-century Athens was a culture that loved youth. Witness their statuary, the public adulation of the young, beautiful and brilliant Alcibiades. Their tragic obsession with death also bespeaks a youthful way of looking at things. It is the youthful disposition to take things too seriously; therefore young heroes won't do in comedy. But old heroes are perfect. Energetic and exuberant with the insouciance that only those over forty can muster when nothing new they learn or experience can ever compete with their memories, eccentric and willful as the aging process makes us, thus more ready to act out their personalities without embarrassment, in love with life from having challenged it and won. Yet frail. They can be silly in their ways: when they endorse old-fashioned education (through the words of Just Discourse, *Clouds* 961ff.) it is with prurient nostalgia (see pp. 167f.). This was the education, they claim, that made the men of Marathon. Likewise Philocleon in the *Wasps* is foolish if lovable when he holds court in his house with the dog as defendant. What is lovable is the freedom with which Aristophanes and presumably his audience allow old people to grow senile. It is another example of the Athenian ability to look publicly at reality straight.

The creaky limbs, the faulty eyesight, all these inadequacies are brought together by Aristophanes in the constant themes of farting and to a lesser degree the process of faulty elimination. As a sneeze was thought in times past to let loose the very soul from its moorings there is no stronger reminder that we are vessel not monolith, creatures of muscle and nervous response not cerebral, than a powerful breaking of the wind. Farting, I suspect, was absolutely basic to the fifth-century Athenian comic sensibilities; not only does it appear in every Aristophanic comedy but in the one surviving satyr play as well (*Cyclops* 328f.). A measure of the broad gap between Aristophanes and Menander is in fact the disappearance of the body as a part of the comic vision. No one farts in Menander.

Moreover, all men in Aristophanic comedies must confront their penises. Erect, cumbersome, painful, the phallus of the Aristophanic plays is a constant reminder of the beast we carry with us. More than that, the phallus is an instrument of self-awareness that makes the comic hero an analogue—through the looking glass—to the tragic hero. The hero of comedy like his tragic counterpart proceeds to awareness, in his case, however, an awareness derived from his sensuality. We eat, we fornicate; therefore we are. The banqueting and love-making with which comedies often culminate are the realization of Homeric *arete* in a comic perspective. But that triumph is won at the same time through a struggle which produces another awareness, a somber one, more acutely parodying the tragic mode of awareness as it is expressed in the Aeschylean notion that knowledge comes through suffering. The signs of this are the painful, embarrassing farts and erections. Erections and flatulence are the human truth, the frail foundation upon which the ideal edifices of banquets and love-making are reared. We pursue love and food in rich fantasies, only to have the penis come up in pain and the gas emit its trumpet sound.

Critics of Aristophanes since the Victorian era have been uneasy in their criticism because the poet is graphic when describing various physiological processes. Moderns can handle belching easily, farting with a blush perhaps, sexual intercourse is common enough nowadays, but masturbation enthusiastically and humorously practiced before the audience as Nikias and Demosthenes proceed to do in the *Knights* is more difficult to take, especially because Nikias and Demosthenes were prominent figures at the time. How could Aristophanes enter so private an area of a man's life? Was this the phallic fun of fertility rites? Aristophanes can be even more explicit in a way that amazes us; consider how he deals with cunnilingus and so specifically attributes it to a certain Ariphrades, whose brothers are known to have been respectable, prominent people:

[Ariphrades is]
not only completely rotten, but he's on to something new,
mucks up his tongue with the dirtiest kicks
down in the whorehouses licking out cunt dew,
messing his moustache, stirring up the girls' lips. (1283–86)

This is not at all an isolated example of Aristophanes'
pornographic propensities. Imagine the crowd of thousands,
the public nature of this description, under the sun, coupled
with a prominent man's name. One cannot say that the
Athenians were so comfortable with their bodies and their
sexual practices that they took no notice. After all, Aristophanes wrote everything to be noticed. Contemporary vase
painting is filled with scenes of heterosexual genital intercourse, homosexual anal intercourse, fellatio, occasionally
bestiality, all of it there to be noticed. Because it is so well
done it was to be admired we may be sure, but whether it
was also to titillate is more obscure. The religious aspect of
their sexuality beclouds the matter.

The Aristophanic allusions to sex seem easier to understand. First of all, it's fun. At the close of the *Acharnians*
the pompous general, Lamachos, goes to the doctor to heal
his battle wound while Dicaiopolis takes his girls off to bed
to cure his great erection. Some Greeks discovered long ago
that we should make love, not war. More than that, sexual
activity is ultimately very animal, spastic and compulsive. It
is the opposite of serious, deliberate, self-consciously human
attitudes. The Greeks, it is said, made god in man's image.
Their statuary poses man as sublime, awesome, beautiful.
One thinks of the charioteer at Delphi, or the bronze Zeus-
Poseidon in the museum at Athens or the many *kouroi*
statues there, or the Apollo in the metope at Olympia.
These are akin to what is almost caricature in the extreme
dignity of the verbal representation of man in tragedy.
Comedy goes to exactly the other extreme: man descends
from pedestal or frieze, begins to masturbate, fart and fuck.
The insistence upon these particular human attributes by
Aristophanes is because they *are* sensual, they are the way
stations to the corporal satisfaction if not satiety promised in
the feast and in the bed at play's end. So it is necessary to
emphasize and to begin with, as Aristophanes did, the anus
and the genitals as comedy's common ground, the source of
joy and laughter.

Nothing perhaps more offends Anglo-Saxon proprieties than Aristophanes' insistent review of what goes on below the belt. The Greeks, as we know, admired, indeed adulated, the human body. Their reverence for it knew no limitations. Nothing offended, as we can tell from Aristophanes and from vase painting. There is a very elegant vase painting of a young man who has drunk too much in the process of vomiting, showing how the Greeks were not at all alienated from their bodies. By contrast the Greek sense of propriety was offended by formal innovation. Picasso's experiments would have enraged men of the fifth century since their sense of propriety was indeed strong.

To prepon they called it, "that which is fitting." It is like our "decorum" or *"comme il faut"* although a more forceful, pervasive idea than what is contained in those words. *To prepon* lies behind the measures and volumes of the architectural members of the buildings, the judicious stance and composed gaze of the statues, the sturdy continuity in architectural expression and art forms over the centuries, the political conservatism, the impulse to categorize literary production by genre, to make canons of the so-called best writers in each category. The question we ask ourselves is whether the tendency toward defining the fitting, seeking it, also meant always adhering to it. How open were the Athenians to altering their experience? More specifically, when Euripides introduced plays that to us seem to depart radically from the tragic norm (*pace* the small sample), how did the audience receive this? With laughter (as it sometimes seems to call for), catcalls, restlessness and confusion or tight-lipped allegiance to the tragic decorum?

One of the harder plays to interpret for this reason is Euripides' *Alcestis;* the scholarly introduction to the play that survives from antiquity indicates that the play was produced in the place of the satyr play. That is perhaps to say that the *Alcestis* is a substitute satyr play or rather like a satyr play. The introduction goes on to say that scholars removed the *Alcestis* (together with the *Orestes*) from the category of tragedy because the ending was more or less (or relatively?) comic. *To prepon* at work again clearly enough. Even if this intelligence had not survived along with the text of the play the *Alcestis* would have excited diverse reactions, for it *is* strange. In a way it is what we expect from so strange and unpredictable a playwright; typically the *Alcestis* is his very first extant play (438), although he was in fact well into middle years by then.

If the *Alcestis* was presented in the place of the customary satyr play it must have fed certain expectations. The drama, however serious it may seem, certainly excited different reactions simply by its place in the program. Since we know very little about the satyr play we cannot easily identify what these reactions might be. One staple of the satyr play was the chorus of satyrs, men with bestial features endowed with erect phalli also found on Aristophanic actors. They are usually in the company of Silenus, a woodland figure, a companion of Dionysus both in triumph and in revels, a man-beast often drunk, but often given to wise, pithy sayings. The subject matter of satyr plays was generally taken from the traditional body of Greek myth and saga; our one example, the *Cyclops*, is taken from the meeting of Odysseus with Polyphemus recounted in the ninth book of the *Odyssey*. Whether tragedy and satyr plays developed independent of each other cannot be known. Certainly the evolved satyr play was dependent upon tragic convention; it is interesting therefore to see tragic structure like that of the *Alcestis* going in the other direction, metamorphosing into a satyr play, for it strains the demands of *to prepon*, either by making tragedy satyric or making the satyr play tragic. The tension in the viewer must have been exceptional. This tension between the conflicting demands of propriety is dramatized within the play when Hercules appears acting out the personality traditionally given to him in comedy, that is, the Falstaffian eater, drinker and lecher, in a setting that is tragic. One could also say that Hercules is playing Silenus in the *Alcestis*, for he is drunk and he does philosophize.

The *Cyclops* follows the Homeric account of Odysseus' arrival at Polyphemus' cave, his entrapment, the blinding of Polyphemus and his escape. The marvelous and moving detail of his escape by clinging to the underbelly of Polyphemus' favorite ram, to whom the blinded Cyclops speaks so mournfully, is not in this drama, probably because it gives a dimension of tenderness to Polyphemus that this two-dimensional account could not sustain. There are very funny moments in this play, as for instance when Polyphemus announces that he is tired of mountain food and wants man meat (246ff.); or Odysseus' speech of common jingoist propaganda: "we made the world safe for Greeks" (289ff.); or the chorus leader's remark during a scene of great terror and fright that he has not been getting any sex recently (439–40). In the play Odysseus remains true to his character in epic and tragedy; he is a serious figure whose long speech, a messenger speech in effect (382–437), is common to tragedy, is in fact a more detailed version of the blinding event Homer puts in Odysseus' mouth in the *Odyssey*. The Cyclops is big, clumsy and crude, uncivilized. Such a figure is always impossible in tragedy; he is a grotesque. He would in fact be out of place in the *Iliad*, which must remind us that the *Odyssey* does have a special quality we would not expect to find in the *Iliad*. Euripides has done nothing to make him sympathetic as Homer has done. The Cyclops' sufferings are part of the fun (at least for those who can find fun in suffering). The chorus and Silenus are ridiculous, the other pole from Odysseus, who is the reality principle in the drama. Odysseus with his messenger speech, his epic action, is the core epic/tragic literary experience against which the chorus and Silenus play. The elegant choral lament (63ff.) on the absence of drink and sex or the chorus leader's concern to know (179) whether all the conquering Greeks had a chance to lie with Helen are the distortions that make Odysseus' part amusing. The same incongruity is dramatized when the chorus prepares to make its stand to help Odysseus (632ff.) and they discover that they are too lame or there is too much dust in their eyes. They offer an alternative reality principle:

> just because I'm worried about my back and vertebrae
> just because I don't want my teeth knocked out
> getting bashed, I'm a rotter? (643–45)

Silenus is the same, getting drunk throughout the action, then unaccountably talking of his physical charms, ugly as he was supposed to have been. Perhaps in his drunken state he fancies that he is good-looking; he inflames the Cyclops, who yanks him off the scene to satisfy his desire. Silenus is an interesting character. He is willing to trade with Odysseus although the Cyclops would punish him if he were to discover this; then he lies about Odysseus to the Cyclops to save himself (Odysseus by contrast declares that he will not abandon his crew [480–81]); he gets drunk; decides that he wants to stay and drink rather than escape. Silenus is life with belt undone, corset removed, fly unzipped and garters down. He is demonstrably without tension, something impossible to find in tragic or comic characters. If we had more evidence of satyr plays we could perhaps see the Silenus figure as an imposing alternative life figure in Athenian culture. Certainly he is common on vase paintings.

Hercules in the *Alcestis* is somewhat like Silenus because while the household of Admetus is deep in grief he arrives blithe and unconcerned (if unknowing) and remains to eat, drink and philosophize with the slave who must serve him. The effect of Hercules' appearance is very different, however. He is remarkably incongruent in the play, superficially because he brings comic nuances into a demonstrable tragedy; then because he is boisterous and assents to life while around him the principals have glumly yielded to death: Alcestis gone to her grave; Admetus to perpetual mourning. Most of all he is incongruous because he alone shows sympathy, altruism, heart, whereas Alcestis, her husband Admetus and her father-in-law Pheres are calculating, self-seeking negotiators.

In a society where women were meant to serve the dynastic ambitions of their husbands, bearing his children, maintaining his household, there could be no finer paradigm of wifely self-denial than Alcestis' legendary willingness to die in her husband's stead when fate had decreed his death. As Iphigenia says to her brother in *Iphigenia in Tauris* (1005f.), "If a man dies there is a real loss to the house, but a woman is a weak support." Phaedrus in the *Symposium* tells Alcestis' story as the supreme act of love; this is interesting in that context indeed, since he is mainly praising the virtues of homosexual love. In a way he is saying that men will find their self-esteem in the love offered them by another male, while women will realize themselves in dying for a male. Alcestis' decision to die answers to the real problem in Athenian society of the desolation and insecurity of a widow. Yes, better dead, and dead with glory. The chorus refrain how Alcestis has got herself the name of best of women. The play is filled with the clichés found on tombstones. Here is another fantasy acted out, that is, ignoring the squalor of their existence, women can dream of funereal marmoreal celebrity.

Euripides has given the material a new perspective. The dying Alcestis first is presented in an emotional scene that lays upon Admetus a heavy obligation of grief. She then rallies enough to insist that Admetus not remarry, that she remain in memory at least as consort and mother in the house. Here is emotional blackmail with a vengeance and Admetus responds (actually quite competitively) with a wildly emotional speech, telling how he shall pass the rest of his days in perpetual mourning: no parties, no new women, no joy, nothing. Ironically what he describes is not unlike the life of a widow, but nothing like of course the typical widower who, as Greek society would quickly concede, will need a new wife for his bed and for stepmother to his children. The exchange between Alcestis and Admetus is quite humorous, first because after the lyrical, dying swan-like quality of her initial appearance she rouses herself on her pillow, so to speak, and like a lawyer with a well-prepared brief, delivers with notable absence of endearment a list of demands. Admetus, victimized by this, replies in an orgy of self-abnegation. The tone is feverish, like Alcestis' initial moments, but hardly an adversary match for her second, cooler speech. He achieves a moment of sheer silliness when he proposes taking to bed a sculptured replica of Alcestis to which he will make love. Short of the phallus and explicit sexual references we are in comedy!

Alcestis dies and minutes later Admetus' extravagant pledges are put to the test when Hercules arrives thinking to pass the night on his way north. When he sees the funereal trappings he insists that he will go instead to another friend. Admetus anxiously invites him in, masking the truth of his wife's death, afraid that he will lose his reputation for being a superlative host. The chorus is shocked but Admetus insists. The public man will win out over the husband. While Admetus is gone to Alcestis' funeral Hercules reappears drunk and happy, scandalizing the grieving slave who must wait upon him. When the slave blurts out the truth of the situation goodhearted, generous Hercules rushes off to wrestle Alcestis back from death. Admetus returns from the funeral repenting his wife's death in a typically masculine self-centered way. He will feel loneliness, the house will be dusty, the children at him constantly; he will feel disgrace. His reaction is a curious mélange derived from his public and private roles. Euripides has chosen to develop the play upon two levels. The one is the mythic, the public and political story of Alcestis and Admetus, in which she is the noblest of all women, the exemplar of wifely devotion, and Admetus is the steadfast widower and noble host and grand gentleman. The other is the private aspect of the tale, the resentful betrayed wife who attempts to secure her position at least posthumously while her husband tries to negotiate between promises made her and the living fact of his needing a housekeeper and nursemaid so that he can get back to the business of cutting a decent public figure. That is to say, mediating between the guilt felt by the survivor in a conjugal relationship and the necessity to return to the living. The play seems humorous in the manner of satyr plays or the works of the Sicilian Epicharmos, that is, Euripides' play is a burlesque of a traditional tragic theme. Euripides flirts with this in his *Electra* when Electra scoffs at the traditional signs of recognizing Orestes or when she complains about the material privations of her life ("no clothes," "my hair's a mess") in place of the conventional tragic expressions of grief and desolation. The *Alcestis* goes further than the *Electra* because there is nothing like a matricide to inhibit the tone of mockery. Yet the *Alcestis* is never really funny because the characters are mean, the verbal sparring too sharp and often bitter, especially when Admetus' father, Pheres, shows his son how selfish he is, how foolish his wife is (614ff.). The ending is "happy," that is, Hercules brings Alcestis back. Again Admetus is put to the test. He had vowed to remain celibate. Hercules arrives with a pretty girl veiled, whom he asks Admetus to shelter in his house. Admetus is frantic, especially when Hercules insists that he take her by the hand. Again, Admetus' private vows conflict with his wish to ingratiate himself as a public man and host with Hercules. He yields to Hercules, takes the girl, the protestations to Alcestis forgotten, but, of course, all ends well, it is Alcestis beneath the veil, and they all live happily ever after.

The play offers a conflict that is no more than an exercise in emotions because unlike most ancient tragedies there is no death to make the action irrevocable, thus to give it definition, to make those who act committed. The resultant detachment means that the conflict can be amusing, which in fact it is in this play. The reverse here is not, however, like that of a *deus ex machina*. The irreconcilable, tragic obstinacy of Philoctetes is not changed by Hercules new direction; the ugliness of Orestes and Electra remains after

Apollo describes a brighter future. Nothing changes when Medea flies away after killing her children. Here instead what each party fondly wishes will succeed: Alcestis will continue to be wife and mother, Admetus will continue to be king, host and gentleman. What we saw was a moment in the conjugal contest in the lives of a typical married couple. The story has been domesticated.

Longinus, the one truly gifted literary critic the ancient world has left us, was the first to relate the *Odyssey* to what we may vaguely call the comic spirit. In discussing the differences between the *Iliad* and the *Odyssey* he concludes by saying:

> These are the details introduced by Homer about the house of Odysseus relevant to portraying character, creating as it were a comedy of manners.
>
> (*On the Sublime* 9)

The *Iliad* is more tragic than the *Odyssey*, goes the common opinion. The *Iliad* portrays men alone, confronting death, separated from family and home. The *Odyssey*, on the contrary, shows a man journeying home, to wife and bed, en route passing time in the company of a variety of people, socializing. The details of ambience loom large in the *Odyssey* whether it be the table service, the food, Calypso's grotto, Menelaus' party, Alkinoos' mechanical men, Eumaios' hut or Odysseus' marriage bed. Odysseus' attachment to the bed is symptomatic of the poet's concern to place his characters *in situ*. The details of living reflect again Odysseus' rejection of immortality and his determination then to get on with the business of living. And this is the world of comedy.

What is technically known as New Comedy, which we know most of all from the Roman adaptations of Plautus and Terence and somewhat from the mostly fragmentary bits of Menander, has a common feature that can also be found in the *Odyssey*. That is the recognition scene. Late comedy abounds with foundling children who are reunited as adults with their natural parents on the basis of some tokens of identification such as beads or a bracelet. One might be inclined to discuss this motif as a manifestation of a particular culture and a particular moment in time, except that something much the same appears in the *Odyssey*. These are the many occasions when some newly arrived person is called upon to identify himself, culminating in Odysseus' giving as his *bona fides* the scar, his prowess at archery, his intimate knowledge of the marriage bed's construction, in other words, his innermost psychic quirks, his manliness and his sexual identity. Here is the wayfarer being integrated once more into his family, into reality, after being both alone and in fantasy land, whether the saga land of Troy or the never-never land of the Odyssean travels. Similarly throughout the poem each stranger is integrated into some social context by identifying himself. This then may be a concomitant ingredient of the comic spirit, the need to be identified and accepted.

Among the extant Euripidean plays are some that have captured the essentials of this mood of comedy, although they were presented at the tragic festival. Structurally, they adhere to the tragic formula. They are not hilarious, as satyr plays are represented as being. They are not technically or formally comedies, as the plays of Aristophanes are. There are no ridiculous situations, crazy spoofs, no political and social asides. Euripides shows in the *Alcestis* that he can invest the tragic form with another content. The domestic bourgeois spirit is there as it is off and on in his *Electra*, done perhaps twenty years later. The *Alcestis* is a satirical etiquette of bereavement, replete with all the clichés of tombstone sentiment. A fitting substitute for a satyr play, yes; perhaps a dark comedy of manners, for the play is bitter, although we can concede that all's well that ends well.

The *Ion*, produced around 410, is a play with a truly happy ending. Likewise the elements of the myth have been invested by Euripides with domestic and personal significance. A girl's reputation, her husband's claims to a position that he married into, his wife's fears of being superfluous because she is barren are some of the reiterated themes. The *Agamemnon* also portrays a domestic situation, but Aeschylus makes it part of a many-faceted view of the workings of the universe, whereas in this play the domestic concerns stand alone. Perhaps this reflects the late-fifth-century middle-class thinking. In the *Ion* Apollo the god takes a girl and she bears his child. At a time when the Olympian gods were still taken absolutely seriously Apollo's action would have had such strong religious and cult associations that the human dimension of the act would have been irrelevant. Now Euripides has fashioned a story of Creusa, who was ravished, as they say, if not raped by the god, left pregnant, forced to conceal the scandal by exposing her son; she is a gentle, sorrowful woman whose life has been altogether scarred by that event. The god Apollo becomes in Euripides' characterization the big man who exploits a girl, leaves her and finally is too cowardly or too self-centered to make amends himself, sending his sister instead ("He did not choose to appear before you since blame for what happened in the past might come out in the open" [1557–58]).

The *Ion* is a play of intrigue, identifications, false discoveries, lyrical sorrow, suspense and, most of all, details. Even the prologue is unusually detailed because the plot, which is complicated, requires an extended, detailed exposition. Ion in his first appearance as he cleans the temple courtyard describes his work and his equipment, branch of laurel as broom (112ff.), golden bowls of water (146) to keep down the dust; then he describes the approach of the birds (152), his enemies, since their droppings dirty his courtyard. He describes them as they alight on the architectural details of the temple ("Look, is that bird going to build a nest under the cornice?" [170ff.]). The detail here is answered by the initial chorus of women tourists, who exclaim over the details of the sculpture and architecture of the temple of Apollo. The chorus is an elaborate piece of *ekphrasis,* the ancients' term for the verbal description of a work of art, something of which they were very fond. The choral ode, even more than Ion's speech, requires an effort of imagination since sets and props so far as we know were not used to create "realistic" staging such as we find today. Partly for these reasons as well Creusa describes so exactly (1006ff.) the golden bracelet with the poison in it, but again it is part of the general emphasis upon detail in the play. Later in the play (1132ff.) in the messenger's speech describing Xuthus' preparations for sacrifice there are more extensive specifics, another try at *ekphrasis* describing (1146ff.) the embroidery on a banner. Finally in the moment of recognition between Ion and Creusa the cloth and its embroidery in which Ion was exposed are fully described (1421ff.). This scene is the culminating moment in the play: Creusa has sought her lost son throughout the play and Ion his parents. The scene turns on material details, the tokens of identity, for which the earlier detailed descriptions form a fitting prelude. The story in Euripides' version leans upon its setting in a way foreign to traditional tragic practice as we know it. Tragedy is abstracted, generalized in so extreme a fashion that the locus of its happening is almost immaterial. Where recognition occurs in that sort of tragedy, as for instance in the *Choephoroi*, its details are accepted and passed by as inevitable and necessary but not crucial. The recognition of Electra and Orestes is part of a tragic or mythic movement that has moved to the heart of the action, to its psychic and religious truths. The recognition in the *Ion*, however, is a moment when the spectators' hearts will beat harder at the revelation of each *detail*. Euripides allows the many details in this play to be the legitimate object of the spectators' attentions, thought and imagination wherever they occur. The movement toward theater of this sort parallels the development toward historical thinking where again the emphasis is upon detail, which is particularly unlike mythical thought (see pp. 181ff.). Notice in fact that an oracular response, that is, a religious, mystical utterance, incomplete while complete, leads Xuthus falsely to assume parenthood whereas the details of material objects lead Creusa to a true identification.

Euripides has constructed the plot so as to tantalize the audience. First there is the elaborate minuet of Xuthus' mistaken identification of Ion as his true son and Creusa's final correct recognition of Ion as her own son. The long exchange between Ion and Creusa early in the play (238–428) is in fact a charming recognition scene of sorts. For although neither knows the other's true identity they each confide in the other their innermost hopes, fears and anguish, which constitutes another kind of mutual awareness. The irony throughout the play is consistently exciting: Creusa the mother of Ion talking to him about seeking her child, Ion telling her that the temple priestess is his surrogate mother, Xuthus embracing Ion as his long-lost son, Ion assuming that he is making sexual advances, Xuthus imagining how he got some girl pregnant, Creusa's account of Apollo's impregnating her. This irony is tantalizing and pleasurable because the audience possesses the foreknowledge of a successful outcome. Tragic irony, on the other hand, typically approximates the chilling, gripping, soul-stabbing recognition that we too must die. The *Ion* presents a series of delusions and confusions that become a staple of the Western comic tradition.

Creusa's situation and Ion's personality, however, make the play more complex. Creusa is a gentle person. We see this as she talks to Ion (248ff.) and when she talks to the old family slave and to the chorus (725ff.). Xuthus by contrast is bluff, hearty, matter-of-fact. When he first speaks to Ion, for instance, he dismisses him as soon as he learns what he wants to know (417f.), whereas Creusa had taken time with the boy (308ff.) after telling him her own sorrows. Likewise after Ion tells of his timidity about going to Athens, Xuthus dismisses him not unkindly but without sympathy (650): "Stop talking like that; think positively." Creusa's gentleness is part of her vulnerability. She has been raped, bereft, ruined. Her description of exposing the child is heart-breaking ("if you could have seen the baby stretching out his hands to me" [961]) and must have struck many resonant hearts at Athens, where the exposure of infants was common enough. Creusa has married a parvenu and, now barren, she sees him planning to take over the position in Athens that she inherited and then shared with him. And he will do this with a son not from her body. A barren woman is no match for a man with a son. The chorus as women who must suffer what Creusa does side completely with her (676ff.). The old family slave urges her to kill them both. Her gentleness remains. She will not kill Xuthus. "My marriage means something to me, and he used to be faithful and good" (977). Ironically Creusa, who once symbolically killed Ion by exposing him, now plans to poison him. Her misery is magnificently expressed in lyrics that would constitute a major soprano aria in modern opera (O heart, how can I be still? [859ff.]). As so often Euripides has taken one of the ugly facets of women's social and familial position as the truly engaging center of the play. In the choral song (1090ff.) woman is the victim, man is the monster echoing Creusa's description of the moment when Apollo came to her (887ff.).

The character of Ion is also developed, or at least one side of it. The boy is first presented cleaning the courtyard. This remains throughout the play the key to his character. Ion is a little sweetheart; cleanliness, good smells and innocence make up his life, purifying and removing the dirt are what he does. Ion is in fact a little prig.

"May we come into the temple?" ask the tourists (219ff.).

"No you may not," replies Ion.

"You may come to the altar steps if you have done the minimal necessaries, but no entrance without killing a sheep," he says a bit later (226ff.).

Later he sings of how he would hate leaving Delphi and the temple, how insecure Athens and its political life would make him (585ff.).

When Creusa's attempted murder is discovered he turns completely vindictive. He rails against the law of asylum that protects Creusa at Apollo's altar (the unjust should not have the right to sit at altars [1314]). Finally the priestess, his surrogate mother, has had enough ("Shush" [1320]).

He doesn't want to examine the cradle the priestess has saved in case it should prove he were born of a slave (1380ff.).

And when Creusa's secret has been revealed he draws her aside (1523ff.): "Listen, mother . . . are you sure you aren't laying this pregnancy on the god to escape the shame of an illegitimate birth?"

And throughout he wonders at the violence of Creusa's feelings about what Apollo has done and he is shocked at the god's behavior.

The qualities of naïveté, innocence and priggishness in the boy make him memorable among Euripides' characters and point at the great distance between Euripidean so-called comedy like the *Ion* and Menandrian New Comedy of a half century later where the characters are the merest façades, no personalities at all. Altogether the *Ion* is one of the most engaging plays in the Euripidean repertoire. To compare it with the complex, deeply religious, awesome *Bacchae* and the intellectualist, wordy *Medea* is to see the extraordinary range and versatility of Euripides. One can then see why he is so often the target for Aristophanes' comic invention. Euripides must have surprised and amazed his countrymen often because he is most un-Greek when he is at his best being unconventional. And yet we must remember that in the *Poetics* Aristotle mentioned favorably *Iphigenia in Tauris* more times than any other save the *Oedipus*.

Intrigue, strategy, identification and happy endings. Eurip-

ides tried out these possibilities of his invention in two
other extant plays, the *Helen,* produced in 412, and the
Iphigenia in Tauris, produced somewhere around the same
time. Iphigenia and Helen are two of the most powerful
figures of the tragic theater. In these plays each tells how
the crucial event of her life (Iphigenia's slaughter at Aulis,
Helen's seduction by Paris) never happened, that a phantom
substitute took her place. These are not stories invented by
Euripides but his decision to build plays about the adventures
of these two women at a remove from the traditional epic/
tragic stream of events is characteristic. This remove is
similar to that of the happy ending, the parody or the
burlesque. Iphigenia and Helen are not serious characters,
but rather curiosities. The plays do, of course, have happy
endings. Helen is reunited with Menelaus, the misunderstanding is explained and they go to Sparta happily. Iphigenia
is reunited with Orestes and by Athena's command at the
play's end she will go to southern Attica to become a priestess
and they will both live happily ever after. We are left free
to concentrate on the details of the action, which are
suspenseful and exciting since in both instances the heroines
must be spirited away from jealous guardians or tutors.
Iphigenia is at the mercy of Thoas, king in Tauris, and
Helen is loved passionately by the king of the land in which
she is staying. In both plays the wandering adventurer
arrives (Menelaus, Orestes) to save the beleaguered maiden.
The circumstance of both these plots is similar to the common
type of plot in New Comedy. A girl who is under the
control of either a suspicious and jealous parent or a
possessive and unsympathetic madam in a brothel meets a
young man who falls in love and schemes to wrest her away
from parent or guardian or madam. Much of these plays
turns on the schemes and stratagems of the young man and
his supporters. Often there is a slave who helps the scheme,
a role that is filled by the priestess Theonoë in the *Helen.*

Apart from the excitement and suspense engendered by
the details of the escape, there is the thrill when in each play
the participants recognize one another. Menelaus in his rags
is not recognizable to Helen, whom he in turn cannot credit
since he has just suffered ten years for the false Helen whom
he at last got back at Troy. Orestes and Iphigenia must rely
on material tokens since they were too young to remember
each other. The reunion of Orestes and Iphigenia is much

like the recognition scenes that are so common in New Comedy, but the reunion between Ion and Creusa is even more so. Generally the young lovers of New Comedy are thwarted because the parentage of one or the other is in doubt. This complication is resolved when identification becomes possible as tokens of babyhood or something similar becomes available.

The ubiquity of identification in New Comedy leads to reunion, which, as we remarked, is a basic theme of the *Odyssey*. Reunion then may be called an element of comedy. Identification, on the contrary, while it too can be found everywhere in the *Odyssey*, is more akin to tragic *anagnorisis*, those scenes of recognition where what has always been true finally becomes clear and the tragic hero can say, as indeed he does in several plays, "Now I understand." The comic identification is in fact this exact revelation. The circumstances of birth which have always been so now become apparent. What has happened is that the playwright has turned from the immutable truths of our human nature or the human condition that, long hidden, become finally and tragically known to the players, turned from this to the merest externals, the surface tokens of that inborn existence, the facts of our biological existence, who our parents are, where we come from. When Jocasta leaves Oedipus for the last time begging him not to proceed with the investigation (for she has guessed the truth), Oedipus imagines that she fears he will discover that he was slave-born. "But," says he (1080ff.), "I call myself a child of fortune . . . the months are my brothers . . . and sprung from such as these I should never want to be anyone else." The several ironies here make this proud declaration almost too much for the spectator to endure. Foundling that he was, exposed in the hills, he calls upon the months as his siblings, laughing at his wife's fears of slavery in his background, yet enslaved to an oracle's doom, child of fortune, self-made by his wits, now to be destroyed by them; child of fortune, not like other children with families, Oedipus is the isolated man, the taboo figure, the man whom he has publicly declared alien in Thebes, for he is the man who has destroyed his family; all this lies within this courageous definition of himself. And we may contrast this with Ion's fear that he will prove to be of slave birth. Fastidious, prissy, comfortable in his cozy, sheltered temple life, he does not want that kind of rude truth to shatter his calm, just as he does not want the culture shock of living in Athens. Ion's dilemma is altogether the common, superficial one whereas Oedipus' response goes to the heart and mystery of one's being.

This change in emphasis is consonant with the decline of the Olympian religion and the obsolescence or failure of mythopoetic thought. The paradigmatic quality of myth allowed the tragic playwright of the fifth century to pose action that reveals something other being immanent. By the end of the fourth century, however, action has come to be viewed as simple, complete in itself. Therefore identification could not possibly reveal more than one's family line. Oedipus will never blind himself again because there is not that much to see.

CHAPTER ELEVEN
THE NEW ATHENS

> . . . in Egypt, land of diverse tribes, graze
> many pedants, fenced in, hugely arguing
> in the Muses' wicker cage . . .
>
> fragment from a poem by Timon

> Living well is the best revenge.
>
> old Spanish proverb

When Alexander conquered Egypt he undertook to build a city in the very west of the Nile Delta, a superb location between Lake Mareotis and the sea. He named it Alexandria. From its start in 331 B.C. a Greek population arrived to grow alongside native Egyptians, Jews and other distinct ethnic groups, and the city prospered. At Alexander's death in 323 his general Ptolemy seized the power in Egypt for himself and established a royal dynasty, based on the native Egyptian tradition of the Pharaohs. The Ptolemaic line died out several centuries later when Cleopatra (VIII) killed herself after the battle of Actium in 31 B.C. Under the early Ptolemies Alexandria became the major cultural center in the whole of the Mediterranean. The literature produced there was created by immigrant Greeks for immigrant Greeks. The colonials looked back to Athens and other obviously Greek places. What they produced more than not ignored the locals. It was a literary movement grown in a vacuum, incestuous, introspective, elitist and alienated.

Many of the principles of Western literary criticism derive

from the premises this literary experiment formulated. This resulted from the Roman encounter with Greek culture and their subsequently being the vehicle and medium of transmitting ancient ideas to what eventually became modern Europe. For the Romans emerged as the major power in the Mediterranean and met the Greeks most thoroughly and intimately in the second century when the great age of Alexandria was a century past and the Alexandrian avant-garde in its turn had become classical (although so slow-moving was the ancient time sense that Catullus in the 60s and 50s of the first century B.C. could be considered innovative for advancing the aims of what had been new in the Greek world two centuries earlier). The Romans took over Hellenistic literature and the critical assumptions that accompanied it. Rome did this at a time when she was rapidly becoming a large city, with an emergent proletariat and a vast empire of subject and, in her eyes, inferior peoples. The climate and conditions for the kind of literature the Alexandrians had produced were perfect. The Romans faced the wealth of Greek tradition and culture with empty satchels. They were ready, eager to take on this alien culture, and in doing so accepted its artifice, its remoteness. Roman literature was to be the projection of a small class. The literary critical principles are consistent with these facts and they remained the principles of criticism in the Western world through the nineteenth century.

The great creative impulse of the Romans, however, which is particularly manifest in their architecture and political structures, also took hold of the Hellenistic models and imposed Rome upon them. Nowhere is this clearer than in comparing the far superior poems of the Latin Catullus with Alexandrian epigrams, elegies and lyrics or when Virgil's *Aeneid* is set against Apollonius Rhodius' *Argonautica*. In the Greek world what Alexandria began was in part dissipated by the failure of the Greek populations in the cities of Greek Asia Minor either to retain their ethnic vitality or to assimilate creatively the surrounding peoples. The vacuum persisted. The epigrams, for instance, which the Alexandrian Age so popularized continued to be composed for over a thousand years in the same language, same meter and on similar themes. Quintus Smyrnaeus of the second century A.D. could write an epic poem (*Post-Homerica*) that reproduces the language and style of the Homeric corpus although considerably more bland, everything being simplified, words, meter, constructions, ideas, persons. To an extent it is quite dull, sterile. The amazing fact is that after so long a time the style was at all viable, that the passage of time did not intrude, that new events, activities, situations did not alter the basic texture. In the Roman world the divergence of the spoken language from the much more conservative, static literary language reveals the isolation of the literature. It is an outgrowth of Hellenistic literature and cultural aims.

The literature of the Hellenistic world begins most importantly in the city Alexandria in the third century B.C. So important was the literary movement of that city that the century itself is often called the Alexandrian Age. Yet what came into being there had its antecedents in the intellectual climate of Athens a century earlier. Demetrios of Phaleron, who was invited by Ptolemy to act as his Minister of Culture, came to Alexandria bringing with him the Athenian intellectual tradition he had acquired as a student of Theophrastus, the successor to Aristotle, who in turn had been the student of Plato.

In 387, on the outskirts of Athens in a park dedicated to the local demigod, Academus, Plato established a school. The Academy, as it was and is known, survived until A.D. 529. Although Plato speaks (in his seventh letter) wistfully of having wanted as a young man to have a political career, a normal ambition for an aristocratic youth of the fifth century, it was not to be. The debacle of the Peloponnesian War, his family's close involvement in the failed aristocratic take-over of 411 and his own aversion to working in and with a completely democratic form of government were inhibitions. Attempts to serve other political figures elsewhere were no more successful. Like many another after him, Plato turned to teaching. His protégés' accomplishments were impressive, however; Plutarch gives a list of political strong men from Sicily to the Euxine who were students of Plato at the Academy.

The founding of the Academy symbolized a definite movement away from the *polis,* a move that had important consequences for Greek literature. Although Plato saw his school as a training ground for young men who would serve their community, he removed them from the normal educative influences of the community they were to serve. In the earliest times the young learned their adult roles within the confines of the family; much later, the family was superseded by the city-state. City-sponsored tragedy and comedy joined epic poetry as the instruments of instruction and revelation. The Academy, however, was isolated; it did not have social roots. It signalized Plato's awareness of the failure of the *polis,* the city-state culture and the legitimizing of a search for an alternative. Myth, tragedy and comedy died with the city-state; their dynamics were assumed by Plato to his own uses in his creative dialogues. But the uses were no longer public.

Pythagoras' creation of a sacred society in Croton in the late sixth century, which lasted until the late fourth century, was the precursor of the detachment Plato was creating. Plato was fascinated by Pythagoras' blend of mysticism and mathematics, fascinated as well by the cleanliness of mathematics, its freedom from the accidents of the material world. Pythagoras was a mystic; his followers were initiates who observed rituals and taboos, ultimately making themselves cut off, a society within a society. Plato, however, addressed himself to the problem of the culture of the *polis,* its survival and its purification. He was at least in this way more "of this world"; yet he sought metaphysical premises and solutions.

The tendency toward cultism and exclusiveness that Plato inaugurated at the Academy was sharply opposed by his contemporary Isocrates. Isocrates was by profession a rhetorician, a speech writer, a teacher of oratory. Isocrates also acquired the objectivity Plato achieved by moving away from Athens to the Academy. Isocrates was endowed with so weak a speaking voice that he had to retire from the rhetorician's natural arena. First, he contented himself with writing speeches for others, but later when he tired of that, he turned to training orators. His school was established in 393, actually before Plato's. It was this presumably that gave him a more objective and intellectualist view of the rhetorician's role. At his cheapest, a rhetorician was a hack writer who wrote legal defenses for clients where the aim was to win the case despite its merits or claims to justice. Otherwise oratory or rhetoric is the practice of verbal lucidity, making things clear, explaining, persuading indeed, but in the best sense, by revealing the truth as it can be seen.

Isocrates' objection to Plato and Socrates was that their pursuit of metaphysical solutions or definitions of reality ignored or obfuscated the situation in which we humans find ourselves. Isocrates preferred, therefore, to use his training to elucidate the social reality about him. This, of course, would be natural for someone who was trained to make legal defenses. The immediate emphasis is pragmatic; then too, the speech writer looks to the facts of the contemporary situation. Isocrates, being a man of great intellect and vision, transferred these instincts and techniques to consider instead the larger problems of the way of life shared by the Greek citystates and their opposition to Persia. In a series of treatises and would-be speeches, he thought over and articulated this subject to the point that what he finally produced was a notion of culture or civilization, something hitherto only hinted at or suggested in Herodotus' distinctions between Greeks and Persians. The sense of culture or civilization that we may say Isocrates created in turn increased Greek selfconsciousness, cultural awareness; and this like Plato's exclusiveness influenced the literature. The fourth century saw mainly the production of prose. The fourth-century orators were heirs to the social function of tragedy, but there was otherwise a great qualitative distinction. These speeches are especially difficult to appreciate out of their context. However elegant, however stylized the prose, they remain a lawyer's brief. Addressed as they are to the particulars of the moment, they remain topical and after two and a half millennia they excite an audience of antiquarians and prose connoisseurs. Only Isocrates consistently rises above the occasion, philosophic and abstract.

The self-consciousness found in Isocrates is reflected in the works of Aristotle. His intellectual tendencies are revealed in categorization, in classification and description. The *Poetics* and the *Rhetorica* are not, as often imagined, how-to-do-it manuals, but rather descriptions, somewhat from the same premises as Northrop Frye's, of verbal production, how it is done, the nature of it. If later ages conceived that which Aristotle called natural as prescriptive, that is largely because he ignored the cultural context in which the objects of his descriptive, classifying technique lay (either because it went without saying or more likely because he did not see the subtleties of cultural relativity). They were natural to an age, but not to all eternity. Aristotle's pupil and successor, Theophrastus, shows the same tendency in his *Characters,* a series of verbal portraits of psychological types, very much like the character studies in Aristotle's *Nicomachean Ethics.* Menander must have been influenced by Theophrastus because many of his types are similar to Theophrastus' character types. While it is an example of the Aristotelian penchant for categorization the *Characters* also reflects the very commonplace Greek habit of typifying humanity, a habit we can trace in an unbroken line back to Homer.

Cultural self-consciousness was particularly heightened by Alexander's extraordinary conquests to the East. Alexander in fact embodied cultural self-consciousness as his father did before him. Coming from Macedonia, the wild and woolly antique counterpart to Wyoming, they felt themselves to be inferior to the demonstrably more advanced, complex and refined culture of the southern Greek mainland, notably Athens, of course. Having as he did a parvenu's enthusiasm for an acquired culture (and, we must not forget, having Aristotle for a tutor), Alexander actively worked to bring about an amalgam of the cultures of the East and West, to make at least some bridges between the two civilizations. Traditionally the Greeks were intellectually curious people; the moral authority of their city-state society had diminished with the collapse of the political, economic and spiritual efficiency of the *polis;* they were, therefore, very open to the influence that centuries-old, highly stable, successful Persian culture had to offer. Things foreign help to intensify a sense of what is native and inherent. They can make one self-protective as well. Some strong sense of cultural self-interest and awareness must have lain behind the scheme to introduce new cities in the East made up principally of Greek-speaking inhabitants imported from the West. Alexander may have talked cultural mix, but he practiced Greek colonialism. The Hellenistic city was prominent for its ghettos, another token of cultural self-consciousness. But the world in a way became smaller in Alexander's time. The expression *ge oikoumene,* the inhabited world, becomes popular, meaning the whole world marked out by human habitation, in a sense the world family. So the limits of the known world were extended to their extremities, but the limits were there and understood, everything within lay to hand, recognizable. And that feeling is everywhere in the literature.

At the same time, as consciousness increased, as everything came to be known and organized into departments of knowledge and experience, an opposing sense of vastness and aloneness appears in the literature. Immediately we can see that the failure of the *polis* as a social fabric, its replacement by a large-scale empire, meant that the individual was no longer in scale with the social environment. The Hellenistic city was the product of intense city planning, a grid city with imposing wide streets, a central piazza and grand façades. But the individual is lost in such a setting. The grid plan was not only monotonous but tended to stifle or deny nature. The remains of the ancient city of Priene on the coast of Asia Minor reveal the sterility of the grid. Priene lies upon a marvelous hillside without acknowledging any of the sensual contours of the landscape. It is the same grid that has defeated the natural beauty of San Francisco and made New York City beyond Greenwich Village a nerveless, mechanical set of troughs. Then too, a fundamental change had taken place in the ethos of the Greek city, as one writer put it, a change from acropolis to agora. Instead of the city as a religious grouping, the Hellenistic kingdoms created a mercantile center; the agora, a rectangle lined with arcades of shops, becomes indeed a shopping center. Furthermore, the planned city could be standardized and exported; the sense of vastness and alienation was exacerbated by traveling far and never reaching someplace new, or someplace peculiar.

The Ptolemaic dynasty had taken over and improved the systematic exploitation of the people and the land which the Pharaohs had originated. It was an extraordinarily pervasive system of control, extending from the centralized royal court through a vast network of royal agents to the smallest hamlets. An efficient bureaucracy of staggering proportions made the system run. Again the individual had no place. The contrast with the tradition is especially emphatic when seen against the traditional concept of the hero, epic or tragic, who acts upon the faith that he is important in this universe, god-marked or god-loved, accountable and autonomous.

The times were often chaotic, dynastic warring moving national boundaries, transplanting whole peoples—and always that sense of loss. Nowhere are the underlying anguish and anxiety of the time better caught than in the remains of the altar to Zeus at Pergamon* (now located in the Pergamon Museum in East Berlin): the figures sculpted in relief on the sides of this gigantic edifice stare out in fear, alarm and

* Although the altar at Pergamon was constructed roughly a century after the high period of Alexandria.

desperation. In contrast, the figures from the temple of Zeus at Olympia (460 B.C.) or the figures from the Parthenon (c. 440 B.C.) show, even when in scenes of war, calm, security, strength, repose in vigor.

The times had changed although there was a marked decline in war among the Greeks. The Greek city-states of the fifth and fourth centuries especially were continually warring against each other; Greeks killed each other, enslaved each other; war was often close to home. Philip and Alexander, however, imposed some kind of stability and order. Yet the third and second centuries show both despair and anxiety, especially in the quietism of the philosophies and the mysticism of the religion. Stoicism, Epicureanism, magic, mysticism and astrology are the experiments of this complicated age. They are not Alexandrian inventions but they flourished in the city and influenced the literature. The Greek-speaking people of the Mediterranean were never, we must remember, united in anything like a nation. Although they shared many things—language, Homer, the Olympic religion being obvious —they were fragmented politically and socially. Each city-state was an anchorstone and focus to their lives. The single most important fact of the fourth century is that the culture of the *polis* that had flourished in the fifth century was simply not sufficient. The political, social and most particularly the religious life of the city-state ceased to function well at all. Consequently the startling culture shocks that Alexander's conquests produced fell upon receptive people, ready for something new, also traditionally intellectually curious. The third century is a period of cultural experimentation and this quality is everywhere in the literature. Particularly good examples are Callimachus' *Hymns* and Theocritus' *Idylls*. The poems in each group vary in tone, purpose and manner within the series in a way that would have been unthinkable to the Greeks of the fifth century. There is something tentative and nervous as well as experimental about this poetry. The sense of a unified whole is absent.

Into the void left by the departed Olympians came Stoicism and Epicureanism. The Phoenician Zeno, who came to Athens in 313, studied there, became famous there, lecturing in public on the philosophical system he created (called Stoicism after the Stoa Poikile, a public, arcaded set of shops where he is said to have spoken). Stoicism was very popular from the start; later it spread over the Mediterranean, becoming the staple of Roman logic and ethics and finally influencing St. Paul immensely in his conceptualizing the spiritual legacy left behind by the Christ.

Epicurus, born on Samos, the son of an Athenian immigrant to that island, around 307 after his student days settled permanently in Athens. He bought a house with a very large and beautiful garden which became the headquarters of his teaching and the residence of his followers, a determinedly private group who excited envy and derision by virtue of their exclusiveness and their supposed constant search after pleasure. Epicureanism also spread throughout the Greek-speaking world although it was never so congenial to such numbers as Stoicism came to be. Both philosophies are known to us more through the writings of Romans because the major original Greek texts of the founders have perished. We must turn to Cicero for the best account of Stoicism and to Lucretius' poem *De Rerum Natura* for his account of Epicureanism.

The innovative feature of Stoicism and Epicureanism is that they formulate systems of social and private behavior. When the comfortable security the traditions of the *polis* conferred vanished with the end of the city-state system, the immediate need was establishing some rules and rationale for conduct. Epicureanism is essentially quietist. It starts from Democritus' atomic theory. In this mechanistic world without gods, good or evil, no life after death, reality no more than an unceasing rain of straight-falling neutral atoms, the only meaning that could be squeezed out of living was happiness, pleasure or contentment. This one true good was not necessarily physical pleasure or any passionate pleasure or joy, nothing so strong or assertive. For that speaks of free will. Instead the good was intellectual pleasure or repose, freedom from cares, the absence of pain. Life was to be pursued in such a way that one would not be upset. The poetic equivalent is the pastoral poem, an invention of the Alexandrian world. It portrays an environment absolutely at variance with the urban world of its poets and their audiences. Theocritus' pastoral *Idylls* (see the first eleven poems of the collection, although the authenticity of some are disputed) are furthermore in an artificial dialect. This emphasizes the remove in which his pastoral figures exist. His shepherds contest in song, they sing of love lost, relaxing in the narcissistic charm of self-pity. All is serene, for no demands are made in pastoral poetry.

Stoicism is the reverse of the coin, the alternative response to the same dilemma. Zeno's ideas rested upon the belief in a supernatural force, a divine power, Zeus, destiny, call it what you will. This destiny or supreme power was, of course, relentless in its unfolding, yet tolerable in that it was deemed to be all-wise, contriving in every instance what is best for mankind in general, no individual man in particular. It was just as lunatic as Dr. Pangloss' dictum—"Everything is for the best." The everything was absolutely unalterable, a universe determined. Man is part of the divine power, a spark, one might say, of the divine fire. The spark is housed in the body, a mere vessel of no consequence. Therefore, whatever befell mortal man—sickness, poverty, death—was inconsequential. The wise man ignores the accidents of life. He orders his life so that through his own will he does what destiny ordains for him. Free will in this system is made compatible with destiny. Happiness is wanting what you get and you get what you deserve. The wise man will ignore a sudden access of wealth or the death of his spouse; the former is not worth notice and the latter is part of destiny's beneficent plan. Epicureanism at its extreme produced psychic marshmallows, Stoicism, unfeeling monsters of rectitude.

Both systems focus upon the problem of the inevitable; they are accommodations to what must have been very strong feelings of impotence. Astrology was popular for the same reason. The pattern of the movement of the stars and planets is reproduced in human events upon this earth. To know the celestial pattern is to be able to anticipate at least the inexorable train of events in human lives, to grow comfortable with it and avoid shock. The interest in the heavenly bodies in part explains why the *Phainomena* of Aratos, which to us seems a rather dullish poem, enjoyed such extraordinary celebrity, not only among the Greeks, but among the Romans as well. In addition to astrology there was magic to enchant and charm, or, to alter fate, or, at least, to speed it up. Magic worked, for instance, where love was concerned and the intended did not seem to be capitulating. It was a popular subject for poetry. Theocritus, in his second Idyll, for instance, portrays a young girl who has been jilted by a very handsome young man and who now devises magical incantations to win him back again. Both mystery religions and salvation religions derived from a similar psychological stance. These religions taught transcendence, something beyond fate and death, ecstasy beyond the body, purity beyond corporal weakness and decay. What in this world could not be altered could be ignored. The inexorable, faceless force, a notion all of these beliefs share, was a fact of Egyptian life; the enormous, smooth, faceless, relentless, royal bureaucracy, which exploited systematically, and indeed for the good, the population, together with a monarch whose position was made unassailable by divine right, was not only enervating by itself, but was a dramatic departure from the ideologies that the *polis*-oriented tradition maintained. Certainly there was a source for anxiety.

For literature, the most extraordinary change or innovation was the establishment of the Library and the Mouseion at Alexandria. The latter, "The House of the Muses," was a research center for which the Library served as a convenient repository of recorded knowledge. There had been nothing like this before in the Greek world. It was the creation of Demetrios of Phaleron, who started his career as the strong man in Athens toward the close of the fourth century. When he fell from favor, he fled, and upon the invitation of Ptolemy I Soter, first of the line and formerly Alexander's general, Demetrios went to Alexandria and in 297 founded the Mouseion. At Athens, Demetrios had studied with Theophrastus, Aristotle's successor at the Peripatetic Lyceum. Theophrastus, far more pragmatic than Aristotle and his predecessors, abandoned the pursuit of first principles or final causes, concentrating instead upon the accession of knowledge. After all, Aristotle had left an enormous body of factual material, treatises and the like. This needed codification. What is more, the Macedonian monarchies were great users of machinery in warfare, and this demanded technology, research. Herein lay the direction of the Lyceum under Theophrastus; and the Lyceum was Demetrios' model for the Mouseion-Library complex. The Mouseion was a residence and study place for scholars dedicated to the Muses. The Library, also Demetrios' creation, was greatly enlarged, probably by Ptolemy II. In its days of prosperity it contained 700,000 papyrus rolls. Calculating with the fact that a large book of the *Iliad* constitutes a roll, we can see that such a number of rolls is hefty, but does not make an immense library by modern standards. Still it was a wonder of the world at that time, unique; it must have provided in every case the standard for copyists. Hesiod called memory the mother of the Muses, now in the literate age of books, the library is the mother of the Muses.

The Library is symptomatic of a new general familiarity with books. Evidence is that in the Greek communities of the third century education became more and more widespread, and as is ever the case, class distinctions appeared among the educated. There were on the one hand the very highly educated and on the other a far larger group of what we might call general readers. There appeared in response to this latter class, as well as, I suppose, in response to the general popularity literacy enjoyed, the man of letters, the critic, persons who wrote because it was pleasant and profitable rather than because compulsion and holy enthusiasm drove them. Markets were very large; a reading public and patron kings made it a prestigious and agreeable occupation. We know the names of over a thousand writers during the Hellenistic centuries. Strangely enough, very little of this enormous literary production survives. Most writers fell victim to the same spirit that had elicited this energetic increase in writing. That is, those who read as a narcotic pastime tend to want it easy; hence the era was marked by the spread of abridged versions, anthologies, school versions and the like. Much was discarded and much fragmented in this process, but so far as we can tell, not necessarily on the basis of superiority or inferiority, all of which seems true to the facts of a large reading public.

In order to make his Library complete, Ptolemy sent round to every city, every source, so as to make copies of every author whose works survived. There is evidence that in some cases, the originals were kept for the Library and copies only given back—such was the arrogance of the creators of the Library at Alexandria. Athens had no library until the second century, neither did Pergamon. The latter library seemed not to have grown beyond 200,000 rolls, in any case; so the Alexandrian Library was indeed extraordinary.

It clearly dominated the literary life of Alexandria, which is not surprising since it was so new, so revolutionary. It introduced profound, new qualities into literature. The Library was part of the lives of two of the three most important literary figures in Alexandria in the third century.

Their works and lives—the little we know of them—are typical (although they are more successful) of Alexandrian writers.

Callimachus (c. 305–c. 240 B.C.) was born in Cyrene, a city of North Africa halfway between the Nile Delta and present-day Tunisia. As a young man, he went to Alexandria and found a modest position as a schoolteacher in the suburb of Eleusis. Then he received a position in the Library to undertake a catalogue of the books. This must have been a stupendous task; the finished work consisted of 120 volumes. What he created was no simple catalogue list, but a literary history, a scientific classification and categorization of the contents of the Library, a universal history of recorded knowledge. Callimachus was enormously productive as a writer. The ancients assert that he composed eight hundred pieces. These range from compilations of facts and learned distinctions to a variety of experimental poetical pieces.

His student, Apollonius (c. 295–?), the only native-born Alexandrian writer, is known, however, as Apollonius Rhodius to distinguish him from all the other Apollonii of antiquity. The appellation Rhodius is his because he supposedly retired to the island of Rhodes sometime after 247. Apollonius was director of the Library from about 260 until 247. As director, he was also tutor to the Ptolemaic crown prince. He composed hexameter poems on the founding of various cities, some epigrams—none of which survive. His major work which does survive is a 5834-line epic poem, the *Argonautica,* which aroused a great deal of controversy, indeed acrimony, at the time. Apollonius and Callimachus were the poles in a raging dispute over the value and indeed the possibility of making a long narrative poem. Callimachus took the position that epic poetry was anachronistic. Apollonius' answer is the *Argonautica,* and the poem does indeed raise the question. For we ask ourselves whether epic poetry does depend upon the adventures of a self-assertive, autonomous hero or whether the pervasive sense of a civilization contained within a so-called narrative epic poem is not the genre's chief justification; furthermore we may wonder whether Apollonius is really making a literary, critical and philosophical statement about the epic genre which happens for that reason to resemble somewhat a traditional epic poem. It is not easy to know which questions one may legitimately ask. Dispute, subtlety and intellectualism mark the Alexandrian literary scene.

The third of the triad, Theocritus, who lived from c. 300 to c. 260, had no institutional position in Alexandria but his poetic patronage of Ptolemy Philadelphus implies that he was on some royal stipend. Idyll 17, a poem in praise of Ptolemy, is the kind of thing poets in pay turn out. We may compare it with the more restrained references to Ptolemy which Callimachus puts to far more subtle purposes in his Hymn to Zeus (85–90), and we may remember that Callimachus was a salaried employee of the Library. Theocritus in an earlier poem (Idyll 16), while poetically and publicly seeking money from Hieron II, tyrant of Syracuse, had painted a rather nice picture of the unsuccessful mendicant Muse (5–12). "His Graces," he says, "come home barefoot, complaining . . . dejected, they sit, heads between cold knees, down in the empty bottom of his coffers."

Theocritus was a native of Syracuse in Sicily, from which he seems to have gone first to southern Italy, then to the island of Kos in the eastern Aegean. There he spent some time before entering the employ of the emperor at Alexandria. He composed a series of poems, called idylls, which are highly polished experiments in poetry. One could call some minuscule epics or hymns (13, 22, 24, 26); some are like mimes; many are love poems. Theocritus is best known for his pastoral or bucolic poems, a new genre that typifies certain aspects of the Alexandrian Age, aspects not unlike the qualities of the eighteenth century with which Fragonard played. These pastoral poems are the subtlest pieces, depending upon an extraordinary delicacy of language for their effect. They do not therefore create much effect in translation.

The Alexandrian period was the time when the concept of literary genres was developed and the individual genres themselves were described and set. This is complementary to library work, particularly cataloguing. Ancillary to this was the work of textual criticism, which formed a major industry within the Mouseion, arising from the fact that procuring and copying texts for the Library revealed naturally considerable variance among copies; a standard text had to be restored. Examining the text of the Homeric poems had the greatest priority both because the Homeric corpus was the most sacred literary heritage and because numerous and divergent texts of the *Iliad* and the *Odyssey* were scattered throughout the Greek-speaking world. The men who worked on the Homeric text were concerned to remove the inevitable accretions to which a tradition of some several centuries is liable. They were therefore at pains to conceptualize the original Homeric aesthetic as well as to formulate the earlier stage of diction and style that could be called Homeric. Propriety was their watchword. Propriety is the notion that most systematically and strongly supports all Hellenistic poetry, derived from and reinforcing an intense self-consciousness that sometimes reduces a poet to absolute frigidity.

Several men involved in Homeric textual criticism also composed epic poems. A certain Rhianos, the contemporary of Apollonius, who composed several epics unfortunately lost to us, also produced an edition of both the *Iliad* and the *Odyssey* from which over forty readings have been preserved. He was in fact known as Rhianos Grammatikos, Rhianos the Grammarian. Strangely enough, Isocrates, the fourth-century prose writer, was called Isocrates Poetes, Isocrates the Poet. Here is an ironic reversal of roles that is reflected in the epic poetry of the time.

The one epic written at that time that has survived intact is Apollonius' *Argonautica*. The *Argonautica* tells the story of Jason's winning the golden fleece, his travels to and from Colchis, where the deed was done, and his love affair with Medea, daughter of the king of Colchis. More than any other work of the period, the *Argonautica* reveals the temper of the times, mankind's sense of the human condition as well as the predominant literary sensibilities of the poets, poetasters and critics. The *Argonautica* is the most serious, important poem of Hellenism, buttressing the claim that epic poetry is the repository and the best revelation of a culture.

While mirrors of their times, men like Rhianos or Apollonius were also very much a part of the tradition. They were the latter-day Homeridae, the rhapsodes who maintained the Homeric poems and sang them. Unlike the earlier Homeridae, these Alexandrians did not pass on the exact *words* of the master, rather they were prepared to re-create the exact *manner* of the master. That they were conscious to an extraordinary degree of epic usage we know from the scholia to the Homeric epics. They were not only capable of making the subtlest distinctions in matters of diction (although often wrongly), but they concerned themselves as well with matters of epic propriety. In the latter matter they therefore involved themselves in re-creating the Homeric mentality, of setting the Homeric tone. The story of Zenodotos striking out the lines at *Iliad* 3.423–26 because it is not fitting for the goddess Aphrodite to set a chair for Helen and thus perform the task of a serving maid is exactly a case in point. It illustrates still further the truth of the complaint of Choirilos of Samos that epic technique has discovered and reached its natural limits. The major fact, then, that confronts anyone trying to compose epic is that the form and the tone are determined, are a given. He must observe this given in one of two possible ways, either accept it or deny it.

One way to deny the form is to pervert it, and to my mind, this is exactly what Apollonius set out to do. He is, however, unlike Euripides, who seems frequently bored with tragic usage and therefore laughs at the ingredients of the form. Time and again we can see Euripides slipping out of the manner and tone of tragedy to mock it. Apollonius in another way, quite seriously, took the materials of epic and put them together with various incongruities that, while legitimate, are bizarre, to create an epic poem that is thoroughly sensible, and by denying much that is Homeric he maintains the sense of Homer throughout. Akin to surrealist painting, this is paradoxical, but, as theologians will tell us, he who is agnostic is lost, whereas the man who denies god is accepting him as much as the true believer. Thus I would call the *Argonautica* anti-epic, rather than call Jason anti-hero. He fits comfortably into the *Argonautica;* he is the hero within that narrative. It is the epic itself that in the face of the tradition is a distortion.

From the very first Apollonius indicates how he will acknowledge Homer by distorting him. Homer's line is made up of formulae; Apollonius avoids the formulae while using Homeric words. Verbal repetition is the essence of Homeric diction; the quality it imparts to the narrative stamps the epic. Its absence, then, in language patterns that are otherwise immediately akin to the older epic language is remarkable, unsettling and, indeed, perverse. Although Apollonius remains relatively simple and direct, the change in his style from that of Homer is important because the formulae have been replaced by the individual words as the building blocks of the line.

Similar to this is the poet's decision to vary Homeric phrases. The notorious example is the poem's opening line, where *klea photon* will remind his learned audience of Homer's using *klea andron*, two metrically similar, verbally different ways of saying "men's famous deeds." The variation shows the poet's control, his sense of artifice and, more important, his manner of playing his poem against the reader's knowledge of Homer. In doing this he exhibits if only in details his conscious manipulation of the elements of epic poetry. Anyone familiar with the *Iliad* and the *Odyssey* in the way that the ancients were would probably notice that Apollonius very frequently alters the formulaic phrase. These stylistic variations in Apollonius are matters of the minutest detail, and very likely no reader would consciously recognize the majority of them. What is important, however, is that they produce for the constant reader of Homer the sense of the narrative style slightly askew or out of focus. Apollonius' audience would know their Homer well, for people with any pretense to education knew their Homer in that era. We know, for instance, from a papyrological document of the mid-third century that a farm steward in Egypt could write a quotation from Homer on the margin of a letter with the expectation that his correspondent would get the intended irony.

The manner in which Apollonius deals with form is more obvious. For instance, Apollonius introduces his catalogue in a way that is certainly a bolder assault upon our senses. The catalogue stands alone and the transitions in the first few lines of the poem are the very boldest; a four-line invocation followed by an extremely condensed résumé of events leading to Jason's departure, which moves abruptly into the introduction to the catalogue. Gone is epic prolixity; gone, too, is the epic assertion of narrative. Gone is the feeling of effort and grandeur that preceded the Homeric Catalogue of Ships. Here Apollonius is being literary, playing with structure rather than securing it. The effect is repeated at the close of the poem. In the fourth book he has moved his ship and crew ever closer to home, finally through a series of relatively inconsequential picaresque episodes (1170–1172), when suddenly he shifts gears and delivers an abrupt epilogue after the manner of the Homeric Hymns. The epilogue in the *Argonautica* fairly sneaks up upon the reader.

Why, we may well ask. This is the result of the professionalism of the *poetes grammatikos* and his audience. He knows perfectly well the structure of his model; he understands the structure in terms of its parts and he can manipulate them at will; by so doing he demonstrates to his reader that he is reordering his Homeric models in some new perspective. The opening fifty lines of the *Argonautica* are, compared to Homer, surreal in their breathless and harsh juxtapositions; so is the conclusion. But as elements *qua* elements their fundamental similarity is unmistakable.

Apollonius wants still further to make it abundantly clear early on in his poem where he stands before his tradition. He moves through action and character to establish the new perspective. Again he shows his seriousness, for he proceeds to the very heart of epic, to the central problem for epic in his time, in searching for a hero. From the time of Homer to that of Apollonius there emerges a revealing change in epic. That is the trend toward the gradual abandonment of the hero in favor of intensified concentration upon his adventures, simply as adventures, or on the historicity of the events, in other words, the arrival of the antiquarian mind. When the hero no longer must be an integral part of the narrative, authors become free to consider the creation of a hero and the mounting of such a figure in the narrative much more objectively.

One of the distinguishing features of Homeric epic is the number of well-drawn major figures; one can think of perhaps ten figures beyond Achilles and Odysseus who are, despite their typicality, in varying degrees individual portraits. These figures believe in their own worth and are conscious of and confident in their own powers, emblems of the heroic age.

In the course of time, however, the question of historicity and veracity impinged upon the saga tradition and upon epic poetry. We have seen it in Hesiod's account of the visitation of the Muses to him. Hereafter poets in the epic tradition had either to acknowledge its fictional nature or proceed to take on the pretensions to truth that Hesiod had arrogated to himself.

If we can judge by the fragments, most epic writers proceeded to do the latter. Certainly poems of the epic cycle bear testimony to a new strength in the conscious historical coloration of epic poetry. We know very little of the various

attempts at epic that were made from the time of Homer
until Apollonius wrote his epic in the third century. We assume that they were not exceptionally vital. Fragments from
Panyassis, supposedly a relative of Herodotus', show that his
revival of epic, as it is often called, his *Heraklea*, was what is
commonly called antiquarian epic. Panyassis' purpose seems
to be the compilation of fact after the fashion of the cyclic
poets. The fragments are aphoristic or instructive, such as the
two describing the function of drinking in a man's life; or
they are compilatory, such as the brief catalogue listing
various divine victims of man's cruelty or power.

> Suffered Demeter, suffered famous Amphigueis,
> suffered Poseidon, suffered silver-bowed Apollo
> forced to serve a mortal man for a year;
> suffered great-hearted Ares at the demand of his father . . .

The fragment is clearly catalogue-like and far more in the
manner of Hesiod than of Homer. Panyassis seems to have
created the orderly presentation of facts or opinions strung on
the adventures of Hercules. He is also said to have written an
Ionika, dealing with the settlement of the coast of Asia
Minor. Here again we may assume that historicity of a sort
other than the saga mentality dominated the poem. As
has been remarked, Panyassis shows the influence of Hesiod,
and perhaps we can see that Panyassis has tried to incorporate into epic thinking the new authenticity Hesiod gave
to his poetry and its objectives. Homer himself seems to
have been re-evaluated in the course of time so that his
epics grew to appear as sources of true knowledge rather
than the particular kind of truth that poetic fiction produces.
He came to be grouped with Hesiod as a teacher. One
thinks of Aristophanes' canon of early teachers in the *Frogs*
(1032ff.), Orpheus, Musaios, Hesiod and Homer, the same
group with whom Socrates anticipates passing time after he
is dead (*Apology* 41a).

The emphasis upon utility and didacticism, perhaps stemming from Hesiod and apparent in Panyassis, shows the gradual obliteration of the central feature of Homeric epic, that
is, the personal drama of the hero from which spring all the
elements of the poem. The potential for passing information
became central, hence the tendency to antiquarianism.

The two possibly superior epics about which we know little

are the Samian Choirilos' poem on Xerxes' campaign into Greece and Apollonius' contemporary Rhianos' poem on Sparta's Messenian War. Both chose true historical subjects for their poems; this is in keeping with the aim that epics become sources or repositories of knowledge. These two men seem to have been able to create a hero for their narratives. Actually we know little of Choirilos' treatment of the Persian invasion of Greece; if he was influenced by Herodotus' conception, which is tragic and epic by turn, then he had at hand the stuff of more traditional epic, that is, both the story and the hero. What little we know of Rhianos' poem comes largely from Pausanias' account of it in his description of Sparta (book 4). In addition to employing a historically true story, Rhianos evidently contrived a hero in the person of Aristomene, a historical figure to be sure, but who, if we can judge through Pausanias, motivated and focused the action in the manner of more typical fictional epic heroes. Despite the evolution of the epic genre a place for the hero could still be found.

While these two writers did choose true events for subject matter, both the Persian and the Messenian wars were considerably remote in time. Convention was influential here. The thinking of the fourth century set up a division between old and new Athenian history with the Persian War as the dividing point. The later period was not thought to have any connection with myth, not to be set within the heroic range, unlike the earlier period, to which, indeed, Herodotus had already given a mythical-epical personality. The fourth-century mentality then shrank from the creation of a truly historical contemporary epic; clearly the conflict between obvious immediate truth and epic's fictional potential was too great. The fabrication of cyclic epics, therefore, went on apace, epics that simply outlined a series of saga or otherwise early events with depersonalized participants in the action. Something of the nature of these poems perhaps comes through in an amusing poem in the Palatine Anthology (11.130) beginning: "I hate those cyclic poets, the ones who keep saying 'and then.'" These poems, of which we have very few remaining fragments, must have achieved the effect akin to what it would be like if H. G. Wells' *Outline of History* were turned into dactylic hexameters. The hero is essentially lost in them.

Apollonius makes a point of emphasizing that Jason is the

hero of the *Argonautica*. He accomplishes this in large pa... by introducing Hercules in a significant fashion as an anti-hero. Apollonius' seriousness needs stressing perhaps since he sometimes appears to be creating a mock-heroic poem or in any case parodying the epic. Such a view, however, does not account for the grimness and solemnity of emotion that appear quite frequently in this strange poem.

Jason has seemed to many an unlikely candidate for hero. The reasons are many, but in general they rest upon the fact that he is morally, spiritually and intellectually impotent, and perhaps a physical coward as well. If we look, however, to the formal elements of the poem, Jason is inescapably the hero. And Apollonius had directed us to consider the formal creation of a hero by playing so emphatically with epic forms. He does not ask us to nominate Jason hero out of our hearts, but from our intellectual grasp of the structure of the poem. Jason is formally the hero, as Apollonius insists again and again. For instance, Jason is the cause of the entire expedition for it is he who so inspires Pelias' fear that the king conceives the plan that constitutes overall the subject of the entire poem (1.5ff.). The poet reminds us of this fact often during the course of the action, for instance when Argos says (3.356f.): "It was for his [Jason's] sake that the others went out as a body from Hellas." When the poet calls upon Erato (3.1ff.) for poetic assistance it is to tell the story of Jason. Perhaps nowhere is he more obviously the hero than when the poet paints in detail his psychological state (e.g. 2.621ff.). Jason's psyche is a matter of general concern; this is not true of any other hero, none of whom actually has a personality. Jason seems unsympathetic; nonetheless Apollonius has contrived formally to maintain Jason's primacy throughout the poem.

The presence of Hercules in the narrative is a means by which Apollonius enlarges and more clearly sets the focus upon Jason. Hercules is in the poem by design, not because the tradition of the voyage of the *Argo* determined his presence. Those who imagine that Apollonius was such a slave to some tradition that he had to bring in Hercules praise the poet for the adroit way in which he manages to dismiss the hero from the narrative by the end of the first book. They are embarrassed to find a traditional superhero who upstages a conventional if somewhat colorless hero. But the embarrassment is important. Like Hercules himself that sensation is in the narrative by design.

Apollonius from the first contrives to establish Jason as a hero with a difference. He is absent from the catalogue, which marks him off as someone separate. The crew can be called his retinue, as the line concluding the catalogue implies (1.228): "These were the many helpers gathered together as helpers for Jason." His position, however, is thereafter made ambiguous by the unanimous decision on the part of the crew to elect Hercules as their leader (337–39). It is suggested to them that they choose the best man, one who will lead them, manage every detail and handle their differences and dealings with the strangers whom they shall meet. Hercules declines and suggests Jason as an alternative—but only because it was Jason who gathered together the band of men. Nonetheless, Jason, cause of the expedition as the fleece is its goal, central to the story as no one else is, appears alone, removed from the crew, structurally by his absence from the catalogue and emotionally by their failure to select him openly and spontaneously as their leader.

Hercules, the crew's choice, is a formidable figure of saga and myth. He was the subject of earlier epics, in one, the Hercules who could assault the gods, the lover of wine, the fighter of monsters, whereas in the other, the Hercules as hunter and all-round athlete. The references to him in the *Iliad* indicate a live oral tradition coeval with that of the Trojan saga and the story of Achilles' wrath. Hercules is, therefore, an important alternative to Jason. He is on one level a counterpart to the heroic values of Achilles; he is still more perhaps analogous to Ajax or Diomedes as a man of considerable physical strength, animal daring and courage— all exemplified in his labors. Beyond this, the tale of the labors has a fairy-tale ring to it so that we may say that Hercules has also moved in the fairy-tale world in which Jason, too, will appear. Finally, through his exploits and his travels he bears affinities with the new heroism that Alexander brought into the Greek world. From the outset, then, Hercules' refusal to accept the unanimously offered leadership of the crew is momentous. And Apollonius keeps his reader aware of Hercules often throughout the earlier part of the poem by such deliberate devices as the description of the *Argo*'s lowering in the water under Hercules' weight (1.532f.) or the crew's recognition that Polydeuces' powers would have been unnecessary had Hercules confronted Amycus (2.145–53).

Between the catalogue and Hercules' refusal Jason is portrayed in a strange fashion. The poet shows us the grief of Jason's parents at his parting; a little sorrow is natural enough but this is a grief so intense as to charge the scene with unrelieved sadness. Then Apollonius describes Jason's arrival at the beach where his comrades are assembled, gathered to meet *him*, as the poet says (32). Then suddenly the poet interrupts Jason's appearance to describe the late arrival of Akastos and Argos, adding that the crew were filled with wonder as they saw them (322) in their resplendent clothing. The two naturally upstage Jason. In a curious and subtle way Jason is deflated.

The description of Jason's departure from the palace (307–16) reinforces this. After having compared him in simile with Apollo in his beauty as he sets forth to the shouts of the populace, Apollonius introduces an old woman, Iphias, the priestess of Artemis. ". . . she kissed his right hand, but had not the strength to say a word, eager though she was to do so, as the crowd pressed on. But she was left there by the wayside, as the old are left by the young; he passed by and was gone afar." The simile gives the first hint in the poem of the majesty that should rightfully belong to Jason as a hero figure, but Apollonius has immediately undercut it with the description of the priestess just as he has used the latecomers' arrival at the beach. True enough in crowds and processions old women will be lost and turned aside. But Apollonius manages to give the description considerable melancholia ("as the old are left by the young"); we see the event from the sorry position of the old woman and the glitter of Jason's triumphal progression is tarnished. The sadness here reinforces the misery of Jason's mother; furthermore, Jason seems not to be master of his actions. He is swept along—no doubt, unseeing, and perhaps not caring—part of the surge of events that he cannot control. The simile speaks against Jason in a small detail. Jason, as analogue to Apollo, has bereaved the priestess of Apollo's sister. Since Apollonius is always so careful to ensure that all points of his similes fit the compared situation, this surely represents a minor intended incongruity reflecting the world in which communications, continuity and coherence are fractured, a world in which the glorious coming of Jason does not make things right.

Apollonius does not employ characterizing epithets in the Homeric manner, but Jason is sometimes described as *amechanos,* "helpless," "dejected." It does seem that it is the force of events that places Jason where he is rather than personal drive.

The bittersweet and out-of-focus quality of the poem reaches an early peak when Jason mistakenly kills the young Kyzikos. The crew of the *Argo* have stopped at the young prince's island home. He receives them graciously, entertains them. They sail away, but at night mistakenly return. Alarms are sounded, Jason's men and Kyzikos' men meet in battle in the darkness of the night. Kyzikos leaves his bride and rushes to battle. Such is the sweet goodness of the new groom, the kind host, the amatory young man. Because of the importance of love in this poem it is horrible that Kyzikos is killed; doubly horrible that he is killed in ignorance by Jason. The poet offers this episode to illustrate seriously and awfully how *amechanos* Jason is. Things happen to him; he does not create them. The battle in which Kyzikos dies is in context as perverse as any episode in the poem. It is the first *androktasia* (see p. 36) in the poem, in fact, almost the only one, with the traditional catalogue-like list of names. The battle is followed by the traditional lamentation and burial. While formal and traditional the episode is startlingly wrong and meaningless. In this situation Jason's qualities as an epic hero seem altogether faulted.

Eventually on the island of Lemnos another kind of Jason emerges, a more positive man, and here he is associated with love. Here Jason becomes more formally heroic on the Homeric model, specifically when he goes forth to an audience with the princess Hypsipyle. He girds himself in a great cloak, which is lengthily described. We seem to be meant to be reminded of Agamemnon's arming in the twelfth book of the *Iliad,* although here one item Jason takes up is fully described and there the description is spread over several articles of Agamemnon's armor. More exactly the description of the cloak recalls the description of Achilles' shield, for the cloak has designs representing the same kind of abstract symbolism that the shield has.

The cloak gives to Jason the splendor and brightness of the sun (1.725f.), recalling the countless times that Homer equates his heroes' martial brilliance with shining fire. Jason goes forth to the city like a star, as Achilles in the twenty-second book of the *Iliad* rushes upon the waiting Hector like a star. There are more points of comparison with that passage in the *Iliad:* the waiting Trojans, the waiting lovesick maidens; the darkness of the night in both cases (22.28;1.777); Achilles rushing across the plain; the star rising over the girls' homes (22.26;1.776); the star of the *Iliad* bringing fever, in the *Argonautica* charming the maidens' eyes (22.31;1.777). As Jason approaches the city the simile helps to place him in the context of a warrior endowed with wondrous might. The entire passage beginning with the description of the cloak suggests the prelude to an *aristeia* that is in general reminiscent of Achilles' preparation for battle at the close of the nineteenth book of the *Iliad*. The one crucial difference is that Jason's *arete* is his sexuality.

When Jason complains of his inadequacy (2.416ff.) the prophet Phineus replies that he is to rely upon the aid of Aphrodite. The whole of the Lemnos episode illustrates this particular dimension of Jason's heroism. Sexual images are central, from the first discussion in Hypsipyle's council hall when her aged nurse Polyxo rises to speak from her seat next to four virgins, unmated, with white hair (indicative of the irrevocable state of virginity). Polyxo's warning of the time when there will be no one to do the plowing is obviously sexual, especially after the barnyard adjective applied to the virgins (cf., too, lines 867ff.). Some of the images from Jason's cloak have to do with incomplete, unfinished states such as Zeus' unfinished thunderbolt, or Amphion and Zethos still working on the walls of Thebes; both reinforce the idea of untried virginity that Lemnos represents. Also on the cloak are images more apt to the setting of the entire poem, that is, the conflict between love and war, or rather love in war and war in love, such as the image of Aphrodite viewing her reflection in Ares' shield, or the race contest of Hippodameia with love and hate clearly warring.

The simile of the star at Jason's approach involves a description of maidens enclosed in their chamber, surely the virginal state again. Jason is described as going through the gates of the city, then arriving at the palace, where maidens open more gates to give him access to the princess, whose name means "High Gates." Gates and portals had the same strong sexual significance for the ancients as they do for ourselves. One of the major themes of love elegy was the lover's lament who has been shut outside the gate when the door is closed. Apollonius shows virginity overcome as a kind of battle encounter.

The traditional hero's panoply with which Jason's encounter with Hypsipyle commences formally demonstrates him to be a hero, but the sexual tones provide more. Jason is a sexual hero, a lover; and this is a type of hero that is probably novel for epic. Odysseus has a number of sexual adventures, and more than once owes his survival to the women with whom he sleeps (even Nausicaa's sexual interest in him provides the motive for her concern for his welfare). But there is an enormous difference in attitude between the two poems; in Odysseus' relationships with Circe or Calypso we are not made to feel that the interest is anything other than simple sexual desire on the part of the females, and certainly Odysseus keeps his affections for Penelope. The women in the *Argonautica*, on the other hand, are interested in Jason in a deeper, more complicated emotional way.

Hypsipyle's feelings for Jason are veiled until he must leave. Then her actions and speeches tell that she does in some way love him (886ff.). Jason's emotions are not revealed. But his manner of approach to Hypsipyle's palace, endowed with radiant sexuality, implies more of a lover, at least as far as externals, than even the magically rejuvenated Odysseus seems to suggest. Jason as a romantic lover is not, however, demonstrative or aggressive; his sexuality is simply the essence of his being. This is important to notice, for despite the formal elements of the traditional heroism and the sexuality Jason remains as *amechanos* as before. Endowed with a romantic sexual panoply that his personality does not complement, he seems to be an unfulfilled Paris.

While Jason and most of the crew go off to enjoy the delights of Hypsipyle and the other Lemnian ladies, Hercules remains behind with a few chosen comrades. The others enjoy an evening of gaiety and sensuality that stretches into days, provoking Hercules' disgust, disgust at the delay, disgust at the sexuality ("Is it a pleasure to stay here to plow the rich soil of Lemnos? . . . Let's leave [Jason] in Hypsipyle's bed until he has filled Lemnos with men children and there will come to him great fame" [1.867–74]). Hercules, the more traditional hero, disapproves. Apollonius is setting

Hercules up as the alternative to Jason's sexuality. Such is the force of this disapproval that the *Argo* departs abruptly.

Hercules, however, is made to disappear from the narrative and the circumstances of his departure show Apollonius again defining the kind of hero that dominates his epic. Hercules' overwhelming strength reduces him in fact to impotence when his oar breaks as he furiously tries to maneuver the *Argo* alone, a portent of his departure and the reasons for it. Shortly thereafter he loses Hylas, who is snatched away by a lovesick water nymph. Hercules' frenzied search for Hylas takes him away forever from the voyage of the Argonauts and the winning of the fleece.

What is Hylas to Hercules that he prizes the boy above the sailing of the *Argo?* Hylas is Hercules' creature, reared by the hero from childhood after Hercules killed his father. There is a hint of Andromache's dependence upon Hector here; it recalls her survival and the death of her family. More specifically Hylas holds a position analogous to Patroclus' relationship to Achilles or that of Sthenelos to Diomedes in the *Iliad.* Hylas is first described (1.131f.) as in the prime of youth. When the water nymph first perceives him he is rosy with beauty and sweet graces as the moon shines down upon him. Apollonius says no more, but Theocritus in his account of the episode (Idyll 13) identifies the young boy as Hercules' beloved. Masculine affection and concern have been traditional heroic qualities since the *Iliad;* heroes operate in a male world. It is this to which Hercules is heir in Apollonius' conception if nothing else. The Theocritan version presents this side too: "As a father teaches his beloved son, so did Hercules teach Hylas all the lore which had made him noble and renowned himself, and never parted from him, neither at noon's onset, nor when dawn . . . sped upward to the halls of Zeus" (13.8–11). This represents what at certain stages of Greek culture constituted the ideal emotional relationship.

For Hylas Hercules demonstrates considerable concern, grief, deep need. This is the version of Apollonius. Taking from Theocritus the potentials of the relationship we may view Hercules as a hero of the type who offers his soul to a young male, although freely seeking sexual satisfaction from females (see Sophocles' *Trachinian Women*). Hercules, alone of the figures in the catalogue, is described as having a young helper. He is a hero of the older epic tradition. Apollonius, by removing Hercules from the narrative in pursuit of Hylas, still more clearly shows Jason as a new kind of epic hero, a romantic hero, a love hero, a man who will move out of the male-dominated context of traditional epic into a new heterosexual tragedy of manners. This is the most important function of Hercules. His earlier appearances went far toward establishing Jason as perhaps nothing more than an ordinary man perversely in hero's clothing. Hercules provides the measure, Jason is found wanting until at Lemnos he is invested with a kind of heroism. Then finally Jason and his peculiar *arete* triumph as Hercules and the tradition for which he stands must withdraw in a pederastic pursuit that has no place in love epic.

Hercules, like two others of the crew, Idas and Peleus, also stands for a martial skill and toughness of personality that is found wanting in the new ambience. This is mirrored on the divine level (3.18ff.) when Athena is helpless and love is not; "It's not strength or force of hands we need," says Hera to Aphrodite, "but love" (3.84). Similarly Jason can ponder (3.182–84) whether he should meet Aeetes in battle, *or* in fact contrive some other plan. Fighting is definitely passé; Jason alone of the heroes seems to understand this.

Yet in contrast to Hercules Jason remains *amechanos* especially emotionally. Hercules' mad dash after Hylas shows an energy and vitality that Jason never musters, and Apollonius chooses to remind us of this at the very end of the epic in his description of Hercules and the Hesperides. Here once again we see the old-style hero who achieves his prize through his own strength and courage, relying on no one. Jason, as we know, must depend upon Medea completely in order to get the Fleece.

Jason's initial conquest of Medea's heart and his subsequent victory in the contest Aeetes sets for him are critical moments in the narrative that call for heroics. Apollonius has introduced two episodes that are reminiscent of Homeric epic. The Homeric coloration highlights alternately the importance and the absurdity of these moments. Among these moments in Jason's relationship with Medea there stands out specifically the embassy of Hera and Athena to Aphrodite, who at their request sends Eros to earth to inflame Medea with love. The dramatic scene is that of Thetis going to Hephaestus in the eighteenth book of the *Iliad*. In one view Jason, as a kind of wandering Odysseus, needs his Athena, who in this epic will naturally be replaced by Aphrodite. As Phineus said, the crew must find their help in Aphrodite. She provides this in the form of her son, Eros. But the embassy of petition that Athena and Hera make strongly reminds one of Thetis' trip to Hephaestus for Achilles' new shield. The reference to Hephaestus in the Apollonian scene as the builder of Aphrodite's house and the explanation for his absence bring to mind the cozy domesticity of Charis and Hephaestus in the *Iliad* scene. This is made sharper by the parallel in the greetings. As Charis says (*Iliad* 18.386) to Thetis: "You didn't used to visit us too often," so Aphrodite says to Hera and Athena (*Argonautica* 3.53f.): "Why have you come, you two, who before did not come too frequently?"

Eros then becomes the invincible shield who will help the hero, the new hero of love. Eros descends to earth majestically in a manner reminiscent of Homer. The description of the descent gives majesty to the otherwise petulant pretty baby boy. The scenes of the conspiring goddesses and the two divine boys at their dice would be out of place in the traditional epic; the goddesses resemble Alexandrian court ladies too much. Since the Ptolemaic court was almost as close as one could get to the divine in the Alexandrian era, such women and their manner as well as the elegance and grace of their lives are a natural counterpart to the more rigorous scenes on Olympus in the Homeric epics. The temptation to see in them a source for the mood of mock-heroic, especially in Eros' descent, is inhibited by the deeply passionate and tragic quality to Medea's love; the story of Jason and Medea is ultimately too serious. Love is a force in life that has many sides, one of which is overwhelming passion. But love has also an ambience of beauty, gaiety and a sense of careless pleasure that the goddesses and Eros and Ganymede provide. They form the sensible divine entourage to Medea's love, and in this sense they are as thoroughly epic as Athena's appearance to Achilles in the first book of the *Iliad* or her appearance to Diomedes in the fifth.

The other scene in the third book in which we are translated back into the world of heroic epic is Jason's victory in the contest of plowing the field and sowing the dragon's teeth, a scene that is meant to be Jason's *aristeia* (see p. 36). The mood is different because Jason is dealing with fantastics and he is protected by magic; yet an *aristeia* it is. Apollonius has very well managed to show the surreal aspects of this *aristeia* by describing Jason's preparations for the contest (3.119ff.), involving magical rites performed at night, his covering himself in a cloak given him by Hypsipyle, which, as the poet says, is a memorial to their continual love-making. This description is opposed to that of Aeetes girding for battle (3.1225ff.) where the king puts on the traditional pieces of armor. The king when accoutered rides forth fierce and proud as any traditional hero, but, of course, ineffectually, because that kind of heroic strength and purpose is now meaningless. Aeetes is only an astonished onlooker in this scene. Aeetes' emotional capitulation marks the success of Jason's *aristeia* on the heroic level, magic, maiden and love apart.

The narration of Jason's contest is filled with similes (sixteen in the last hundred and fifty lines of the third book) as the *androktasiai* of the *Iliad* are. Apollonius has for the most part introduced similes that recall those of the *Iliad*, that is, a vigorous horse (1259), lightning in the stormy sky (1265), a rocky reef in a pounding sea (1294), a raging boar facing hunters (1359). The comparison of Jason to a falling star (1377ff.) is particularly effective in recalling the style and feeling of heroics in the *Iliad*. With this event the third book ends in high epic allusion as it had begun with the embassy to Aphrodite.

But the third book belongs to Medea, which at first glance seems fatal to any heroic pretensions on the part of Jason. Medea, however, appears as Jason's victim, or more specifically Eros' victim. She is as much *amechanos* in the face of love as Jason has been earlier in facing the entire expedition to Colchis. To this extent they parallel each other and sustain a mood throughout the poem of helpless victims in a world they never made, culminating finally in their lack of enthusiasm toward their so long delayed marriage (4:1161ff.), when they are forced into sexual intercourse (to make the mood more obviously wrong the poet surrounds the couple with the customary features of a joyful celebration [4.1128–69]). Medea has her magic as Jason has his sexuality; beyond this they are helpless people acted upon far more than acting. In the third book each has his moment of individual heroism, Jason's the more typical, Medea's the more novel, that of a lovesick woman. From her love springs the decisive action of the third book, but this is balanced by Jason's killing of

Apsyrtos in the fourth, an act that springs if not from love then at least in part from deep concern.

Although Medea contributes the aid that settles the course of action there are constant intimations that Jason controls the situation. The motif of Theseus and Ariadne suggests that Jason is the user and Medea the used. More importantly the numerous allusions to Nausicaa of the *Odyssey* evoke a Medea under the spell of the stranger Jason. In creating the Nausicaa-Medea equation Apollonius shows the same determination he exhibits elsewhere to show the perversity of his epic world. Medea changes subtly from the sweet young thing whom we know Nausicaa to be into the witch who is ultimately capable of anything (and in this we are meant to be reinforced perhaps by Euripides' conception of her). Apollonius has contrived a particularly remarkable description of Medea in the third book (828–90). It begins with the light of day, the maiden's washing away the tears of the lovesick night. The bath, the ointment, the perfume, the veil gleaming like silver, her entourage of fragrant maidens—all combine to display lightness, goodness and innocence. As the maidens hitch up the chariot for Medea we are reminded of Nausicaa off to the seashore for the family washing. The impression of Medea as a Nausicaa figure is intensified at 869ff. by the description of her departure in the chariot with her lovely maidens dancing along beside. As if to set the parallel still more firmly Apollonius compares Medea to Artemis and the lengthy simile recalls a similar one in the sixth book of the *Odyssey* (6.102ff.). These portraits, however, surround a description of the magical charm that Medea is transporting to the temple of Hecate, a goddess associated with the night (quite the reverse of the atmosphere of the opening passage). During the nighttime incantations, we are told, Medea has created the charm herself, got from a flower sprung from the blood spilled by the eagle who chews Prometheus' liver (it reads like a recipe). With this description Medea, the witch, the mysterious and strange, stands revealed. Apollonius manages this Jekyll and Hyde perversity nicely with the remark (3.867f.): "She brought the charm out and set it in the fragrant girdle which went about her ambrosial bosom." Another time the poet achieves an equally unsettling juxtaposition. In the beginning of the fourth book Medea is wracked with anguish and she decides to leave her family. Both her anguish and her departure (4.11ff.) are the pitiable tale of an innocent maiden in trouble; indeed, the simile Apollonius employs (35ff.) emphasizes exactly this: she is like a servant girl afraid, alone in a strange land, stealing away from a house where her mistress maltreats her. Then Apollonius intrudes the other Medea (50ff.): "Now Medea decided to go to the temple. For she was not ignorant of the road, since often before she had wandered that way in search of corpses and deadly roots from the earth, things which sorceresses are usually out looking for."

Medea's fairy-tale features, her magic are dangerous for Jason. His love of Medea is finally fatal to his pretensions to be a traditional hero. Medea's world, her family are far from the traditional heroic world scaled to normal men. Jason by attaching himself to her becomes lost in this other world. Partly Jason's seeming inability to function well, to deal with his environment, stems from its fantastic quality. Odysseus' travels through the more magical parts of his never-never land show him deserted by the Olympian gods, symbol of the fact that he cannot function among fantastics as a typical saga hero. Apollonius has located the major part of his story in such a setting. While the myth calls for it, the poet emphasizes it, and in this fairy-tale world Jason is lost. From the first Aeetes (Circe's brother, we should remember) shows a barbarity (3.377ff.) that stuns Jason; the contest Aeetes demands is grotesque. Naturally Jason is at a loss (cf. 3.423, 432). Jason is out of his context and when Medea instructs him in what he must do (3.1026ff.), the magical directions show that Jason's task will be every bit as complicated as Odysseus' various adventures, if not more so, because normal man is made to go to the final limits of fairyland in this elaborate ritual.

As if to symbolize this Apollonius has devised two voyages for the *Argo*, the first (in the first and second books) in essence as realistic as any *periplous* known to the Greeks, but the second (in the fourth book) an adventure in a fairytale world of strange people and impossible geography. Here Jason meets Medea's aunt, the witch Circe, surrounded by grotesques rather than simply men transformed into animals. Here in this fairy-tale setting he finally takes Medea's virginity. Perhaps most significantly it is in this final portion of the epic that Jason most decisively acts when he murders Apsyrtos. To be sure, he acts at Medea's suggestion, but Jason must make the choice ("if this pleases you" [4.419]).

Jason does the killing and Apollonius makes Jason's endeavors the more individual by having Medea turn her eyes away at the act. The death of Apsyrtos is accomplished first by trapping him with gifts. Consistent with the main theme of this epic, the primary gift is a cloak, which before Hypsipyle gave to Jason. The cloak bears in its very texture the odors and memories of love-making; Apollonius recounts the time when Dionysus made love to Ariadne upon the very cloak after she had been deserted by Theseus. Once again sexuality, especially Jason's, gives him victory.

The poet makes a comment upon this by the way in which he breaks the narrative with an apostrophe to Love which works so much evil for mankind; this comes between the description of the cloak and the murder of Apsyrtos. The poet's sudden subjectivity provides a sharp focus on the killing of Apsyrtos. The event is, of course, unheroic, and an evil crime. Again we witness the perversion of the hero, but set within the perverse, bizarre arena of the final travels. Jason has traveled far in this narrative and in a sense he is a victim of Medea in this unnatural world (cf. the emotional trap laid for Jason beginning with 4.345ff.). Apollonius has contrived a strange story and a strange man in Jason. The murder of Apsyrtos, however, reflects the rhythm of love and hate in the poem, a motif first introduced in the song Orpheus sings in the first book (496–511). The poem is offered by Orpheus to quell the ugly mood of quarreling between Idmon and Idas; its theme is suggested by the quarrel, that is, the alternation of love and hate or strife as the two opposing and ruling forces in the universe. More than a piece of Alexandrian pedantry, a display of Empedoclean philosophy, the theme of the song grows out of the quarrel and furthermore offers elaboration of a motif that runs through the entire poem, the conflict of love and hate (or destruction). The theme appears formally as in the design on Jason's cloak, where Aphrodite is shown looking at her reflection in Ares' shield. Dramatically the theme appears in the warmth of the reception offered by the Doliones and their leader, Kyzikos, to Jason and his crew, soon to be reversed in their sudden and wanton murder; or the theme may be seen in the women of Lemnos killing all their menfolk only to seek out sexual relationships with Jason and his crew. Again and again love and hate alternate and often seem to grow the one out of the other; it is a rhythm in which Jason himself is caught rather than one that he has created.

The fleece is perhaps symbol of Medea's virginity. The fourth book begins with Medea's anguish; she has betrayed her people and her father in helping Jason. Her anguish is shown as occurring in her room, which she leaves finally after having left a cutting of her hair for her mother, a memorial to her virginity, she says. She precedes this by kissing her virginal bed and the folding doors on both sides of it, and then she strokes the walls of her room. Shortly thereafter it is she who offers to Jason the fleece and he responds by vowing marriage (4.86–87, 95–98). One might say that the golden fleece represents on one level Medea's maidenhead and Jason's acquisition of this is his triumphant heroism, a natural consequence of his innate sexuality. Medea in her Nausicaa-like dream of wish fulfillment (3.616ff.) has already confused the fleece and herself, confused her role and Jason's in contesting for the fleece; it is she in her dream who yokes the oxen, she who bestows the fleece and in all this within the dream she seems to be giving up her virginity. And finally when Jason and Medea consummate their love they lie on the fleece so that it is bound up by the poet in their feelings to each other.

Jason's extraordinary passivity needs noticing. Partly this seems to come from Apollonius' view of mankind as helpless figures, or at least in his own time, contrasting an Alexandrian Jason to a Homeric Hercules. This is more important and more obvious. There is, however, another technical factor in Jason's passivity and that has to do with his sexual qualities. His sexuality is not either pederastic or simple animal need. He is endowed always with the romantic qualities of beauty, grace and charm. His females, Hypsipyle and far more notably Medea, love him with a passion. As the fourth book shows, Jason cares for Medea as well. This is a new kind of sexuality, at least for epic poetry, namely heterosexual love, and I believe that the reason why Jason appears essentially passive is because the epic tradition could not even for Apollonius accommodate itself to a male exhibiting strong feelings of love and affection for a female. One is reminded of the peculiar revulsion that Pentheus feels toward the disguised Dionysus in Euripides' *Bacchae* (453ff.), because the stranger displays in his good looks what Pentheus calls effeminance, some electric quality designed for seducing women. No self-respecting male would either be so handsome or so unnecessarily interested in the female sex, that is the implication. To the Greek mind it is not masculine.

Compare the successful development of feeling that Theocritus manages in his Hylas poem. This, however, is homosexual love, sanctioned in poetry for some time, a kind of love in any case perhaps dignified and built into the institution of culture, as the initial speech in Plato's *Symposium* signifies. Nothing of this sort existed for heterosexual love, certainly not in epic, at least so far as men were concerned. A Phaedra might be lovesick in tragedy, a Medea might go mad for love, but no man shows his passion. Apollonius wished to achieve Jason's heroism through his sexuality, as is evident in the way in which Jason approaches Hypsipyle and by the manner in which the poet removes Hercules from the narrative. Nonetheless, the poet fails, I believe, in exhibiting Jason as a fitting sexual hero, a counterpart to his anguished Medea. To do so successfully would have been too daring.

Perhaps also Apollonius is influenced by the misogynistic strain that runs through so much of Greek literature, apparent already in the *Odyssey*. Once Jason has Medea under his spell, once he has contrived (with Eros) to be her lover, then he himself is caught somehow. To be sure, Medea is special, being a witch, but she is also very much a woman, and she leads Jason further and further away from the normal world he knows where alone he can possibly exercise any control. And this is perhaps not so much the enchantment of a witch as it is of a woman; and, too, this may be a misogynistic element more in the genre than in the culture.

The late fourth century and the third century was a period when women were growing increasingly freer of the restraints that family, tradition and law had placed upon them. They became personalities in their own right; many poems are evidence to this. The New Comedy at Athens also portrays many less circumscribed women. In the movement toward greater freedom, it has been suggested that courtesans led the way. Already long since much freer than their sisters, preferred as companions intellectual and otherwise by numbers of males, they were the models. No wonder that New Comedy shows so many so prominently. And how fitting that they should herald in an age and a literature in which personal, heterosexual love should triumph.

Beyond this, Apollonius may very likely have had the alternative desire to indicate the failure of will among his contemporaries. By leaving Jason's emotional reactions hidden, he allowed himself to portray a hero as *amechanos*, which may very well have been part of his aim. The poem is ambiguous; when it is perverse, one feels the poet's control; but its ambiguity, on the contrary, seems to me to be irresolution on the poet's part.

The features of Apollonius' *Argonautica* are found all or severally in the writings of his contemporaries. Most of all this poetry demands erudition from its audience, which one would expect from poetry born and cradled in a library. Heroes are everywhere passive or insignificant. Love is a considerable fact in the lives of the poets or their characters. A new sensibility abounds, personal, impressionable, responsive. Poets delight in the strange and unknown; magic intrudes upon the world of Olympian coherence and control. Humor and sentimentality play with classical austerity and severity. The classical world seems pretentious by comparison.

The new poetic was vigorously advanced by Callimachus.

Judge poetry by some critical technique,
    not with a Persian measuring tape.
Don't expect from me a big-sounding poem;
    Zeus thunders, not I . . .
    [Apollo said to me]
"Feed the sacrificial beast until fat,
    keep the Muse fine.
This I command: where carts have not gone
    walk there. Drive your chariot
not in the tracks of others, not on the wide road
    but on unworn roads, even if your way is narrower."
                        (*Aitia* frag. 1, book 1)

Callimachus here and elsewhere advocates subtlety, delicacy, newness, lightness, qualities that are absent from the public poetry of previous centuries, particularly epic with its long narrative, swollen by digressions, worn smooth with repeated and clichéd expressions. The reiteration and obviousness that public theater demands also contrast with the lean Muse whom Callimachus' Apollo advocates. To judge by the poetry of Callimachus that survives, his aesthetic also had no room for the kind of seriousness that Homeric epic and fifth-century tragedy and comedy particularly reveal, a seriousness that informs everything of Greece in the Classical Age. The lines of Callimachus speak the frustration and fatigue of someone who has been cataloguing the monuments of a literary tradition. We must also remember that Callimachus belonged to the immigrant generation in Alexandria. They were Greeks in a foreign land, and were probably obsessed with things Greek. The burden of the tradition of Greek poetry would have been all the heavier for them, not having the more open cosmopolitan mentality of successive generations of Alexandrians. What Callimachus cannot see because he is too close is that epic, tragedy and comedy of that type, even Pindaric choral music, were mostly public, civic, group literature. The *polis* declined, public poetry declined. What once again surfaces is the natural inclination toward personal poetry. In so vast a world, lacking social scale, one has mostly himself to contemplate and to celebrate. In the centuries before the *polis* exercised its absolute hold on poetic imaginations, men and women wrote of their private world and feelings. Style then becomes so much more important because it is the expression of an individual personality, a specific taste. Callimachus is the Hellenistic poet par excellence, highly self-conscious, stylish, stylized, ironic, always aware of himself in his poetry. Here is the tombstone epitaph he fashioned for himself:

You are walking past the tomb of Battus' son
skilled at song, and laughing together to the correct degree in wine.

Wine and proportion, measured abandon, decorous silliness, song and shared laughter, an ironic glance at the world through poetry, irony that you, gentle reader, will comprehend and enjoy.

Callimachus' poetry was wide-ranging; little of it survives, unfortunately. A major piece was the *Aitia,* a poem of seven thousand lines on the subject of origins or causes for things (*aition* is the Greek word for "cause"). It betrays the antiquarian mind of the poet, who is interested in the curiosities of love and tradition, reasons why cults and other institutions are said to be as they are. The poem does not, so far as we can tell from the fragments, have any ongoing organizing principle, being episodic, a series of narrative vignettes in elegiacs. In each episode Callimachus was free to be as subtle and careful as he chose, having to sacrifice nothing to an overarching narrative scheme. The quality of his poetic technique and the excitement engendered by the nature of the curiosities that formed his subject matter were the redeeming features of what might otherwise seem inconsequential poetry. Erudition was called for in poet and reader. Callimachus, we know, wrote learned treatises that were more or less the compilations of fact. The *Aitia* satisfied the demands of that sort of intellectual curiosity while meeting aesthetic needs as well.

Curiosities formed a major interest of the Alexandrians. Some sought out especially bizarre or extraordinary curiosities. In a way, the pastoral feeds this appetite because it portrays what is to urban dwellers a very *exotic* world and people. The collecting of curiosities was called *paradoxagraphia*. The marvels of every age and every country were written up in books to be published. It is a clear instance of men with a compulsion to write and nothing to say. Undeniably we are among men of letters in a literary age writing for an audience who needed titillation. Yet *paradoxagraphia* is a definite stance before the classical tradition, based as it is upon the typical, the general and the symmetrical. The paradox celebrates the unique, the unexpected and the accident and proves that freedom exists in the world.

Men wrote cookbooks, books of fishing, books on medical practice, compilations of extraordinary rivers—all of these in poetry. They stood as a landscape or still life does for a painter, ready to be transmuted. Facts formed the basis of the poems, but few of these poets bothered to check their facts. So many composed poems of this sort we cannot dismiss it as a freakish movement. The influence of Hesiod to this movement is obvious. Yet, while it does not seem that Hesiod labored under a compulsion to exhaust his subject, his facts, nonetheless, ring true, are seriously presented. Callimachus relates his encounter with the Muses on Helicon in the *Aitia* and one is reminded of Hesiod. Callimachus compliments Aratus by remarking that he has skimmed all the honey from Hesiod's verse. Hesiod compiled facts using his facts architectonically to create a theological fabric, a moral vision. The Alexandrian poets allow the facts themselves to stand as sufficient enchantment or reason to engage the reader. The poems of this sort that survive whole are not many, but in their own way they do intrigue. The penchant for fact betrays the Alexandrian emphasis upon precision and detail. This can be seen, for instance, in the way in which Theocritus in his *Idylls,* which is not one tenth the size of the Homeric corpus, mentions far more trees and plants than Homer does. Instead of the typical or generic tree or plant, there are precise, realistic, botanical details. In the same way, Theocritus creates real Sicilian landscapes in some of his *Idylls* rather than portraying a stereotyped nature scene.

Aratus, the most famous of the poets of fact, wrote the *Phainomena,* a poem of 1154 lines of dactylic hexameters. He versified the work of Eudoxos of Knidos on meteorology. The first part of the poem is a description of the heavenly bodies, their names and celestial positions. Now and then, Aratus bows to poesy; his hommage, for instance, to Hesiod is a narration of the ages of man (100ff.). A comparison of the passage with the Hesiodic original shows how banal Aratus is; there are only clichés, which augment the blandness of his general style in the other parts of the poem. Now, this poem was immensely popular with the Greeks and later the Romans, so it must have some quality we can no longer appreciate. Is it the *tour de force* of setting this amount of factual material to verse? That, of course, is not easy. The number of givens is inhibiting, particularly the proper names. Still, Aratus has not done anything extraordinary with his language. The stuff of the poem, the meteorology, does not necessarily excite, but perhaps in a society where astrology enjoyed considerable vogue, a poetic review of the celestial phenomena would be inherently interesting. The latter part of the poem (733–1154) is a change in tone, being a disquisition in verse of how animals, birds and nature in general foretell storms. There is something curious, cunning and delightful about this information. Here is a sample:

> Even before the rain, oxen begin to sniff
> looking to the sky; ants rush
> to bring up eggs from their hollow nests;
> swarming centipedes can be seen
> climbing walls; out wander earthworms
> which men call the dark earth's guts.
> Tame birds, and the rooster
> preen, cluck in great voice—
> sounds like drips of water upon water.

(954–62)

Two poems of Nicander have survived. They are also poetic paraphrases of prose scientific works. The one on snakes and the treatment for their bites is peculiarly compelling. The names of the snakes and the herbal remedies provide a marvelous and exotic sound amid the common Greek poetic diction. Strange visions of reptiles and the vast range of herbals make the poem at least titillating. The diction between these image-provoking terms is pedestrian, the style is pedestrian, dactyls without distinction marching resolutely on their course; still there is that weird charm. Here is one of the more imaginative and exciting passages, which at least gives a sense of the temper that pervades the poem. This is part of a description of the human reaction to the bite of what Nicander calls the Cocytos:

In his head, shadowy darkness settles in. Suffering,
he is dry in his gullet at one moment, dry with thirst;
From his very fingertips, cold grips him often; a winter's
  hailstorm
all over his limbs fiercely weighs him down.
And again he vomits up often from his belly a mess of bile;
the skin goes yellow all over. A damp sweat
colder than falling snow passes over his limbs.
Sometimes his skin is the color of dark lead,
Sometimes cloudy, sometimes like copper flowers.

Theriaka, 63–67

Here are directions for making a bed of herbals out of doors that will repel snakes:

Cut and scatter under you
Flowering willow or stinky hulwort
which has a horrid odor; add viper's bugloss,
marjoram leaves or some wormwood
growing wild in the mountains in a chalk valley.

Theriaka, 63–67

A similar fascination with strange names, queer sounds marks the 1474-line epic poem of Lycophron. Called *Alexandra,* it relates the description by a slave of the prophetic utterance of Cassandra (here called Alexandra). It is an amazingly obscure poem. Fifty per cent of Lycophron's vocabularly is rare words, 10 per cent, words that occur nowhere else in the extant Greek literature. The patience with which Lycophron worked to assemble the mass of alternative, arcane names for obvious mythological figures was immense. The effort of his readers at comprehending them, we may assume, was assuaged by the pride they took in having such encyclopedic learning at their control. The slave begins:

> Not as before calmly
> did the maiden give forth her oracular voice,
> but poured forth a shout, undescribable, all mixed up . . .
>
> (3–5)

Thereafter, the slave tries to remember the "shadowy obscure paths of her riddling oracle." Lycophron brilliantly creates the obscurity; however, it is one of recherché allusions, and pedantry, rather than the garbled utterance traditionally associated with the prophet. The *Alexandra* is a marvelous reflection of the overwhelming weight of the centuries-old tradition, accrued now to the degree that it has become insupportable, no longer to be assimilated. Learning and scholarship, which were hallmarks of Alexandria, emblems of the Library, are the curious curse of Apollo, dulling, crippling, obfuscating the clear, true-speaking voice of Cassandra, who like all the possessed has the gift of poetry in her soul. Lycophron's *Alexandra* is poetry drowned in a sticky mess.

Lycophron's slave speaks just as darkly as his mistress, in fact. Here he describes Paris' ship off Tenedos as it makes for Troy:

> The centipedes, fair-faced daughters of Phalacra,
> stork-colored, struck with their broad blades
> the maiden-slaying Thetis.

The moderate obscurity of Phalacra (the place in the Troad where Paris got the wood for his ships) and the ugly contrivance for the Hellespont (Thetis, daughter of Neleus, old man of the sea; "maiden-slaying" refers to Helle, who drowned where the sea waters are now known as the Hellespont) quite sink the nice image of the many-oared ships as centipedes. Things get worse; here is Cassandra speaking:

> When you, the wolf, have snatched the heifer
> without wedding, bereft of her offspring, two doves,

fallen into a second net of foreign snares,
plunder caught by the birdcatcher.

The wolf is Paris, the heifer is Helen, unwed to Paris; the
doves are her daughters; the net is the seduction, the second
is Paris' (the first, Theseus'), foreign because Paris is from
Troy, Theseus from Athens. In this passage, in fact, Lycophron has taken some of the common elements of similes
(wolves, cows, doves, snares) of the Homeric and archaic
period and applied them in literal fashion to the participants
of the myth.

These pieces are curious. Set beside the glories of fifth-century Athens, they often repel. Yet they were popular in
their time and many of them thereafter. They represent only
a small part of this kind of *oeuvre:* the rest have perished.
But they are more than curiosities; they are a fundamental
of the Alexandrian Age.

In the formation of the city of Alexandria, there was
considerable effort to duplicate the political and social structure of Athens. Alexandria was to be the cultural heir to
Athens as well. The early Ptolemies, for instance, encouraged
tragedy; but continuity and vitality cannot be willed into
existence. The world was much changed, and symbol of that
change was the Mouseion and Library. Literature was the
object of study rather than a part of civic life. Culture became
a cloak or masque one self-consciously put on, rather than
absorbing it uncritically at one's mother's knee or beside the
village elders. Culture resided in the Library and the Mouseion
as the possession of a special few, no longer a celebration
watched, heard and talked about from theater to agora to
local street. Gone was the deep, abiding, natural affinity;
the umbilical cord was cut. But in a world of change, of
vastness, an ecumenical world, where there appeared a
jumble and mélange of traditions, religions, peoples, the bits
and pieces of Greek culture, like the gymnasia that appeared
around the world, like the appearance of Athens whether
distorted or watered down in the city of Alexandria, gave one
a sense of belonging to something. The poets were mostly
migrant people in an alien land. The Greek culture of Alexandria was a migrant culture in an alien land, standing out in
relief, not a pervasive, assimilated, omnipresent, ubiquitous
fact of life, like the air we breathe. The Library and Mouseion encouraged the alienation by institutionalizing literature
and the culture of which it was a part.

We do not know too much about the very popular street mimes. They were small dialogues, witty bits of social commentary, caricature, parody, extravagant emotion. Seven literary mimes composed by a man known as Herodas or Herondas have come to light in the last century, and they are no doubt similar to the more popular, earthy variety. Herodas' mimes are like comedy routines on American radio in the thirties and forties; one thinks of Jack Benny, George Burns and Gracie Allen, Fred Allen, or the routines Imogene Coca and Sid Caesar did in the earlier days of television. The remarkable feature of Herodas' art is his finished verbal portrait of various characters within these dialogues. The influence of Theophrastus' characterization or at least the mentality that represents is very strong. In his second, Herodas portrays a pimp at court trying to exact damages from a man who tried to steal one of his girls. In the fourth, two women at the temple of Asclepius at Kos are portrayed wandering in a typical tourist's awe and amazement (one is reminded of the first chorus in Eurpides' *Ion*). In the seventh, Herodas has a brilliant portrait of a shoe salesman. What Herodas has created is far simpler, more direct, smoother than the works of what might be considered the Alexandrian avant-garde, and perhaps they noticed him enough to criticize him. His eighth, which exists only in fragments, seems to be an oblique reference to his unhappy reception from hostile critics.

Many of the street mimes had a strong Egyptian flavor as did stories of the times. They were naturally in the Egyptian language, but some of them were also in Greek. Critics sometimes ponder why a Greek should have wanted to read this very clearly Egyptian sort of literature. But the answer is surely that the Greek culture imposed by the group around the Mouseion-Library required such an initiation in learning, such compliance, such agreement with aims and styles and was so devoid of immediate humanity that many Greeks turned away. One is reminded of the last fifty years of teaching Eliot, Pound and the rest of the obscurant, migrant poets who have been pursuing that elusive bird, Western culture; it will not work. The Alexandrian literary crowd was evidently a hostile, competitive group, at least Callimachus was. There have come down to us several stories of his feuding with Apollonius. The issue was whether long, sustained poetic narrative was any longer possible. Callimachus argued against it: "A great book is a great evil," he is supposed to have said. Apollonius, they said, withdrew from Alexandria because of the derision from the circle of Callimachus that greeted his *Argonautica*. At the same time, we can discern echoes of several of the poets in each other's writings. Consider the way in which Theocritus' twenty-second Idyll, the Hymn to the Dioscuri, has a passage (27–134) very much like Apollonius Rhodius' second book (1–97), describing a boxing match between Polydeuces and Amycus. The particular detailing of Theocritus, the generalizing of Apollonius tell much about the different preoccupations of these two poets. It also hints at much in the relationship of the two. Literary Alexandria must have had an incestuous, gossipy atmosphere producing feuds and backbiting, all taken so seriously that it was incorporated into poems. For example, Callimachus closes his Hymn to Apollo with the following:

Envy secretly spoke into Apollo's ear,
"I don't like the poet who will not sing vast as the sea."
Apollo pushed Envy with his foot and said:
"The Assyrian river is great but it carries erosion
  of earth and much trash upon its waters."
Not from every source do the Melissai carry water to Deo
but from where it is pure and clean and sparse . . .
Hail, Lord: But let blame go where Envy dwells.

And to make it more pointed, his second line has strong verbal parallels to a line in the *Argonautica*. One can read this as Envy being Apollonius' determination to rival or envy the great pieces of classical and preclassical Greek poetry; blame, on the other hand, would be the common Alexandrian tendency to be harshly critical. Obviously, numbers of the Alexandrians wrote poetry to which they were so close that they muddled their egos and their poetic styles.

The least controversial and the most popular literary effort of the Alexandrian period was the epigram. As the Greek word implies, epigrams were elegiac pieces to be cut into stone, generally funerary markers. Simonides made very beautiful epigrams in the early fifth century and the tradition remained strong. The Alexandrians considerably widened the scope of the genre: the epigram was no longer confined to

stone, nor to thoughts of death. It became the medium for
the occasional poem, for a versified thought, most of all for
thoughts on love and sex. In the Hellenistic period, the private
self was probably best transmitted through the metaphor of
love; it was, however, a love without the passion and tragedy
with which the nineteenth-century novelists endowed that
metaphor for the human dilemma. Vast numbers of epigrams
have survived, most of them strikingly similar, many of them
in fact serious imitation or variations on one another. Specimens were gathered together in anthologies in the third century and later. What remains from these has been collected
into what is called today the Greek Anthology. Reading
through the Anthology is to notice how routine and banal
these epigrams can be. The epigrams are analogous to
popular Anglo-American dance songs of this century, most
of which make light listening but are tiresome. Occasionally
one gets a Cole Porter or a Paul McCartney, but they do not
keep ASCAP in business.

The most conventional was the love poem. Asklepiades,
one of the celebrated poets of the genre, wrote this rather
shallow piece:

> Hanging on to your virginity? Why? In Hades
>   You'll find no one to love you.
> Love's pleasures are here among the living;
>   By Acheron we'll lie, dust and ashes.
>
> (5.85)

Leonidas from southern Italy was heavy-handed, pedantic
and detailed, but popular in writing dedicatory epigrams. It
was the custom to offer up to a patron god objects relating
to your profession or your salvation (after a shipwreck).
Here Leonidas imagines a fisherman having made a dedi-
cation:

> Hook easily gulped down and long poles,
>   line, creel and weel.
> Cunning device for men at sea
>   to catch their fish.
> Sharp trident, Poseidon's weapon
>   the two oars from his boat
> the fisherman, Diophantes, offers to his patron god
>   as is right, what's left of his old trade.   (6.4)

A woman, Nossis, also from southern Italy, wrote on the family:

> Here's Melinna. Look, how dear her face,
>   how sweetly she looks at me.
> How closely daughter resembles mother every way;
>   beautiful when children are like their parents.
>
> (6.353)

A very common theme was physical, sexual relations; these were not exactly what we would call pornographic, because the ancients were so much more open and accepting of sexual habits and quirks that it would be harder to appeal to their prurient interests. Homosexual relations were commonly discussed in love poetry since males tended to merge their physical passions and their affections when taking another male to bed whereas they took women to satisfy their lusts and to bear their children. But the Alexandrian Age is witness to a real revolution in this regard. Heterosexual relations became dignified by poetry; love between man and woman became a serious poetic concern, as we can see in Apollonius' *Argonautica;* and heterosexual love from a woman's point of view became an especially poignant subject. It is, for example, the subject of Theocritus' second Idyll about the lovesick girl who is trying to win back her man through magical charms. But the writers of what the ancients called *pornographia* created poems that were obviously considered respectable enough to become part of collections of epigrams. Here is one by the famous Dioskorides:

> If you want a little love from your pregnant wife,
>   don't bring her to bed face up, belly big,
> you'll be right on a giant wave, it's not easy—
>   she rowing for dear life, you slipping to and fro.
> Turn her over; get your pleasures in her rosy ass.
> Teach her how men make love to boys.
>
> (5.54)

Callimachus, a versatile poetic genius, also left his mark on epigrams. As one would imagine, he made a set of epigrams far superior to the standard. Here is one of death and sorrow, the original tone of the epigram, said for a fellow poet:

> They told me you were dead, Herakleitos; I cried,
> > remembered the times we two talking
> put the sun to bed. You, Halicarnassian friend,
> > are ashes now, I guess, gone a long, long time.
> Still, your nightingales live. Hades who takes
> > everything won't get his hands on them.
> > > > > (Epigram 2)

One of Callimachus' most successful experiments was what the ancients called a little epic (*epyllion*). In about one thousand lines of hexameter narrative in a modification of the diction of Homer, Callimachus told the story of Theseus killing the bull of Marathon. Callimachus was experimenting with several things at once. The story is an *aition*, giving the reason for the naming of the Attic deme Hekale and the establishment of the sanctuary of Zeus Hekalos. The formal *aition* has been expanded, given drama, local color and emotion, which the several *aitia* of his aitiological poem could not sustain. More importantly, it is an epic account reduced. Callimachus makes it clear that length and grandeur do not suit him, or perhaps do not in his opinion suit the times. The *Hekale* is an experiment in achieving epic narrative without the vast perspective. We cannot tell if Callimachus was successful because so little of the poem survives. The story is that Theseus set out for Marathon to kill the bull, stopped off at the cottage of an old woman, Hekale, because of a heavy rain. Next day, having enjoyed her hospitality, he goes to Marathon, kills the bull, returns by way of Hekale's cottage to find that she has died. Truly grieving for her, he determines to repay her hospitality by establishing various institutions in her honor. The traditional epic poet would have concentrated on Theseus, his nobility and glory, his *aristeia* in contest with the bull would have been much dilated. Hekale very likely would not have appeared. Callimachus concentrated on Hekale, which means he not only places the focus on a non-heroic figure, but takes the emphasis away from action, movement, drama. A passage much cherished in antiquity was the description of the meal that Hekale set for her chance visitor. A brief passage preserved records the conversation of two crows, an episode more magical than human, not exactly within the epic convention. The ancient Greek tendency would be to locate the heroic male figure in such a poem and to follow his adventures, particularly looking to his *aristeia* as being some kind of crucial moment for him. Callimachus has radically changed perspectives, bringing what should be the background to the foreground, insisting that the hero or the heroic world take into account the non-heroic ambience. The poem in an oblique way shows or implies the sensitivity of the hero to something, some person other than himself, not at all true to the traditional epic way of viewing things, where the hero is megalomaniac.

Callimachus has rejected the kind of unity and grandeur of scope that Aristotle describes (and so often then in the mind of his reader prescribes) for the literature of earlier antiquity, and Theocritus often does the same thing. Theocritus has created a brilliant variation on epic poetry in his thirteenth Idyll. This is a short piece, 75 lines, narrating, as we earlier mentioned, how Hylas, the beloved of Hercules, was pulled into a pond by the nymphs, causing Hercules to seek him in an anguished search. While much too short for true epic, the poem is endowed by Theocritus with all the touches of Homeric prolixity and grandeur.

[Hercules]
never parted from him [Hylas], neither when midday came,
nor when white-horsed Dawn rode up to the house of Zeus,
nor when the chirping chickens looked to their bed,
their mother's wings flapping on the smoke-stained perch.

(10–13)

So when Jason, son of Aeson, sailed after the golden
fleece, the best men followed along with him,
chosen from every city, the *crème de la crème*,
and with them came also to rich Iolkos the man
of labors, son of Alkmene, queen of Midea.

(16–20)

These and several more in a short poem fill the field, leaving small space for the dramatic moment when Hylas is snatched into the well by nymphs. But, with one simile, Theocritus not only once again intrudes the Homeric manner, but also conveys the sense of Hylas' fall, encapsulated so perfectly, so shockingly poignantly that the real lack of action in the poem goes unnoticed.

> Down he fell, headlong into the dark water
> as a flaming star falls from the heavens
> headlong into the sea, and some sailor says to his
>   comrades:
> "Get your gear together, boys, it's a sailing breeze."
>
> (49–52)

Hylas falls, all is silent, all is over. The falling star, star in the darkness, the voice out of the velvety dark, the cry of departure. The voice come from nowhere, a command of finality: all is silent.

Callimachus also changes the traditional perspectives in the six hymns from his hand that survive. It is remarkable that as a collection these hymns do not at all maintain the same tone. Although all are hymns, more or less after the model of those known as the Homeric Hymns (see p. 96ff.), the collection resembles a miscellany. The ancient Greek hymn to a deity had some fixed elements: an invocation to the god complete with several of his epithets or titles; a description or narrative account of the god's birth; and a listing of his powers or attributes. Homeric Hymns, those to Apollo, Demeter, Hermes and Aphrodite, are long narrative poems, each a divine adventure, a genuine epic episode. Callimachus has managed to play with each of these hymnal elements and conceits.

The Hymn to Zeus, for instance, begins with the god's birth, and after a transitional passage (54–66) ends with his powers. But the birth becomes an occasion for a kind of scholarly disquisition. The poet wonders about the true facts of Zeus' birth:

> I am in doubt since your birth is disputed,
> Zeus, they say you were born on the hills of Ida,
> Zeus, or in Arcadia. Which, O Father, lies?
>
> (5–7)

There follows the narrative of Rhea's birthing Zeus. The narrative is so laden with place names and personal names that the action is lost in them. When there is a choice, the less common name is used: Parrhasia, for instance, instead of Arcadia. Learned footnotes replace the allusive digression or simile of the Homeric Hymns, such as the following:

The goddess did not repay her with empty favor, no,
she named the river Neda, which, large by the city of
the Kaukones which is called Lepreion,
joins Nereus [the sea], this ancient water,
the grandson of the Bear, Lykaaon's daughter drinks.

(37–41)

The first part of the poem ends with Zeus' growing up to
assume his powers. This transitional passage finishes the first
part by returning again to the question of truth or falsehood
in the tradition. The ancient poets did not tell the truth, Callimachus says (59ff.), when they said that the sons of Kronos
drew lots for their spheres of power. If I am to tell lies at
least may they be persuasive ones, he adds (64). And very
neatly he turns then to proclaiming that Zeus' sovereignty
derives from his superiority. This launches the second portion,
the description of Zeus' power, into which he manages to
insert a complimentary testimonial to the reigning Ptolemy
(84ff.). Unlike the poet of the Homeric Hymns, who emerges
only to ring up or down the curtain on his poetic narrative,
which, true to early epic practice, stands apart in a kind of
poetic limbo, Callimachus draws himself and his time into
the poem. Callimachus, the poet/professor, manages the birth
of Zeus. The power of Zeus is made clear and valid by a
Ptolemaic analogue here on earth.

Instead of summoning Apollo in the opening to the second
hymn with the traditional invocation, the poet takes roughly
forty lines to establish the god's arrival and presence, describing the assembled, waiting young men (1–21), then the
effect of Apollo's presence upon various mythological figures
(22–31), followed by a description of the god's physique,
clothing and face (32–41). He is thus arrived. The Hymn to
Artemis begins as a charming portrait of a little girl (Artemis) on her father's (Zeus') knee, first asking for as many
epithets or titles as her brother Apollo has (6–7). In this way
Callimachus very cleverly plays on the typical hymnal practice of introducing the god's titles. Then she asks for arrows,
ritual title, clothing, maiden attendants, a city. In this way,
the poet manages to bring in the goddess' powers and attributes, another feature of hymns. And he has enough
homely details to create a portrait of the little girl, a conversational tone (8), too small to reach her father's beard
(26ff.), sweet enough to offset Zeus' problems with dreadful

Hera (29–30), a tough little miss who once pulled out the hair on the chest of one of the Cyclops.

Theocritus' twenty-fourth Idyll, which is meant to be a heroic narrative of baby Hercules' vanquishing snakes in his crib, is hilarious and homely in the description of Amphitryon. He is awakened by Alkmene, rushes to the children's room, sees that Hercules is in fact not hurt, then like any good, working father whose wife and children have roused him for nothing out of his sleep, "back he went to his bed; he concentrated on sleep [63]."

Callimachus is particularly adept at establishing a scene or a mood in a few lines, as he does in the Hymn to Artemis. It is an Alexandrian cast of mind to concentrate upon a detail, a feature, to bring it out until it is transformed. The Hymn to Artemis is relatively long, mostly concerned with the adult goddess; so the tender scene at the start, by emphasizing the childishness of young Artemis, becomes the traditional hymnal description of the birth of the god. The Alexandrian analysis of literature broke it down into its components, gave these components freedom or independent existence. The Alexandrians were then free to translate any components into something else, as we have noticed Callimachus doing. Theocritus is doing the same sort of thing when he creates a dialect for some of his Idylls that is Doric but yet made up of words and forms drawn from a variety of dialects within Doric, producing therefore an artificial language not to be spoken by anyone. Presumably in any case, Theocritus spoke the Alexandrian *koine* and wrote it as well. Doric was an artifice like the present-day sung dialect of country & western or rhythm and blues.

Theocritus' first Idyll betrays the same self-conscious use of parts to create an unanticipated whole. Thyrsis meets a goatherd who promises him an elegant cup among other things if he will sing a song of Daphnis. Thyrsis agrees, sings the song, the cup is handed over, all in a neat 152 lines. The Daphnis song (64–145) is eighty lines; the goatherd makes his offer (15–63) in forty-eight, of which thirty-three describe the cup (27–60). Theocritus has made a poem that is a diptych. The description of the cup balances in several ways the Daphnis song. First, the description is far more complex . . . verbally and imagistically more intriguing. The cup is *worthy* of the song. The description, a piece of *ekphrasis*, of which the ancients were exceedingly fond, is as poetry, as verbal technique, the equal of the Daphnis song, which is much simpler verbally, among other things having a refrain, the whole being a kind of easy mood chant. Then the images on the cup elucidate the prevailing emotion of the Daphnis song. Daphnis is dying in love, but he denies himself out of conviction, and so he dies. In the song, he bids good-bye to the landscape, the wild animals, love. The mood is one of yearning and the cup reinforces this. It has three scenes: a girl set between two courting suitors; an old man angling for fish; and a young boy fashioning a cricket cage beset by two foxes, one after grapes, the other after the lunch in his rucksack. Each of the scenes has to do with appetite, with seeking. The sense is that yearning is a constant in every age of man, also common to the wild animals. Even the goatherd wants the song, and Theocritus has made the cup so beautiful that we and Thyrsis yearn for it. Theocritus has ignored the classical age's sense of proportion. He has taken the relatively smaller acccount of the cup, structurally less significant than the Daphnis song, and by the richness of his description made it the focus from which emanates the sense that guides us in understanding the poem as a whole.

Likewise, the Alexandrians had a marvelous gift of humanizing description. Herodas is a case in point. They could evoke personalities because they believed in human personality, something one does not get a sense of in the classical, more austere and impersonal period. Two passages stand out in Callimachus. In the Hymn to Delos (217ff.), a messenger brings the ever jealous Hera news that the island of Delos has given Leto (pregnant by Zeus) asylum, so that she can deliver her baby. The deferential nervousness and fear in the panting (as Callimachus notes) messenger's voice, bearer of ill tidings, is very well caught. The portrait closes with the comparison of the messenger to a hunting hound ever on the ready, repeating the tension and the subservience that were in the messenger's speech. In the "Bath of Pallas," Athena puts out Tiresias' eyes because the lad has seen her nude at her bath. Her best friend is Tiresias' mother, Chariclo, and the poet emphasizes this (57–67) relationship so that when the goddess has blinded the youth, the poet can turn to the interesting reaction of Chariclo to her erstwhile friend's ugly gesture and Athena's subsequent response to Chariclo. Here again the Alexandrian sensibility shows through. The

great female goddess, the youthful male's sexual advances
(in this myth translated to an innocent glance), his destruction (here simply blindness) are commonplaces of a myth
type (see p. 187); and it is the kind of myth that traditionally
stands in such a hymn as this. But Callimachus' narrative is
really about two friends whose friendship is destroyed.

The best of the hymns is to Demeter (VI). Again, a mythical element is given very different perspectives. Erysichthon
cuts down a tree sacred to Demeter and is punished. This is
still another variant of the story of the great female goddess
and the young male who is destroyed. But Callimachus has
another purpose. The story is told of Erysichthon's impious
act and Demeter punishes him by causing him to suffer hunger without relief. The hymn has begun with reference to the
sacred basket and to Demeter's sad search for her daughter,
her refusal to eat and drink. Full belly, empty belly. Erysichthon begins to eat and eat and eat. What could be a
horror story is immensely funny. Callimachus describes (66ff.)
the mother making excuses for her son's disappearance while
he is in the back room gorging, then the cooks and butcher
saying no, everything being cooked, even the cat:

But the mules too they led out from the wagons;
and he ate the cow, which his mother was saving for sacrifice;
he ate the race horse, and the war horse,
even the cat before whom the mice used to tremble.

(107–10)

The worship of Demeter derives from the legitimate fear
of earlier centuries that there would be famine. The hymn is
Callimachus' ironic portrait of that fear, its psychological
essence, compulsive eating. And it is very comic.

Earlier in this chapter, Apollonius' *Argonautica* was singled
out as the best expression of the age. But there is another
work far more memorable, if only because it is shorter, but
more memorable too because it falls more sympathetically
into the human dimension. It is Theocritus' fifteenth Idyll
and most of all memorable because it is completely em-
blematic of the Alexandrian Age. It is essentially a mime,
the story of two rather vulgar, simple women off to see an
exposition at the palace. The women, their vulgarity, especially their attempts at politesse, the sympathy of the poet,
the easy mime dialogue, the contrived Doric dialect, the

sense of urban crowding, the great attention to detail (e.g. the man who tries to silence them) and finally the elegant, ornate, pedantic, overdone, heavy Adonis song which is their goal have all the Alexandrian sensibilities. The depiction of these two women, Sicilian emigrees in Alexandria, trying at gentility, sentimental, pushing along in the throng, aiming at culture, erudition and splendor which is dispensed to them from on high, is in fact an extraordinary portrait of the society of Alexandria in relation to the Library. The self-consciousness of the women is a reminder of the age, which is why one can probably best describe Hellenistic poetry, or at least Alexandrian poetry, as poetry of criticism. The women of the *Idylls* stand to the age as heroic portraits in the *Iliad* do or as the figures in tragedy do.

> The two speakers are Gorgo and Praxinoa. Eunoa, Phrygia and Eutyches are slaves.
>
> G: Praxinoa home?
>
> P: Gorgo, dear! It's been so long. I am at home. Amazing that even now you could come. Eunoa, get a chair, put a cushion on it.
>
> G: Very nice.
>
> P: Sit down.
>
> G: What a silly I am! Hardly made it with my life,
> 5   Praxinoa; huge crowd, so many carriages, everywhere soldiers' boots, men in cloaks, everywhere. And this road! Goes on forever. You live farther and farther away.
>
> P: That's my reckless man. At the ends of the earth he takes a shack, not a house, so we don't have any neighbors,
> 10   just to be nasty, the mean bastard, oh, always the same.
>
> G: Don't talk about your man, Dino, that way with the little kid here. See how she's staring at you. Cheer up, Zopyrious, sweet child; she doesn't mean Papa.
>
> P: Good Lord, the child understands.
>
> G: Pretty Papa!
>
> 15 P: Well, that Papa, couple of days ago, yes, a day or so ago, I said "Papa, buy me some soda and some rouge at the market." So he comes back with salt, him a great hulk of a man!

G: Same with mine. No sense of money, that Diokleidas. What does he get yesterday with seven drachs?
20   Five fleeces—real dog hair! lint pickings from old
wallets! dirt, nothing but work. But, come on, put
on your dress and get your stole. Let's go to the
house of our rich king Ptolemy to see the Adonis.
I hear it's really something that the Queen's putting
on.

P: To the rich belong the riches.

25   G: When you've seen this you'll have something to tell
those who haven't. Time to get going.

P: It's always festival for those
who don't work. Eunoa, get a move on! Pick up
that spinning lazy dog. Just try that again. Cats
like soft beds. Move! Hurry! Get some water. Oh,
I ask for water, she brings soap. Never mind, give
30   it here. Not so much, idiot. Now the water. Oh,
you slob, why spill on my dress? Oh, stop. Well,
I'm as washed as the gods will allow. The key,
where's the key to the big chest? Fetch it here.

G: Praxinoa, my, that long gown goes very well on
35   you. Tell me, how much did it come to right off
the loom?

P: Don't remind me, Gorgo. I laid out more than two
minas of silver; and I put my whole life into
making it.

G: Your plan certainly worked, you'll have to admit
that.

P: Bring me my stole and my hat, set it on right! No,
40   child, I'm not taking you. Cry all you want, but
it's not good getting you hurt. Let's go. Phrygia,
take the kid and play with him. Call the dog in,
lock the front door. My God, what a crowd. How'll
we get through this mess . . . and when? Like
45   ants beyond number, zillions! You've done many
good things, Ptolemy, since your father died; no
criminal sneaks up behind, the way Egyptians do,
to hurt you, oh, the games they used to play, made
50   of cheating, all alike, lousy tricks, to hell with them
all. Sweet Gorgo! What'll happen to us? The king's
cavalry! Dear fellow, don't run me over! That
chestnut horse reared. Look how wild he is. Eunoa,
you crazy, get out of the way! He'll do in the

55 man leading him. Thank God, the baby's at home.
G: Cheer up, Praxinoa, look, we're behind them now;
they've gone.
P: Well, I'm pulled together. Horses and
cold snakes, I've been afraid of them since I was
a child. Let's hurry; the crowd is overrunning us.
60 G: Did you come from the palace, mother?
OLD LADY: Yes, child.
G: Easy
to get in?
OL: The Greeks got into Troy by trying, you
pretty things. Everything succeeds through trying.
G: Now she's said her oracle off the old lady goes.
P: Women know everything, even how Zeus took
Hera.
65 G: Praxinoa, look what a crowd is at the doors.
P: Incredible! Gorgo, give me your hand; Eunoa,
take Eutyches' hand; don't get separated from her.
We'll all go in together. Stay close, Eunoa. Good
grief! My stole is already ripped in two. For the
70 love of god, sir, if you don't want trouble, watch
out for my stole.
MAN: Okay, I'll try, but it's not my fault.
A real crowd, all-
right, pushing like pigs.
M: Cheer up, lady, we're okay.
P: Well, dear sir, I hope you'll stay okay right on for
75 guarding us so. Nice, thoughtful guy. Our Eunoa's
getting squashed. Come on, you poor thing, push.
Fine. "All inside," said the man who locked up the
bride.
G: Praxinoa, come here. Take a look at the hangings
first. How delicate, how beautiful; you'd think they
were for the gods.
80 P: By Athena, imagine the weavers who worked on
these! What artists, to draw everything so accurate.
They stand like they're real, they whirl around like
real living beings, not woven figures. Mankind is
so smart! And himself, thrice-loved Adonis, loved
right up to shores of Acheron, how marvelous he
85 is in his silver chair with the first down spreading
over his cheeks.

ANOTHER Will you damn women shut up, chattering like that
MAN: on and on; doves, that's what. Wears you down,
that broad accent all the time.

P: Well, who is he? What's it to him, if we chatter?
90   Get your own slaves to order about. We're Syra-
cusans you're trying to order. As you can see,
Corinthians by descent, just like Bellerophon. We
talk Peloponnesian dialect. I imagine it's allowed
for Dorians to speak Dorian. O Persephone, may
there never be more than one master over me. You
95   don't bother me. Don't waste your time.

G: Shush, Praxinoa. The Argive woman's daughter is
about to sing the Adonis song; she's that clever
singer, the one who sang the lament last year with
such success. There, she's clearing her throat. I
just know she'll sing something beautiful.
(There follow forty-five lines of an elegant song in
the Hellenistic style, sensuous, allusive, pastoral
and erotic, describing the death of Adonis.)

145   G: Praxinoa, that woman is the smartest thing! Lucky
to know all that, twice lucky to have a voice like
honey. Well, time to go home. Diokleidas hasn't
eaten. He's all nasty, you can't go near him when
he's hungry. Goody-bye, Adonis, lovely, lovable;
bring us luck when you come again.

FURTHER READING

Ancient Greek literature became the object of scholarly pursuit from the time of the establishment of the Library at Alexandria in the early third century. Probably more has been written on this subject than any other. It became a science in nineteenth-century Germany; see W. Jaeger's description of Berlin in the 1920s and '30s *Five Essays* (Montreal: Casalini, 1960). The interest remains high, as the surveys of contemporary scholarship published annually in the journal *Lustrum* reveal. Nevertheless random reading in the books and articles cited by *Lustrum* will suggest that to a large extent the scholarship has become an end in itself. The discipline needs perhaps a moratorium on most publications. When what has been researched becomes digested more thoroughly the professionals may better ascertain the fundamental trends and goals of the study. (See my, "Impressions on the Present State of Classical Studies," *The Philosophical Forum* [new series 1968], 207ff.) If it would amuse the reader to contemplate what a college classics course is read B. R. Rees, ed., *Classics: An outline for the intending student* (London: Routledge, 1970). What follows is a selection from the vast number of scholarly pieces on the subject of ancient Greek literature. The principles of selection are based upon the desire to acquaint the non-specialist with some interesting and relatively easy accessible items that will at first illuminate the subject and then help in showing the way to further study. Hence the items are generally in the English language, most often from American journals if articles, relatively general in approach, recent, with bibliographies that direct the reader back, thought-provoking and not necessarily in agreement with the ideas advanced within this book.

Above all else, the reader should locate The Oxford Classical Dictionary, second edition, (Oxford: Oxford University

Press* 1970), a superb reference that belongs, as they say, in every home. It is interesting, well written and has good bibliographies. For those who would like a brief statement of how the pieces of ancient literature survived to our time, L. D. Reynolds and N. G. Wilson, *Scribes and Scholars,* second edition (Oxford: Oxford University Press, 1974) is the best account.

The reader may wish a complete survey of ancient Greek literature. H. J. Rose, *A Handbook of Greek Literature,* third edition (London Methuen, 1948), is a crisp, unadorned and uninteresting survey with all the facts but peculiar emphases (for example, only brief remarks on Herodotus). A. Lesky, *A History of Greek Literature,* second edition (London: Methuen, 1966), translated from the German, is more thoughtful, more aware of the social context and just as thorough. W. Jaeger, *Paideia* (New York: Oxford University Press, 1945), volume 1, is an account of the transmission of Greek culture through the literature, a kind of history of ideas of the eighth through the fifth centuries, treating the same authors with whom this book deals. For the reader of French A. and M. Croiset, *Histoire de la littérature grecque,* second edition (Paris: Fontemoing, 1913–47), five volumes, is infinitely superior to the books mentioned above, for although it is out of date in details it is far more humane, far more attuned to our own literary critical sensibilities. For the reader of German U. Wilamowitz Moellendorf, *Die griechische Literatur des Altertums,* third edition (Leipzig-Berlin, 1912), is filled with fascinating insights, the result of a profound penetration of the subject by a man generally considered to be the finest product of the German philological tradition. It is continually amazing that nothing written by this truly titanic classicist has ever been translated into English except his memoirs. Since his style is as elusive as a Delphic oracular response very few classicists have any real access to him.

As I said, classical scholarship was and is a considerable industry. The history of it from its beginnings to the end of the Hellenistic Age has been brilliantly treated in R. Pfeiffer, *History of Classical Scholarship* (Oxford: Oxford University Press, 1968). J. E. Sandys, *A History of Classical Scholarship* (reprinted New York: Hafner, 1958), three volumes, is

* I have in every instance written Oxford University Press for Clarendon Press.

a dull but useful survey of the subject from the beginning through the nineteenth century. Both can be supplemented by J. W. H. Atkins, *Literary Criticism in Antiquity* (London: Methuen, 1952), two volumes. Sandys' work is much improved if read in conjunction with the useful G. Highet *The Classical Tradition* (New York: Oxford, 1957, paperback), a survey of the influences of classical literature upon Western European authors.

Most readers probably would not care to consider the scholarship prior to this century. Maurice Platnauer, ed., *Fifty Years (and Twelve) of Classical Scholarship,* revised with appendices, second edition (Oxford: Blackwell, 1968), contains some very stimulating essays on more recent scholarly trends and achievements in the study of various ancient authors. The journal *Lustrum,* published from Göttingen, appears annually with superb review articles on the scholarship of various authors. Those relevant to this book are:

Aristophanes: volume 2 (1957), pp. 52–112

Euripides: volume 13 (1968), pp. 289–405

Greek Archaeology and Literature: volume 1 (1956), pp. 87–120; volume 6 (1961), pp. 5–37; volume 11 (1966), pp. 5–32; volume 15 (1970), pp. 5–36

Herodotus: volume 11 (1966), pp. 71–138

Homer: volume 1 (1956), pp. 7–86; volume 2 (1957), pp. 294–97; volume 11 (1966), pp. 33–70; volume 15 (1970), pp. 99–122

Menander: volume 10 (1965), pp. 5–212; volume 11 (1966), pp. 139–44; volume 13 (1968), pp. 535–71; volume 16 (1971–72), pp. 5–80

Sophocles: volume 7 (1962), pp. 94–288

The Classical World, a publication of the Classical Association of the Atlantic States, publishes excellent surveys of scholarship. An index to these is contained in volume 67, number 4 (February 1974), pp. 221–24.

Most important of all is the annual French publication, *L'année philologique* (Société d'Édition "Les Belles Lettres"), begun by a man named Jules Marouzeau and continued by a woman named Juliette Ernst. Each volume is a listing of every article and book in every tongue relating to any and every part of antiquity. It is overwhelming. With the titles of books are listed the reviews; titles of articles are followed by a précis. In the last five years most English-language articles have an English-language précis. *L'année philologique* is fun to browse through. The arrangement is obvious even to those who do not know French.

Among American journals *Arethusa, Arion, Classical Journal* and *Greek, Roman and Byzantine Studies* are freest of pedantry and generally interesting, sometimes valuable. Classicists as a group are trained as philologists first, historians second, rarely as literary critics. The problem this training produces can be seen in varying degrees in C. P. Segal, "'Ancient Texts and Modern Literary Criticism," *Arethusa*, volume 1 (1968), pp. 1–25; R. Sonkowsky, "Scholarship and Showmanship," *Arion*, volume 1 (1962), pp. 102–7; H. D. F. Kitto, *Poesis: Structure and Thought* (Berkeley: University of California Press, 1967), who demands a criticism based on historical awareness; P. Green, *The Shadow of the Parthenon: Studies in ancient history and literature* (Berkeley: University of California Press, 1972); M. Thorton and A. A. Lund, *Time and Style. A psycholinguistic essay in classical literature* (London, 1962). The classicist who thoroughly understands modern literary criticism is quite rare. William Arrowsmith is perhaps the best example; although he has written little, it is always stimulating, especially the individual introductions to his translations in *The Complete Greek Tragedies*, edited D. Grene and R. Lattimore (Chicago: Chicago University Press, 1959–60).

I began this book by remarking on the Greek language. It can be learned rather easily and at home by following F. K. Smith and T. W. Melluish, *Teach Yourself Greek* (London: English Universities Press Ltd.). Then when one has mastered the language he or she must get the Loeb Classical Library translations of the ancient Greek authors (published by Harvard University Press). These have the Greek text on one side, the English translation on the other. The translations are at best grotesque, at worst incomprehensible, yet if one compares the Greek and the English and asks why the translator says what he says eventually a rather good knowledge of the literary language will develop. Try Arrian's *History of Alexander,* Euripides' *Alcestis* or Plato's *Crito* for starters, then go on to Homer and Herodotus. B. F. C. Atkinson, *The Greek Language* (London: Faber & Faber, 1931), is a dull survey of the language that may help. G. E. R. Lloyd, *Polarity and Analogy* (Cambridge: Cambridge University Press, 1961) contains important observations on antithesis in the Greek language and the importance of opposites in early Greek philosophy. W. B. Stanford's *The Sound of Greek* (Berkeley: University of California Press, 1967), is very hypothetical yet instructive and contains a small recording of Professor Stanford's beautifully musical Irish voice reading some Greek poetry. If Greek did not sound like that it ought to have.

A decent knowledge of history goes hand in hand with studying the literature. The Cambridge Ancient History (Cambridge: Cambridge University Press) in its several volumes is authoritative. There is also J. B. Bury's *A History of Greece,* third edition revised (London: Macmillan, 1951), and N. G. L. Hammond, *A History of Greece* (Oxford: Oxford University Press, 1959). Best of all, even if much outdated in detail, is the many-volumed nineteenth-century *History of Greece* by George Grote, whose judgments and insights cannot be surpassed.

The survey that follows adheres as much as possible to the scheme of the chapters of the book.

HOMER AND THE HEROIC AGE

I have discussed Homeric scholarship in the final chapter of my *The Iliad, the Odyssey and the Epic Tradition* (Garden City, N.Y.: Doubleday, 1966 [now published by Peter Smith, Gloucester, Massachusetts]). Pages 111–205 of that book contain various critical remarks on the *Iliad* and the *Odyssey.* Some of the material of this chapter is contained in my "Male and Female in the Homeric Poems," *Ramus,* volume 3 (1974), pp. 87–101. The single best background book on the Homeric poems, however, is P. Mazon, P. Chantraine, P. Collart, R. Langumier, *Introduction a l'Iliade* (Paris: Société d'Édition "Les Belles Lettres," 1943), for it has a survey of all the problems of these two poems which confront the scholars. As I remarked in the book on Homer Milman Parry's theory of oral composition, which dominates Homeric scholarship, has become an orthodoxy culminating in such pieces as A. B. Lord's *The Singer of Tales* (Cambridge: Harvard University Press, 1960). Lord fittingly enough was Parry's student and protégé. See also J. A. Notopoulos, "Studies in Early Greek Oral Poetry," *Harvard Studies in Classical Philology,* volume 68 (1964), pp. 1–77. Orthodoxies produce revisionists. A principal one—and fittingly Oedipal—is Parry's son, the late Adam Parry. *The Making of Homeric Verse,*

The Collected Papers of Milman Parry, edited by Adam Parry (Oxford: Oxford University Press, 1971), has a superb essay by Adam (pp. i–lxii) on his father's theory, its strengths and frailties. An equally important essay is A. Parry, "Have We Homer's Iliad?" *Yale Classical Studies,* volume 20 (1966), p. 177–216. G. S. Kirk, *The Songs of Homer* (Cambridge: Cambridge University Press, 1962), pp. 55–101, is a lucid examination of the problem whether such complicated, integrated, strikingly individual poems can be the product of a tradition. Nowadays one imagines a specific Homer whose impress upon the poems is unmistakable. This leads to works like P. Vivante, *The Homeric Imagination* (Bloomington: Indiana University Press, 1970), a work with which I have little sympathy (see my review in *The American Journal of Philology,* volume 95 [1974]), for Vivante proceeds to discuss the poems as though in every detail they betray the thoughtful intent of a single poet, as though the *Iliad* and *Odyssey* were equivalent to *Paradise Lost, Remembrance of Things Past* or indeed a longish lyric poem. Milman Parry made the oral theory too rigid, its poetics too mechanical. Certainly the *Iliad* and the *Odyssey* are not "routines" but nonetheless they *are* conventional, clichéd and traditional. A. B. Lord answers the revisionists in "Homer as Oral Poet," *Harvard Studies in Classical Philology,* volume 72 (1967), pp. 1–46. D. Young, "Never Blotted a Line? Formula and Premeditation in Homer and Hesiod," *Arion,* volume 6 (1967), pp. 279–324, is useful. G. S. Kirk, ed. *The Language and Background of Homer* (Cambridge: Heffer, 1964), is a collection of typical scholarly essays on Homer that illuminates the perimeters and potentials of the field. A similar collection is C. H. Taylor, ed., *Essays on the Odyssey, Selected Modern Criticism* (Bloomington: Indiana University Press, 1963). See also J. N. H. Austin, "The Function of Digression in the *Iliad,*" *Greek, Roman and Byzantine Studies,* volume 7 (1966), pp. 295–312; S. Bernadette, "The Aristeia of Diomedes and the Plot of the *Iliad,*" *Agon,* volume 1 (1968), pp. 10–38; "Achilles and the *Iliad,*" *Hermes,* volume 91 (1963), pp. 1–16; H. W. Clarke, "Telemachus and the Telemacheia," *American Journal of Philology,* volume 84 (1963), pp. 129–45; J. A. Russo, "Homer Against his Tradition," *Arion,* volume 7 (1968), pp. 275–95; C. P. Segal, "The Phaecians and the Symbolism of Odysseus' Return," Arion, volume 1 (1962), pp. 17–64; C. H. Taylor,

"The Obstacles to Odysseus' Return. Identity and consciousness," *Yale Review,* volume 50 (1961), pp. 569–80; J. A. Russo, "The Structural Formula in Homeric Verse," *Yale Classical Studies,* volume 20 (1966), pp. 219–40; J. A. Russo and B. Simon, "Homeric Psychology and the Oral Epic Tradition," *Journal of the History of Ideas,* volume 29 (1968), pp. 483–98; C. S. Littleton, "Some Possible Indo-European Themes in the *Iliad,*" in *Myth and Law Among the Indo-Europeans,* J. Puhvel, ed., (Berkeley: University of California Press, 1970). See also M. Nagler, *Spontaneity and Tradition: A Study in the Oral Art of Homer* (Berkeley: University of California Press, 1972); N. Austin, *Archery at the Dark of the Moon: Poetic Problems in the Odyssey* (Berkeley: University of California Press, 1975).

E. Vermeule, *Greece in the Bronze Age* (Chicago: University of Chicago Press, 1964), and H. L. Lorimer, *Homer and the Monuments* (London: Macmillan, 1950), and A. J. B. Wace and F. H. Stubbings, eds., *A Companion to Homer* (London: Macmillan, 1963), give the vast array of historical fact known about the so-called Heroic Age, which H. M. Chadwick tries to describe in *The Heroic Age* (Cambridge: Cambridge University Press reprint, 1967) by comparing Greek and Teutonic epics. M. I. Finley, *The World of Odysseus* (New York: Viking, 1965), is an attempt to isolate the historical realities in the Homeric narrative. H. V. Routh, *God, Man and Epic Poetry,* volume 1 (Cambridge: Cambridge University Press, 1927), has, among other things, a provocative offbeat account of the mood of that period as seen through the *Iliad* and the *Odyssey.* W. Jaeger, *Paideia,* volume 1, second edition (New York: Oxford University Press, 1945), pp. 3–56, is an enduring discussion of the aristocratic outlook of the Homeric epics.

HESIOD, THE LYRIC POETS AND THE ARCHAIC AGE

B. A. van Gronigen, *La Composition littéraire archaïque grecque* (Amsterdam, 1958), is fundamental to the subject of this chapter. A. R. Burn, *The Lyric Age of Greece* (London: St. Martins Press, 1960), is a handy detailed history as is M. I. Finley, *Early Greece: The Bronze and the Archaic Ages* (New York: Norton, 1970). P. N. Ure, *The Origin of Tyranny* (Cambridge: Cambridge University Press,

1922), and A. Andrews, *The Greek Tyrants* (New York: Harper, 1963), are expositions of the most important political fact of the seventh and sixth centuries.

Much of my discussion of the *Works and Days* comes from my essay "The Rhythm of Hesiod's *Works and Days,*" *Harvard Studies in Classical Philology,* volume 76 (1972), pp. 23–43. Hesiod is generally studied from three aspects: 1) his relationship to second-millennium literature of the Near East; 2) his role in the origins of Greek philosophical speculation; and 3) his linguistic and stylistic relationship to the Homeric poems. For 1) the best account is P. Walcot, *Hesiod and the Near East* (Cardiff: Wales University Press, 1966); also helpful are T. B. L. Webster, *From Mycenae to Homer* (London: Methuen, 1958), and C. H. Gordon, *The Common Background of Greek and Hebrew Civilizations* (New York: Norton, 1962). For 2) see F. Solmsen, *Hesiod and Aeschylus* (Ithaca: Cornell University Press, 1949); F. Teggart, "The Argument of Hesiod's *Works and Days,*" *Journal of the History of Ideas,* volume 8 (1947), pp. 45–77; E. A. Havelock, "Thoughtful Hesiod," *Yale Classical Studies,* volume 20 (1966), pp. 59–72. Professor Havelock's *Preface to Plato* (Cambridge: Harvard University Press, 1963), especially pp. 36–196, should be read in this connection. *Preface to Plato* is one of the truly brilliant, original books; it deals with the changes in the psychology of communication and ratiocination as the Greeks went from an oral to a literate culture. It is also the most intelligent accounting for Plato's hostility to the poets. See also E. A. Havelock, "Pre-literacy and the Pre-Socratics," *Bulletin Institute Classical Studies,* volume 13 (1966), pp. 44–67; D. J. Stewart, "Hesiod and the Birth of Reason," *Antioch Review,* volume 26 (1966), pp. 213–31. The great danger in studying Hesiod's contributions to Greek philosophical thinking is to imagine him as an intellectual. Poetry is not the medium for an intellectual. Even if he must use poetry because there is no other developed verbal medium at hand he ceases to be an intellectual when he becomes a poet. J. Burnet, *Early Greek Philosophy,* fourth edition (London: Black, 1930), gives the translated texts of the philosophers and a discussion of the major figures. There is a very curious book, E. Vandvik, *The Prometheus of Hesiod and Aeschylus* (Oslo: Dybwad, 1943), which makes Hesiod into a kind of Christian moralist. For 3) see T. G. Rosenmeyer, "The Formula in Early Greek Poetry," *Arion,* volume 4 (1965), pp. 295–311; C. Angier, "Verbal Patterns in Hesiod's *Theogony*," *Harvard Studies in Classical Philology*, volume 68 (1964), pp. 329–44; M. S. Jensen, "Tradition and Individuality in Hesiod's *Works and Days*," *Classica et Mediaevalia*, volume 27 (1966), pp. 1–27; B. Peabody, *The Winged Word. A Study in the Technique of Ancient Oral Composition as Seen in Hesiod's "Works and Days*," (Albany: SUNY Press, 1975); C. P. Edwards, *The Language of Hesiod in Its Traditional Context* (Oxford: Oxford University Press, 1971). See also W. Sale, "The Dual Vision of the *Theogony*," *Arion*, volume 4 (1965), pp. 668–99; S. Bernadette, "Hesiod's *Works and Days*. A first reading," *Agon*, volume 1 (1967), pp. 150–74; T. Feldman, "Personification and Structure in Hesiod's *Theogony*," *Symbolae Osloenses*, volume 46 (1971), pp. 7–41. Another important study of the history of thought relevant to this period is B. Snell, *The Discovery of the Mind* (Cambridge: Harvard University Press, 1953), pp. 1–89, 136–52.

The Homeric Hymns chiefly engross scholars who would like to know how far these poems are oral, that is, their relationship to the technique and aesthetic that the Homeric poems suppose. See M. L. Lord, "Withdrawal and Return. An epic story pattern in the Homeric Hymns to Demeter and in the Homeric poems," *Classical Journal*, volume 62 (1967), pp. 241–48.

Hesiod is certainly better known to us as a historical figure than is Homer. The other poets of these centuries are very shadowy figures; their poetry survives only in fragments except for the relatively large corpus of Pindar's poems. It is hard to say anything sensible about the poems or the poets. C. M. Dawson, *"Spoudaiogeloion:* Random Thoughts on Occasional Poems," *Yale Classical Studies*, volume 19 (1966), pp. 37–76, emphasizes the Homeric and Hesiodic allusions and adaptations, drawing examples from most of the poets of the period. This seems to me the best if perhaps almost the only possible critical approach. The standard discussions are C. M. Bowra, *Greek Lyric Poetry*, second edition (Oxford: Oxford University Press, 1961), and *Early Greek Elegists* (Cambridge: Heffer, 1960). Bowra has collected every last tidbit of information and he uses the poems as possible proofs of biographical fact. The whole, however, is not at all criticism; see M. S. Silk, *Interaction in Poetic Imagery* (Cambridge: Cambridge University Press,

1974), a brilliant critical study of the lyric poets. N. Rudd, "The Style and the Man," *Phoenix,* volume 18 (1964), pp. 216–31, is also interesting, as well as D. L. Page, "Archilochus and the Oral Tradition," in *Archiloque: Entretiens sur l'antiquité classique,* volume 10 (Genève: Fondation Hardt, 1964), pp. 117–79; J. A. Notopoulos, "Archilochus the *aoidos,*" *Transactions and Proceedings of the American Philological Association,* volume 97 (1966), pp. 311–15; A. J. Podlecki, "Three Greek Soldier Poets: Archilochus, Alcaeus and Solon," *Classical World,* volume 63 (1969), pp. 73–81; W. Jaeger, "Solon's Eunomia" and "Tyrtaeus on True Arete," in *Five Essays* (Montreal: Casalini, 1966).

In addition to the van Gronigen book cited earlier, there is now G. M. Kirkwood, *Early Greek Monody. The History of a Poetic Type* (Ithaca, 1973), with literary interpretations of Archilochus, Alcaeus, Sappho and Anacreon. Sappho's poetry survives in merest fragments apart from the two larger pieces quoted here in the text. The newly discovered fragments measurably detract from our estimation of her poetic abilities. Nonetheless Sappho has always enjoyed great celebrity (see, however, M. R. Lefkowitz, "Critical Stereotypes and the Poetry of Sappho," *Greek, Roman and Byzantine Studies,* volume 14 [1974], pp. 113–23) as a figure of either mysterious beauty or strange perversion. One thinks of the plays and novels, for instance P. Green, *The Laughter of Aphrodite* (1965); A. Krisler, *No Man Sings* (1956); M. Holland, *Sappho, a drama in verse* (1948); L. Durrell, *Sappho, a play in verse* (1958); not to mention Grillparzer's nineteenth-century play *Sappho* and von Kleist's eighteenth-century version. The extremes may well be *Sappho, a tragedy in five acts,* by Stella (a pseudonymn for Mrs. Estelle Anna Blanche Robinson Lewis) (London, 1875), and *Sappho Was a Right-on Woman; A Liberated View of Lesbianism,* by S. Abbott and B. Love (New York: Stein & Day, 1972).

The choral poets are better known and there is far more written on these. Their working conditions are hypothesized by S. Gzella, "The Competition Among the Greek Choral Poets," *Eos,* volume 58 (1969–70), pp. 19–32. For Bacchylides see D. S. Carne Ross, "The Gaiety of Language," *Arion,* volume 1 (1962), pp. 65–88; G. M. Kirkwood, "The Narrative Art of Bacchylides," pp. 98–114 in *The Classical Tradition. Literary and historical studies in honor of Harry Caplan* (Ithaca: Cornell University Press, 1966). C. P. Segal,

"Croesus on the Pyre. Herodotus and Bacchylides," *Wiener Studien,* new series, volume 5 (1971), pp. 39–51, is a comparison of two narrations of the same event pointing up essential differences in interpretation which shows among other things Herodotus' affinities for tragedy.

Since I do not appreciate Pindar's poetry I probably cannot evaluate the criticism of Pindar very well either. J. H. Finley, *Pindar and Aeschylus* (Cambridge: Harvard University Press, 1955), seems to me vague and muddy, showing the influence of Pindar's vagueness upon Professor Finley, who is elsewhere strong and lucid. See his superior "Pindar's Beginnings," an analysis of Pindar's debt to Theognis and Simonides, in D. C. Allen and H. T. Rowell, eds., *The Poetic Tradition* (Baltimore: Johns Hopkins Press, 1968). Pindar often seems to be making veiled topical references. The topicality is examined in W. Mullen, "Pindar and Athens: A Reading in the Aeginetan Odes," *Arion,* new series, volume 1 (1973–74), pp. 446–95; see also W. Mullen, "Place in Pindar," *Arion,* volume 6 (1967), pp. 462–91. C. G. Starr, "Pindar and the Greek Historical Spirit," *Hermes,* volume 45 (1967), pp. 393–403, relates Pindar to Herodotus. E. L. Bundy, *Studia Pindarica* I–II (*University of California Publications in Classical Philology,* volume 18, 1 and 2 [Berkeley, 1962]), is the best study of Pindar's poetry showing how the so-called topical allusions work within the poem. C. A. P. Ruck and W. H. Matheson, *Pindar: Selected Odes* (Ann Arbor: University of Michigan Press, 1968), is an important book. The interpretive essays feature musical composition as an experience analogous to the Pindaric ode. This idea is very suggestive for it accounts for the peculiar lack of thought continuity or connection in Pindar's odes, as though the language were there to serve other structures, volumes and tonalities—language as texture rather than as semantic or significant. C. M. Bowra, *Pindar* (Oxford: Oxford University Press, 1964), is the standard work, which, however, tends toward literal meanings, historical readings. D. C. Young has some excellent readings of Pindar in *Three Odes of Pindar, Mnemosyne,* Supplement 9 (Leiden: Brill, 1968), and *Pindar Isthmian 7 Myth and Exempla, Mnemosyne,* Supplement 15 (Leiden: Brill, 1971); earlier he brought out the excellent article "Pindaric Criticism," *Minnesota Review,* volume 4 (1964), pp. 584–641, which is reprinted in *Pindaros und Bakchylides,* Wege der Forschung series number 134 Darm-

stadt, 1970), pp. 1–95. See also J. Stern's discussion of
Nemean 5 in *Classical Philology*, volume 66 (1971), pp.
169–73. See also C. P. Segal, "Pindar's Seventh Nemean,"
*Transactions and Proceedings of the American Philological
Association*, volume 98 (1968), pp. 431–80; R. W. B.
Burton, *Pindar's Pythian Odes. Essays in interpretation*
(Oxford: Oxford University Press, 1962); M. A. Grant,
Folktale and Herotale Motifs in the Odes of Pindar (Law-
rence: University of Kansas Press, 1967), which locates
Pindar's work in the saga and oral traditions.

ATHENS IN THE FIFTH CENTURY

Apart from the standard histories mentioned earlier there
are such books as A. R. Burn, *Pericles and Athens* (New
York: Collier Books, 1949). A. Zimmern, *The Greek Com-
monwealth: Politics and Economics in Fifth-Century Athens*,
fifth edition revised (Oxford: Oxford University Press, 1931)
is still very useful. W. G. Forrest, *The Emergence of Greek
Democracy* (New York: World University Library, 1966),
is an excellent survey of the formation of Athens' *polis*.
Behind it lie C. Hignett, *A History of the Athenian Constitution* (Oxford: Oxford University Press, 1952), and J. W.
Headlam, *Election by Lot at Athens*, second edition (Cambridge: Cambridge University Press, 1933). The latter is
an amazingly clear-eyed analysis of the Athenian democracy.
It is an inspirational book as well, revealing a society of
men who deliberately sought to rid their group of any
outstanding person so as to destroy all bases of power
in order to achieve true egalitarianism. That it most likely
resulted in the collapse of Athens is immaterial. A free
society of that sort from time to time is worth the catastrophe
it produces. G. Gilbert, *The Constitutional Antiquities of
Sparta and Athens* (New York: Macmillan, 1895), is another
fun book to browse in for those who treasure strange laws
and interesting political arrangements. The book is somewhat outdated but contains most of what we know of the
governmental systems of Athens and Sparta. I. T. Hill,
*The Ancient City of Athens, Its Topography and Monu-
ments* (Cambridge: Harvard University Press, 1953), is the
definitive study of the physical city. C. G. Starr, *The Ancient
Greeks* (Oxford: Oxford University Press, 1971), is a good
account of the ordinary life.

W. K. Lacey, *The Family in Classical Greece* (London: Thames and Hudson, 1968), is a superb collection of the evidence. R. Lattimore, *Themes in Greek and Latin Epitaphs* (Urbana: University of Illinois Press, 1942), an exhaustive study of the sentiments found on tombstones generally from periods after the fifth century, is nevertheless instructive of family feelings. P. E. Slater, *The Glory of Hera. Greek Mythology and the Greek Family* (Boston: Beacon, 1968), is an excellent psychoanalytic study of certain attitudes and feelings in myth which are expressive of characteristic situations within the ancient Greek family.

Slater is an example of the relatively few thrusts of the social sciences into antiquity. Another—and brilliant too— is A. W. Gouldner, *Enter Plato: Classical Greece and the Origins of Social Theory* (New York: Basic Books, 1965, the first part of which has been made into a paperback entitled *The Hellenic World: A Sociological Analysis* (Harper Torchbook). This book must be read. It offers consistently valuable insights into the Greeks. To compare it with something like H. D. F. Kitto, *The Greeks* (Baltimore: Penguin, 1957), is to realize how far away from the mainstream of twentieth-century intellectual activity the discipline of the classics is. E. R. Dodds is one classicist who has tried to understand these newer disciplines. His *The Greeks and the Irrational* (Berkeley: University of California Press, 1951) is the result, more or less an anthropological investigation of what lies beneath or behind the celebrated rationalism that the Greeks seem to have imposed upon everything in their culture. This is a first-rate book that is basic to understanding the Greeks. Even the footnotes are fascinating. Light-years away from these, but still filled with facts and references, is H. Licht, *Sexual Life in Ancient Greece* (New York: Barnes & Noble reprint, 1952), a kind of coy nineteenth-century Kinsey Report of the subject.

The subject of Greek myth and religion is immense. M. P. Nilsson, *A History of Greek Religion*, second edition revised, New York: Norton paperback, 1952), is basic. Also W. K. C. Guthrie, *The Greeks and their Gods* (Boston: Beacon paperback, 1955); H. Lloyd Jones, *The Justice of Zeus* (Berkeley: University of California Press, 1971), a very useful survey; J. Harrison, *Prolegomena to the Study of Greek Religion*, third edition (New York: Meridian paperback, 1957); W. K. C. Guthrie, *Orpheus and Greek Religion* (New York: Norton paperback, 1966); W. C. Greene, *Moira: Fate, Good and Evil in Greek Thought* (Cambridge: Harvard paperback, 1944); F. M. Cornford, *From Religion to Philosophy* (New York: Harper, 1957); C. Kerényi, *Gods of the Greeks* (London: Thames and Hudson 1951), also his *Archetypal Images in Greek Religion* (Princeton: Princeton University Press, 1963); B. C. Dietrich, *Death, Fate and the Gods* (London: University of London Athlone Press, 1965); W. Otto, *Dionysus* (Bloomington: University of Indiana Press, 1965), a stimulating if manic book; H. W. Parke and D. E. W. Wormell, *The Delphic Oracle,* two volumes (Oxford: Blackwell, 1956); H. W. Parke, *The Oracles of Zeus* (Cambridge: Harvard University Press, 1967); J. Pollard, *Seers, Shrines, and Sirens* (London: Allen & Unwin, 1965).

Mythology, of course, is one expression often of religion and yet it is separate. The distinction is hard to draw and hard to maintain. The standard works are H. J. Rose, *A Handbook of Greek Mythology,* fourth edition (London: Methuen, 1950); R. Graves, *The Greek Myths* (Baltimore: Penguin, 1955). The former is exceedingly thorough, indicating every source and every variant, very necessary when one sets out to generalize. The latter tries to give an anthropological, sociological or psychological structure to the material. M. P. O. Morford and R. J. Lenardon, *Classical Mythology* (New York: McKay paperback, 1971), is good because there are numerous quotations of the myths in the literature as well as interesting remarks on their later transformations. But see also E. A. S. Butterworth, *The Tree at the Navel of the Earth; Some Traces of the Pre-Olympic World* (Berlin: de Gruyter, 1970) a discussion of the religious practice before the arrival of the Indo-Europeans, a good book until it begins to dissect the *Odyssey* too literally; J. Campbell, *The Hero with a Thousand Faces* (New York: Meridian paperback, 1956). *The Masks of God: Occidental Mythology* (New York: Viking, 1964), pp. 1–290, is an excellent comparativist's review of some of the main elements in Greek mythology. See also C. Kerényi, *The Heroes of the Greeks* (London: Thames and Hudson, 1959); L. R. Farnell, *Greek Hero-Cults and Ideas of Immortality* (Oxford: Oxford University Press, 1921). Recently G. S. Kirk, *Myth: Its Meaning and Function in Ancient and Other Cultures* (Berkeley: University of California Press, 1970), describes the structuralist movement and how it relates to ancient Greek mythology, thereby rendering it comparable to other myth systems. As the line over the review in the *TLS* said, the book is "Lévi-Strauss without tears."

G. Devereux, "Greek Pseudo-Homosexuality and the 'Greek Miracle,'" *Symbolae Osloenses*, volume 42 (1968), pp. 69–92, argues that Greek creativity is related to the prolonged adolescence that homosexuality affords. A curious but thoughtful book that relates both to the common practice of male homosexuality in Greece and to the religion is T. Vanggaard, *Phallos. A Symbol and Its History in the Male World* (London: International Universities Press, 1972). O. Brendel, "The Scope and Temperament of Erotic Art in the Greco-Roman World," pp. 3–108 of *Studies in Erotic Art*, T. Bowie and C. V. Christenson, eds. (New York: Basic Books, 1970), is an important review of one of the more common themes in ancient art.

H. I. Marrou, *A History of Education in Antiquity* (New York: Sheed & Ward, 1956), contains a brilliant, realistic, witty discussion of the extant evidence for educational practices, mostly in Athens. B. Snell, *The Discovery of the Mind* (Cambridge: Harvard University Press, 1953), is an excellent account of the growth of consciousness in Greek culture from Homer to the later more nationalist period. See also L. Versenyi, *Man's Measure: A Study of the Greek Image of Man from Homer to Sophocles* (Albany: SUNY Press, 1974).

The emergence of the Sophists is treated exhaustively in W. K. C. Guthrie, *A History of Greek Philosophy*, volume 3 (*The Fifth-Century Enlightenment*) (Cambridge: Cambridge University Press, 1969). The fragments of their sayings together with the flotsam and jetsam of bibliographical material that survives are to be found in K. Freeman, *The Pre-Socratic Philosophers*, third edition (Cambridge: Harvard University Press, 1966). Their place in Greek cultural history is defined by E. A. Havelock in *The Liberal Temper in Greek Politics* (New Haven: Yale University Press, 1957); the juices of his imagination sometimes move him to describe these men as British leftists of the '30s but the book is basically sound. J. H. Finley's "Euripides and Thucydides" and "The Origins of Thucydides' Style" are to be found in *Three Essays on Thucydides* (Cambridge: Harvard University Press, 1967). Both are sensitive, subtle analyses of Thucydides' language revealing his part in this intellectual movement; at the same time one gains an excellent impression of the language of what we really might call the Athenian avant-garde.

Athenian imperialism is the subject of R. Meiggs, *The Athenian Empire* (Oxford: Oxford University Press, 1972). D. Kagan, *The Outbreak of the Peloponnesian War* (Ithaca: Cornell University Press, 1969), is an excellent analysis of the reasons for the hostilities.

A good introduction to Sparta is the ancient Plutarch's *Life of Lycurgus.* Sparta was not only a reality in antiquity, it was also a myth and an ideology. See E. N. Tigerstedt, *Legend of Sparta in Classical Antiquity* (Stockholm: Almquist & Wiksell, 1965); E. Rawson, *The Spartan Tradition in European Thought* (Oxford: Oxford University Press, 1969). See also W. den Boer, *Laconian Studies* (Amsterdam: North-Holland Publishing, 1954); A. H. M. Jones, *Sparta* (Oxford: Blackwell, 1967).

HERODOTUS AND THUCYDIDES

R. G. Collingwood, *The Idea of History* (New York: Galaxy paperback, 1956), pp. 1–30, raises basic philosophical questions about the nature of early Greek historiography. J. B. Bury, *The Ancient Greek Historians* (New York: Dover paperback, 1958); M. Grant, *The Ancient Historians* (New York: Scribner's, 1970); and S. Usher, *The Historians of Greece and Rome* (London: Hamish Hamilton, 1969) place Herodotus and Thucydides in the tradition of ancient history writing. P. Walbank, "History and Tragedy," *Historia,* volume 9 (1960), pp. 216–34, discusses the relationship of epic, tragedy and history. See also A. Momigliano's essay on oral tradition and history, pp. 211–20 in *Studies in Historiography* (London: Weidenfeld & Nicolson, 1966). The influence of tragedy is again posed in H. P. Stahl, "Herodots Gyges-Tragödie," *Hermes,* volume 96 (1968), pp. 385–400. J. de Romily, *Time in Greek Tragedy* (Ithaca; Cornell University Press, 1968), is basically a discussion of the Greeks' time sense and narrative continuity.

R. Lattimore, "Composition of the History of Herodotus," *Classical Philology,* volume 53 (1958), pp. 9–19, is a brilliant reconstruction of the means of writing available to Herodotus and how his style in part derives from this factor. In this connection we might mention J. A. Davison,

"Literature and Literacy in Ancient Greece," *Phoenix* 16 (1962), pp. 141–56; 219–33. Herodotus' oral qualities, his folkloric tendencies are much noticed, first in W. Aly, *Volksmärchen, Sage und Novelle bei Herodot und seinen Zeitgenossen* (Göttingen: Vandenhoeck & Ruprecht, 1921). That leads to questions of Herodotean veracity, as in B. Baldwin, "How Credulous was Herodotus?" *Greece and Rome*, volume 11 (1964), pp. 167–77; J. A. S. Evans, "Father of History or Father of Lies. The reputation of Herodotus," *Classical Journal* 69 (1968), pp. 11–17; and also to his intent and style: see F. J. Groten, "Herodotus' Use of Variant Versions," *Phoenix*, volume 17 (1963), pp. 79–87; M. Miller, "The Herodotean Croesus," *Klio*, volume 41 (1963), pp. 58–94, an essay that explores the storytelling function of Solon; M. Lang, "Herodotus and the Ionian Revolt," *Historia* 17 (1968), pp. 24–36, concerns again Herodotus' veracity; Herodotus' Eastern sources are discussed in R. Drews, *The Greek Accounts of Eastern History* (Cambridge: Harvard University Press, 1973); K. H. Waters, "The Purpose of Dramatization in Herodotus," *Historia* 15 (1966), pp. 157–71, is an excellent article with many examples discussing the informational value of the speeches in Herodotus. D. M. Pippidi, "Sur la philosophie d'histoire d'Hérodote," *Eirene*, volume 1 (1960), pp. 75–92, is another excellent essay with many, many examples devoted to showing how Herodotus does not develop one law or thought but has in fact many contradictions, or ambiguities, we might say. Herodotus has bothered historians since antiquity; see Plutarch (*de Malignitate Herodoti*), who condemned his prejudices.

H. R. Immerwahr, *Form and Thought in Herodotus* (Chapel Hill: University of North Carolina Press, 1966), is stimulating and original where J. L. Myres, *Herodotus, Father of History* (Oxford: Oxford University Press, 1953), is conventional. Immerwahr looks to the relationship of Herodotus' stories for the unity and the meaning of the history. The second chapter, on style and structure, is particularly good. C. W. Fornara, *Herodotus: An interpretative essay* (Oxford: Oxford University Press, 1971), has a thought-provoking discussion of Herodotean unity and interesting remarks on the influence of tragedy upon Herodotus. The first chapter is a very intelligent survey of the scholarly background to the subject. W. P. Wallace, "Thucydides," *Phoenix,* volume 18 (1964), pp. 251–61, is a compelling statement of Thucydides' manipulation of his reader; G. W. Bowersock, "The Personality of Thucydides," *Antioch Review,* volume 25 (1965), pp. 135–46, shows Thucydides to be less the model objective historian he has traditionally been presumed to be; R. Syme, *Thucydides,* British Academy Lecture on a Master Mind (Oxford, 1963), is a brilliant summation of the historian as one would expect from the great former Camden Professor of Ancient History in Oxford University. J. H. Finley, *Three Essays on Thucydides* (Cambridge: Harvard University Press, 1967), is excellent on the language of Thucydides and its origins; the third essay deals with the unity of Thucydides' writing. See also A. Parry, "Thucyides' Historical Perspectives," *Yale Classical Studies,* volume 22 (1972), pp. 47–61.

G. B. Grundy, *Thucydides and the History of His Age,* second edition (Oxford: Blackwell, 1948) is a long, detailed, excellent account of the historical realities that we must understand so as to understand Thucydides' sometimes less than obvious allusions. A. W. Gomme, *A Historical Commentary on Thucydides,* volume 1 (Oxford: Oxford University Press, 1945), pp. 1–88, is an excellent account of what Thucydides takes for granted, the reasons for his silences, and what other sources there are to the history of the period Thucydides describes. The influence of medical writing upon Thucydides is described in C. N. Cochrane, *Thucydides and the Science of History* (London: Russell, 1929), a book that supports the notion that Thucydides was what is called today "a hard-nosed scholar." The influence of tragedy is described by F. M. Cornford, *Thucydides Mythistoricus* (London: Routledge & Kegan Paul reissue, 1965), a book that is a very profound statement about the continuing pervasive influence of tragic logic throughout the fifth century. Cornford's chapters 8 and 13 (pp. 129–52; 221–43) contain some of the best observations on Aeschylean dramaturgy to be found anywhere. J. de Romilly, *Histoire et raison chez Thucydide* (Paris: "Les Belles Lettres," 1963), is an excellent account of the implications of Thucydidean selectivity, of his manipulating, of his investing action with moral nuances. See also A. Thibaudet, *La Campagne avec Thucydide* (Paris: Éditions de la Nouvelle revue française, 1922); V. J. Hunter, *Thucydides: The artful reporter* (Toronto: Hakkert, 1973).

TRAGEDY

As the title indicates, P. W. Harsh, *A Handbook of Classical Drama* (Stanford: Stanford University Press, 1944), systematically sets out the few known facts for each tragedy, relates the plot and suggests the major problems in interpretation. A. Lesky, *Greek Tragedy,* translated from the German by H. A. Frankfort, (New York: Barnes & Noble, 1965), is an excellent survey of the subject. Lesky's first chapter, "What Is Tragedy?" is a particularly good discussion of what seem to be the features common to all the extant tragedies. Compare this with the remarks on tragedy in N. Frye, *Anatomy of Criticism* (Princeton: Princeton University Press, 1959), pp. 206–23, where tragedy is discussed more as a phenomenon of culture. H. D. F. Kitto, *Greek Tragedy,* second edition (London: Methuen, 1950), is particularly good on Aeschylus and Sophocles, especially good on the way in which Aeschylus used his characters in dramatic tension with the chorus. His discussion of Euripides suffers from his inclination to see Euripides as a falling away from the norm rather than as an alternative.

A. W. Pickard-Cambridge, *Dithyramb, Tragedy and Comedy,* second edition, revised by T. B. L. Webster (Oxford: Oxford University Press, 1962), is a good review of various theories of the origin of tragedy as well as an assemblage of the evidence. See also A. C. Schlesinger, *Boundaries of Dionysus: Athenian foundations for the theory of tragedy* (Cambridge: Harvard University Press, 1963). The best discussion of the early social role, the early need for tragedy is G. Thomson, *Aeschylus and Athens: A study in the social origins of drama* (New York: Grosset & Dunlap reprint, 1968). G. F. Else, *The Origin and Early Form of Greek Tragedy* (Cambridge: Harvard University Press, 1965), has among other things interesting remarks on the role of the poetry of Solon in the formations of tragedy. The origin and nature of tragedy as the ancients saw it is found in Aristotle's *Poetics,* which G. F. Else has studied and commented upon exhaustively in *Aristotle's Poetics: The Argument* (Cambridge: Harvard University Press, 1957), which features a translation and an exploratory commentary.

The relationship of myth to tragedy is a complicated and little-understood subject that puzzles classicists often because they have no systematic understanding or theory of myth. The following books are all suggestive: H. Musurillo, *Symbol and Myth in Ancient Poetry* (New York: Fordham, 1961); J. P. Vernant, *Mythe et pensée chez les Grecs* (Paris: Maspero, 1965), *Mythe et tragédie en Grèce ancienne* (Paris: Maspero, 1972); but they pose a rather intellectualist function for myth. See R. Y. Hathorn, *Tragedy, Myth and Mystery* (Bloomington: University of Indiana Press, 1962). The relationship of ritual in cult worship to myth is equally obscure; see J. Fontenrose, *The Ritual Theory of Myth* (Berkeley: University of California Press, 1966); J. P. Guépin, *The Tragic Paradox, Myth and Ritual in Greek Drama* (Amsterdam: Hakkert 1968); W. Burkert, "Greek Tragedy and Sacrificial Ritual," *Greek, Roman and Byzantine Studies*, volume 7 (1966), pp. 87–121; J. Lindsay, *The Clashing Rocks, A Study of Early Greek Religion and Culture and the Origins of Drama* (London: Chapman & Hall, 1965).

The indispensable book for studying Greek tragedy is A. W. Pickard-Cambridge, *The Dramatic Festivals of Athens*, second edition, revised by Gould and Lewis (Oxford: Oxford University Press, 1968). Here is all the evidence we have for the production of the plays, the conventions of the theater, the role of the theater in Athenian political life. The book poses some difficulty for those who do not know Greek. T. B. L. Webster, *Greek Theater Production*, second edition (London: Methuen, 1970), is easier. See also P. Arnott, *Greek Scenic Conventions* (Oxford: Oxford University Press, 1962).

There are numerous essays discussing one or more tragedies or tragedy in general. Some of the more distinguished are R. Lattimore, *Story Patterns in Greek Tragedy* (Ann Arbor: University of Michigan Press, 1964); B. Snell, *Scenes from Greek Drama* (Berkeley: University of California Press, 1964); T. G. Rosenmeyer, *The Masks of Tragedy. Essays on six dramas* (Austin: University of Texas Press, 1963). W. Arrowsmith, "The Criticism of Greek Tragedy," *The Tulane Drama Review*, volume 3 (1959), pp. 31–57, advances the notion of tragedy's role as being a forum for ideas not yet established in the community, tragedy, therefore, as a catalyst or springboard; see also W. Arrowsmith's "A Greek Theater of Ideas," in J. Gasner, ed., *Ideas in the Drama* (New York, 1964). R. D. Dawe, "Some Reflections on *ate* and *hamartia*," *Harvard Studies in Classical Philology*, volume 72 (1967), pp. 89–123, treats two fundamental Greek concepts that lie behind the action of a majority of the tragedies. See also J. H. Finley, "Politics and Early Attic Tragedy," *Harvard Studies in Classical Philology,* volume 71 (1966), pp. 1–13. J. Kott, *The Eating of the Gods. An interpretation of Greek tragedy* (New York: Random House, 1972), is an attempt to show the contemporary relevance of the plays, to take them away from history, a stimulating discussion with particularly interesting footnotes. J. Jones, *Aristotle and the Art of Tragedy* (Oxford: Oxford University Press paperback, 1960), a most important book, insists that action, not character, is the main feature of tragedy. The book runs counter to the criticism that looks to the hero as a continuation of the emphasis on the person or hero figure begun in the Homeric epics; it opens up criticism to a re-emphasis upon myth in tragedy, to psychoanalytic interpretation. What is more, it seems the best reading of Aristotle's *Poetics.* See also W. Kaufman, *Tragedy and Philosophy* (Garden City, N.Y.: Doubleday, 1968), another attempt at a new criticism of tragedy with good results when applied to the *Oedipus.*

AESCHYLUS

A. J. Podlecki, *The Political Background of Aeschylean Tragedy* (Ann Arbor: University of Michigan Press, 1966); J. de Romilly, *La crainte et l'angoisse dans le théâtre d'Aeschylus* (Paris: "Les Belles Lettres," 1958); *Aeschylus: A Collection of Critical Essays,* ed. M. H. McCall (Englewood Cliffs, Prentice-Hall, 1972); R. S. Caldwell, "The Pattern of Aeschylean Tragedy," *Transactions and Proceedings of the American Philological Association,* volume 101 (1970), pp. 77–94, on the importance of the father-child relationship in Aeschylean drama; C. J. Herington, "Aeschylus: The Last Phase," *Arion,* volume 4 (1965), pp. 387–403, a study of the last plays as being a new kind of drama, differing from all other tragedy, E. A. Havelock, *Prometheus* (Seattle: University of Washington Press, 1968), relates the hero to twentieth-century intellectuals, half martyr, half scapegoat; F. Will, "Prometheus and the Question of Self-awareness in Greek Literature," *American Journal of Philology,* volume 83 (1962), pp. 72–85; C. Kerényi, *Prometheus: Archetypal Image of Human Existence* (New York, 1963); H. Lloyd-

Jones, "The Guilt of Agamemnon," *Classical Quarterly*, volume 12 (1962), pp. 187–99; W. C. Scott, "Wind Imagery in the Oresteia," *Transactions and Proceedings of the American Philological Association*, volume 18 (1970), pp. 30–39; J. J. Peradotto, "Patterns of Nature Imagery in the *Oresteia*," *American Journal of Philology*, volume 85 (1964), pp. 379–93; R. Kuhns, *The House, the City and the Judges. The Growth of Moral Awareness in the Orestia* (Indianapolis: Bobbs-Merrill, 1962); G. Murray, "Hamlet and Orestes," in *The Classical Tradition in Poetry* (New York: Vintage paperback, 1957), pp. 184–210.

SOPHOCLES

V. Ehrenberg, *Sophocles and Pericles* (Oxford: Blackwell, 1954), is an example of the view that considers Sophocles to be the most typical, the finest specimen of Greek art, thought and understanding at the peak of the classical period. J. C. Opstelten, *Sophocles and Greek Pessimism*, translated from the Dutch by J. A. Ross (Amsterdam: North-Holland Publishing Co., 1952), disabuses us of the notion that the Greek tragic view of life was indeed pessimistic. C. H. Whitman, *Sophocles: A study in heroic humanism* (Cambridge: Harvard University Press, 1951), relates the Sophoclean hero to the Homeric hero, probes Sophocles' use of a Homeric sensibility; B. M. W. Knox, *The Heroic Temper; Studies in Sophoclean Tragedy* (Berkeley: University of California Press, 1964), is also concerned with the hero as the staple and focus of the tragic. The first two chapters are the best account of the Greek tradition of the hero from Homer to Sophocles; A. J. A. Waldock, *Sophocles the Dramatist* (Cambridge: Cambridge University Press, 1966), is a necessary antidote to the numbers of books that concentrate so on Sophoclean thought and religion that one would believe Sophocles were either a don or a divine. He was in fact a poet and a dramatist and Waldock has good insights into the structuring of his dramas. *Sophocles, A Collection of Critical Essays*, T. M. Woodard, ed. (Englewood Cliffs: Prentice-Hall, 1966), is a particularly good collection from Nietzsche to Heidegger to Virginia Woolf to Oswald Spengler, illustrating how Sophocles more than Aeschylus and Euripides is accessible to understanding and interpretation.

But, of course, no two people agree. See for instance the

very good essay by E. R. Dodds, "On Misunderstanding the *Oedipus Rex*," *Greece and Rome,* volume 13 (1966), pp. 37–49, where the idea of Oedipus' freedom, his pursuit of truth is emphasized, and the opposite view of T. Gould, "The Innocence of Oedipus: the Philosophers in *Oedipus the King*," *Arion,* volume 4 (1965), pp. 363–86, 582–611, and volume 5 (1966), pp. 478–525. See further *Twentieth Century Interpretations of Oedipus Rex; a Collection of Critical Essays,* M. J. O'Brien, ed. (Englewood Cliffs: Prentice-Hall, 1968); B. M. W. Knox, *Oedipus at Thebes* (New Haven: Yale University Press, 1957), is a superlative investigation of the language of the play showing how the figure of Oedipus mirrors Athens, how the character may well be the symbol of Athens.

Less is written on the other plays. See W. M. Calder, "Sophocles' Political Tragedy, *Antigone*," *Greek, Roman and Byzantine Studies,* volume 9 (1968), pp. 389–407; C. P. Segal, "Sophocles' Praise of Man and the Conflicts of the *Antigone*," *Arion,* volume 3 (1964), pp. 44–66; T. M. Woodard, "*Electra* of Sophocles. The Dialectal Design," *Harvard Studies in Classical Philology,* volume 68 (1964), pp. 163–205. C. R. Beye, "Sophocles' *Philoctetes* and the Homeric Embassy," *Transactions and Proceedings of the American Philological Association,* volume 101 (1970), pp. 63–75, and W. M. Calder, III, "Sophoclean Apologia: *Philoctetes*," *Greek, Roman and Byzantine Studies,* volume 12 (1971), pp. 153–74, are contrary readings of the character of Neoptolemos.

EURIPIDES

Less is written about Euripides because he has been considered by classicists generally to be "bad," "incompetent" or "decadent" whereas, of course—or at least in my view—he is being experimental and original. The influence of the Sophist movement which is unmistakable in his plays makes him seem to be an intellectual. Many see him as an ancient George Bernard Shaw, forgetting that GBS could never have written the *Bacchae* or the *Trojan Women,* or the *Ion* for that matter. The great critic of Euripides in the nineteenth century was A. W. Verrall, who was convinced that Euripides had contrived great messages in his plays. He imposed an immensely literal interpretation upon the plays, which made for some astounding interpretations. See A. W. Verrall, *Euripides the Rationalist. A Study in the History of Art and Religion* (Cambridge: Cambridge University Press, 1895); *Essays in Four Plays of Euripides: Andromache, Helen, Heracles and Orestes* (Cambridge: Cambridge University Press, 1905); *The Bacchants of Euripides and Other Plays* (Cambridge: Cambridge University Press, 1910). W. Zurcher, *Die Darstellung der Menschen im Drama des Euripides* (Basel: Reinhardt, 1947), has been influential on much subsequent Euripidean criticism, emphasizing the rhetorical nature of Euripides' dramatizing, creating a kind of debate drama where neither action nor the character nor story itself matters so much as the energy and force of the conflicting opinions. And, indeed, some of Euripides' plays do seem like debates, if not altogether, then in part. But like much other criticism it is a generalization that the particularities of the plays will not sustain.

G. M. A. Grube, *The Drama of Euripides* (London: Methuen, 1941), was for a long time the standard piece of criticism, more a survey than an interpretation. Then there was the slighter L. H. G. Greenwood, *Aspects of Euripidean Tragedy* (Cambridge: Cambridge University Press, 1953), which has, however, a good survey of Euripidean scholarship. A hard book for the novice is S. J. Conacher, *Euripidean Drama, Myth, Theme and Structure* (Toronto: University of Toronto Press, 1967). L. S. Morrow has written an extremely thoughtful dissertation, *Euripides' Treatment of Women* (University Microfilms 74.24,374: Ann Arbor, Michigan). See also G. Meremans, *Les femmes, le destin, le siècle dans le théâtre d'Euripide* (Cuesmes: G. Beugnies Cie, 1972). Also see E. M. Blaiklock, *The Male Characters of Euripides: A study in realism* (Wellington: New Zealand University Press, 1952); G. Zuntz, *The Political Plays of Euripides* (Manchester: Manchester University Press, 1955), which reaches the conclusion that Euripides is not topical but speaks to the general political atmosphere; A. P. Burnett, *Catastrophe Survived; Euripides' Plays of Mixed Reversal* (Oxford: Oxford University Press, 1971), which makes more literal, realistic readings of the plays, ignoring ambiguity, absurdity, elements of humor, which are the contemporary staples of Euripidean criticism. Burnett's readings of the plays are based on the belief that Euripides was working with conventional plots to which the myth or legend was made to fit.

B. F. Dick, *"Lord of the Flies* and the *Bacchae," Classical World,* volume 57 (1964), pp. 145–56, points up how like contemporary thought Euripides' ideas seem. W. Arrowsmith, "Eliot and Euripides," *Arion,* volume 4 (1965), pp. 21–35, deals with *The Cocktail Party,* the *Alcestis* and along the way Verrall's criticism of Euripides.

There are many essays on the individual plays, for instance, J. R. Wilson, *Twentieth Century Interpretations of Euripides' Alcestis* (Englewood Cliffs: Prentice-Hall, 1968); C. G. Wolff, "The Design and Myth in Euripides' *Ion," Harvard Studies in Classical Philology,* volume 69 (1965), pp. 169–94; J. de Romilly, "Phoenician Women of Euripides. Topicality in Greek Tragedy," translated by D. H. Orroh, *Bucknell Review,* volume 15 (1967), pp. 108–32; A. W. H. Adkins, "Basic Greek Values in Euripides' *Hecuba* and *Hercules furens," Classical Quarterly,* volume 16 (1966), pp. 193–219; N. A. Greenberg, "Euripides' *Orestes;* An interpretation," *Harvard Studies in Classical Philology,* volume 66 (1962), pp. 157–92. H. Parry, "Euripides' *Orestes,* The quest for salvation," *Translations and Proceedings of the American Philological Association,* volume 100 (1969), pp. 337–53, sees the play as a study in madness for which there is no remedy; see also J. A. LaRue, "Prurience Uncovered. The psychology of Euripides' Pentheus," *Classical Journal,* volume 63 (1968), pp. 209–14; W. Sale "The Psychoanalysis of Pentheus in the *Bacchae* of Euripides," *Yale Classical Studies,* volume 22 (1972,) pp. 63–82. R. P. Winnington-Ingram, *Euripides and Dionysus; An interpretation of the Bacchae* (Cambridge, 1948), is a detailed, subtle, sensitive, line-by-line reading of the play, just about the best analysis of a tragedy in the English language; read also E. R. Dodds, *Euripides' Bacchae,* second edition (Oxford, 1960), pp. xi–xxxviii.

COMEDY

Very little has been written about Attic comedy, very very little in English, and what there is does not often seem worth reading. K. J. Dover, *Aristophanic Comedy* (London: Batsford, 1972), is a good introductory book to Aristophanes, discussing technical problems of production as well as offering interpretations (not always conventional) of the plays. Dover also briefly takes up the evidence for the comic theater after Aristophanes. C. Whitman, *Aristophanes and the Comic Hero* (Cambridge: Harvard University Press, 1964), chapter 1, pp. 1–20, is a good discussion of the major views on Athenian, or more specifically Aristophanic, comedy. By concentrating upon the hero Whitman looks more to the fictional, or really fantastic aspects of comedy, seeing it more as a view of man comparable with, or better, complementary to, the heroes of epic and tragedy and the views of man they imply. So it is that he sees comedy more as an abstraction. That critical approach is challenged by W. Arrowsmith, "Aristophanes' *Birds:* The Fantasy Politics of Eros," *Arion,* new series, volume 1 (1973), pp. 119–67, who insists upon the historical background to Aristophanes' plays although the evidence is meager and interpretation is slippery. But some scholars do indeed use Aristophanes as a historical document; see e.g. V. Ehrenberg, *People of Aristophanes; A sociology of old Attic Comedy,* third edition (New York: Shocken, 1962). See also L. Strauss, *Socrates and Aristophanes* (New York: Basic Books, 1962; D. J. Stewart, "Aristophanes and the Pleasures of Anarchy," *Antioch Review,* volume 25 (1965), pp. 189–208.

The nature of comedy in antiquity is discussed in a very interesting way in A. Cook, *The Dark Voyage and the Golden Mean: A Philosophy of Comedy* (Cambridge: Harvard University Press, 1949); comedy and tragedy are opposed and the ramifications of each are displayed so as to show how the whole of human existence is encompassed by the two views. Furthermore the comic or tragic affinities of each piece of literature are discussed. See also my translation of Euripides' *Alcestis* with a commentary (Englewood Cliffs: Prentice-Hall, 1974), principally pp. 1–10, which develop the idea that the *Alcestis* is comic, amusing or unsettling. The idea comes from my "Alcestis and Her Critics" *Greek, Roman and Byzantine Studies,* volume 2 (1959), pp. 111–27. B. M. W. Knox, "Euripidean Comedy," pp. 68–96 of *Rarer Action: Essays in Honor of Francis Fergusson,* A. Chase and R. Koffler, eds. (New Brunswick: Rutgers University Press, 1970), is a brilliant assessment of the comic elements in Euripides' *Electra, Ion, Iphigenia in Tauris* and *Helen,* pointing out that the Western comic vision starts here (if not before in the *Odyssey*) rather than in Menander, Plautus and Terence. See also L. A. Post,

"Menander and the *Helen* of Euripides," *Harvard Studies in Classical Philology*, volume 68 (1964), pp. 99–118. See also W. M. Hart, *High Comedy in the Odyssey*, University of California Publications in Classical Philology, volume 12, number 14 (1943), pp. 263–78.

ALEXANDRIAN LITERATURE

Most histories of ancient Greece end with the death of Alexander in 323 B.C. as though the whole world were forever eclipsed in that woeful event. But in fact much more was to come, most immediately the Alexandrian Age of the third century. It is a period that has much more human interest, for we seem to know much more about the lives of the people at this time. A survey of the period is contained in W. W. Tarn and G. T. Griffith, *Hellenistic Civilization*, third edition, (London: Arnold, 1952). F. E. Peters, *The Harvest of Hellenism* (New York: Simon & Schuster, 1970), pp. 17–260, concentrates upon politics and philosophy; J. P. Lynch, *Aristotle's School* (Berkeley: University of California Press, 1972), describes the new scholasticism; P. M. Fraser, *Ptolemaic Alexandria* (Oxford: Oxford University Press, 1972), volume 1, is an immense work (the footnotes form an entire second volume of over a thousand pages), but it is extremely informative and well written, covering all the facts of the physical city, then its social and economic existence, and finally devoting roughly five hundred pages to the scholarly, scientific, philosophic and literary achievements. While the judgments may sometimes be routine all the facts are there. It is the most recent thorough survey of the whole literature. A. Couat, *Alexandrian Poetry*, translated by J. Loeb (London: Heinemann, 1931), is again a survey with that characteristic French way of making epigrammatical judgments. Couat calls Alexandrian literature decadent; when a poet (Callimachus) can laugh at his own tradition, says Couat, this is decadence. The opinion and the question it raises are engrossing particularly in our time when people alternate between laughing and crying at what confronts them. R. Pfeiffer, mentioned earlier (p. 421), has excellent remarks on the scholarship of the Alexandrian period, which is basic to the literature. See also T. B. L. Webster, *Hellenistic Poetry and Art* (London: Methuen, 1964). The best piece on Apollonius Rhodius is probably P.

Handel, *Beobachtungen zur epischen Technik des Apollonios Rhodios*, Zetemata Monograph Number 7 (München: Beck, 1954). There are, however, several interesting essays in English; my own is "Jason as a Love-Hero in Apollonios' *Argonautika,*" *Greek, Roman and Byzantine Studies,* volume 10 (1969), pp. 31–55, which forms the basis for the discussion of Apollonius in the present text; see also J. F. Carspecken, "Apollonius Rhodius and the Homeric Epic," *Yale Classical Studies,* volume 13 (1952), pp. 35–143; and G. Lawall, *"Apollonius' Argonautika:* Jason as Anti-Hero," *Yale Classical Studies,* volume 19 (1966), pp. 121–69.

The best piece on Callimachus may be somewhat hard going for the reader without Greek. It is K. J. McKay, *The Poet at Play* (Leiden: Brill, 1962), a study in detail of Callimachus' language and the poetic effects achieved with it. No other criticism exists in English.

For Theocritus there is C. Lawall, *Theocritus' Coan Pastorals. A Poetry Book* (Cambridge: Harvard University Press, 1967), which seeks to establish the pastoral vision as first created by Theocritus, a view of man of equivalent value to that of epic, tragedy and comedy. T. G. Rosenmeyer, *The Green Cabinet* (Berkeley: University of California Press, 1969), is a discussion of Theocritus and the European pastoral poetry without emphasizing chronology or tradition but rather establishing through a discussion of all the poems despite their relative age a sense of what the pastoral is, a stimulating and thought-provoking book displaying wide learning.

The profile of the Hellenistic Age becomes ever more obvious as the sands of Egypt continually yield up papyrus fragments and they are studied. A hint of what is being learned is contained in the three volumes entitled *New Chapters in Greek Literature,* ed. by J. E. Powell (Oxford: Oxford University Press, 1921–33).

TRANSLATIONS

The work of every ancient author mentioned in this book is translated for better or for worse in the Loeb Classical Library, published by the Harvard University Press. The translations are often dreadful, dry and stilted, yet it is handy to have most everything translated (together with the original text) in one place.

What follows are my favorite translations. I am actually no judge since I can always discern the Greek through the English and so while listening to that faraway voice I ignore the language unfolding before my eyes. The problem of translation is well stated by J. Ciardi, "Translation: The Art of Failure," from *Dialogue with an Audience* (New York: Lippincott, 1961). For Homer see the discussion in my *The Iliad, the Odyssey and the Epic Tradition*, pp. 252–57, and my review of Fitzgerald's *Iliad* in a forthcoming issue of *Parnassus*.

R. Lattimore has translated the *Iliad* (Chicago: University of Chicago Press, 1951) and the *Odyssey* (New York: Harper Torchbook, 1967) into a rather routine American English which, however, evokes for me more or less the Homeric hexametric line. R. Fitzgerald's translations of the Homeric poems both published by Doubleday (1961, 1974), which are highly praised by poets, sound to me like lyric poems more than epic. E. V. Rieu's translation of the *Odyssey* (Baltimore: Penguin, 1946), although in prose, delights me; but one senses a little too much Noël Coward in the style.

R. Lattimore has translated Hesiod's *Works and Days* and *Theogony* (Ann Arbor: University of Michigan Press, 1959) with his customary skill and lack of flair. D. Wender is the most current translator of Hesiod (Baltimore: Penguin, 1973). R. Lattimore translates most of the major pieces of the poets of the archaic age in *Greek Lyrics* (Chicago: University of Chicago Press, 1955). The interesting feature is that he tries to do this in the meter of the original poem. I am not sure that the effect intended is achieved. W. Barnstone, *Sappho* (Garden City, N.Y.: Doubleday, 1965), has nice translations facing the Greek text. He includes, however, the merest fragments, the merit of which escapes me. R. Fagles, *Bacchylides* (New Haven: Yale University Press, 1961), translates everything faithfully and beautifully. R. Lattimore, *The Odes of Pindar* (Chicago: University of Chicago Press, 1947), is an interesting study in translation. Pindar is well-nigh incomprehensible. At best the poems are a verbal trip; like a light show they produce a sensual experience; perhaps a subliminal meaning evolves. In any case Lattimore is faithful but the effect does not transfer from Greek into English. Pindar demands to be translated with a line-by-line commentary. C. Ruck and W. Matheson (see p. 430) have done a better job with Pindar although the effect has a kind of self-consciousness and contrivance that are not like Pindar. Perhaps one senses a certain tentative quality in Ruck and Matheson.

Tragedy is very well translated in R. Lattimore and D. Grene, eds., *The Complete Greek Tragedies* (Chicago: University of Chicago Press, 1959–60). The translations are literal enough to satisfy most who know Greek yet usually the translations have a pleasing way of using English. Some achieve poetry; see, for instance, John Moore's translation of the *Ajax*. Since tragedy is read and studied far more in in English than in Greek these translations have great authority. Whether they can be successfully supplanted is doubtful although William Arrowsmith is trying to do so in a series at the Oxford University Press based on the premise that Greek tragedy deserves genuine poets for translators and needs good commentary. The second of these propositions seems sounder and is the motive for the Prentice-Hall series of translated tragedies for which I did the *Alcestis*.

Comedy was translated in the nineteenth century by Benjamin Bickley Rogers, once while on vacation on the Riviera far from the Greek text back home in England— the wedding of genius and memory! The translation is good and famous but there are others that are better. The anonymous translator in *The Complete Greek Drama*, edited by W. J. Oates and G. O'Neill, Jr. (New York: Random House, 1938), is excellent, managing to get a great deal of the literal meaning across while at the same time achieving a relatively vigorous style. It is not as rough, tough, aggressive and fast as Aristophanes. I doubt that it would play in a theater. Two volumes of translation, *Aristophanes: Four Plays*, D. Parker, R. Lattimore, translators (Ann Arbor: University of Michigan Press, 1969), and *Aristophanes: Three Plays*, D. Parker, translator (Ann Arbor: University of Michigan Press, 1969), are lively, indeed wild versions. There is considerable effort to recover the incredible energy and vulgarity of Aristophanes. But vulgarity just doesn't work for educated people in English. These translations are on speed and desperate. One gets tired just reading them. They are funnier than any other translations, which, however, does not concede too much.

Aubrey de Selincourt translates Herodotus perfectly to my taste (Baltimore: Penguin, 1954). Rex Warner does a fine translation of Thucydides (Baltimore: Penguin, 1954). It

reads, however, like a political journalist in the Sunday
Times. Thucydides himself is far more tortured than that,
and he varies his style, too, as he struggles with his meaning.
Warner misses all of the majesty. Therefore it is probably
better to try the translation by R. Crawley. It is nineteenth-
century prose but one likes the dignity and the sonorous
beauty. It does remind the reader of Thucydides—after all,
he was trying for grandeur—although at times it fairly
smothers him.

E. V. Rieu (Baltimore: Penguin, 1959) translates Apollonius
Rhodius well and A. S. F. Gow has very fine prose translations of Theocritus in his edition of the poet (volume I, Cambridge: Cambridge University Press, 1952). See also the verse
translation by B. Mills (Lafayette: Purdue University Studies,
1963). L. Casson, *The Plays of Menander* (New York: New
York University Press, 1971), is as lively as that pedestrian
playwright can be.

No one has come along to rescue poor Callimachus from
the Loeb Library.

INDEX

INDEX OF CITED PASSAGES
Line references are in italics.

INDEX OF MODERN AUTHORITIES CITED